THE END OF
PAX AMERICANA

ASIA-PACIFIC: CULTURE, POLITICS, AND SOCIETY

Editors: Rey Chow, Michael Dutton,
H. D. Harootunian, and Rosalind C. Morris

Duke University Press *Durham and London* 2022

THE END OF PAX AMERICANA

The Loss of Empire and Hikikomori Nationalism

NAOKI SAKAI

Printed in the United States of America on acid-free paper ∞
Project editor: Lisa Lawley
Typeset in Garamond Premier Pro and Din by Typesetter, Inc.

Library of Congress Cataloging-in-Publication Data
Names: Sakai, Naoki, 1946- author.
Title: The end of Pax Americana : The loss of empire and
Hikikomori nationalism/ Naoki Sakai.
Other titles: Asia-Pacific.
Description: Durham : Duke University Press, 2022. | Series: Asia-pacific:
culture, politics, and society | Includes bibliographical references and index.
Identifiers: LCCN 2021016456 (print)
LCCN 2021016457 (ebook)
ISBN 9781478013976 (hardcover)
ISBN 9781478014911 (paperback)
ISBN 9781478022213 (ebook)
Subjects: LCSH: Postcolonialism—Social aspects—East Asia—History—
20th century. | Postcolonialism—Social aspects—Japan—History—
20th century. | Hikikomori. | Social isolation—Japan. | East Asia—Foreign
relations—United States. | United States—Foreign relations—East Asia. |
Japan—Foreign relations—United States. | United States—Foreign relations—
Japan. | BISAC: HISTORY / Asia / General | HISTORY / Asia / Japan
Classification: LCC DS518.8 .S253 2022 (print) | LCC DS518.8 (ebook) |
DDC 320.540952—dc23
LC record available at https://lccn.loc.gov/2021016456
LC ebook record available at https://lccn.loc.gov/2021016457

Cover art: Workers at the Kidoura shipyard in Kesennuma, Japan, 2012.
Courtesy Daniel Berehulak/Getty Images.

*Dedicated to
Harry D. Harootunian
in friendship, admiration,
and gratitude*

Contents

Acknowledgments

This volume consists of articles and manuscripts for speeches that I have written and delivered in the last two decades in a variety of locations in Asia, Europe, and North America. Although each is modified and edited for inclusion here, without too much difficulty a reader might detect inconsistencies, revisions, and minor contradictions that I have failed to resolve. Some of the problematics I repeatedly tackled, such as racism and translation, were inversely formulated, articulated to different topics, and contrarily conceptualized. As a matter of fact, in the editing process for their inclusion I encountered a certain difficulty in reducing incongruities and, on rare occasions, outright contradictions in my original versions. Apparently, time is one reason for this challenge. As the situation changes and as my thinking advances, many times I discover how inadequate and insufficient my previous grasp was. As recently as 2016, for instance, I was forced to acknowledge that the end of Pax Americana would come in a much more drastic and catastrophic fashion than I had previously anticipated. Until then I thought of Donald Trump as nothing more than a bad joke. Another reason is not unrelated to the time factor; it is input from my fellow scholars from whom I have learned so much that often forced me to reconsider the ways I posed problems and programmed perspectives.

I want to acknowledge my exceptional gratitude to Harry D. Harootunian, who helped to create many opportunities for me to pursue an academic career, introduced me to rigorous inquiry, and taught me how not to ignore the sense of justice in intellectual life. Therefore I dedicate this book to him.

In the 1980s, at the University of Chicago, I became increasingly suspicious of the disciplinary formation of area studies with regard to power and governmentality, but it was William Haver, a fellow graduate student, who taught me that, as long as one works in a certain field of specialization, one cannot evade the responsibility for critically examining how knowledge is produced within and under what conditions one's expertise is sanctioned. In the last three decades, I have tried to be responsible for the demands of critical scholarship, although I am not certain that I have succeeded in this mission at all. My acknowledgment also goes to Jon Solomon, with whom I have been in constant dialogue about the disciplinary knowledge of area studies and the politics of the will to know. I acknowledge his great assistance in providing me with many opportunities to reflect on my own argument and to broaden the theoretical scope I had assumed. In this volume he kindly allowed me to include the introduction to the fourth volume of *Traces: A Multilingual Series of Cultural Theory and Translation*, which we coedited. Of course, I want to express my gratitude to Takashi Fujitani for his exceptional generosity. When he discovered Edwin O. Reischauer's "Memorandum on Policy towards Japan" at the National Archive at College Park, he contacted me and allowed me access to this amazing document. It was the discovery of this historical source that finally confirmed my speculation, for which I did not have any documentary evidence until 2000. I had conducted my research on U.S.–Japan complicity after the Asia-Pacific War, on the one hand, and the structural homologies between prewar Japanese imperial nationalism and American imperial nationalism, on the other. Reischauer's memorandum finally confirmed my hunches and predictions. I have been exceptionally fortunate in their friendship.

In addition to these three friends, in myriad ways I have received tremendous inspiration from Sandro Mezzadra, Lisa Yoneyama, Brett Neilson, Rey Chow, Brett de Bary, Gavin Walker, Lim Jie-Hyun, the late Tetsuo Najita, J. Victor Koschmann, and the late Masao Miyoshi.

I cannot express adequately how much I have benefited from my dialogues with Richard Calichmann, Isomae Jun'ichi, John Kim, Joyce C. H. Liu, Wang Hui, Iyotani Toshio, the late Hirota Masaki, Mayumo Inoue, Nojiri Ei'ichi, Guarne Blai, Katsuya Hirano, Itagaki Ryûta, Thomas LaMarre, Nich Vaughan-Williams, Hyon-Joo Yoo, Toba Koji, Andrea Bachner, Wu Peichen, Étienne Balibar, the late Watanabe Kôzô, Boris Buden, Uno Kuni'ichi, Charles Prado-Fonts, Uemura Tadao, Atsuko Ueda, Goh Byeung-Gwon, Iwasaki Minoru, the late Etsuko Terasaki, Myriam Suchet, Kang Naehui, Stefan Tanaka, Darko Suvin, Kim Chul, Tomiyama Ichiro, Kim Heisook, Toshiaki Kobayashi, Lee Hyoduk, Tsuboi Hideto, the late Kyoko Selden, Narita Rui'ichi, Nakano Toshio, the late Michael Marr, Tim Murray, Nishitani Osamu, Nayoung Aimee Kwon, Steffi Richter, Lydia Liu, Sun Ge, Komagome Takeshi, Boreth Ly,

Morinaka Takaaki, Yann Moulier Boutang, Sun Ge, Yan Haiping, and Muto Ichiyo, as well as many others.

In the preparation of this volume, I combined some separate publications into chapters, so each one does not necessarily correspond to a single article or lecture. Chapter 1, "History and Responsibility: Debates over *The Showa History*" was originally prepared for a public lecture at Hanyang University in Seoul and later included as "History and Responsibility: On the Debates on the *Shōwa History*," in *Mass Dictatorship and Memory as Ever Present Past* (ed. Lim Jie-Hyun, Barbara Walker, and Peter Lambert, Basingstoke, UK: Palgrave Macmillan, 2014, 120–138). Chapter 2, "From Relational Identity to Specific Identity," was originally delivered at the University of British Columbia in August 2013 and later published as "From Relational Identity to Specific Identity: On Equality and Nationality" in *Values, Identity and Equality in 18th and 19th-Century Japan* (ed. Peter Nosco et al., Boston: Brill, 2015, 290–320). It was later translated into Japanese and published as「関係的同一性から種的同一性へ—平等と国体(ナショナリティ)について」("From relational identity to specific identity: On equality and nationality," trans. Noberto Ono, in『江戸の中の日本、日本の中の江戸』, ed. Peter Nosco et al. (Tokyo: Kashiwa-shobo, 2016, 246–291). Chapter 3, "Asian Theory and European Humanity," was first prepared for *Postcolonial Studies*. It was published as "Theory and Asian Humanity: On the Question of *Humanitas* and *Anthropos*" (*Postcolonial Studies* 13, no. 4 [2010]: 441–464). Chapter 4, "'You Asians': On the Historical Role of the Binary of the West and Asia," was first delivered at the Millennium Regional Conference "'WeAsians' between Past and Future" held in Singapore in February 2000 and was included in the conference publication of the same title (ed. Kowk Kian-Woon, Indira Arumugam, Karen Chia, and Lee Chee Kenge, Singapore: Singapore Heritage Society/National Archive of Singapore, 2000, 212–247). It was later reprinted in *South Atlantic Quarterly* as "Millennial Japan: Rethinking the Nation in the Age of Recession" (ed. Harry Harootunian and Tomiko Yoda, 99, no. 4 [2000]: 789–817). Chapter 5, "Addressing the Multitude of Foreigners, Echoing Foucault," was prepared by Jon Solomon and me as the introduction to the special issue "Translation, Biopolitics, Colonial Difference" of *Traces: A Multilingual Series of Cultural Theory and Translation* (Hong Kong: Hong Kong University Press, 2006). And Chapter 6, "The Loss of Empire and Inward-Looking Society," came from two separate manuscripts: "Trans-Pacific Studies and U.S.- Japan Complicity" and "The End of *Pax Americana* and the Nationalism of *Hikikomori*." The former was prepared as a chapter in *The Trans-Pacific Imagination: Rethinking*

Boundary, Culture and Society (ed. Naoki Sakai and Hyon Joo Yoo, Singapore: World Scientific, 2012). The latter was delivered as a public lecture at the University of Hong Kong in October 2014—and also at Kobe University a month after—and later published as "On Nishikawa Nagao's *Neo-Colonialism*: The End of *Pax Americana* and the Nationalism of *Hikikomori*," *Shisô*, no. 1095, July 2015. The publication of this article prompted the Japanese anthology 『ひきこもりの国民主義』(The nationalism of hikikomori [reclusive withdrawal], Tokyo: Iwanami Shoten, 2017), in which the latter was included.

While I was writing this book, Gail Sakai read every part of the manuscript and gave me a large number of valuable suggestions and supportive criticism, without which I would never have completed this task. Once again I want to express my gratitude to her. Finally, I would like to privately dedicate this book to the memory of my father, Haruyoshi Sakai, and to my mother, Katsuko Sakai, who passed away late in 2018 while I was working on the manuscript for this volume.

INTRODUCTION

In the late twentieth and early twenty-first centuries, countries in Northeast Asia underwent unprecedented social transformations, some of which were undoubtedly traumatic, while some others were welcomed by local residents almost with a sense of euphoria. No matter how one narrates, interprets, and evaluates these transformations, they are so drastic that, at this point in time, all of the conventional historical narratives feel inadequate to take account of what has been happening in this increasingly wealthy part of the globe. Many of us, including the majority of intellectuals and scholars resident in or coming from this geopolitical area of the world, are not yet intellectually or even emotionally ready for this new reality. How can we come to terms with the historical prospect that, in a decade or two, East Asia may well be the center of gravity in the global economy? Or, to put it a slightly different way, how should we prepare ourselves for the end of Pax Americana, for the end of the geopolitical order that has been accepted in the last several decades?

By now, after four years of Donald Trump's presidency, the prospect that Pax Americana can soon end will not be especially surprising to many, including U.S. citizens. In so many tangible ways, the hegemonic dominance of the United States of America has deteriorated, and in a visible way the features that used to persuade many peoples on the earth to respect, adore, and fear the United States as a global hegemon have been chipped away. Perhaps America's extraordinary military capacity is still sustained through its global network of military bases and international collective security agreements, such as the North Atlantic Treaty Organization and the Security Treaty between the United States and Japan, that have been built step by step since the end of World War II; yet American military superiority is not easy to maintain today. It is important to emphasize at the beginning of this book, however, that I am not concerned with counterproductive international policies, incoherent or simply irrational assessments, unrealistic propaganda, and almost self-destructive resolutions in the spheres of international politics as adopted by the U.S. government in these last four years; these have helped to render the prospect of the end of U.S. global hegemony not only visible but also plausible. I have been pursuing issues concerning Pax Americana for more than two decades, and, as a matter of fact, every one of the original essays that have been modified and reorganized as chapters for inclusion in this volume was written and published in periodicals and anthologies before the inauguration of the Donald Trump administration in January 2017. For some people, it may be very hard to dissociate the end of Pax Americana from the name Donald Trump, but I purposely did not include any assessment or evaluation of the Trump presidency itself in this volume. Instead, for the last three decades, I have been observing many developments and changes that have occurred in East Asia and Europe, and I have been wondering if I could find some common problematics among these incidents and transformations that may appear unrelated to one another at first glance. What I have undertaken is to seek some common themes and to understand these vicissitudes from the perspective of Pax Americana and its future. In this respect, I would like to stress that I do not want readers of this book to look for some rosy picture of the future, particularly in East Asia. My focus is on the loss of empire rather than the end of colonial subjugation.

Before offering congratulations on the century of East Asian prosperity to come, therefore, we must remember that we cannot afford to overlook the era of Pax Americana during which the historical conditions for the present were prepared and came into existence. This peace associated with the global reign of the United States of America continued to be exceptionally bloody even after World War II and succeeded in prolonging the basic colonial-imperial order of the modern international world, which Carl Schmitt called "the spatial structure of international law" (2006, 140–212), despite the orchestrated rhetorical disavowal of the essentially colonial character of America's peace in the postwar world. By no means, however, do I mean to suggest the internal collapse of the United States national economy or a decline in American domestic polity with the end of Pax Americana. The prospect of the United States of America as a national society is a matter that requires a different set of inquiries.

I do not predict that the end of Pax Americana will be somewhat comparable to the end of Pax Britannica. Therefore, I do not anticipate Pax Americana will be followed by some other structure of global hegemony such as Pax Sinica.

What I want to indicate by "the end of Pax Americana" is, first of all, this sense of growing historical irrelevance, the sense that, in some way, our conventional categories for historical narrative are rendered increasingly extraneous; we are in one way or another facing the proliferating sense of worthlessness of such categories as the West, the Rest of the World, and so forth, whose cogency we used to take for granted. These basic categories by which we used to envision the world, comprehend global events, and imagine our futures now seem unhinged, dislocated, or ineffective as far as the historical perspective from East Asia is concerned. Of course, this geopolitical designation "East Asia" itself is not beyond question.

The history of East Asia since Japan's defeat in 1945 will remain incongruous in some fundamental sense unless we take full account of its hegemonic domination by the United States of America. What makes Japan's surrender to the Allied Powers so significant in retrospect is the subsequent history of the American reign in Northeast Asia as well as in the international world at large. If the reality of Pax Americana were discounted, it would be utterly unlikely to find coherent historical interpretations, evaluations, and judgments about the area's major events, social transformations, cultural trends, and collective anxieties in the post–World War II era; this is true not only of military, economic, and diplomatic interstate maneuvers but also of everyday life, communal sentiments and emotions, mass media, and domestic politics. By no means has the presence of America's military forces and its economic intervention, ways of life, political values, and, most importantly, its introduction of consumer capitalism remained accidental or trivial to the ways in which Asian people have constructed their own national, ethnic, or racial identities, invented the types of their daily life, and shaped their desires and anxieties in the midst of consumerist interpellations. As soon as American global strategy was outlined in the Truman Doctrine after the Second World War, Northeast Asia was one of the target regions of the world where the United States attempted to establish its hegemonic domination over local political forces by means of the incentives of "development"; this was a symbolic word that could mean all sorts of things and that served significantly to justify American efforts to "modernize" an underdeveloped Asia against the tides of anticolonial nationalism and Maoist socialism.[1] The idea of "modernization" was newly marketed by the promoters of modernization theory, and countries in North East Asia were often regarded as experimental fields for American modernization theory.[2] American domination has been absolutely overwhelming to virtually every person born, raised, working, and dying in this northeastern part of what has been labeled Asia.

Of course, we cannot afford to forget that the word "Asia" itself marks a specific historical reality generally referred to as "modernity" since the ascendance of Europe to the throne of the world more than two centuries ago. Prior to American domination, Asian people had been subject to the colonial governance of European and Japanese states. It was under Pax Americana that many constituted themselves as peoples and acquired their state sovereignties. The United States' hegemony was an indisputable reality for peoples in the Philippines, Japan, Korea, Taiwan, Vietnam, and even China, where their lives were fashioned largely in accordance with and in reaction to its overwhelming presence and "the American way of life."

In the famous Policy Planning Staff Memo of 1948, George Kennan estimated that more than 50 percent of global wealth was produced by the population of the United States of America alone, which then constituted no more than 6.3 percent of the planet's population. At stake in his shrewd design of the containment strategy were two concerns: how long the United States could possibly maintain this unprecedented global domination, and what policy arrangements would facilitate global peace under American leadership lasting for as many decades as possible. My guess is that Kennan was not optimistic enough to believe that Pax Americana would last more than half a century. Seven decades later, the United States still occupies the position of global hegemon, but it no longer enjoys such a one-sided preeminence as Kennan witnessed in 1948. Particularly in the last two decades (including the last three years of the Trumpian tragicomedy in which all the destructive and fatuous instincts of American reactionaries have been on display), a self-inflicted collapse of American global leadership has been observed virtually everywhere in the world, but it should not be forgotten that the gradual decomposition of Pax Americana has been under way for a much longer time. And wide differentials in the standard of living and the per capita average income that used to exist between North America and countries in Northeast Asia can no longer be taken for granted. In the late twentieth and the early twenty-first centuries, a large-scale historical transition occurred, and consequently some fundamental changes in the structure of the international world ought to be recognized, not only in Northeast Asia but also globally, in spite of the continuing existence of elements that facilitated Pax Americana in the first place.

The fatigue or exhaustion of Pax Americana can be observed today, but the phenomenon has been a rather long and gradual one. Over time I noticed certain symptoms indicating the recession of the U.S. global hegemony in East Asia, but it never struck me as a one-time blow or surprise, unlike the fall of the Berlin Wall. For the last two decades, I have attempted many times to understand how the dominant position of the United States of America in international politics has altered and been redefined. The essays collected in this volume were all written, delivered as public lectures, and published in academic journals and anthologies during the last twenty years, with the exception of Edwin O. Reischauer's "Memorandum on Policy towards Japan" and "Statement on Racism," prepared by William Haver and me, which are included as appendixes at the end of the volume. Since I wrote these essays in response to ongoing historical changes, I could not preliminarily delimit their themes to focus on or organize their systematic analysis. Compiling them together in this volume, I tried to streamline my arguments so that readers can follow these chapters as an assembly of interconnected treatises on a set of well-defined problems; unfortunately, they cannot be read as a series of coherent and continual narratives. Rather, they should be read as chapters, each of which serves as a historical witness to ongoing events.

Despite the accidental and disparate situations in response to which the chapters of this volume were initially produced, they are backed by one overarching inquiry. In recent decades, I have been concerned with the general problematic of "the dislocation of the West." By this, I want to offer a diagnosis of a historically long duration in which the modern international world is being transformed. Definitely it is not "the decline of the West" or "the disintegration of Western civilization." In this respect, the chapters of this volume have been prepared as historical case studies on the basis of which the systematic and theoretical monograph titled *The Dislocation of the West* will be written.

Why should I evade idioms such as "the decline of the West" by any means? Above all else, the West or any other civilizational identity—Asia, Christendom, Islam, or Africa—must not be regarded as something substantial or as an enduring body that germinates, grows, wanes, or declines. My aversion to organicist **tropisms** that depict communities, nations, cultures, civilizations, and societies derives from my concern for what is generally described in terms of racism. Of course, my stance in all the chapters in this volume can be summarized as "antiracist," and I do not hesitate to criticize racism and denounce a variety of forms of racist practice, but my concern for racism goes beyond opposition or denunciation of it. Hostility toward racism, I believe, must be informed by how it is possible to envision the world without relying on racial identities. As soon as I commit myself to antiracism, however, I am obliged to acknowledge that my task to comprehend what I oppose and denounce as racism is not an easy one at all. More broadly speaking, my inquiry into racism must begin with an acknowledgment that it is extremely hard or virtually impossible to apprehend the conception or conceptions of race. Whereas we face the reality of racism and racial discrimination persistently everywhere in the world, the very relationship between the concept of race and the reality of racism has never ceased to be an enigma.

For us to be effectively oppositional to racists, our apprehension of racism must include how certain social formations are facilitated by the constitution of essentialized categories called race, ethnicity, or nationality. In other words, we must not take the very concept of race for granted, and our apprehension of racism needs to be accompanied by a critical assessment of the categories of race themselves: how they are constituted socially and relationally; under what historical conditions they came into existence. Since I determinedly commit myself to the denunciation of racist practices for the first time (my stance is outlined in "Statement on Racism"; see appendix 2), the problematic of racism has continued to proliferate. My hostility toward racism, which cannot be divorced from an endeavor to know how race is constituted, how racism is practiced, or how racial identity is performatively installed, has never given me uncomplicated answers; my denunciation of it scarcely offered me any help in objectifying what can be subsumed under racism, consolidating the target of my criticism, recognizing who my enemies—tentatively called racists—are, or positioning myself on the positive outside of racist discourse. The more I have wanted to understand racism, the greater difficulty I have encountered in systematizing critical knowledge on race and racism. In short, I have never been assured that I could ever speak from the outside of racism despite my persistent commitment to antiracism.

It goes without saying that there are many sites outside academia where racism is routinely practiced. But the most crucial issue I have to tackle is the insidious relationship between knowledge production and racism. It is in this respect that the very topic of race and racism did not allow me to remain indifferent or nonchalant about my own profession. For the last four decades, I have been engaged in academic disciplines of area studies—even though I have never been fully comfortable there—and all my writings, not only those included in this volume but also the majority of my previous publications, are academically and professionally classified in the fields of area studies. It is undeniable that since the late 1970s I have worked as a member of area studies departments at universities, have been recognized in its fields, have registered in its academic associations, and, on occasion, have been invited to participate in conferences concerning area studies scholarship. Ever since its inauguration in the late 1940s, the disciplinary genre of area studies has been an ensemble of institutional sites of academic and professional activities, just like those of cultural and social anthropology, where racism has frequently been refuted and disavowed but at the same time institutionalized and practiced. One might trace it back to the scholarly intelligence activities associated with the colonial administrations of European and Japanese imperial powers during the interwar period or earlier. These disciplines are epistemologically, socially, and politically associated with the topoi in which racial recognition plays an essential role. The term "race" may be displaced by other terms such as "ethnicity" and "nationality," but regardless of which specific discussions are under way, area studies as a disciplinary genre cannot sever its fatal bonds with colonialism and colonial administration.

It is not for the sake of giving a kind of summary of the many articles included in this volume that I decided to reproduce the text of "Statement on Racism," which William Haver and I composed in the 1980s. On the contrary, it indicates the beginning of a confusion and uncontrollable proliferation of problems of and about racism as a result of which I had to wrestle with a number of issues—the discourse of "the West and the Rest," the loss of empire, the nationalism of *hikikomori* (reclusive withdrawal), the putative unity of the West, the modern international world, anthropological difference, specific identity, and so on. Even if these issues may appear fragmented and mutually disconnected, I would like readers to apprehend that they had to be raised in my pursuit of the problematics of racism. Moreover, I believe that the end of Pax Americana must be grasped from this generalized perspective of racism problematics and the modern international world. As a matter of fact, all the chapters of this volume are explicitly or implicitly underlined by my conviction that area studies as an institutional formation of knowledge production cannot be appreciated in its historical significance outside the context of Pax Americana.

The End of Pax Americana and *Hikikomori*

The end of Pax Americana has been anticipated with a variety of premonitions. For the first time in the 1990s, I was compelled to speculate on what the end of Pax Americana would possibly engender as well as what we should expect with this emerging reality of global geopolitics. What prompted me to seriously consider the end of American global hegemony, however, was not directly related to a policy adopted by the U.S. government or an incident in North America. Instead I was urged to critically consider the prospect of the end of Pax Americana, first because I witnessed the advent of a social phenomenon generally called "hikikomori" (reclusive withdrawal) in Japan. With this term, some social workers, sociologists, and mental health experts there referred to a group of young people (mostly men, but some women too) who refused to emerge from their bedrooms or their parents' homes and thereby alienated themselves from social life in general. Besides the people suffering this reclusive withdrawal from social life, the Japanese word "hikikomori" also signifies the phenomenon of this type of extreme social alienation. The social phenomenon of hikikomori was first reported in mass media in the late 1980s, but I only became aware of its gravity in the 1990s. It was in the middle of a long recession, when Japanese public opinion drastically shifted in a reactionary direction, that I faced the questions concerning hikikomori and its implications.

Although hesitant, I began to use the idiom "nationalism of hikikomori" to roughly group an assembly of sociopolitical issues related in one way or another to emerging reactionary, discriminatory, and exclusionary political trends observable in Japan during what is widely termed the Two Decades of Loss (失われた二十年), from the 1990s through 2010. It is, however, necessary to clarify my use of "hikikomori" in the idiom "nationalism of hikikomori" as part of the umbrella title of this volume, for fear that it could easily be misapprehended; here, in fact, this idiom does not directly refer to the hikikomori people who suffer from reclusive withdrawal at all; instead, it designates a parallel sociopolitical tendency witnessed in many postindustrial societies, sometimes discussed nowadays with the phrase "inward-looking society." By "nationalism of hikikomori," therefore, I designate a social and political constellation based upon the fantasy built around the image of a nation as an enclosed space of security and comfort, almost a fantastic equivalent to the enclosed space of a bedroom for hikikomori people. The adherents of this type of nationalism fear that their national space is vulnerable to the intrusion of aliens from outside the nation. As a matter of fact, in their political orientation and conduct, hikikomori people have little in common with those who speak loudly for the nationalism of hikikomori or have behaviors largely inspired by this type of jingoism.

I had to face the question of Pax Americana and its future when I examined sweeping changes occurring in societies on the western shores of the Pacific. When I was invited to deliver a lecture at the University of Hong Kong in the midst of the Umbrella Revolution in 2014, I discussed the topic of the end of Pax Americana. Later, while selecting essays in preparation for this volume, I decided to include "hikikomori" in the title of the whole book.

In the last two decades, I have dealt with a number of topics, discussions of which have culminated in my analysis in chapter 6 of this volume, "The Loss of Empire and Inward-Looking Society." However, as a preliminary caution for readers, it must be noted that its central focus is neither state policies of the countries on both shores of the Pacific nor the international and military maneuvers adopted by transpacific alliances. Although I do not completely overlook the United States' global prerogatives, international treaty negotiations, transpacific economic collaborations, or military maneuvers based on Cold War collective security arrangements, my primary thrust is rather with what Michel Foucault once called the microphysics of power.

Accordingly, my discussion of the end of Pax Americana and the nationalism of hikikomori must be located in the constellation of several problematics, each of which may appear, when apprehended in isolation, to be unrelated to others. Let me go back to these problematics that have motivated my research in the last twenty years.

The Modern International World and Europe

I was first introduced to the problem of internationality when with Jon Solomon I prepared the introduction (reproduced in this volume as chapter 5, "Addressing the Multitude of Foreigners, Echoing Foucault") for the fourth issue of a multilingual series called *Traces*, published in Chinese, Korean, Japanese, English, and Spanish.[3] In seeking the broadest scope from which to discuss modernity, we must take into account the long-term geopolitical arrangement that has characterized the modernity of the modern world in the last several centuries. There are many ways to define modernity, of course, one of which is to refer to a new phase in global history in which the Eurocentric spatial order of international law became dominant. This historical phase is said to have begun in the late fifteenth century and continues to the present. It is a rough span of chronological time in which a new geopolitical area called Europe came into existence and a new type of sovereignty—territorial state sovereignty—was first accepted as the legitimate form of government. A new regime, internationality, became the rule of interstate diplomacy among these states in the area called Europe, each of which fashioned itself as a legitimate territorial state sovereignty; consequently a distinction between the international world and the rest of the world was accepted as basic doxa underlying the operation of international diplomacy. This paved the way for a new polity of the nation-state on the one hand and modern colonialism on the other. The nation-state could not be found before the eighteenth century, while modern colonialism can be traced back to the conquest of the Americas in the late fifteenth or early sixteenth century. By the modern international world, therefore, I do not mean an enduring and homologous structure that has existed ever since the discovery of the Americas. In order to investigate the structure of the modern international world, however, we might as well presuppose a new regime of diplomatic equilibrium, which I tentatively call internationality, a system of interstate relationships according to which the new styles of government were gradually endorsed. Colonialism had existed since antiquity in a variety of forms, but modern colonialism is unique and must be distinguished from its older versions since it has been promoted, authorized, and legitimated within the scope of this interstate balance of internationality.

In discussing the formation of Europe, Michel Foucault raised two distinct principles with respect to government: the first is called the *raison d'état* prior to the eighteenth century; the second, the liberal art of government after the eighteenth century (2004a, 2008). We know that, in transition from the raison d'état to the liberal art of government, new historical positivities, such as "life" and "labor," were also introduced. One may add new objects of governmentality such as "peoplehood" and "population," and a field of knowledge summarily called the "social sciences" to the list of eighteenth-century inventions. While the former agenda was closely tied to mercantilist incentives, the latter assumes the liberal dynamics of competition and progress. Yet what Foucault stresses both in the raison d'état and the liberal art of government is that imperial domination by one state over others was deliberately evaded in the international world or Europe then. It prevented sovereigns and governing authorities from seeking to occupy an imperial position over other states. Raison d'état postulated that every state had its interests and had to defend them and that the state objective could not be to assume the unifying position of a total and global empire.[4]

Of course, his analysis is deployed within an assumed domain of historical occurrences, a privileged area that he elsewhere calls "our society" or "the West." To my knowledge, he never explicitly queried how our society or the West was constituted, how he was justified in relying upon the framework of the history of Western civilization that has supposedly continued to exist since Greek antiquity, in which a wide variety of documents of Greco-Roman antiquity are assumed to be relevant to us, the Europeans of the late twentieth century. As Foucault did not explicitly refer to non-European cases, his historical assessment implicitly highlights a striking contrast between developments in Western Europe and in other areas, such as Northeast Asia, and illustrates that the interstate regime of internationality was a prerogative unique to Western Europe in the seventeenth and eighteenth centuries, a prerogative that would be exploited in the history of the modern international world.

While we are no doubt heavily indebted to Foucault's insights and analyses, we must never lose sight of his Occidentalist blindness. Nevertheless, it is important to note that he did not forget to remark the very historicity of Europe; he called this historically unprecedented geopolitical formation "Europe" that was independent of imperial subordination. Europe is not some transhistorical substance for him. Europe became "Europe" precisely because it was characterized by this regime of international equilibrium; it is in this respect that internationality was something unique to Europe. This internationality was nothing but a prerogative resulting from this principle of equilibrium that was absent in Northeast Asia, at least until the late nineteenth century.

Before the nineteenth century in Northeast Asia, interstate diplomacy had never been apprehended in terms of internationality; it was never exercised on the basis of mutual recognition among equal states. It had never accepted the protocol of formal equality, thanks to which, no matter how small, poor, or militarily weak a state may be, it was allowed to behave as an equal in the game of interstate recognition. Hence the idea of a treaty was a challenge to Northeast Asian actors in interstate diplomacy in the nineteenth century. In this respect, Europe was born as an area where the prerogative of internationality prevailed. What distinguished it from the rest of the world was the conviction on the part of Europeans that Europe was an international world, while the rest of the world was not.

The Nation and the Modalities of Individual Identification

In chapter 2, "From Relational Identity to Specific Identity," I outline the drastic change that occurred in the modality of individual identification in modernization in Northeast Asia and that inaugurated the possibility of the new community called "nation." I have tried to give a more detailed explanation to this pair of concepts, relational identity on the one hand and specific identity on the other, in the sphere of the interpersonal relationship, which I coined in my study of the stillbirth of Japanese as an ethnos and as a language in the eighteenth century (Sakai [1997c] 2015).

Initially, I introduced this pair so as to describe the drastic change that occurred in ethics or, more specifically, in the structure of imperative statement. It was a part of my attempt to correct an error I had committed in my early study of the invention in fantasy of ethnic/national language in the eighteenth-century discourse, *Voices of the Past: The Status of Language in Eighteenth-Century Japanese Discourse* (Sakai 1991). In analyzing Confucian ethics, I presumed, even though I acknowledged that the concept of judgment in the propositional form could not be found in Confucian or pre-nineteenth-century discourses in Northeast Asia, that the basic pattern of the ethical imperative could be construed in the propositional form of an imperative statement, just as it is, for example, in Kant's moral philosophy: "One must do this" or "One must not do that."[5] In fact, none of the ethical imperatives takes either an individual or anonymous general subject as "one," as an agent of ethical conduct. In Confucian discourses, an agent of moral action is never divorced from the specific position of enunciation, as determined in the network of kinship, in clan or some rank-related positions. Accordingly, a basic imperative should never be construed in such a way as "One must respect one's elder brother" or "One must take care of one's children." Instead, a Confucian virtue is expressed in a statement such as this: "A son is expected to respect his father," or "A husband is obligated to take care of his wives." As far as a person's ethical conduct is concerned, the acting agent is always and already determined in his or her relationality to others, primarily in the network of kinship. It follows that all the major ethical values carry the sense of familial obligations in Confucian or premodern discourses in Northeast Asia, and that the abstract notion of the individual human being, of a human agent stripped of all familial relations, could not exist there.[6] Therefore, when the project of modernization was thematically taken up in Northeast Asian societies for the first time in the late nineteenth century, so-called Enlightenment intellectuals could not avoid a question of how to eliminate the modus operandi of Confucian ethics. As I discuss in chapter 2, as far as the modernization of subjectivity was summarized by the invention of individualism, Enlightenment intellectuals could not evade the question of how to liberate the personhood totally incarcerated in the network of kinship into an individuality independent of all these kinship constraints.

Accordingly, I argue that one of the tenets of modernization in some countries in Northeast Asia, where Confucianism dominated many aspects of everyday life and government, must have been to introduce a new modality of individual identification, to manufacture subjects who identify with a large collectivity without the mediation of kinship, clan, and rank-related hierarchy. I call this new modality of identification "specific identity" in contrast to "relational identity," the old modality of identification. I believe that this explains why, for progressive intellectuals of the late nineteenth and early twentieth centuries in Northeast Asia, it was so important to get rid of the legacies of Confucianism and open up the social possibility of the individual human being who is directly identified with the new imagined community of the nation.

Modernization implies a host of social changes, from the sphere of the money economy, to the registration of population, to the institutions of legislative procedures, to the reorganization of the heterosexual relationship in terms of the idea of romantic love, to the rearrangement of familial networks (the invention of the modern family), to the introduction of scientific and technological rationality in everyday life, to the creation of individualized subjects effectively capable of responding to the new tactics of government as members of the new community called the nation, and so on. But for the massive transition from relational identity to specific identity, the nationalization of population would not have been possible. Neither could the individuation of subjectivity have been accomplished in countries in Northeast Asia. What I overlooked in my initial study was this radical biopolitical transformation that occurred in the sphere of everyday life for individuals in the late nineteenth century.

Even in the sphere of diplomacy, the comprehension of the interstate relationship could not be emancipated from the old form of relational identity. Hence, a tributary worked between two semiautonomous sovereigns as if they shared some kinship relation, which obliged the sovereign to follow some moral dictates in relation to his vassals. Without fail, tributary diplomacy reintroduces some pseudo-paternalistic relationship of subordination between a father and his legitimate offspring. Thus the interstate relationship also had to be fashioned as if it were a kinship relation that was quite often reinforced by some marital arrangements. Just as there was no explicit conception of formal equality in a familial network according to Confucian ethics, likewise there was no place for the protocols of formal equality in diplomacy as long as it was dictated by the tributary system.

Internationality thus meant much more than the sheer juxtaposition of states: it may appear to help build a new type of international diplomacy; yet we must not overlook the other aspect of the modern international world. Foucault's discussion of Europe is indispensable precisely because, perhaps unwittingly, it casts light upon this difference, which I have called "civilizational difference" or "anthropological difference," and which Stuart Hall, among others, called "the West and the Rest" (Hall 1996, 184–227). It is a difference that may appear pertinent to geographical order, of the region designated initially as Europe and later as the West, in contrast to the rest of the world. But, as Jon Solomon and I explore in chapter 5 in this volume, it is a sort of ethical imperative masquerading as an epistemic judgment that serves to differentiate two types of humanity: *humanitas* and *anthropos*.

Anthropological Difference and "the West and the Rest"

A plurality of people inhabits the world, and frequently the world is imagined as a common space where differences among people are encountered. In order to distinguish the plurality of peoples from the plurality of human individuals, we often rely upon categories for collective identities, such as family, kin, race, nation, ethnos, religion, and culture. The most commanding category for collective unity in the modern international world is presented in language; a language is represented as expressing the primordial union of a people. The individuality or indivisibility of one's soul or ego is most often associated with the imaginary unity of one's body, a body supposedly proper to a human individual. If one's proper body is somewhat a marker of human individuality, the image—or figure, trope, or schema—of a language gives the sense of an individual or indivisible collectivity. While it is possible to experience an encounter of an individual and another or one set of individuals with another set, an encounter of a collectivity with another—or among plural collectivities—cannot be experienced unless it is symbolically construed in such an expression as "Britain meets China." One individual encounters another individual, but it is only through a symbolic representation that one collectivity—such as nation and race—encounters another. We understand that an encounter of collectivities occurs when individuals involved in it are recognized as representatives of different collectivities. Since there are always multiple categories for collectivities, a single encounter among individuals is always open to different categorizations. Hence, an encounter of collectivities always implies that individuals involved in such an encounter identify themselves with their respective collectivities. This is a mundane truism, of course. No matter how rudimentary it may sound, however, let us not undervalue this logical cliché.

How does the symbolic representation of collectivity work in the interstate balance of internationality? How does internationality modify and transform the manner in which collectivities are represented? What modification and transformation in the symbolic representation of collectivities allow for the emergence of a new collectivity called "nation" in the modern international world?

Collectivities can be said to encounter each other only when individuals identifying with them come across one another. For example, China and Britain never meet; it is only a person regarded as a representative of China and another regarded as a representative of Britain that can in fact meet. It is always the encounter of individuals identifying with two different collectivities that allows us to say collectivities encounter one another. It follows that, for instance, the West and the East never meet because this context is only an individual identifying with the West meeting another identifying with the East, leaving aside the question of how to specify identification in this instance.[7] When we say that collective identities meet, it is assumed that individuals encounter each other and that each of these individual participants identifies with one or other collectivity.

This encounter gives rise to a series of choices: what collectivities these participants select for their identification; through what procedures they identify with the collectivities of choices; to what positionalities they ascribe their own choices in relation to the other participants' choices; and so on. The encounter thus marks a locale of identification when collectivities are constituted. In other words, this encounter is the very site where what Michel Foucault termed "microphysics of power" is carried out.

The West is one such category, and it is often used as if it were a trope for a unified collectivity, like a language whose visual representation is often ascribed to an area on the cartographic plane. Habitually, it is believed that the West is one of these collective identities and furthermore is cartographically determinable since the phrase itself comes etymologically from the directional adverb "west." Yet, on what grounds is it possible to claim that the West can be configured cartographically? What sort of microphysics of power serves to articulate the West to a geographic location?

It is generally believed that the West and the Rest is one of the most significant ways of ordering differences among peoples by geographic location.[8] Here I have adopted the notation the "West and the Rest," following Stuart Hall. The West and the Rest is not a juxtaposition of two separate and preconstituted entities, namely, the West and the Rest, but rather it is a discourse that institutes the very differentiation of the West from the Rest. When the Rest cannot be postulated, neither can the West be identified. It follows that the Rest cannot exist when the West cannot be postulated. Both the West and the Rest are effects of some differentiation, without which neither can be sustained. In other words, the West and the Rest symbolize positionalities whose stability is sustained only as long as they are incorporated into the quest for anthropological difference.

I propose to understand the world in which the West is distinguished from the Rest as a schema. This schema world enables us to make different social relations comprehensible, as though these relations were synthesized and accommodated in a coherent configuration. But the presumed coherence of this configuration is never more than a presumption that cannot be factually verified. In this sense, too, the world is a schema. As far as the world projected as a schema is concerned, let us call this performance through the schema of the world "worlding."[9] The schematism of the world, or "worlding," which gives sense to our experiences with the things and people we encounter, allows us to imagine heterogeneous social relations—races, social classes, genders, nationalities—as forming a coherence, along with a certain cartographic representation of the world, as well as the narratives of world history. One may argue that worlding or the schematism of the world serves as a passive doxa or prejudicial ground that provides us with a fantasized coherence among things and people we encounter in this lifeworld. In other words, it gives us the facticity of our being in the world in a typically anthropocentric and Eurocentric manner. This modern schema of the world allows us to comprehend a wide variety of power relations in an imaginary configuration of hierarchies in which the West is considered the center. Therefore, the modern world is structured, spatially as well as temporally, by the opposition of the West and the Rest. The West is a figure rendered sensible through the worlding of modernity, and it is always a putative unity. It is putative, first, in the sense that the world is imagined as a putative coherence, and, as long as it is only determinable within the world, the West can only be identified as such in the last instance. But this last instance never comes; the West is always in suspension, so to speak. Second, it is in the sense of a project toward an actualization in the future. The West is a teleological order that is not only spatial but also temporal.

However, this teleological intensity of the West has been perceptibly eclipsed in the last several decades so that it is increasingly dislocated, not only in the cartographic representation of the world but also in the chronological order of world history. It is less and less plausible that the West is more developed than the Rest in the chronological order of the world; it is increasingly dubious that the West can designate an assemblage of advanced or progressive collectivities, in contrast to less advanced or, more straightforwardly and condescendingly, primitive societies. Not only among the local tribes in New Guinea and the Congo basin but also among indigenous whites of Alabama in the United States and Northamptonshire in the United Kingdom, what was once characterized as "feudal remnants" can be found nowadays among those indigenous people.

The West is a relatively recent designation in the development of the schematism of the modern international world.[10] Until the late nineteenth century, the term "West" was not in common circulation even in Western Europe, although *xiyang* (西洋 or *seiyô* in Japanese), which signifies the West today, was widely used in Northeast Asia before the mid-nineteenth century; this was mainly because it used to designate the Far Western periphery of the earth in the old Sinocentric world. This compound of Chinese characters—*xi* + *yang*—remained unaltered, but its connotation was completely altered in the late nineteenth and early twentieth centuries. This change implied the collapse of the Sinocentric worlding; xiyang no longer indexed a periphery with the Middle Kingdom in the center of the world. The Middle Kingdom was now located in the Far Eastern periphery of the world.

The use of the West was preceded by that of Europe, and, as mentioned above, Europe was already the space of international interstate competition in the seventeenth century, whereas the surface of the earth outside Europe was recognized as virgin land with the potential for colonial conquest. Yet European forces had to wait to be endowed with superior military, economic, and epistemic capabilities in order to overwhelm, conquer, and subdue—or annihilate—local inhabitants in other parts of the rest of the world. In this respect, we must keep in mind that European superiority was first established after the discovery of the Americas. Even two hundred years after this initial conquest of the Americas, European states could in no way challenge the governmental authority of the imperial reign, for instance, in China. Consequently, what Stuart Hall (1996) called "the discourse of the West and the Rest" first became the regulatory dynamics of international politics in the Atlantic theater. Having begun in the Americas, this bifurcation of the world reached Northeast Asia in the late eighteenth and early nineteenth centuries with the development of industrial capitalism and modern technologies in Western Europe.

As a consequence of the imposition of this new bifurcation of the West and the Rest on peoples inhabiting regions to be subsumed under the name of Asia, no people in Northeast Asia could possibly escape this wave of modernization. No matter whether local intellectuals could knowingly reflect upon it or not, modernization in Northeast Asia was, if not explicitly, accompanied by the schematism of the West and the Rest. Consequently, modernization was never felt as an internal progress among the inhabitants of the Rest; it was perceived as an imposition on peoples in Asia by some external forces. As a result, it was comprehended that most Northeast Asian societies were conquered and colonized through modernization by European powers (and later by the United States and Japan), and they had to drastically change their ways of life in the spheres of government, economy, and cognitive and cultural activities as well as social interaction. In this process, the dichotomy of the West and the Rest, which still serves to sustain Pax Americana today, became globally recognized. It was in this bifurcated design of the worlding of modernity that modernization was pursued by the political, industrial, and intellectual elites of local societies in Northeast Asia.

Modernization brought about new forms of legitimacy and community. Under the reign of international law, each state sovereignty had to be legitimated through mutual interstate recognition, while the new community of "nation" that had begun to anchor the legitimacy of the sovereign state since the eighteenth century had to consolidate its authenticity through a number of cultural and aesthetic institutions, including that of the national language. But only by means of the modern regime of translation could the national language be represented as the unity of a linguistic medium native to a certain population.[11] As I argued in *Voices of the Past: The Status of Language in Eighteenth-Century Japanese Discourse* (1991), the national language is recognized as an individuated and unified medium supposedly inherent in the national population only when it is represented in contrast to other languages. In other words, the new practice of translation in terms of the modern regime of translation is part and parcel of the biopolitical technology of internationality whereby the identification and individuation of a national community is accomplished together with a subjectivation of an individual as a native speaker of a language.

What happened in Northeast Asia—Vietnam, China, Korea, and Japan—in the process of modernization was the collapse of the authority of the Classical Chinese language, whose presence in societies of Northeast Asia had paralleled the role of Latin in Western Europe as a universal language in some respects (although in other respects the significance of Latin can in no way be compared to that of Classical Chinese). From the ruins of Classical Chinese emerged new national languages—modern Chinese, Korean, Vietnamese, Japanese, and so on; these serve to define the cultural identity of each of these nations today. The aesthetics of national communality was elaborated upon in modernity, and the formation of the national community was accompanied by a revolutionary change, which I have already referred to as the transition from relational identity to specific identity in the mode of individual identification. But for this revolutionary change, the aesthetics of nationality, thanks to which an individual feels that he or she belongs to a nation, would never have been institutionalized. What must be emphasized is the aesthetics of nation building in the modernization of these societies; the emotional-sentimental dynamics of national belonging is closely affiliated with the invention of national language as well as with the subjective technology of nationality whereby subjects of the nation are made to feel together in imagination.

Humanitas and Anthropos

One of the most profound transformations that the modern international world gave rise to can be found in the disciplines of knowledge production. From the late eighteenth century when universities began to be modernized in Europe, the discourse of the West and the Rest helped to establish what is referred to as "anthropological difference."[12] By this, two types of knowledge production were differentiated from one another in the fields of the humanities and social sciences. While one is about a type of humanity, "humanitas," the other is about a different type of humanity, "anthropos." The first, under which disciplines such as philosophy, psychology, and sociology are subsumed, was supposedly about "us" or European humanity—let us not forget Foucault's use of "us"—while the second, in which disciplines such as Indian philosophy and cultural/social anthropology are included, was about "them," or exotic people somewhat distinct from "us." Nowadays it is indeed really arduous to see on which empirical ground this anthropological difference can be ascertained, but regardless of whether there can ever be an empirical ground for this difference, anthropological difference has served as an epistemic judgment as well as a practical imperative in the organization of humanistic and social scientific knowledge at the modern university. What is significant in this assertion of anthropological difference is that it pretends to be based upon empirically verifiable facts: what is put forth is, as a matter of fact, a rule of conduct in the guise of empirical verifiability in the fields of academic knowledge production. Thus, the logical status of anthropological difference is, to say the least, ambivalent.

As I explore in chapter 3, "Asian Theory and European Humanity: On the Question of Anthropological Difference," this difference has been very closely associated for a long time with the mission of European humanity, and it regulates how one must conduct oneself in order to fashion oneself as European when engaged in knowledge production; this is most explicitly expressed in Edmund Husserl's last public lectures and posthumous publications. In short, even though it might appear to justify itself on some constative and empirical grounds, anthropological difference is, in the final analysis, concerned with how one fashions oneself in the practice of knowledge production. In this respect, it is a reactive response to the putative identity of the West; it is nothing but a quest and investment.

It was once argued that those who fashion themselves as European—or as Westerners nowadays—ought not to accept the definition of their status being exclusively as an object of study. Thus, the Westerner is not of an empirical determination of human type even though the claim of Western identity is made on epistemic grounds. Before being known, described, and recognized, they are expected to take an active attitude in knowing, describing, and recognizing. Instead of being passively inspected, classified, compared, and analyzed, Westerners are supposed to apply their own means of inspection, classification, comparison, and analysis to some object, which might well be themselves. The dual characteristics of this subject/object structure—Foucault succinctly calls it an "empirico-transcendental doublet" (1966b, 323–339; 1973, 312–328)—is attributed to the Westerner, who, at the same time, is an object of empirical inquiry and a subject reflecting on the very procedure of that inquiry. Supposedly only Westerners actively engage in transcendental reflections on, improvements in, and inventions of the means of knowing. When a group of people is characterized exclusively by their communal mores and local histories, they are determined in terms of their objective characteristics. They are thereby overlooked for their subjective faculties. In other words, in this epistemic and/or practical operation, the West insists on being determined, not in terms of its characteristics as an object of knowledge, but rather for its subjective faculties and productivity. This is why the idea of theory, a faculty of reason, to critically examine, incessantly improve upon, and newly innovate the very means of knowing has been singled out as the exclusive endowment of European humanity. Until the twentieth century, as Edmund Husserl insisted, philosophy, the science of theory par excellence, ought to be understood as the spiritual shape of this type of humanity, distinguished from "anthropological types," such as Chinese, Indians, Eskimos, and Gypsies.[13]

It is now essential to apprehend what sort of logical and conceptual maneuver this anthropological difference entails. What sort of difference is it? Where does its inherent ambivalence derive from?

It is often assumed that anthropological difference is something empirically observable, and thus it is possible to construe this constative difference in terms of two species, two already substantialized beings. Just as a group of white horses can be distinguished from a separate group of black horses in the generality of horses, anthropological difference is reduced to the difference between one group of humanity called Europeans and another group of humanity called non-Europeans. What is operating here is an attribution of anthropological difference to discrimination between two distinct species, to a species difference (*diaphora*) in classical logic in this case.[14]

In the discourse of the West and the Rest, it is postulated that there is a fundamental difference in life attitude toward knowledge production between Westerners and non-Westerners. As if reflecting the mythological vision of global migration in the early modern period, Westerners travel around the world and observe, inspect, and gaze at exotic people and their peculiar behaviors encountered on their migratory movements, while non-Westerners are described, analyzed, and compared in a passive way by distant observers or travelers. It is assumed that non-Westerners are destined to be stationary, reactive, and traditional, whereas Westerners are dynamic, active, and restless by nature. Hence, the adjective "indigenous" is rarely attributed to Westerners in this perspective of gaze, where an inspecting look is cast at the stationary indigenous or native inhabitants by mobile migrants even though the vast majority of the European or Western population, in fact, do not participate in global migratory movement.

Flows of Knowledge and Flows of Migrants

One of the signs intimating the end of Pax Americana in the last few decades is a radical change in the perception of migratory flows in the world. Of course, it is misleading to claim that the fantasized vision of global migration has not shifted before. In the 1920s and '30s, an anti-immigrant rhetoric of "Europe for Europeans" flourished, and it propagated an entirely false vision that intruders from outside Europe had invaded Europe and caused European civilization to decline. The political rhetoric of "America First" evokes a similar narrative of anti-immigrant racism on the acute sense of the loss of empire. Operating in the nativist exclusion of immigrants is the perception of the fantastic vision of global migration in reverse. The West is no longer the center from which values and commodities symbolizing modernity emanate. On the contrary, Europeans who used to travel far, move freely, and settle in their colonized places in the peripheries of the world are no longer capable of migrating. It is now fantasized that the assumed division of migratory labor that used to characterize the modern international world has been reversed: such adjectives as "indigenous," "native," and "stationary" must now be attributed to the inhabitants of Western Europe and North America. We must seriously consider how we can study the indigenous population of North America—it goes without saying that I am not talking about Native Americans—independently of the discourse of the West and the Rest. But, before going into this redefinition of indigenous or native people, one simply cannot overlook the disciplinary formation in the humanities and social sciences at American universities, a disciplinary arrangement that contributed greatly to the transformation of American universities and developed in the age of Pax Americana: area studies.

In selectively inheriting the legacies of the colonial studies of prewar empires, the disciplines of area studies were established at universities and institutions of higher education in the United States after World War II. With the remarkable expansion of these programs, the humanities and social sciences were transformed and reorganized on the basis of new interdisciplinary configurations. Initially, in the late 1940s, the Social Science Research Council's task force intended to create area studies programs that were to cover Western Europe as well, but in subsequent decades area studies were confined to those areas supposedly outside the West, namely, geographic regions regarded as the Rest in the discourse of the West and the Rest. Consequently, until the end of the twentieth century, area studies were assigned exclusively to geographic areas outside the North Atlantic. In other words, in higher education in the post–World War II world under the Pax Americana, the idea of area studies reproduced the centuries-old bifurcation of the world between humanitas and anthropos.

In due course, it has been expected that area studies experts inevitably embody the posture of humanity endowed with the capacity for humanitas, observing particular instances of humanity for the production of knowledge on anthropos. Before the 1990s, when the effects of globalization began to manifest on American university campuses, the imagined positionality of area experts was incarcerated in the fantastic vision of a migratory division of epistemic labor, the dichotomous staging of traveling Europeans who observe, inspect the natives, and collect data on them on the one hand, and on the other of the indigenous residents who are observed, inspected, and recorded by area experts. As a matter of fact, many area experts fashioned themselves as the most typical Westerners. But as the number of international students from the Rest increased in campus classrooms, it became increasingly difficult to project onto a vast plurality of people the simplistic dichotomy of two kinds of humanity differentiated in terms of anthropological difference: European or Western humanity endowed with a theoretical capacity, vis-à-vis the natives of the Rest whose knowledge lacked in self-critical reflection or innovative self-transcendence.

It used to be almost indisputably accepted that those from outside the West specializing in area studies were routinely regarded as "native informants"; they had a lot of native knowledge about an area but were supposedly incapable of either critically reflecting upon such native knowledge or of evaluating the procedure of knowledge production, innovating new operations of describing, classifying, or judging. In short, these indigenous scholars were supposed to be incapable of theory. To the extent that the focus of anthropological difference is displaced from the domain of epistemology to the classification of humanity, those affiliated with the West are presumably theoretical, whereas the native informants are in due course nontheoretical or antitheoretical. Let us remember that this fantastic vision of the global division of intellectual labor is not confined at all to the West or to the so-called white population. Ironic though it may sound, this vision is endorsed rather enthusiastically by a large number of indigenous scholars resident in the Rest. This is why the idiom "Western theory" is still endorsed uncritically and circulated widely in academia in Asia, Africa, and Latin America.

Yet what has been increasingly noticeable in the last few decades is that this Eurocentric division of intellectual labor is becoming irrelevant, and that area studies experts cannot be neatly accommodated in the bifurcated vision of theoretically oriented Europeans versus nontheoretical natives of the Rest. Can one seriously argue that Euro-American area scholars are theoretically oriented while Asian or Asian American specialists in area studies programs are alienated from so-called theories? Does an inherent property of a person, such as one's birthplace, ethnicity, nationality, or native language—of course, a human being is never born with his or her langue; a language is always a later acquisition, so the term "native language" in the sense of inborn language is no doubt an oxymoron—determine whether or not one is endowed with capacity for self-critical reflectivity or theoretical reasoning? Is the fantastic vision of migratory flows in this respect any different from the prejudicial assumption of the gendered division of labor, namely that women are less theoretical by nature while men are born to be better at abstract thinking like mathematics? Are you not familiar with many men who are hopeless in mathematics?

Today we live in a globalized academic world where we constantly interact with intellectuals of different ethnicity, from different continents, and of different genders. These fantastic visions of migratory flows and of the global, ethnic, and gender divisions of intellectual labor are much easier to dispute than before the 1990s. What is at stake nowadays is not how to contest these fantastic visions of divisions of labor. As a task, that is all too easy. What we must concern ourselves with is knowing how the enterprise of area studies, whose original design was thoroughly enmeshed with these fantasies of division of labor in the discourse of the West and the Rest, is still sustainable even in the twenty-first century. It seems that the disciplines of area studies are still captured in the worlding of modernity. Our task nowadays is to seek to discover how to transform the discipline of area studies in such a way that it could survive as an intellectual project even when Pax Americana is gone.

Allow me to examine, once again, how appropriate the topic of Pax Americana is to the problematics mentioned so far. First of all, it is undeniable that the United States' global policies were designed to reconstruct the system of international law that had been destroyed twice over, by two world wars in the twentieth century. It was claimed that Pax Americana asserted itself on the grounds of the universal validity of the system of international law within the scope shaped by the structure of the modern international world. The United Nations headquarters was not located in Europe but was symbolically shifted to New York City instead. Second, the U.S. government publicly denounced the ideologies of colonialism and old colonial governance and, at least nominally, supported anticolonial nationalism, not only in Europe but also in countries later designated as part of the Second and Third Worlds. In this respect, Pax Americana was constructed to resurrect the old vision of internationality beyond Europe, recognizing each nation-state's autonomy in terms of the idea of territorial state sovereignty; it was legitimated as an extension of the modern international world. Thereupon, the Allied Powers initiated a drastic move by which the equation of "Europe = the realm of interstate governmentality dictated by international law" was canceled and the international world was expanded to cover the entirety of the earth's surface. It is no accident that, in East Asia, the former colonies of Vietnam, North and South Korea, the Philippines, Taiwan, China, Indonesia, Malaysia, and Burma gained independence within approximately one decade after Japan's defeat.[15]

Of course, this is not to say that all the old colonial power relations ceased to exist. On the contrary, the United States gradually built a hegemonic order that controlled the western shores of the Pacific through a number of measures, including a network of American military bases where colonial extraterritoriality was guaranteed by status of forces agreements. It is in the relationship of American military personnel stationed in satellite countries of the United States with the local citizens that the remnants of old colonialism are starkly visible.

At the same time, some features of the modern international world and the discourse of the West and the Rest have continued to prevail in the realms of academic knowledge, the humanities, and the social sciences in particular.

Transpacific Complicity and Pax Americana

In many respects, the transpacific alliance between the United States and Japan after Japan's unconditional surrender to the Allied Powers represents a newly revised colonial government on the western shore of the Pacific. In the 1950s and '60s, the Japanese state and conservative forces benefited greatly from Pax Americana, which was progressively consolidated from the late 1940s through the 1950s. As I discuss in chapter 6, the decision to pardon Emperor Hirohito for war crimes so as to use him as an American puppet under the Allied Occupation of Japan proved to be exceptionally successful in turning Japanese nationalism into an instrument of American control over Japan's domestic politics. It can be argued that the United States of America imitated the strategy of colonization devised by the Japanese military in the prewar Manchu-kuo in order to fabricate a satellite state, which appeared independent. In this sense, the Japanese state forged after World War II was America's Manchu-kuo. With Hirohito as a prime example, Japanese political actors, many of whom were war criminals released by the United States Occupation Administration who could have been blackmailed anytime if necessary by American agencies, were favored and supported by the U.S. government. Around the U.S. "Confinement Strategy," the American supreme commander while Japan was under the Allied

Occupation, and then the Central Intelligence Agency after Japan's independence in 1952, constructed an alliance between Japan's war criminals, such as Kishi Nobusuke and Shôriki Matsutarô, and an American anticommunist campaign in East Asia. In this respect, Japanese national politics dominated by conservative forces—mainly by the Liberal Democratic Party since 1955 with only brief interruptions—can be characterized as a semicolonial regime of war-criminal conservatives, including the recent administration of Prime Minister Abe Shinzô (安倍 晋三).

As explained chiefly in chapter 6, the United States of America inherited the Greater East Asia Co-prosperity Sphere from the Japanese Empire. But American policy makers did not have knowledge of these areas for colonial governance, so they had to rely upon Japanese expertise on colonial administration that was acquired by Japanese bureaucrats and colonial officials, mainly during the interwar period, even though Japan was defeated in the Asia-Pacific War; they deliberately assigned the role of "empire under subcontract" to the postwar state of Japan, which was led mainly by former war criminals and anticommunist ideologues. As a result, with a massive infusion of capital investment in its industry, the Japanese economy rebounded rapidly in the 1950s and could sustain high economic growth for more than three decades, well into the 1980s.

Since the United States inherited the Greater East Asia Co-prosperity Sphere (except, of course, mainland China and North Korea), the Japanese public was allowed to resume the status of colonizers in relation to their Asian neighbors under the pretense of empire under subcontract. Predictably enough, whereas the Japanese public experienced Japan's surrender to the Allied Powers and the loss of empire and its colonies in their relationship to the United States, they never underwent the sort of humiliation expected of them vis-à-vis peoples of Asia. They did not realize that they were also defeated by those whom they used to look down upon as their colonial servants. The majority of Japanese failed to expose themselves to the gaze of Asian peoples and undergo the experience of shame necessary for them to decolonize themselves. The loss of sovereignty over old colonies is not sufficient; one must undergo radical transformation in the manner of self-fashioning in order to decolonize. In this manner, the Japanese nation missed the chance for decolonization through the important process of the loss of empire.

Indeed, here I use "the loss of empire" as something positive, as a sort of affirmative action. In this regard, I learned much from the scholars of British cultural studies who studied the problem of loss of empire in Great Britain.

In the 1980s, scholars like Paul Gilroy confronted social phenomena generally discussed in reference to this expression, "loss of empire."[16] In the late 1940s and the 1950s, the British Empire lost many of its colonies, and the British public could no longer take for granted the colonial prestige and the sense of superiority toward the inhabitants of their former colonies. Yet, immediately after the collapse of the British Empire as former colonial masters, they were not infected with the disillusionment and anxiety often associated with decolonization; the moment of disillusionment came about thirty years later, for a variety of reasons. In the interim, as the most important satellite state of the United States, Britain could continue to maintain an exceptional status in international politics and, as a core country of the Allied Powers, Britons were allowed to behave as victors under Pax Americana, although, in relation to their former colonial subjects, they were clearly losers. Yet, in the 1970s and '80s, even ordinary British people could not overlook the fact that Britain was no longer an empire, and thus some began to appeal to the nostalgic image of old England. Yet others harbored a strong sentiment of resentment over the reality of this loss of empire. The first visible sign of the loss of empire was widespread anti-immigrant racism. Reactionary political figures such as Enoch Powell attracted many followers, and since that time England has never escaped a persistent substantive anti-immigrant racism. Many in Britain were and still are vulnerable to this sentiment of resentment, which is easily triggered when certain sociopolitical and emotional conditions are in place. Brexit of 2016 cannot be comprehended without regard to this British loss of empire and a deliberate manipulation of mass media. In chapter 6, therefore, I exemplify this with Kazuo Ishiguro's *The Remains of the Day* (1989), a novel that skillfully captures the anxiety and resentment evoked by the loss of empire.

The British example of the loss of empire was very important in my apprehension of what the end of Pax Americana implied for many Japanese. Please allow me to reiterate. In the 1990s, I discovered the social phenomenon of hikikomori in Japan; I learned that a large number of young Japanese, somewhere between one and two million, had withdrawn from public life, and that an increasing portion of the Japanese population exhibited an inward-looking attitude in everyday life. Mass media's coverage of hikikomori coincided with the emergence of the reactionary political movement of the Japanese Society for History Textbook Reform (新しい歴史教科書をつくる会); this society successfully mobilized a large number of Japanese citizens and attempted to erase from middle and high school history textbooks any description of the colonial and wartime atrocities caused by the Japanese state and military. Instead of dealing with historical facts about Japanese colonialism and war crimes, they simply wanted to deny and reject what Japanese soldiers and citizens did before and during the war, including the notorious wartime sex slavery generally referred to as "the Comfort Women problem." They simply refused to dialogue with non-Japanese or those Japanese concerned about Japanese responsibility for the country's colonial and wartime ventures; they withdrew from any possible occasions where they would be forced into responsibility for or responsiveness to charges of accountability. The significant fact of their disavowal is that they tried to hide in a safe place in order to evade the possibility or potentiality of an encounter with non-Japanese or Japanese critics who were likely to hold them accountable; their evasion of colonial or wartime responsibility was played out entirely in fantasy.

The underlying premise of their movement was to confine themselves to a closure by which to avoid encounter with foreigners or "masochistic" (self-critical) Japanese. Ten years later in 2006, these reactionary movements were followed by street demonstrations organized by the Association of Citizens Who Denounce the Privileges Accorded to Resident Koreans and Chinese (在日特権を許さない市民の会, often abbreviated as Zaitokukai 在特会). These demonstrations publicized many openly racist statements. Although there have been innumerable incidents of racial discrimination and violence in modern Japan, since the end of World War II there have scarcely been any street demonstrations that have openly advocated for discrimination against certain ethnic or racial groups. Perhaps the Association of Citizens Who Denounce the Privileges Accorded to Resident Koreans and Chinese is the first such movement in which resident Koreans and Chinese, the majority of whom were actually born and raised in Japan, were accused of enjoying not excessive privilege but simply an equality under the law. In addition, what is immediately obvious is that the overwhelming majority of the association's members are embarrassingly ignorant of the ethnic groups they choose to attack, of their histories, and of their social conditions. It is apparent that, even though they hate the resident aliens of Korean and Chinese ancestry, this hatred does not stem from any actual encounters with them. It seems plausible that they hate these resident aliens based entirely on their fantastic projection. With this in mind, I want to pose the crucial question: to what extent is the nationalism of hikikomori one of the consequences of their fantastic wish to evade a collective shame, of their disavowal of the loss of empire?

This nationalism of hikikomori is a unique historical occurrence in its own right; it cannot be analyzed without regard to the history of postwar Japan, the rapid media revolution—digitalization in communication technology, the development of social media, the collapse of neighborhood communities, and general atomization—taking place in Northeast Asia or the postcolonial conditions in Asia at large. Yet it is also true that it shares many features of the inward-looking society observed in many postindustrial countries. As outlined above, I attempt to situate the nationalism of hikikomori in the history of post–World War II Northeast Asia under Pax Americana. Moreover, I also approach it from the viewpoint of the modern international world, one from which I have conducted an extensive historical analysis of the formation of the national community as well as a particular subjective technology whereby subjects have been manufactured for the nation-states.

When I examined the drastic changes undergone by societies on the western shores of the Pacific, I could not escape the question of the myth of Japan's successful modernization that used to give its people a sense of colonial self-esteem. Perhaps we should apprehend the emotive-sentimental impact of the loss of empire against the backdrop of an overly optimistic vision of Japanese modernization.

By the end of the 1960s, having somehow recovered from the trauma of wartime miseries, the devastating effects of American aerial bombing and overseas atrocities, the vast majority of Japanese people conceded that Japan's subsequent modernization was something positive and that they were proud of themselves for this extraordinary accomplishment, despite the fact that Japan's postwar success was possible only under Pax Americana. Underlying this affirmative attitude toward Japan's past—despite its colonialism and defeat in the Asia-Pacific War—there was a sense of collective superiority as a nation. The Japanese public was convinced at that time that, in East Asia, only Japan had succeeded in creating a modern political system and a modern governing bureaucracy, in appropriating the spirit of modern scientific and technological rationality, in competing with Euro-American nations in industrial capitalism, and in establishing an exceptionally high standard of living and education in Asia. South Korea and Taiwan were still very poor countries with a per capita income less than a tenth of Japan's. Even though Japan was defeated in World War II—the Asian-Pacific War—and lost sovereignty over Korea and Taiwan, it could still enjoy the status of empire between Japan and its former colonies, at least in terms of economic measure and as an "empire under subcontract." As is typical of the legacy of colonial domination, the gap between the suzerain nation and its former colonies was still tangible in terms of the standard of living and the degree of modernization.

During the 1980s and '90s, however, a number of significant political reforms were implemented in Taiwan and South Korea, thanks to which parliamentary democracy seemed to take root in these former Japanese colonies. In some respects, the Republic of China (Taiwan) and the Republic of Korea (South Korea) appear more politically modern than Japan does. Furthermore, one must

TABLE I.I Per Capita Gross Domestic Product in Five Countries (1982–2012)

Year	U.S.A.	China	Japan	South Korea	Taiwan
1982	14,410	327	10,615	3,040	4,466
1992	25,467	1,028	21,057	9,443	11,901
2002	38,123	2,884	26,749	18,878	21,613
2012	51,704	9,055	35,856	36,950	38,357

Figures are IMF estimates in current U.S. dollars.

not overlook the fact that these political changes were accomplished against the backdrop of rapid economic growth.

The statistics presented in table I.I amply show trends in the per capita gross domestic product (GDP) in five countries, the United States of America, China, Japan, South Korea, and Taiwan, in the last four decades (figures are in per capita GDP purchasing power parity values).[17]

In the early 1980s, the per capita GDPs in Taiwan and South Korea were about 45 percent and 30 percent that of Japan, respectively; ten years later, in the early 1990s, they were 56 percent and 44 percent; and in the early 2000s, they were 81 percent and 71 percent. In the same period, from 1982 through 2012, China's per capita GDP increased from 3 percent (1982) to 5 percent (1992), 11 percent (2002), and then 25 percent (2012), while Japan's remained almost the same in relation to that of the United States (74 percent in 1982, 83 percent in 1992, 70 percent in 2002, and 69 percent in 2012). What is noteworthy here is that, during the decade of 2002–2012, finally Taiwan's per capita GDP exceeded that of Japan (at 107 percent). Incidentally, in 2017, Taiwan's per capita GDP (purchasing power parity values) exceeded those of both the United Kingdom and France.

Of course, per capita GDP is one of many indicators and cannot be emphasized in isolation. However, referring to the trends observable among these countries helps us to appreciate how drastic the social changes have been in the last four decades on the western shores of the Pacific. It also means that Japan's position relative to other countries in East Asia was being redefined in the late twentieth and early twenty-first centuries, just as Western Europe's or the United States' position was being reassessed in the international world. As I elucidate the notion of empire under subcontract in chapter 6, Japan used to enjoy prestigious status under the American confinement policy, and it benefited greatly from the special treatment it received from the United States. Under the political climate of the Cold War and thanks to the global conditions set in Pax Americana, Japanese people were allowed to behave as if they continued to be part of a nation of colonial suzerainty, even though Japan had lost its overseas colonies (except for Hokkaido, Okinawa, and other small islands). As a result, many in the Japanese nation have failed to kick their old colonial habit of looking down on their Asian neighbors as less developed and less modernized.

But with the global hegemony of the United States of America having crumbled gradually since the 1970s, a new configuration of interstate politics has finally emerged in Northeast Asia. In not being able to liberate itself from its reliance on Pax Americana, the Japanese public finds it increasingly difficult to view the position of Japan with its Asian neighbors through an optimistic view of modernization theory, according to which Japan was the only genuinely modern society in all of Asia. As a telling indicator of the Japanese attitude toward the outside world, let me mention other signs of their loss of empire.

The Inward-Looking Society

I want to draw attention to another statistic, namely that the number of Japanese college applicants to American universities has steadily declined in the past three decades. In the 1980s, many Japanese students were visible on many university campuses in the United States. Their presence at American universities was then apprehended as a manifestation of the trend toward globalization at large, at a time when compact Japanese automobiles began to dominate the American market. As time passed, Japanese students were outnumbered by South Koreans, and the globalization of higher education in the United States became all the more indisputable. In the last two decades, a larger number of students have also begun to arrive at American universities from India and China.

Since the 1990s, the composition of the American university student body has undergone a drastic change. In 2016 the total number of international students (both undergraduates and graduates) studying at American universities exceeded one million, out of which 363,000 were from China, 196,000 from India, and 55,000 from South Korea.[18] In spite of this general increase in the number of international students from Asian countries studying on American campuses, however, the number of Japanese students in the United States has reflected an entirely different trend. In 2017, it was 18,753. As of 2017, the total number of students from Japan at American universities was far less than that from Taiwan (22,454), while the total population of Taiwan is less than one-fifth of Japan's.

It is not merely the number of Japanese students at American universities that has declined; the level of young Japanese people's intellectual curiosity about the outside world has also shrunk drastically.

Recently a scholar friend of mine who works in political science in Japan drew my attention to a thought-provoking datum: only 5 percent of Japanese people in their twenties have ever applied for passports. In the last five years, the percentage of Japanese in their twenties who have applied for passports has fluctuated between 5 and 6 percent. Fifteen years ago the figure was about 9 percent, which was already shockingly low, so it is now obvious that fewer and fewer young Japanese are interested in going abroad. Regrettably, I have found no access to passport application statistics for the years of the twentieth century, so I cannot discuss a longer trend in passport application figures among the Japanese population in this twenty-to-twenty-nine-year age range. Since about 24 percent of the total population of Japan own passports, this is an astonishingly low figure.[19] Of course, one must not overlook the economic adversity in which an increasing number of young Japanese have found themselves in the last few decades. Perhaps a factor here is that the younger generation of Japanese are much less well paid in comparison to those of other industrialized countries.

According to a 2015 survey of Japanese corporations, 63.7 percent of new employees responded negatively to the question, "Are you willing to work abroad?," while 36.3 percent responded affirmatively (9.1 percent would work in any country; 27.2 percent would not work in certain countries).[20] In 2001, only 29.2 percent answered negatively to the same question, while 70.7 percent answered affirmatively (17.3 percent would work in any country; 53.1 percent would not work in certain countries). Evidently a drastic change has occurred in the attitudes of new employees toward potential work overseas.

These statistical data seem to confirm the tendencies that I have observed about Japanese society in the last three decades. I am now convinced that it is valid to portray today's Japan as an inward-looking society.

In his brilliant study of the imaginary formation of nationhood in what is called Thailand today, Thongchai Winichakul (1994) coined the idiom "the geo-body of a nation"; he explored how modern cartography contributed to the process in which the kingdom of Siam was transformed into the modern vision of the Thai nation, how the technology of modern cartography gave rise to a collective imagining that allowed residents in Siam to imagine themselves as members of a new collectivity called a nation. A nation is a particular form of modern community whose imaginary constitution is closely tied with a geographic enclosure; it is embodied in a national territory, a geographic space bound by national borders. Therefore, a nation is not only a collectivity of people connected to one another through what John Stuart Mill (1972, 187–428) called "sympathy"; sympathy that binds a nation together is invoked by the image of a geo-body; a nation also signifies a collectivity of people who are geographically bound, who are distinguished from the rest of humanity by the fact of their residency within a determinate territory insulated from the outside world. It follows that their membership in this community—exclusive membership which is indeed called "nationality"—is marked by a national border and that all the individuals living outside this border must be regarded as aliens, excluded from the nationality or from the sympathy that is supposed to be extended to every member of a nation. In other words, for a nation to exist, it is essential that fraternity, the bonds of national comraderies, must never be shared with foreigners. By virtue of the fact that it encircles an enclosed space on a modern map, the figure of a geo-body symbolically represents the very exclusiveness of a national community in ways similar to a border wall that symbolically represents a barrier or obstacle to supposedly prevent foreigners from intruding into the interior of the nation.

By now it is evident why I have adopted the term "hikikomori" (reclusive withdrawal) to describe a certain nationalism that has characterized Japanese society in recent decades while dissociating the term from the hikikomori people who actually suffer from social alienation. Confinement to one's bedroom is one thing, while imaginary confinement to the geo-body of a nation is quite another. Hikikomori people are afraid of the social space outside their bedrooms or their parents' homes, but they are not necessarily afraid of a possible intrusion from the world outside their nation. On the other hand, the nationalism of hikikomori suffers from a phantasmatic fear of intrusion from outside the national territory, and shares little with hikikomori people's physical confinement. This is why the nationalism of hikikomori is insistent upon the building of a wall, in fantasy or actuality, at the national border to supposedly prevent alien intruders from entering the national interior.[21] Therefore, it is important to note that the nationalism of hikikomori is not unique to Japan, while hikikomori as a sociological phenomenon may, at least statistically, appear particular to it; it is universal in the sense that the nation-state cannot be built without this fantastic mechanism of exclusion based upon the geo-body of a nation. Every formation of a modern community called nation potentially includes the nationalism of hikikomori.

Strategic Directives: How to Get out of National History

Before closing this introduction, I would like to remind readers about the strategy or methodology I try to adhere to in selecting, compiling, and modifying the chapters in this volume. The word "strategy" is perhaps more appropriate than "methodology" in this instance since I do not believe in the sort of epistemic metaphysics usually implied in the concept of methodology, according to which knowledge is produced within the dichotomous configuration of the object of knowing, passively given as empirical data on the one hand, and the subject of knowing, who actively selects and synthesizes such data to form knowledge or experience, on the other. I do not deny that I owe much to the tradition of transcendental criticism and am largely a product of such a legacy of Enlightenment, but I am hesitant to uncritically endorse the classical premises of modern subjectivity.

In writing, selecting, and modifying the chapters for this volume, I have been concerned with two problematics that for more than three decades have guided me with regard to how I conduct my research, make judgments, and construct narrative accounts: (1) how to write history against the narrative premises of national history, and (2) how not to overlook possible or potential links of knowledge production, particularly in the humanities, with such aspects of social reality as racism and colonialism. Of course, it is not easy to determine what is connoted by racism or colonialism. The definition of such terms alone could easily be beyond my ability. Yet I have never wittingly neglected these problematics in my scholarly endeavors.

Obviously some chapters included in this volume address social and political incidents and phenomena normally attributed to Japanese history. Many of the topics I deal with, such as hikikomori (reclusive withdrawal) and the Tokyo War Crimes Tribunal, are usually discussed by experts working in the disciplinary fields of Japanese history, Japanese literature, or area studies on Japan. Yet, since my earlier publications, I have never abandoned attempts to discuss these topics against the discourse of Japanese history or area studies on Japan (Sakai 1991; 1997b, 1–12). In addition to deliberate efforts to critically scrutinize the idea of national history and its workings, I invert the relationship between the nation and national history, so to speak. Instead of assuming that some incident legitimately belongs to a national history because it happens to a particular nation, I always ask how an incident is made to appear to belong to a national history, and what the conditions and the rules of discourse are by which the incident is ascribed to that history. In other words, a nation is never a given, an entity existent prior to its representation, or a substance that is always and already there before being mentioned or narrated. Thus, the national history must be subsumed under a discourse or a set of discourses in which the nation is constituted. What must be investigated is how some thought or idea is ascribed to the nation, how it is modified by an adjective "Japanese" to constitute "Japanese thought." Instead of writing historical accounts within the framework of a national history, I always attempt to write a history that historicizes national history; I resort to a kind of historiography whereby the nation is constituted through imagination and narration. This is also one reason why, in discussing the inward-looking society, I always foreground the discussions of certain sociopolitical phenomena with an analysis of the nation form. By critically examining the operation of the nation form, I have always displaced a national history with one that is otherwise. I have never ceased to get out of national history. Yet I also don't accept that I can get out of national history by entering world history or that, in the present, the outside of national history exists positively. For world history, for instance, is not outside of national history or national histories but rather no more than a horizon within which national histories are juxtaposed, a horizon I call "internationality." In this respect, an outside of national history is yet to come, even though I would never give up this prospect.

This is to say that, in order to comprehend racism in its historical nature, one must consider the emergence of the modern social formation, the emergence of a new type of community that we customarily call the nation. In every chapter of this volume the question of racism is, if not thematically discussed, ever present as a basso continuo.

Thereupon let me proceed to the second strategic directive. As you will discover in reading the chapters included in this volume, I have never neglected the problematic of racism. I simply could not forget about it. In view of my preoccupation with this problematic, I have decided to reproduce "Statement on Racism," which William Haver and I composed together in 1987, as one of the appendixes to this volume. When we were working on the question of racism in area studies at that time, I simply could not imagine what an important role it would play in the next three decades of my scholarly career.

Of course, racism is extremely difficult to pin down. Yet it must not be reduced to social discrimination in general. Racism is a specific way to discriminate against a person or group of people since the phrase "racial discrimination" loses its connotation unless it is contrasted with equality. The question of racism is necessarily associated with the social formation in which the idea of equality is somewhat assumed. In this world, however, no society exists in which the idea of equality is fully actualized. In other words, the idea of equality is intelligible only as long as it is only partially realizable. It is precisely in this respect that equality is something particular to modernity, and equality as a socially institutionalized imperative can only be found in modern societies where discrimination in terms of rank, caste, clan affiliation, and heritage is delegitimated. Paradoxically, racism is viable only in such social formations in which the idea of equality is taken for granted. In this respect, equality is a necessary condition for racism, but it is not a sufficient condition.

THESE ARE SOME OF the problematics that have compelled me to write various essays over the past twenty years. This volume's chapters testify to my struggles and wagers; by no means can I claim that my inquiry has been complete or has arrived at some conclusive insight. They touch upon a group of problematics or concerns that may appear exceedingly diverse; when placed in one volume, they may seem indifferent to and disconnected from one another under one totalizing system. Yet I believe these problematics are intimately interwoven. As a matter of fact, these diverse concerns of mine form a constellation around the central problem: What is the West and, by implication, what is the non-West? The sign "the West" may connote a geopolitical referent, a civilization, a tradition, a political order, an ethnicity, a race, a culture, or a type of humanity. Regardless of whether it is or is not any one of these, or all or some combination of them, one thing is certain: as a concept, it is overdetermined. In short, as a concept, it cannot be coherent. First of all, that the West is overdetermined means that it may be possible to conjure up partial determinations of it in some specific conjunctures, but it also means that it is impossible to do so with an overall coherence in the final determination. In other words, no one is completely determined with regard to positionality in the difference of the West and Asia, the West and Africa, or the West and the Rest. In chapter 4, "You Asians," which is the oldest publication among the chapters included in this volume, therefore, I want to demonstrate the political possibility that anybody can occupy the positionality of Asia (Africa, Latin America, or the Rest); anybody can be Asian because nobody is finally determined as either Western or Asian; anybody who fashions himself or herself as a Westerner can be so only putatively; I wanted to highlight the overdetermined nature of such a civilizational or racial identity. Yet this does not mean that I must surrender any attempt to produce a coherent narrative to deal with the contradictions and dissonances among partial determinations of the West. On the contrary, this is where my optimism of will is located. The question is how to discover the possibilities of practice from the overdetermined nature of the West.

1. HISTORY AND RESPONSIBILITY
Debates over The Showa History

I asked myself, "How many times do I have to explain that it is not *kokka shakai-shugi* (socialism of the state 国家社会主義) but rather *kokumin shakai-shugi* (socialism of the nation 国民社会主義) that is the proper and more appropriate rendering of 'National Socialism'?"

More than two decades ago, the *Asahi Journal*, a left-oriented weekly periodical published by Asahi Shimbun, one of the largest national papers in Japan, still existed, and its weekly issues were readily available in virtually every bookstore in Japan as well as at kiosks in major railway stations. Recalling the political climate of the 1980s and 1990s, some aging baby boomers may well portray those times as the "good old days" with a certain nostalgia.

I was asked to contribute an essay to this journal, so I submitted my manuscript, but the editorial office returned it for further work. First, I did not understand what was wrong with my essay, but after a few exchanges, I learned that everything hinged upon one small detail. I translated "National Socialism" as "kokumin shakai-shugi." Obviously the editor was enraged, and he politely but emphatically delivered his opinion that this was a gross mistake and totally unacceptable. He was determined that I should use the commonly accepted and more respectable term "kokka shakai-shugi" (state socialism).

In English and other modern European languages, the word "nation" is not definable singularly. Neither is it easily classified in East Asian languages. It means different things according to varying contexts—historical, disciplinary, semantic, geopolitical, and so forth. To understand the concept of "nation," therefore, is to appreciate the indexical instability of this word and its polysemic variability.

In modern Japanese, the English word "nation" has been rendered into such terms as *kokumin* (nation 国民), *minzoku* (ethnic nation 民族), and occasionally as *kokka* (state 国家). These different renderings are the result of Japanese scholars' endeavors to respond to the European conceptions of nation as well as of their theorization of how the concept of nation could be actualized and concretized in the Japanese modernization projects of nation building. Taking into account the distinctly modern character of what the nation connotes—national community, national governance, peoplehood, and so on—one may as well presume it safe to say that, in Japan before the Meiji Restoration (1868), there was no equivalent in common parlance to "nation." Both kokumin and minzoku were neologisms invented to translate the English word "nation" in the late nineteenth century. Until the era of the Fifteen-Year War (1931–1945), kokumin and minzoku were sometimes used interchangeably, but the international trends of the 1920s and 1930s alerted many Japanese intellectuals to differentiate kokumin (political nation) from minzoku (ethnic nation) under the international climate of fascism. Let us not forget that, generally speaking, the Japanese government remained hostile, not only to *minzoku-shugi* (ethnic nationalism 民族主義) but also to the idea of minzoku until the collapse of the Japanese Empire in 1945. To manifestly demonstrate that primary education was designed for the manufacture of kokumin (political nation), for instance, the Konoe Fumimaro (近衛 文麿) administration issued an imperial ordinance to change the name of *shôgakkô* (primary schools 小学校) to *kokumin gakkô* (schools of or for the nation 国民学校) in 1941. As far as state-imposed nationalism was concerned, Japanese nationalists insisted on the principal distinction of the nation of Japan as a political community from the conception of a nation as an ethnic community. As a political community whose principle of integration could be sought in the ideal—a nationalist may well say, "We are together and form one nation as long as we dream together and share the same vision of the future we strive toward together"—Japan could have been able to accommodate as many ethnicities as the situation allowed for.[1] It was commonly acknowledged that the nation of Japan consisted of different breeds of people, different in language, familial formation, religious belief, historical consciousness, and even eating habits. Except for a relatively small number of national extremists who believed in the purity of a racial and ethnic constitution, the Japanese nation was a multiethnic alliance, provided that individuality and multiplicity in ethnicity were far from immediately identifiable.[2]

As soon as the war in Asia and the Pacific ended and the multiethnic empire of Japan disintegrated in 1945, however, kokumin and minzoku began to be used almost synonymously among the Japanese, as far as Japanese nationality was concerned. In reference to their own nationality and ethnic identity, the Japanese ceased to differentiate the nation of Japan as a political community from the nation as an ethnic or cultural one. This stands in sharp contrast to prewar nationalism, indeed. And from the 1950s up to the 1990s and even now, many in Japan are totally indifferent to both what was at stake in distinguishing the political nation (kokumin) from the ethnic nation (minzoku) and why ethnic nationalism was abhorred by the Japanese state bureaucracy before the loss of the empire.

Indeed, historically, there have been many versions of national socialism. What I discussed in my essay for the *Asahi Journal* was nothing other than Nationalsozialismus or National Socialism, usually abbreviated as Nazism. So I had to clearly indicate that the sort of national socialism I was discussing was not a socialist polity imposed upon people by state authority or bureaucracy, but instead one that supposedly emerged from the people, supported by a grassroots movement against state bureaucracy.

I do not believe that the type of modern community called "nation" has ever been constituted without the mediation of the state. In this respect, every nation derives from state policies, and every nationalism of an existing nation is state imposed. What was at issue in my exchanges with the editor was not the historical genesis of nationality, but rather my concern with how a nationalism justifies its own genesis and how it puts forth the logic of its own legitimacy. From this perspective, there was no doubt, as I saw it then and see it now, that Nazism was hostile to the idea of the nation created by the state. It was an antistate ideology to such an extent that it denounced even the state endeavor to impose a common language to create a nation.

For the Nazis, the nation ought to be something natural; a human being was not cultivated into it, but the nation was rather a matter of whether one was born into it or not. Accordingly, the socialism advocated by the Nazis was not the type of socialism imposed by the state. In this sense, it was definitely not kokka shakai-shugi (socialism of the state). As a matter of fact, National Socialists themselves insisted emphatically that their political legitimacy did not derive from the state, but instead from the nation.

In *Mein Kampf,* Adolf Hitler argues that what allows for the existence of a superior humanity is not the state, but the nation endowed with the necessary abilities to produce higher culture and also, for the brand of socialism he promotes, that the state is neither an end nor a cause for the existence of the nation: "The state is a means to an end. Its end lies in the preservation and advancement of a community of physically and psychically homogeneous creatures. This preservation itself comprises first of all existence as a race and permits the free development of all the forces dormant in this race. Of them a part will always primarily serve the preservation of physical life, and only the remaining part the promotion of a further spiritual development. Actually the one always creates the precondition for the other" (Hitler 1999, 393).

For Hitler, the question of nationality—which is not clearly distinguished from race but instead reiterated as "nationality of unified blood" in *Mein Kampf*—is intimately associated with another question of which species of humanity manifest those peculiar features that make them creative founders (*Begründer*) of culture. For him, the Aryan is indeed the most superior species endowed with the originality to initiate and create art, science, culture, and human values in general. Cultural accomplishments may appear to be achieved by exceptional individuals, Hitler argues, but these are always rooted in the "community of physically and psychically homogeneous creatures." They serve the development of spiritual forces in the same race, while others may work for the subsistence of the whole community. Nonetheless, no cultural genius is independent of the national substratum shaped by the underlying integrity of physical and psychic homogeneity since the community is formed organically. Insofar as this community is assumed to be culturally homogeneous, in a conceptual sense it should be best described by minzoku (ethnic nation).[3] But in the sense that it is supposed to consist in a community of physically homogeneous creatures, it is no doubt a race. An ethnic nation is no different from a race when its identity is characterized in terms of a "community of physically and psychically homogeneous creatures."

In the Hitlerian apprehension of nationalism, the conceptual distinctions among the three terms nation (kokumin), ethnicity (minzoku), and race are gradually erased. Nation slides into ethnicity; the ethnic nation slides into race. He would adamantly reject both that the nation derives from the state and that the state creates a hierarchy of more or less cultured classes. Instead the state should exist only to preserve the ethnic nation that is culturally homogeneous.

By now it should be obvious that, while I am sure the editor must have believed that fascism is abhorrent, he had nonetheless internalized a conceptual configuration that was not entirely dissimilar to that of Hitler and of National Socialism.

War Crimes and Responsibility

Soon after the end of the Asia-Pacific War, the Japanese public could not remain insulated from news of the atrocities, the genocide, and the acts of extraordinary cruelty committed by the Nazis. Neither could they stay totally ignorant of the crimes and violent acts committed by their own Japanese nationals during the Asia-Pacific War since the International Military Tribunal for the Far East—commonly known as the Tokyo War Crimes Tribunal—was held in Tokyo from 1946 to 1948; in these trials some atrocities committed by the Japanese military were investigated and a comparatively small number of war criminals prosecuted. The proceedings of the tribunal were widely publicized through mass media in Japan, even though news releases were strictly censored by the offices of the Supreme Commander for the Allied Powers (SCAP) in charge of the occupation of regions in East Asia. In addition, the Tokyo War Crimes Tribunal was often compared to the Nuremberg Trials, held in Germany earlier in 1945 and 1946, in which Nazi war criminals were interrogated and prosecuted under criminal categories that included "crimes against humanity."

The Tokyo War Crimes Tribunal had a different organization than the Nuremberg Trials; they were conducted under different historical conditions and for different strategic considerations. For instance, the category of "crimes against humanity" was never applied to Japanese war criminals there.[4] One must not forget a historical context particular to postwar Japan: it was a strategic decision by the United States of America that the Emperor Hirohito of Japan would be deliberately immune to all charges of crimes, atrocities, violations of international law, and other criminal actions committed in his name and under his command by the Japanese government and Japanese military.[5] In due course, at the same time, the pardoning of Emperor Hirohito implied that every subject working for the Japanese state under the jurisdiction of the Meiji Constitution was relieved of legal responsibility, at least in theory, since every Japanese government and military act of aggression had been ordained by the emperor. This decision by the U.S. government to exempt Hirohito from legal liability was for the sake of American postwar strategy in the Far East. War criminals were prosecuted and executed by the Allied Powers under the auspices of the United Nations. But within the legal system of the Japanese state, no legal procedure exists whereby to arrest, interrogate, prosecute, or punish those who committed racist, colonial, or genocidal crimes during or prior to the Asia-Pacific War.

Yet the feasibility of a comparison between Germany and Japan in postwar academic and journalistic discussions on fascism cannot be completely ignored since both German and Japanese political developments have been discussed in journalism as well as in academia since the 1930s. Not surprisingly, some may well argue that it is inappropriate to attribute the name "fascism" to the kind of oppressive regime that developed in Japan in the 1930s. This regime was undeniably antiparliamentarian, jingoistic, anti-intellectual, and anti-Marxist, yet it manifested certain socialistic orientations such that calling it "fascism" does not seem totally off the mark. However, as Maruyama Masao (丸山 眞男) insisted in his famous studies of Japanese fascism (Maruyama 1964, 1966), it has been widely accepted that the system that developed to promote totalitarian policies was hostile toward grassroots ethnic nationalism. In prewar Japan, minzoku-shugi (ethnic nationalism 民族主義) was commonly denounced by the government, and its followers were often regarded as pariahs in Japan's annexed territories, for it was viewed as a political ideology for a separatist movement. It is hard or in fact impossible to demonstrate that such an antistate nationalism as minzoku-shugi could possibly be accepted occupied as a part of the state apparatuses in Japan in the 1930s. As a matter of fact, some historians have attempted to portray this oppressive regime in terms of a system of total war in consideration of the absence of the Völkisch tendency within it.[6] Nonetheless, from the late 1940s until the 1990s, Japanese fascism continued to be depicted in reference to German National Socialism (and sometimes to Italian Fascism). Therefore it one would naturally assumed that the Nazi emphasis on the national or Völkisch features of National Socialism were fairly well known in postwar Japan.

Surprisingly, however, very few Japanese intellectuals were aware—the general public even less so—in the 1980s that Nazism was a sort of minzoku-shugi that detested state-centered rationalization and favored the idealized image of people's communality. Precisely because the postwar image of the Third Reich emphasized the rationalistic character of Nazi policies—the precision of planning with which Germany's remilitarization was executed, the cold-blooded rationalism that guided the management of the concentration camps, the idealization of scientific and technological knowledge, and so forth—it was widely assumed that National Socialism was somewhat organized and directed by the scientific and technocratic spirit of state bureaucracy.

What are the historical conditions and prevailing images of the evil called fascism that nurtured this misrecognition of the ethnic nationalist character of Nazism for so long in postwar Japan? Why did the Japanese immediately accept that the oppressive nature of fascism had to be attributed, or straightaway equated, to the coercive oppression of the state? How could they manage to agree that national people (minzoku) were always passive and, therefore, incapable of victimizing others or themselves, while the state was an agent of active oppression or a victimizer that imposed rules and commands on passive people against their will?[7]

Decolonization Aborted

In order to address these questions in broader contexts, please allow me to shift our focus to a different set of problems that were volatile in Japan after the loss of the empire. These are the problems of war and colonial responsibility that have haunted the production of knowledge in the humanities and social sciences there since those engaged in the postwar production of knowledge were wittingly or unwittingly implicated in a new and precarious process of decolonization; in it the Japanese would be forced to fashion themselves differently from before, even to the extent that they would cease to adhere to their nationality. As a matter of fact, some were no longer Japanese. Under the occupation of the Allied Forces, a large number of the Japanese with Taiwanese and Korean ethnic backgrounds ceased to have Japanese nationality as they were decolonized and liberated. Even among those who remained of Japanese nationality after the defeat, postwar decolonization could have compelled them to reflect upon and call into question what they had previously believed themselves to be. Decolonization could have brought about serious reconsideration of their national identity, a pungent doubt about the nation as a social imaginary, or a critical skepticism concerning the rhetoric of patriotism.

Nevertheless, I can never claim that the decolonization of the mind, in the sense of radical self-doubt and self-refashioning of peoplehood, has ever taken place in Japan since the loss of the Japanese Empire. Nor do I believe that the potentiality of decolonization was totally absent. At this point I cannot evade presenting this question: what prevented the Japanese public from submitting themselves to a complete process of decolonization?

There are many aspects of decolonization, but to the extent that it occurs as a historical process of transformation and concerns a person's or people's relationship to the past, it is not completely off the mark to say that decolonization is first of all a matter of historicity. Of course, it is of crucial importance whether we approach the question of historicity from the standpoint of a single person or of people, but let me tentatively postulate this problem in terms of collective history. By historicity I suggest the calling into question of collectivity's present in relation to the past as well as the future. On the one hand, our historicity is very much informed by the awareness that the present state of affairs, upon which our continuing lives are based, owes itself to what happened in the past in such decisive ways that we cannot change the present state of our being without fundamentally altering our relationship to the past. We do not choose the modality of our being—what and how we are in the present—and we are confined to this present, so to speak, by our historical conditions. On the other hand, our historicity implies that our present is conceivable only in relation to our future, which is essentially indeterminate and open. In other words, our present is meaningful in the modality of anxiety in relation to our hope, fear, aspiration, and despair. Thus, we are at a juncture in the projectile of historical time, which is simultaneously open to the future as well as delimited by the past.

In August 1945, the Japanese Empire was defeated and subsequently collapsed, and this drastic change of state sovereignty suddenly gave rise to a wide spectrum of alternatives. As the annexed territories were liberated from the jurisdiction of the Japanese state, more than 30 percent of the subject population was removed from the national population. This portion, who used to be Japanese nationals, instead ceased to fashion themselves as such and began to identify with different nationalities: Korean, Chinese, and so forth. As a result, the multiethnic nation of Japan was then open to alternative modes of identification. The multiethnic national integration having been discarded as the principal legitimacy for the government, all of a sudden the very idea of minzuku-shugi (ethnic nationalism) earned general popularity not only among the minority population who aspired to non-Japanese identities but also among those who continued to retain Japanese nationality.

Now let me focus on the other portion of the population who continued to identify with the defeated Japanese nation. In order to capture this moment of opening to the future, it was necessary for these Japanese nationals to examine their relationship to the past and to find an alternate way of belonging to the community. The responses were not at all monolithic.

I understand that the problem of historicity in postwar Japan was most explicitly addressed in the discussions of war responsibility, even though, among the populace retaining Japanese nationality, there were many who rejected the topic of war responsibility entirely. Even among those who entertained such discussions, a variety of positions existed. One might refer to the views of Maruyama Masao and Yoshimoto Takaaki (吉本 隆明), perhaps two of the most famous discussants of Japanese war responsibility. For Maruyama, at issue was the war responsibility of the leadership of the Japanese nation for failing to prevent the war from starting and continuing, whereas Yoshimoto held intellectuals responsible to ordinary people for inflicting subsequent disasters upon the nation and ordinary folks (Maruyama 1964, 1966; Yoshimoto 1962, 1976).

It is important to keep in mind that, for Maruyama and Yoshimoto, the war responsibility of the Japanese nation toward the portion of the nation who ceased to be Japanese after the war, or to peoples beyond Japanese sovereignty, was entirely outside their scope. *The Showa History* (『昭和史』) was another attempt by Marxist historians to address the issues of war responsibility by analyzing how Japanese capitalism paved the way for the Japanese state through its ultimate defeat and how imperialist policies were necessarily prompted by contradictions inherent in Japanese society and international politics (Tôyama, Imai, and Fujiwara 1955). It was a historiographic attempt to examine the Japanese relationship to the past, the historicity of which could be summarily addressed as one of war responsibility.

Yet, soon after the publication of *The Showa History*, a protest was launched by those who regarded Marxist historiography as "too inhuman."[8] The ensuing disputes were later called "the debates on *The Showa History*" (*Showa-shi ronsô* 昭和史論争); in them some of the problems concerning kokumin shakai-shugi (socialism of the nation), mentioned above, were unveiled.

In order to pursue the problem of historicity in war responsibility, it is essential to discern two types: legal responsibility and political or historical responsibility.

As to legal responsibility, it may appear unavoidable to assume the continual existence of the subject who is to respond to the charge of guilt or to be held culpable for it. In legal disputes, it is supposed that the one who has committed a crime must be the same as the one who is perceived as culpable for the crime or is held responsible for what was initially violated. Without the supposition of a continual existence of an individual accountable for the criminal act, the case of legal responsibility will not sustain. In order to justifiably demand responsibility, therefore, there must be the assumption of a persistent and continual existence between the agent of a guilty action and the subject accused of that action. In modern jurisprudence, the identity of the agent of crime with the indicted is an absolute requirement, and accusation by association is entirely rejected. A family member of a murderer, for instance, cannot be held culpable for the murder, barring proof of involvement in the criminal action. Neither can a member of the nation whose troops have committed genocide be punished for that atrocity simply because he or she shares national membership with them. As long as the validity of legal responsibility is built on the individual identity of the perpetrator and the accused, this responsibility vanishes when the indicted dies; it cannot be transferred from one generation to another. The indicted can be a legal person such as a corporation or national state. In such a case, the legal responsibility persists until the state or another kind of organization that has been indicted for a crime ceases to exist. The case of the Japanese state's responsibility for the system of the Comfort Stations (従軍慰安所) and the case of Union Carbide's culpability for the Bhopal gas tragedy are typical examples of such legal responsibility. Of course, the responsibility of an individual person, a nation, or a corporation is not exclusively legal, and it can also constitute a case of political or historical responsibility.

When it comes to the problem of historical responsibility pertaining to past injustices involving racism, sexism, military violence, or colonialism, however, one cannot necessarily proceed with the same set of assumptions for legal responsibility. Perhaps it is still fruitful to appeal to Hannah Arendt's distinction between legal and political responsibilities. It is important to keep in mind, however, that there are some that fall clearly within the purview of legal responsibility among the crimes of racism, sexism, war, and colonialism, but what is at stake, particularly in view of what is often referred to as Japan's postwar responsibility, cannot be satisfactorily attended to through the protocols of legal responsibility, even though it is true that many of those in positions of authority—political leaders, commanders in military hierarchies, administrative officers in the decision making of governments, corporations, and other institutions, and so forth—have never been prosecuted or interrogated.

In this respect, the preliminary stage in the question of Japan's postwar responsibility has never been adequately addressed. For one thing, the subject of historical responsibility is not necessarily an individual; many cases exist in which the national state or the nation as a whole must be regarded as the ultimate agent of a criminal act. Hence, it is relevant to say, for example, that the Japanese are responsible for the crimes committed through the institution of the Military Comfort Station (従軍慰安所). Similarly, one may argue that the West is responsible for racist violence in many places in the world. In these instances, the subject is not specified as an individual. Yet the subject of historical responsibility is not merely a collective. It is also a matter of responsibility that reveals itself in a dialogic situation involving addressers, addressees, and witnesses in a variety of social positions. Here responsibility is primordial in its gist: it is responsiveness, that is, the obligation to respond to the charge of past crimes or wrongdoing and concerns with the fact that an individual who identifies with the Japanese nation ought to respond to another individual or individuals, either Japanese or non-Japanese. We now have to confront a paradox.

It is indisputable that a nation such as Japan is accidentally and almost arbitrarily constituted. It is impossible to presume the persistence, substance, or transhistorical identity of the Japanese ethnos or nation. No nation is formulated on any continuing ethnic base; the collective identity projected in nationalist narrative is nothing but a case of fictive ethnicity. The history of modern Japan is one of the best illustrations of the arbitrary and inconsistent constitution of the nation. In the process of colonization and through the policies of multiethnic integration, the Japanese state attempted to create a nation involving the population of the Japanese archipelago, Taiwan, the Korean peninsula, and other Pacific islands. However, as noted above, about a third of the population lost its Japanese nationality as soon as the Japanese Empire collapsed. Furthermore, among the people who were supposedly Japanese, various discriminations have existed, and consequently since the beginning of the Meiji period—not to mention the periods prior to the establishment of the modern nation-state—a number of groups had no sense of affiliation with the nation.

Nevertheless, the persistent existence of the Japanese nation must be assumed in order for us—let me note this "us" is not confined to those who regard themselves as Japanese—to engage in historical responsibility or responsiveness. A person born after the collapse of the Japanese Empire cannot be held culpable, for instance, for Japan's colonial or war crimes in the legal sense, but the same individual is not free from the historical responsibility of the Japanese nation. Even though those who committed colonial, racist, or sexist crimes in the Japanese Empire have all passed away, the Japanese nation as a collective is not exempt from historical responsibility. Strange though it may seem, in the case of historical responsibility every individual is vulnerable to culpability by association in terms of nation, race, ethnicity, or religious faith, while in the legal sense nobody can be held responsible by association.

Please keep in mind, however, that I am not saying that those who are historically responsible are invariably guilty of Japan's past crimes. As many have remarked, historical responsibility must be clearly distinguished from historical guilt, for the concept of responsibility assumes the acceptance of one's obligation to respond when called upon. The concept of responsibility is built on a structured situation where one is addressed by somebody else about an event that one has executed. Therefore, just as with legal responsibility, the concept of historical responsibility requires four constituent moments: an addresser who asks about an addressee's responsibility, an addressee obliged to respond to the addresser, the third party or witness who is neither the addresser nor the addressee, and an event about which the addresser calls upon the addressee.

As a matter of fact, I must speak of a fourth constituent moment, that is, the supposed presence of a witness or witnesses who are neither the addresser nor the addressee and who testify to the event of a responsive dialogue between the addresser and the addressee. This moment constitutes the dimension of objectivity or historical truth in the performativity of responsibility. Since I have discussed this issue extensively elsewhere, here let me exempt this inquiry into the dimension of universality in responsibility (Sakai 2008).

When the addresser and the addressee are of the same nationality, it is not necessary to consider the nation in our inquiry into historical responsibility.

Of course, there are many cases—such as the history of slavery in the United States—in which the issue of historical responsibility can never be overlooked, even though both parties may belong to the same nation. Only when the addresser and the addressee are of different nationalities, however, does the nation emerge as the indispensable topic under dispute. The nation is problematized when the addresser calls upon the addressee from outside the presumed closure of the national community. Japanese national subjectivity is particularly at stake, therefore, when someone who does not identify with the Japanese nation, a non-Japanese (*hi-kokumin* 非国民), problematizes some conduct that the Japanese executed in connection with the non-Japanese or with Japanese who have lost Japanese nationality. Thus, my query is about how Japanese historians have sustained this opening to the outside of Japanese nationality in order to keep the problem of historical responsibility viable. In other words, how have they articulated their historiography to the problem of historicity?

It is to elucidate the problem of historical responsibility that I want to examine the debate on *The Showa History*, the intellectual debate about Japan's war responsibility and the writing of history that captured many historians and literary critics in the 1950s.

The Showa History and National Humanism

The Showa History (『昭和史』), published in 1955, was written by three leading Marxist historians of the time, Tōyama Shigeki, Imai Sei'ichi, and Fujiwara Akira. The book analyzed the transformations in Japanese society and the emergence of Japanese fascism from the first decade of the Showa period until the end of the Asia-Pacific War (1931–1945). It was an extensive analysis of Japanese imperialism and capitalism, and it established the standard historiography of the early Showa period among the progressive readership of postwar Japan. What prompted the debates on *The Showa History* was the article "A Question to Present-Day Historians" (「現代歴史家への疑問」) by Kamei Katsuichirô, a well-known literary critic who was a Marxist in the 1920s but converted to Japanese Romanticism (日本浪漫派) in the 1930s.

In this article, Kamei poses the question of why people want to know about history and argues that when we want to study history we are invariably possessed by "a desire to confirm the origins of our life in our own ethnicity and the trends of times" (1956, 58). Underlying this desire in fact is a question about "who the Japanese are at all." Let me note in passing that the conceptual specificity of "the Japanese" is deliberately left undetermined. Perhaps, for Kamei, it is so self-evident that he need not bother to discuss it. Yet we cannot overlook that this tactic of his narrative performance gives rise to a certain rhetorical force. Thereby he establishes an intimate rapport with the readership that is supposedly exclusively Japanese. In due course, any reader who is not Japanese is not welcome in Kamei's utterance.

Several paragraphs later, Kamei introduces another unspecified term, "human being, man or people" (人間). Since Kamei claims that historiography's mission is "to describe human beings" and that "history is man's history," the task of the historian is to present an alluring (魅力的に) portrayal of human beings. Man lives in his own times to the best of his ability and then dies. "Can the historian be judgmental without trying to re-live the conditions and the environment of the past era?" (Kamei 1956, 6). Many tropes of man, human, humanity, humaneness, and humanism proliferate. Here it is necessary to emphasize that Kamei does not differentiate between "man" and "the Japanese" and also that "the Japanese" equates to "a person of Japanese nationality" without any qualification. So his notion of the Japanese moves freely and almost randomly from the broad generality of "man" to the historically specified particularity of "the Japanese nationality." I must note that the rhetorical force of his argumentation derives largely from his demonstrative but deliberate oversight of what constitutes "the Japanese."

Kamei's argument continues this way: the historian must be in sympathy with the Japanese of the past since his task is to relive the "man" of the past. Thus, he insists that the historian must be endowed with literary talent. And this talent is the faculty of the imagination to re-present or remember the experience of the past that he never actually lived, but as if he had personally experienced it. To interpret Kamei's argument analytically, I think, this faculty is one to narrate a myth rather than the faculty of representation in order to describe the past event as it occurred. What is at issue is not historical objectivity but, instead, a literary sentimentality by means of which to produce a sense of togetherness as a national community, as an ethnic nation of the Japanese, among the members of the very nation to be imagined. According to Kamei, the principal task of the historian is to fabricate a fictive ethnicity, a fiction that is acceptable only among those who want to live by this fiction.

Kamei Katsuichirô feels that the authors of *The Showa History* lack this literary talent of the faculty of imagination to represent the past as it was lived by the nation. It is no more than "a history where the human being, that is, the nation, cannot be found.... I termed this feature [of *The Showa History*] the absence of 'the nation' or of the human being" (Kamei 1956, 22).

What is glaringly obvious by now is this: Kamei deliberately conflated the three distinct categories of humanity (*ningen* 人間), Japanese ethnos (*nihon minzoku* 日本民族), and Japanese nation (*nihon kokumin* 日本国民). Therefore, not only covertly in his argumentative demonstration but also overtly in his performance, he repressed the conceivably logical possibility that could have crushed his reasoning outright: anybody could have asked, "Are you saying that the non-Japanese are not humans?" After all, what was being unambiguously asserted by Kamei is the prototype of national humanism in which humanity is primordially defined as nationality, as the fact of belonging to a certain nation. According to him, those who are qualified as human are those with a specific nationality. Yet he managed to prevent this unambiguous national humanism from manifesting itself in his argumentation by only addressing "us, Japanese," a restricted audience that presumably would never ask such an upsetting question. No matter whether or not his article, which was published in a leading Japanese monthly journal, *Bungei Shunjū* (文藝春秋), was actually read by people who did not identify with the Japanese nation, he preliminarily excluded from his putative audience those who would not consent to such a conformity. By setting the stage for his narrative address, he deliberately and decisively ignored those readers who would challenge his assertion about historiography.

If this is not a case of blatant racial discrimination, where else can we possibly find a more overt instance of racism? Is forming an exclusive group by putting up a sign "off-limits for non-Japanese" not an obvious case of racial preference? When, for the reason of your ethnicity, you feel entitled to ignore somebody asking a question in front of you, does this sense of entitlement not constitute an instance of racism? Is the formation of an exclusive club of humanity whose membership is granted only to the Japanese not a case of blatant racism? Thus, Kamei's racism manifests itself in his irresponsibility, his refusal to respond to a potential inquisition addressed by some humans without Japanese nationality.

What we have so far recognized in the performativity of Kamei's argument is a version of national humanism that we have cursorily surveyed in the Hitlerian rhetoric concerning cultural genius. National humanism consists of a series of category confusions that are not merely oversights, but are deliberate in the sense that this confusionism—humanity = nationality = race—constitutes a series of declarations or imperatives: "I adhere to my conviction that the non-Japanese are not human"; "We are not obliged to respond to those whom we do not admit as human"; and "I will not engage in any dialogue with those who do not belong to the Japanese nation." And let us not fail to notice the communalistic aspect of national humanism: it is undoubtedly an invocation for communal solidarity, an evocation of camaraderie.

But is it only during the period of the Fifteen-Year War (1931–1945) that this type of fascism was dominant in Japanese society? We must admit, therefore, that fascism continued well beyond the Fifteen-Year War. Without inhibition, Kamei Katsuichirô resurrected the rhetorical strategy of national humanism ten years after the loss of the Japanese Empire. This prompts us to once again confront the problem concerning the extraordinary popularity of fascism—not only National Socialism but also Italian Fascism and clerical fascisms—in Europe and elsewhere in the 1920s and 1930s, but herein, the context at issue is postwar Japan.

Already in the 1950s, the strategic maneuver of literary sentimentalism was deliberately adapted to the fantastic reconstitution of national communality at the level of individual identification. It intimated the coming of a literary strategy used extensively by literary critics, such as Etô Jun (江藤 淳), in the 1970s and 1980s that would prove most effective in its appeal to those who felt left behind by a neoliberal economy, those who would be classified as *makegumi* (the class of losers 負け組) in an increasingly atomized society. It is due to this alluring communalism that many were said to have been attracted to what is known as fascism in the interwar period.

Humanity and the Nonnational (非国民)

Now, let us see how the authors of *The Showa History* responded to the accusation launched by Kamei. In the first edition of their book, before receiving Kamei's criticism, the three authors had touched on the issues of history and responsibility in the preface. It was stated that they ~~authors~~ wanted to describe the history of the Showa period up to the moment of Japan's defeat as "representatives of the Japanese nation" (「私たち国民」). In the 1955 edition, the subject of responsibility as the accused was identified as the Japanese nation, whereas the plaintiffs were also the Japanese as a nation. Their initial question went this way: "Why were we, the nation, involved in the war, carried down, and helpless in preventing the war from continuing?" Even though the accused and the plaintiffs are identical as referents, the form of inquiry necessarily postulates a conflict or split between one portion of the nation and another: hypothetically, one group of the Japanese are opposed to another group of the Japanese. When the opposition between plaintiffs and accused is obscured, however, the question of war responsibility vanishes. The issue of war responsibility can persist only as long as the subject demanding an answer and the subject responding are differentiated from one another. It is important to recognize that the authors of *The Showa History*, at least, evaded such a conception of the nation, advocated by Kamei, as a homogeneous and integrated community by focusing on the element of class struggle. Class antagonism disrupts the fantasized homogeneity of the nation.

Nevertheless, the historical responsibility of the nation as a whole was never clearly articulated in *The Showa History*. This was a weak link that did not escape Kamei's scrutiny. He asks,

> Why was invasion into Manchu-kuo and China undertaken? The problem would be simple if "the ruling class" alone were guilty. Moreover, we must take into account our contempt towards the Orientals that have grown step by step among our nation ever since the first Sino-Japanese war. . . . There must have been a great number of soldiers who literally believed in the Holy War and died uttering "Long Live the Emperor." There must have been military officers who sincerely loved the country and died for it. Are these dead people all idiots who were manipulated by the ruling class? (1956, 25–26)

Instead of yielding to Kamei's simplistic rhetoric, it is worth noting the semantics implied here in the concept of the nation. The laxity of Kamei's use of "the Japanese as a nation" can be blamed partly on a semantic inherent in the very concept of the nation. The nation is a principle by which to create the bonds of fantastic communality among the residents of a state territory, despite the disparities and conflicts of economic, ethnic, class, gender, tribal, religious, or geographic nature. Depending upon the relative positions within kinship networks, namely, the configurations of social ranks and other societal elements, each individual is endowed with particular privileges, obligations, and ethical norms. Yet, as a member of the nation, an individual is encouraged to transcend these differences encountered in concrete form in everyday life. Whereas individuals are discriminated from one another in their relational identities in terms of familial positions within kinship, the configuration of social ranks, professional status, and so forth, every individual is entitled to be treated formally as equal in the nation. An individual belongs to the community of the nation, just as an animal belongs to its own species in the classificatory system of zoology.[9] While it is impossible to uphold the principle of equality in human relations regulated by kinship, the nation is a community that, at least in theory and imagination, consists of equal individuals. Through its commitment to the principle of formal equality, therefore, the nation legitimates itself, no matter how disparate, fragmented, and discriminatory the actuality of the national society might be. The modern community we call the "nation" has to be built on both the premise of equality and the fantasy of homogeneity. This is the reason why formal equality was hardly recognized as a social norm before the formation of the nation-state in East Asia and elsewhere. Yet, as soon as the Meiji Restoration destroyed the feudal rank system of the Tokugawa Shogunate, the Japanese state declared that no member of the Japanese nation was born either above or below its other members, at least in theory. A new national community of the Japanese was built on the premise that every member of the Japanese nation was equal under the gaze of the one sovereign, the emperor of Japan.

It may appear that Kamei tried to remind his readership of the historical responsibility that both the ruling class and the ruled classes ought to hold. Let us recall, however, that, from the outset, he excluded the voice of the non-Japanese by emphasizing sympathy among the nation while completely neglecting the plausibility of someone speaking from its outside. As a matter of fact, he foreclosed the possibility of addressing not only the legal but also the historical responsibility for war crimes by thus excluding the non-Japanese from addressing the problem of Japanese responsibility.

However, what is particularly astonishing about the debates on *The Showa History* is not present in Kamei's presentation. Given the historical circumstances of the time—the onset of the Cold War and in the midst of anticommunist fervor—it is apprehensible that Kamei invoked anti-Marxist rhetoric and called for national sympathy rather than the ethics of class struggle.

What I found rather recondite to appreciate is the fact that the authors of *The Showa History* completely failed to draw attention to the laxity of Kamei's use of the concept of nation. They too were entirely oblivious to the concrete possibility that there could be readers outside the postwar membership of the Japanese nation who could have been absorbing their debates. In the Japanese Empire and even in the annexed territories, the state promoted education in the medium of the standard Japanese language in the last decades of colonial rule. How many former Japanese subjects would have become incapable of reading Japanese in the ten years since the end of Japanese colonial rule? Despite Kamei's overt exclusion of the non-Japanese from the forum of these debates, of course, there must have been a large number of people who had been educated in the Japanese national education system and hence could easily read the debates on *The Showa History* in the 1950s, both outside and inside the shrunken Japanese territory. It seems to me that Tōyama, Imai, and Fujiwara also acquiesced to the sort of national humanism I detected in Kamei's argument.

In his review of *The Showa History*, Matsuzawa Hiroaki (松澤 弘陽) drew attention to the very dichotomy of the national (kokumin 国民) and the nonnational (hi-kokumin 非国民) that continued to serve as an important tool of political justification throughout the Asia-Pacific War (1931–1945) and thereafter (Matsuzawa 1959, 109).[10] The term "hi-kokumin"—also rendered as "nonnational" or "antinational"—carried a very strong emotive connotation, just like such pejorative terms as "communists" and "Reds." Those who wanted to justify their political agenda often appealed to this dichotomy and labeled their opponents hi-kokumin; they tried to characterize them as spies or infiltrators in the nation. By layering this dichotomy onto the distinction of the ruled and the ruling class, the authors of *The Showa History* attempted to exorcise the ruling class from the interior of the nation, thereby postulating the configuration of the plaintiffs and the accused. This is to say that the nation was assigned to the position of plaintiff and the ruling class to that of the accused. For Tôyama, Imai, and Fujiwara, too, the Japanese nation was not an agent whose historical responsibility must be addressed by the non-Japanese. For the authors of *The Showa History*, too, the Japanese nation were victims deserving of sympathy. Not surprisingly, Matsuzawa observed, "the [*Showa History*] authors' uses of the basic terms suggest that the nation consists of the people, who have the objective features of a shared ethnicity in common, minus the ruling class." In ostracizing the ruling class by calling them hi-kokumin (non-Japanese), they succeeded in reserving the position of the plaintiffs for the nation. But Matsuzawa expressed his doubt in due course: "Was the subjective responsibility of the nation somewhat obscured in *The Showa History*?" (1959, 110).

Just like Kamei Katsuichirô, the authors of *The Showa History* foreclosed the plausibility of someone asking about the nation's historical responsibility. As far as the historicity of the Japanese national is concerned, Tôyama Shigeki, Imai Sei'ichi, and Fujiwara Akira were accomplices of Kamei rather than serious interrogators.

This explains why Kamei's narrative strategy of national humanism was so pervasive. This is to say that, in 1955, the regime of ethnic foreclosure that would later be called the cultural nationalism of Japan had already been fully institutionalized. Captured in this regime were not only romantic racists like Kamei Katsuichirô but such Marxists as the authors of *The Showa History* who also could not escape the allure of national humanism. After all, they were no different from Marxist nationalists.

It is commonly accepted that fascism was one of the most popular topics of academic discussion in the humanities and social sciences in postwar Japan. A huge number of monographs and articles were produced about war responsibility, the presence or absence of resistance in Japan, the conversion of intellectuals from Marxism to ultranationalism, and emperorist fascism (天皇制ファシズム). Yet, in facing such a blatant indifference to the problem of how fascism was so attractive to many intellectuals and ordinary folk, I start to wonder whether the question of fascism has in fact ever received serious examination in Japan. Have Japanese intellectuals ever critically confronted the problem of fascism in post–World War II history? Do they continue to absolve the nationality of the Japanese for the oppressive and coercive nature of the modern state? Will they return to the idolization of national camaraderie as the only remedy for their current helplessness? Will they ever be able to commit themselves to a strategy of a nonnational or nonethnic community beyond national humanism? Will they continue to blame kokka shakai-shugi (socialism of the state) rather than kokumin shakai-shugi (socialism of the nation)?

It goes without saying that today this situation is not particular to Japan, but the utter absence of a critique of racism in Japan distresses me. It is clear that the affinity of nationalism with racism has not been the unique purview of the German people. It is a problematic inherent in any nation-state.

2. FROM RELATIONAL IDENTITY TO SPECIFIC IDENTITY

On Equality and Nationality

If it is necessary to include in the structural conditions (both symbolic and institutional) of modern racism the fact that the societies in which racism develops are at the same time supposed to be "egalitarian" societies, in other words, societies which (officially) disregard status differences between individuals, this sociological thesis (advanced most notably by L. Dumont) cannot be abstracted from the national environment itself. In other words, it is not the modern state which is "egalitarian" but the modern (nationalist) nation-state, this equality having as its internal and external limits the national community and, as its essential content, the acts which signify it directly (particularly universal suffrage and political "citizenship"). It is, first and foremost, an equality in respect of nationality.—ÉTIENNE BALIBAR, "Racism and Nationalism," 1991

Equality and Confucian Premodernity

The question I want to address in this chapter is related to the problem of how to conceptualize social justice independently of the aesthetics of nationality; in other words, how to put forth the idea of equality against the social imaginary of the national body (國體). In short, I am concerned with the problems of social justice and equality outside of the scope of modern national community. Of course, my question requires some explanation.

Let me start my inquiry into equality and nationality by pointing out the topic of fairness that is often mentioned when social justice is discussed. Yet we cannot address the question of fairness independently of a particular type of social formation in which we live. We usually take for granted that justice means fairness, but this apprehension of fairness must be historicized. To accept it as a truism or as a socially concretized form of universality, as a matter of fact and as Paul Standish claims, is to take a step toward a commitment to equality and to the kind of universalism that implies that we are all equal qua human beings.[1] We are not talking about fairness in a social formation in which human beings are identified in terms of their ranks and statuses. So my starting point is to recognize that we live in a social formation of historical specificity whose legitimacy consists in the principle that every human being ought to be regarded as equal.

Then, let me dare to ask, who are these human beings who ought to be regarded as equal? Who are these human beings among whom the universalism of equality is accepted? Of course, it is "we" who are entitled to be treated as equal, but by "we" I assume the situation of the symposium, from which this chapter in this volume emerges, where the shifter "we" unambiguously designates the participants and audience of the international symposium who live in a variety of places—Kyoto, Los Angeles, London, Hong Kong, Tokyo, New Haven, Ithaca, Seoul, Vancouver, and so forth—but in each of these places, it is taken for granted or, more truthfully put, it is supposed to be taken for granted that we are all equal qua human beings. In this respect, the types of social formation in which we all live are ones whose legitimacy does not accept social behaviors that discriminate against some people on the grounds of social rank, birth, gender, and other sorts of heritage. In these places, the universalism of equality is a shared imperative upon which we expect our social relations to be built. As every one of us is fully aware, this imperative is frequently betrayed. Nevertheless, we hold on to the universalism of equality; we do not easily give it up as an imperative that should be shared.

Even in today's world, there are places where it is not taken for granted that we are all equal qua human beings. Accordingly, it is important to acknowledge that the universalism of equality is valid only for those of us living in the type of social formations that one might call modern, advanced, or Western, in which it is socially illegitimate not to endorse the universalism of equality. All the participants of the symposium, it seems to me, happen to live in such social formations where nobody will be likely to object to the universalism of equality that we are all equal qua human beings.

Here, please allow me to take a brief diversion to a particular national context. This will help, I hope, to clarify a few problems that I want to address with respect to the idea of equality on the one hand and the concept of nationality on the other. The national context I refer to is that of Japan; historians tell us that a drastic transformation of governmental structure took place there around 1868 so that the principle of equality, perhaps for the first time, came into being on the islands of Japan. The assemblage of feudal states under which people lived in the Japanese archipelago prior to the Meiji Restoration is referred to today in history textbooks as "the Baku-Han system." This Baku-Han system, a feudal federation of the peripheral polities of *han* (domains) and the unifying authority of the *Bakufu* (shogunate), was not a centralized system of modern state sovereignty but an alliance of provincial hans, each of which was recognized as a fiefdom by the Tokugawa Shogunate or Bakufu, the most powerful of all the domains. The continuing existence of each han and its bureaucracy was authorized by the legitimacy of kinship lineage.[2] The succession of political authority from one domainal lord to another was dictated by the rules of kinship legitimacy; the very division of the ruler and the ruled was authorized also by the law of kinship heritage.

According to historians of early modern Japanese history, the Baku-Han system suffered from frequent peasant rebellions, and peasants legitimated their insurgence in terms of semi-Confucian ideologies.[3] What is remarkable about the thought of the Tokugawa peasantry is that, among the ethical norms and virtues which they appealed to in order to justify their uprisings, the idea of equality was never included. The peasantry did not believe that the ethical value of equality could be appealed to in order to justify, rationalize, and sanction their rebellions against political authority. But as soon as the Baku-Han system was destroyed and the Meiji state established in 1868, some rebellious peasants began to incorporate the idea of equality as a means of asserting their legitimacy (Hirota 1990).

Probably some vague notions of equality were promoted on such occasions as sacred rituals, religious sermons, or fairy tales even prior to the Meiji Restoration. It is very difficult to deny that, even in premodern societies, people aspired to a sense of equality. But it is extremely difficult to determine what type of social reality equality designated or what sort of conduct it normalized. What is of decisive importance is that, even in the so-called modern societies in which we supposedly live, it is far from easy to determine what reality it designates and what conduct it normalizes.

The idea of equality seems haunted by this metaphysical conundrum of extreme difficulty in determining what the concept of equality signifies empirically. This is perhaps the very reason why the universalism of equality never ceases to invoke dispute. It seems that the ideal of equality is reinvigorated and renewed in the element of conceptual uncertainty; it challenges the existing manner of social conduct and calls into question prerogatives taken for granted in social discrimination against certain people.

Perhaps it is not entirely useless to introduce a preliminary distinction between the concept of equality as an idea and the concept of equality as an institutional reality. Of course, how an idea of equality is actualized in social reality is a crucial question not to be evaded, but what normativity, regularity, archetype, and rationality are involved in the process of its actualization must be dealt with elsewhere. It seems to me, however, that no matter whether it is equality as an idea (an abstract universality) or as an institution (a concrete universality) that regulates people's everyday conduct, the ethical value of equality requires a specific social setting, without which it cannot serve as an instance of universal social justice. Historically speaking, this social setting in which equality has been an accepted virtue or imperative is usually called "the nation."[4] Even though, as I will come back to argue for the relevance of equality as an idea beyond the nation, I would not claim that equality could never have been actualized outside a new type of community called the nation, the way we apprehend what equality can mean is marked by the kind of social relations institutionalized in the nation-state. Therefore, it is not misleading to say that equality was actualized together with the new form of community called the nation. At the same time, I insist, the idea of equality, in the final analysis, betrays or proves incompatible with the aesthetic regime of "nationality," as demanded by the consolidation of the nation.

The problem of modernity is closely associated with how people undergo social transformation as a result of which they acquire a new mode of identification. Modernity may be discussed in terms of its multiple aspects. And one of them is how to represent modernity as a struggle through which old identities were discarded and new subjectivity was manufactured. This testifies to the historical truism that the words "subject" and "subjectivity," in the modern sense, were scarcely used prior to the eighteenth century. With regard to its conceptual affiliation with the infinitesimal calculus and the ecstatic and historicist temporality inherent in it, the philosophical concept of subjectivity, which has played such important roles in historicism and humanism, was newly invented. In modern societies, the modality of identification for individuals was transformed so drastically that the topic of subjectivity became relevant in the discussion of identity. This is to say that, in so-called premodern societies and prior to modernity, the concept of subjectivity was irrelevant and without much significance. Of course, in premodern societies, subjectivity carried its significance in the sense of subjection to dominant power or being subject to an authority, but it was only with Kantian Enlightenment that subjectivity acquired the implications of autonomy and self-transcendence.

Even though the historical passages of social transformation are far from identical, there are not many social formations in East Asia—Northeast Asia in particular—that have avoided fundamental changes and have not achieved a certain stage of commonality. In this sense, I do not hesitate to say that modernity in Northeast Asia is thorough. Thanks to the consequences of modernization, peoples in China, South Korea, Taiwan, and Japan have come to share in common a certain regime of self-recognition, of individual identification, and of subjectivity.

Let us not forget that many intellectuals have addressed the problem of modernity in relation to Confucianism in Northeast Asia. From the mid-nineteenth century until the twentieth century, for intellectuals of this region, the problem of modernity could never manifest itself without reference to Confucian premodernity; it concerned itself with how to liberate people from the legacies of Confucianism. What was then called a feudal remnant was symbolized by the various conventions associated with a variety of Confucian heritage. However, we must keep in mind that what they meant by this name of an old teaching was far from unitary or coherent.

Presumably Confucianism is the general name to cover a vast archive of statements including groups of institutionalized conduct, an archive that arguably has existed for approximately the last twenty-five centuries, or still exists, mainly in Northeast Asia. I am not sure if the name justifiably summarizes these vast and diverse discourses. Furthermore, I am in no position to judge whether or not there is a definite set of characteristics that distinguishes Confucianism from other ethico-political doctrines and practices. Neither am I concerned with what this tradition is. Therefore, what I refer to as Confucianism is very narrow, even at the risk of oversimplification. Here Confucianism is primarily no more than an assemblage of doctrines, social conduct, moral rules, rational regimens in knowledge production, and so forth, which were understood to form some kind of heritage, under such titles as the Teaching of Chou, Gong, and Kongtzu (周公孔子之教), Confucian Learning (儒學), and the Teaching of the Sage Kings (先王之教), during the Meiji period or the few centuries preceding the Meiji Restoration, chiefly in Buddhist temples, domainal schools (藩校), and private academies in large cities in the Japanese archipelago. Furthermore, it may well contain some elements that could be attributed to other religious and ethico-political traditions. If necessary, I would be willing to give up the use of the term "Confucianism" and adopt "popular morality" (通俗道徳), as Yasumaru Yoshio in fact did (Yasumaru 1974), for I do not want to be bogged down in a discussion over the authenticity and lineage of Confucianism. By Confucianism I also include its bastardized varieties that were practiced in the everyday life of nonelite social classes. What is at issue is what sort of social transformation was called for in modernity in Northeast Asian societies, what subjectivation was pursued, and how new subjectivity was articulated to the general conception of community.

Of course, I do not deny Confucianism's lineage with similar developments in China, Korea, Vietnam, and so forth; so I am not concerned exclusively with "Japanese" Confucianism. Rather, I am concerned with what social change was called forth by referring to so-called Confucianism negatively and what future Northeast Asian intellectuals projected by denigrating it. Therefore, my first focus is on the transformation of moral conduct under the auspices of Confucianism at the very point of transition from the Baku-Han system to the nation-state.

In describing how Northeast Asian intellectuals came to apprehend the new sort of social justice, I want to underline the following theses:

Confucian ethics presumes a general comprehension of social relations and the mode of individual identification.
This comprehension of social relations and individual identity is incompatible with the new mode of individual identification necessary for the installation of the nation-state.
Neither Confucianism nor popular morality can be reduced to a set of beliefs that an individual adheres to in personalized interior life. It implies a network of social relations, practical rules regulating one's behavior, protocols and manners that define mutual recognition, rationality in knowledge production, and so forth.

In short, it is misleading to comprehend Confucianism as totally reduced to the conventional notion of "inner faith" after the model of Protestantism.[5] But it was the accusation of precisely this lack of "interiority" that writers such as Kitamura Tōkoku (北村 透谷, 1868–1894) directed at Confucianism and the other "religious traditions" in Japan in the 1880s and '90s. It must be noted that such a comprehension of faith and religious belief is premised on the transformation of the mode of identification. Let me note here, as I will come back to this topic later, that the convention of "inner faith" is closely affiliated with the idea of equality; equality as an idea becomes available when the social conditions for the convention of inner faith are made available. Now, let us return to the discussion of justice in modern Japan.

Society of Mutual Dependence and Society of Independent Individuals

In the transition from the old Baku-Han (shogunate, domainal) system to a modern nation, the hierarchical model of social relations, set out in Confucian norms, made way for an epistemic regime of formal equality, and individual identity was recast accordingly. In 1882, fifteen years after the Meiji Restoration and some thirteen years before the annexation of Taiwan, Fukuzawa Yukichi (福澤 諭吉, 1834–1901), a leading social philosopher of the period, noted a radical change in the morality of people in his *On Moral Education* (Fukuzawa [1882] 1959, 349–364), a thesis that tries to defend new education against the critique of surviving Confucians.

Fukuzawa observed that what used to be respected as social norms under the reign of the Tokugawa were deliberately transgressed and overlooked by people in the reign of "Enlightenment." No longer did anyone pay much attention to the principle of seniority among the members of a family. An elder brother could not automatically presume that he would occupy a more prominent public rank than his younger brother unless he could proves himself more knowledgeable or skillful in his profession. The Teaching of the Sage Kings about the relations between father and son, master and vassal, husband and wife, and elder and younger siblings could hardly be put into practice today. Fukuzawa ([1882] 1959, 357–358) asserted that the basic sense of moral order, which Confucianism upheld as universally valid, was not honored at all, and he speculated that if we should ever resurrect a gentleman of the Genroku era (1688–1704) in present-day Japan he would undoubtedly deplore the fact that the way of human morality had perished in the world of darkness.

No doubt this is a bit of hyperbole on the part of Fukuzawa for the sake of the rhetorical force of his argument. I do not think that the collapse of the Confucian habit could happen so easily in Meiji Japan; neither do I believe that the old moral rule of seniority could dissipate so fast within two decades after the Meiji Restoration. The point of his argument, however, does not rest on the accuracy of his empirical observation, so let us continue to listen to him.

Fukuzawa argued that this radical change in mores already discernible in 1882 could not be attributed solely to the degeneration of Japanese morality. What was significant in what may appear to be the general moral decay of Japanese society since the Meiji Restoration was that all these violations of Confucian values were totally licit and justifiable according to the newly emerging consensus of the Japanese public. Since the opening of Japan to the West and the replacement of the polity, the desires of people in all corners of the country had been redirected toward progressive goals that simply could not be shut off. This is to say that the mode of public opinion had been changed once and for all such that the function of moral education, if not entirely removed, must be fundamentally reconsidered in order to be relevant to the new historical situation. And, he continued, the solidarity of masters and vassals that used to be divided into some three hundred rival unities or domains (han) now is integrated into a single great han (or domain) so that the ways of loyalty and righteousness should naturally differ from before.

Fukuzawa criticized the conservative scholars with a Confucian background for their lack of understanding of the fact that the social formation they inhabited, then, after the Restoration was not of the feudal, decentered polity, like the Tokugawa Shogunate; they refused to acknowledge that they were living in the new society of a nation-state. Consequently, he claimed that the old virtue of loyalty (忠) was utterly irrelevant now. In short, the country (國) was no longer a han or domain; it was transformed into a nation-state. Therefore, Fukuzawa ([1882] 1959, 357–358) argued, the spirit of domainal autonomy had to be replaced by the doctrine of national sovereignty (國権論).

Yet it is disingenuous to conceive of this transformation of polity simply in terms of a quantitative change from multiplicity to oneness, from three hundred governments to a single one, for instance. It also involves an irreversible qualitative change. The fundamental nature of ethics changed in tandem with the installation of the nation-state. "In the old days, the order of society was in the mode of codependency [相依るの風], with individuals being lodged in the reciprocal [相依り相依られ] relations of master and vassal, father and son, husband and wife, and the elder and the younger, and thus loving and respecting one another. The Teaching of the Sage Kings was established after the fact of these mutually reciprocating relations" (Fukuzawa [1882] 1959). Confucian ethics would, therefore, be irrelevant unless these social relations of codependency are cherished. In the Teaching of the Sage Kings, human beings are predetermined in terms of their positions within those reciprocally defining relations. On the contrary, in "the teaching of Autonomy and Independence" (自主独立論) which Fukuzawa advocated, "we must first establish our self as an independent substance, attribute an exclusive value to it, and maintain all social relations based upon the priority of one's self" (Fukuzawa [1882] 1959). The two teachings, Confucianism and the new ethics, are incompatible not only because they are justified on the basis of two entirely different types of governance but also because the fundamental views of the human being, the social nature of man, and the very conception of morality itself are radically different according to these two ethics. It goes without saying that these two different ethical orders continued to compete with one another during the Meiji period and well into the twentieth century. In addition to the massive impacts of capitalist development, the struggles of these ethical orders contributed a great deal to the transformation of social formations in the Japanese archipelago.

What Fukuzawa means by "the teaching of Autonomy and Independence" is not immediately clear, other than that it refers to his fundamental insight into the relationship between the individual and the nation as can be found in his famous thesis, "Only when the individual is independent can the nation of such individuals be independent" (「一身独立して一國 (*ikkoku*) 独立する」; Fukuzawa [1880] 1969, 30). Although I translate the Japanese word *kuni* (or *ikkoku*) as the "nation" in this quote, kuni can be polysemic. It could signify a country in the sense of a territorial state sovereignty, a country in the sense of countryside, or a domain (han) that used to be ruled by the feudal lord. What is certain in his assertion about the individual's autonomy and independence is that he is concerned with the totality of a society that individuals gather together to form, namely, the nation. After bypassing kinship mediation through which each individual acquires his or her concrete status in society, Fukuzawa proposes envisioning a social formation in terms of two contrasting poles, the individual and the nation, as the totality of a community.

Apart from his insistence that Confucianism hinders an individual's independent behavior and thinking and prevents people from desiring to live without relying upon others, by the teaching of autonomy and independence he seems to be indicating some feature, hitherto unavailable, of a radically different way of conceiving social relations and individuals. This was more like a new epistemic regime in which the human being and social relations were conceived of anew and without which the typically modern relationship between the individual and the totality of the society could not be thought of. Of course, what Fukuzawa was genuinely concerned about was the construction of the nation in Japan, of turning multitudes in the Japanese archipelago into the Japanese nation.

Today this new regime is so integral to our commonsensical views of people and societies that it is very difficult for us to appreciate its newness during the early years of the Meiji period. Above all else, I must note that, to the newly emerging nation in the 1870s and '80s, Fukuzawa first had to preach the doctrine of individualism, a revolutionary thesis that logically the individual exists before he or she is in certain social relations. He proposed thinking of social relations and morality, starting with the premise that each individual is an independent substance and that social relations are secondary and accidental, rather than essential, to the primary indivisibility of the individual.

No doubt, his kind of individualism was, above all else, a declaration of his political and ethical stance. It goes without saying that many intellectuals and political leaders affiliated with the Meiji state considered Fukuzawa's agenda too radical in a monarchy that was fast transforming itself through massive policy borrowing from Western Europe and North America. He appreciated the fundamentals of liberal capitalism, and, as we know, the Japanese nation would relentlessly pursue its own future set up in the modernization agenda of liberal capitalism in the century to come. Furthermore, we should not overlook its epistemic significance, which can be rendered evident when contrasted to the Confucian premise of the human being and social relations.

Relational Identity and Specific Identity

The basic values of Confucianism are defined in one way or another in implicit reference to particular kinship and clan relations, and this is one reason why the Confucian view of the social nature of the human being is frequently summarized by the juxtapositions of kinship and clan relations—father and son, master and vassal, husband and wife, the elder and the younger, and friends— or sometimes of the so-called Five Orders or Companies (五倫), which were believed to distinguish humans from other animals. Except for the relation of a friend and another friend—strictly speaking, even this relation is not a symmetrical one—all the threads of constant relations with which Confucian values were woven are unequal ones. The so-called Five Constancies (五常) are moral virtues that manifest themselves on the occasions marked by these Five Orders. On the one hand, as Fukuzawa points out, the Five Constancies necessarily give rise to the system of one-sided obligations. On the other hand, these relations help define the individual in terms of webs of irreplaceable rapports and exchanges; it is claimed that, despite asymmetry and hierarchical obligations, this system of Confucian humanism serves to maintain the welfare of all involved in the long run. As the number of kinship relations engaged in grows—one is a father in relation to his son, and a younger brother in relation to his elder sister's husband, and a husband in relation to his wife, and a vassal in relation to his superior in his administrative service, and so on—one's individual concreteness also increases. So this concreteness is nothing but the sum total of the rules of conduct about what one has to do and how one has to act in relation to a particular person who also occupies a concrete position in webs of kinship and rank relations. Confucian ethics is universalist in the sense that its moral norms are valid and binding anywhere and anytime, but an actual conduct of ethical imperative must differ each time, dependent upon whom one's conduct is directed at. For each practical norm, the position of an acting individual is defined in relation to other individuals toward whom his or her conduct is addressed. Thus, this type of ethics helps us to envision the inner workings of a feudal or caste-based society in which one's station in life is limited by birth, marriage, or kinship.

For the sake of comparison, let me contrast this Confucian society with an entirely different organization, an organization of social relations among individuals and a credit card company. Through a contract, each of the credit card holders has a relation with the company that guarantees that an individual card holder will be able to perform a monetary transaction with a third party with the use of his or her card. The company creates a network of people, but to join this network does not mean that the individual is identified in terms of his or her relations with the other individuals. In the community of the individual card holders and the credit card company, the individual remains totally individuated and is interchangeable with other individuals; each of the card holders is an atomized unit alienated from other members of the community. What ensures the individual card holder's membership in the community of a particular credit card is the one-to-one contract between the individual and the credit card company. From the viewpoint of this credit card company, its card holders constitute the totality of a community, but from the viewpoint of the card holders, the totality of their community is invisible except through their contact with the company. The credit card company symbolically represents the totality of their community as far as each of the credit card holders is concerned. Yet, no card holder of this community needs to be affiliated with other card holders at all. Essentially all the members can be indifferent or unrelated to one another. In this respect, the community of credit card holders forms a society of strangers. Of course, it is quite possible for different individual clients to form some personal relationships among themselves, but these are no more than an accident to the community.

In contrast, no individual can remain individuated in the network of Confucian ethics because he or she is connected to other individuals, each of whom occupies a different and unique position in the network, and forms some reciprocal relations with other members of the kin. In other words, Confucian ethics requires a structured collectivity of individuals who are related to one another through kinship and other relations of obligations. Confucianism assumes the existence of related individuals who are acquainted with one another. In other words, Confucian ethics would never work in a society of strangers; it can only be effectual in a society of acquaintances.

In this community of Confucian ethics, therefore, an individual is never linked to the whole without a detailed kinship mediation. As a matter of fact, the totality of the network within which one's identity is defined is never given directly. To belong to a certain family is always to occupy a particular position within the webs of kinship relations, and one's particular position within it is dependent upon *the persons one is in a relation with*. The system within which a person is identified is built upon a series of *personal* relations, that is, relations of "you" and "me."[6] I have children and, in this respect, I am a father in my personal relation with them. I am then obligated to certain norms in my relation to them. But, in the company of my mother, I am a son. The norms I am to follow in my conduct in the relation to my mother are entirely different from those that govern me in the relation to my children. What I am obligated to is thus dependent upon whom I am with; my *personal* relation to my interlocutor is the most significant factor that determines the ethical scope of personal conduct. And how I identify myself in this modality of kinship communality is best expressed by the use of the honorific. In each instance of being with a certain person in the network, I must express my relationship in reference to my addressee, to someone who happens to be my interlocutor in a specific instance of discourse, by carefully selecting nominal words in the vocative case, the positionality of the speaker in enunciation and, of course, ethical norms to follow.[7] What allows me to enter or occupy a position in the network of kinship is a *personal* relation—what Émile Benveniste (1971) called "the I-and-you polarity" and insisted that only the first and second pronouns ("I" and "you") could be called personal (195–204)—marked in the act of enunciation. My identity is therefore determined relationally as far as my ethical conduct is concerned.

Unless delimited by the degree of kinship, the network generally called "family" cannot be distinguished from its neighboring kinship relationships. In other words, the network of one's relatives can be expanded almost indefinitely in social formations dominated by Confucianism which used to allow for polygamy. At the sixth or seventh degree of consanguinity, one's family could easily be the size of a small city. Furthermore, through marriage, a family can be extended and connected to different families. Unlike the modern family, whose membership is delimited by monogamous marriage and the second degree of consanguinity (parent-child and siblings), the social network of family according to Confucian ethics is much broader and more amorphous. While a person's membership in the family is usually marked by his or her surname, it is extremely ambiguous for female members of the family. Hence, it is not as easy to distinguish insiders from outsiders to the family in the case of its Confucian conception, as in the case of the modern bourgeois family.

Of course, the transformation of the family never happens overnight. In the modernization of Japan, it took more than one century to eliminate the remnants of the *ie* (家) heritage and institute the family of *katei* (家庭); this was triggered in the Meiji Restoration when the Japanese leadership decided to join the modern international world as a territorial, sovereign state. Inevitably, this process of modernization has been marked by many hybrid forms of family, as Nishikawa Yûko argued in reference to the ie family/katei family doublet (「家」家族／「家庭」家族二重体), which had characterized the modern family until the 1970s when the ideal of the modern family began to hollow out.[8]

In modern social formations as well, the family continues to play the decisive role in the identification of the individual human being, but a new and previously nonexistent dimension is integrated into the new way of identifying an individual. That is nationality, the belonging to the nation. This results from the new principle organizing the vision of the world or, more specifically, worlding, according to which certain structural assumptions are accepted in our everyday life. One such assumption is the regime of internationality that is based upon the speciation of humanity by nationality. All humanity must be classified into nations; the genus of humankind must be subdivided into the species of nations, to follow the language of classical logic. And this configuration of speciation, or classifying humanity into species of nations, is then called "internationality." As configured in the international world, a new vision of the world regulated by the system of international law becomes a seminal variable in the identification of the individual human being.

In the new community called the nation, a human being is identified as an individual, and the mode of its identification may as well be called specific identification in contrast to the relational identification prevalent in Confucian ethics and the popular morality prevalent in premodern societies.

Equality and the Individual

It is important to note that essentially there is no room for equality in this conception of the human being and social relations as defined in relational identification. Basically, the moral principle of formal equality is absent in Confucian ethics. By this I am not saying that Confucianism does not allow for antiauthoritarianism or the encouragement of impartiality among people. Rather, I suggest that the liberal idea of formal equality is not viable in the Teaching of the Sage Kings. For, in Confucianism, two people who constitute a reciprocal relation are never defined as two interchangeable entities, outside the instance of discourse in which they speak as "I" and "you" in the dialogic encounter of the addresser and the addressee. Since the individuality of each person is a consequence of many relations in which that person is engaged, no individual is conceived of as interchangeable with another, irrespective of the context of the enunciation, as in the community of credit card holders.

In discussing individuation, it is first necessary to discard the confusing implications of this term "individual." And, of course, we must guard against the so-called individualism, moral stance, or political ideology with which this word is often endowed. Since the nineteenth century the term "individual" has gradually gained some appearance of self-evidence such that it has been circulated widely, designating the human being as an indivisible ontological unit or an atom, but the logical connotations of this word are extremely confusing. Supposedly "individual" derives from the classical logic where things in the universe are classified according to the formula of individual–species–genus. A group of things constitutes a genus as long as they share a common characteristic. Horses, for instance, constitute a group, and it can be designated as a genus, horse. But, among horses, there are, for example, black and white horses, so the genus of horse can be classified into its subsets, a species of white horses and one of black horses. A genus can thus be further divided into species or subsets, but this process of classification reaches a limit where things constituting the species can no longer be split. This is where an individual is identified as an atomistic unity that cannot be further divided. According to Aristotelian metaphysics, therefore, an individual is also an indivisible and supposedly the most basic and concrete component of the universe. Nowadays few people take this ontological thesis implied in Aristotelian metaphysics seriously, but its legacy is still present in the basic concepts of classical logic.[9] Until the nineteenth century, the classical classificatory scheme hardly applied to human beings, so a human being was rarely designated as an individual. Yet, with the rise of capitalist liberalism, the use of "individual" as the term to connote the unit of humankind has been popularized, and today "individual" is used almost indiscriminately to designate a human being.

However, this use of the term "individual" gives rise to a number of logical contradictions. For instance, a human being is capable of reflecting on itself. Reflection implies a separation of an image or figure to be reflected upon and the agent of seeing that views such an image or figure. Thus, man or woman is regarded as an animal separating itself from itself to use the faculty of reflection. The concept of self-consciousness is another instance that illuminates the human being as divided from itself. In modern philosophical and psychoanalytic language, the term "subject" is used instead of "individual" so as to avoid this type of logical confusion.

This is one of the reasons why Fukuzawa Yukichi, famous for his insistence upon the equality of humanity, believed that Confucian ethics must be repudiated in order for the very idea of equality to be introduced to Japan.[10] Yet it is important to keep in mind that, whereas Fukuzawa insisted upon formal equality, he did not hesitate to embrace racial inequality or the hierarchy of ranks developed by colonialism and capitalism. More generally, Fukuzawa never denounced social inequality or the hierarchy of positions introduced into society as a result of competition or work. Essentially, his idea of equality was of opportunity and meritocracy. The better educated ought to be given higher positions than those less knowledgeable or talented; those who earn more wealth through industriousness and enterprise must be more respected than those who are less wealthy. He absolutely endorsed the principle of formal equality but would never denounce the actuality of social inequality. Thus, the debate over what equality could possibly mean was already imminent in Japan as soon as the agenda of modernity was introduced.

However, why was the principle of formal equality absolute for Fukuzawa Yukichi? What he attempted to achieve by endowing an ultimate value to the self or one's single body (一身) was to open a social space in which the individual was stripped of these kinship relations. Or, more precisely, he attempted to install the epistemic regime whereby the individual could be posited as devoid of properties that are attributes of mutually reciprocating relations. Instead of being postulated as already and always caught in the webs of kinship relations, the human being is first posited as an autonomous individual independent of these relations.[11] Clearly what was at stake in his argument about formal equality was the necessary condition for the possibility of a new communality called the nation.

You can probably see that this diagnosis need not be limited to the period of Japanese history subsequent to the Meiji Restoration in which the polity was transformed from the Baku-Han Shogunate system into a modern parliamentary monarchy. This is a large-scale historical transition, generally depicted as that of modernization, in which a state sovereignty whose legitimacy is sought in some symbolic representations of kinship is replaced by a new one capable of postulating its population as an assembly of autonomous subjects through individuation as well as totalization. All the polities in Northeast Asia had to go through a similar process to individualize and totalize their populaces, regardless of whether it was the Republicanism of South Korea, the Chinese Communist Party, the Taiwanese Guomingtang, or the Japanese emperor system.

The Public and the Private

Once again, please allow me to introduce a disclaimer here. I do not mean to say that a transition in the modality of an individual's identification from the relational identity of Confucian ethics to the specific identity of nationality summarizes the process of modernization in subjectivity in general.[12] That would be an absolute misunderstanding of my argument. The principle of relational identification cannot be eliminated tout court. First of all, I cannot imagine a social formation in which relational identity is totally eliminated. Neither can I endorse the liberal notion of individualism to such an extent that every social relationship would be construed in terms of atomized and substantialized individuals, for I believe that the relational identity is much more fundamental to human sociality than the specific identity. Furthermore, as I explain below, the individuation at issue concerns one modality of specific identity, an explication of which seems to require an apprehension of what Michel Foucault called "pastoral power." And the liberal notion of individualism is, in the final analysis, no more than a symbolic expression of the commodified human relationships in capitalist societies. Without personal relations, a human being is unable to learn basic sociality, and as long as humans are social beings, it is impossible to eliminate relational identity in the modality of identification.

What was brought about in Japanese social formations through modernization was not the abolition of relational identity, but an emphasis on the experience of being stray, isolated, or alone, an experience of being alienated from others. Aloneness was regarded as a privileged attitude that was associated with the opening of a new social space that was viewed as public. The negative connotation of being alone or isolated was partially reversed. The modernization of Japanese social formation did not lead to the abolition of relational identity; it rather brought about the delimitation of the realm of the relational identity. In this delimitation that marks the coming of the modern society, it is necessary to take two different stages into account. The first is concerned with the distinction between nature and ethics. Perhaps the Song rationalism (宋理学) best expresses this cosmological tendency; the ethical order was often conceptualized after the model of Five Constancies and ontologized as the law of the universe in Confucian ethics. In other words, Confucianism did not know how to segregate the realm of natural law from the domains of human affairs. As Franz Borkenau observed about the feudal worldview in Europe, the law of nature and the law of ethical conduct were not clearly distinguished from one another, so it was impossible for scholars such as Thomas Aquinas to conceptually differentiate natural law from ethical law. Both are laws created by God (Borkenau 1934, 1965).[13] To use the language of Enlightenment, the alienation of practical reason from theoretical reason was a prerequisite for modernity; but for this alienation, modern science would never have emerged in the early modern period. Undoubtedly, in the process of introducing scientific knowledge to Japan, China, Korea, and so on, the severance of the domain of natural law from that of ethical law was one of the accomplishments of modernization in Northeast Asia, but this was not sufficient. Another stage was in demand.

And this is the most important issue for Fukuzawa's denunciation of Confucianism. The Five Constancies must not dictate the entire sphere of human affairs; they must not be valid in every moment of an individual's as well as collective lives. The universalism assumed in the moral dictates of the Five Constancies should be curtailed to a clearly discernible domain, namely, the sphere of privacy. Outside the sphere of privacy stretches the sphere of the public, in which the Five Constancies are totally irrelevant. The two spheres of privacy and public communality must never be confused with one another, and the transgression of the public with the private would be condemned as corruption. Confucian ethics must be delimited and cannot apply beyond the sphere of private affairs, and when it interferes with the public sphere, it is nothing but nepotism. The domain of affairs about which Confucian ethics is qualified to speak, then, would be confined to the modern family. From the viewpoint of modernizationists, therefore, Confucianism is typically a confusionism in ethical conduct!

Let me note that Fukuzawa's insistence upon human equality was accompanied by his demand that a person's identification be liberated from the constraints of social rank (身分). Only when people are conceived of as comparable indivisible units and as individuated individuals can there be a social space in which equality is properly practiced. And this social space cannot be that of the private; it is outside the domain where family etiquette dictates one's conduct; it is a public sphere in which not the Five Orders but instead the principle of formal equality ought to prevail. This public sphere is the nation. It goes without saying that the positing of an autonomous and independent individual definitely leads to a new way of apprehending individual identity, of an aesthetic investment in community identification, which Fukuzawa called "nationality" or "national body" (*kokutai* 國體).

Nationality and National Body (國體)

The model of a credit card holder community helps us apprehend the basic premises upon which a new community called "nation" is constructed, but it is also important to note that, by no means can we induce the structure of the national community from this model. On the one hand, the nation is essentially a society of strangers. In this respect, the model of a credit card community helps us apprehend the new and modern community called the nation. On the other hand, the nation is also what Benedict Anderson (1983) called "the imagined community." Precisely because the nation is a society of strangers, it structurally requires the supplement of the imaginary. A society of strangers lacks such innate cohesiveness as naturally endows a social formation built on the regime of relational identification. In order for such a social formation to be prevented from fragmentation and atomization, it must be tied together by the imaginary bonds of sympathy. This is why the nation as a society of strangers is at the same time a society of sympathy. It is in this context of the imaginary formation of the national community that nationality and national body must be understood.

That nationality and national body are juxtaposed here is due to the fact that the word "kokutai" (national body 國體) was first introduced during the early part of the Meiji period as a translation of the English word "nationality." Against those "imperial scholars" who proposed implementing the superiority of Japan within the union of religion and the state, as evidenced in the words "a line of emperors for ages eternal" (一系萬代), Fukuzawa argued for an institutionalized consciousness that would integrate the nation. In addition to the "flawless" imperial line, he insisted upon the necessity for the "forms in which things are collected together, made one, and distinguished from other entities":

> Thus kokutai [the national body] refers to the gathering together of a species of people who share suffering as well as pleasure, the creation of a distinction between fellow countrymen and foreigners, the fostering of more cordial and stronger bonds with one's countrymen than with foreigners. It is living under the same government, enjoying self-rule, and disliking the idea of being subject to foreign rule; it involves independence and responsibility for the welfare of one's own country. In the West it is called "nationality." (Fukuzawa [1882] 1959, 27)

Moreover, nationality was to be expressed through certain emotions, that is, a "sentiment of nationality" (國體之情): "A sentiment of nationality may originate in the identity of race, or religion, or language, or geography. Although the reason may differ from country to country, the most important factor is for a race of people to pass through a series of social changes and embrace a common sentiment for the shared past" (Fukuzawa [1882] 1959, 37; [1875] 1973, 23).[14]

This represents a nearly exact rendering of John Stuart Mill's explanations of nationality and "the society of sympathy" as displaced onto the situation in Japan.[15] The definition of this nationality is based upon the desire to ascribe the sense of nationality to either race, the permanence of the governmental body, or language and customs. It was on the basis of these definitions that various and quite distinct discussions of the national body consequently developed in modern Japan. Furthermore, there were instances in which "nationality" was translated into other such words as *kokusui* (national essence 國伜) and *kokuseki* (national registry 国籍; Oguma 1995).[16] It cannot, of course, be concluded that Fukuzawa's interpretation dominated subsequent views of the national body. Yet, even today, his interpretation of nationality remains most fundamental among many other conceptions of the national body (國體). While the other judiciary, theocratic, and historical definitions of the national body have served to justify, rationalize, or mystify the imaginary unity of the nation that is supposedly represented by the symbolic presence of the modern emperor (天皇), Fukuzawa's presents the most articulate and persuasive apprehension of nationality in the service of the national community.

In considering the problem of Japanese identity, however, it is necessary to refer to "nationality" in order to understand from the perspective of the present why this notion has played such an important role as a device by which to produce sympathy among the Japanese nation. Moreover, Fukuzawa argued that it was impossible to construct the nation without a distinction between Japanese and non-Japanese, a demarcation of its insiders from its outsiders. A nation is never humanity in general. A nation cannot exist unless a portion of humanity is distinguished from general humanity. From this standpoint, he regarded "the distinction between fellow countrymen and foreigners" (「自他之別」) as absolutely essential. Only when it is possible to discriminate one portion from other portions of humanity is it feasible to imagine a community of people among whom sympathy would prevail and outside whom antipathy should dominate. The imaginary constitution of the national community is thus premised upon how the speciation of humanity is carried out systematically and universally: a portion of humanity must be distinguished from other portions.

Although Fukuzawa ([1875] 1973, 177) rejected a type of Christian image of the emperor denoting "impartial and universal brotherhood" (「一視同仁四海兄弟」),[17] the idea that the "sentiment of nationality" should accompany the enlargement of the Japanese Empire and extend beyond the residents of the Japanese mainland was later widely accepted.[18] In this way, "impartial and universal brotherhood" came to be understood as attaining a broad universalism, one that extended beyond the residents of the Japanese archipelago as the Japanese nation expanded its territory and population.

In the history of the modern emperor system until the inauguration of the New Constitution in 1946, the first half of the idiom "impartial and universal

FIGURE 2.1. The emperor's baby. The aesthetic regime sustaining the emperor system projects an imaginary relationship between the emperor (= the pastor) and the national subject (= the stray sheep). The central trope (one gaze, equal love 「一視同仁」) determined each individual subject of the nation to be an infant seeking the emperor's love (emperor's baby 「天皇之赤子」). Thus, tropes plagiarized from Christian missionaries formed the basic structure of Japan's nationalist aesthetics. In this respect, the Japanese individual was subjectivized according to pastoral aesthetics, at least until the end of the Meiji Constitution (1945). Source: Getty Images.

brotherhood," that is, "one gaze, equal mercy" or "one gaze, equal love" (*isshi dôjin*「一視同仁」) was irreparably associated with the figure of the emperor; the idiom symbolically expressed the very relationship between the emperor and the individual subject, between the state and individuated Japanese, as being between the one who provides charity and love to his subjects individually and the one who craves such love. It is no accident that the figurative representation of the relationship between the emperor and his subject—his subject was also called the emperor's baby (「天皇之赤子」)—showed an eerie resemblance to that of the shepherd and a stray sheep (see figure 2.1).

The Judeo-Christian origin of this power structure—one of many origins of the emperor system or emperorism—was carefully concealed by Japanese state bureaucracy, but its character as a pastoral power was perhaps unwittingly disclosed in a series of events leading to the official decision on the part of the U.S. Occupation Administration to allow the Showa Emperor to survive.[19]

Pastoral Power and Equality

Although I am hesitant to attribute any causal relationship between the emergence of equality as a virtue or practical principle and the introduction of the emperor system in the Meiji state, it is likely that the idea of equality was apprehended against the background of this figurative representation of the individual and the whole.[20] From the outset, the emperor system was introduced as a sort of pastoral power.[21] I have only discussed the new sense of social justice that was actualized in Japan in the nineteenth century, but I suspect that it is widely applicable to a number of other historical contexts, including those in Northeast Asia, Europe, South Asia, Latin America, and North America.

Here, allow me to make a third disclaimer. The term "pastoral power" was invented by Foucault, and, starting with an analysis of this power, he proceeded to extended discussion of biopower (*biopouvoir*) in modern European societies (2004b; 2007). In his discussion of pastoral power, Foucault read the texts of ancient Judaism and Christianity. In due course, I would never argue that Foucault's description of pastoral power is directly applicable to the Japanese emperor system, which is characterized unambiguously not as an ancient formation of power, but as a modern one. Hence, his inquiry into biopower is conducted in the milieu of a new social arrangement, population. In his analysis of pastoral power, for example, the relationship between the pastor and the cohort of his followers seems to be a personal one in which they are present to each other in the personal vocative of "I" and "you." If one seeks an analogous situation in a modern setting, what would probably come to mind are the institutions of confession in the Catholic Church and of psychotherapy, in which the confessor and the repentant or the analyst and the patient are put in personal proximity. The emperor system is very different from this description of pastoral power precisely because personal proximity is absent. Instead, the sense of personal vocation is counterfeited, so to speak, by the technology of reproduction—photography and printing—and the system of modern education in the emperor system. The individual's relationship to the emperor is mediated by the modern technology of mass communication, universal national conscription, universal education, and so on, in addition to the invention of the modern national language as Japanese. Consequently the structure of community produced by the emperor system is similar, with respect to the formal configuration of national subjectivity, to the one I outlined in the model of the credit card community. By no means, however, can we overlook the fundamental difference between the credit card community, where sympathy is absent and where members are completely indifferent to each other emotive-sentimentally, on the one hand, and the national community, whose unity is brought about by the dictate of sympathy on the other. Why can the figure of the emperor generate nationwide sympathy while no sense of solidarity at all is expected from the credit card community?

The most crucial question to be confronted lies in the dimension of aesthetics. The notion of pastoral power is irrelevant to the credit card community precisely because the matters of feeling are not appropriated into the governing structure of the communality of credit card membership. Indeed, members are thoroughly individuated in this type of community, but they are not totalized at all. Certainly every holder of a credit card knows he or she belongs to the card's community but does not form an intimate relationship with the card issuer. In other words, the community of credit cards lacks an affective symbol of its totality. In the emperor system of the Meiji Constitution, every child of the Japanese nation was taught at school that the photographic portrait of the emperor connects the child to the symbol of state sovereignty and that to be present with the figure of the emperor is to be present with the totality of the Japanese nation. While the old pastorate Foucault discussed in his analysis of ancient governmentality in early Christianity was actualized in the space of dialogic and personal proximity in which the element of sociophysical distance mattered, the new one was deployed in the space of, and in, representation. Emperorism was set up on a new surface in mass mediation, that is, operative in "population."

As the reign of the constitutional monarchy was consolidated, photographic portraits of the emperor and the empress were placed inside picture frames and hung on living room walls in ordinary households. Prior to the late nineteenth century, the picture frame was scarcely in public use in Northeast Asia; paintings, calligraphic pieces, and wall hangings were displayed without the use of picture frames. For ordinary people in Japan, the use of picture frames was introduced into their everyday life for the first time along with images of the imperial couple, images that also represented the idea of the modern nuclear family based upon the conjugal union of one man and one woman. As Japanese society opened to the international world, the use of the picture frame became popular. It was by means of modern reproduction technology that the image of the emperor gradually penetrated the private life of the individual.

The telling example of this historical change can be found in the introduction of the school shrine called Hôanden (奉安殿), a tiny building within the school campus in which photographic portraits of the emperor and the empress were preserved.[22] While the initial propagation of emperorism was very much dependent upon the availability of new technology—photography, mobile printing, and later cinema and television—the space, which this new pastorate inhabited and grew in, was of a different order from that of the ancient pastorate.[23] It was essentially pastoral power in the element of mass media; it should be characterized rather as part of biopower.

It is also important to keep in mind that the formation of the modern family (近代家族) played an indispensable role in the transition from relational identity to specific identity. Interestingly enough, the mass-produced portraits of the emperor and empress also indicated the transformation of the very notion of the family from the kin that is sustained by the polygamic ethics of personal relations to the modern family based upon the monogamic conjugal union of one man and one woman.

Here we must take up the problematic of individuation once again. Individuation is an operation of power—part and parcel of pastoral power—that creates a setting, a mold of subjection so to speak, in which an isolated human being is placed. It is an art or *technē* of subjectivation by which a person is stripped of all personal relations but one: his or her relation with the pastor. Being a stray sheep, already isolated from the flock, a person is placed in a dialogic relationship with the shepherd, or the leader of the group, who is willing to be sacrificed for the sake of this single and lonely sheep. Not for the sake of the group as a whole, but for this stray sheep alone, the shepherd is willing to risk his own life. It is under the gaze of such a shepherd that a stray sheep acquires the sense of security and assurance.

Accordingly, what Foucault called "individuation" has little to do with the indivisibility of a human being as an ontological atom. The assertions of this famous biblical trope of shepherd and stray sheep are twofold. First, a person previously engaged in a variety of relations with persons of many ranks and statuses is isolated; he or she is redefined and reconstituted as a subject solely in terms of a dialogic relationship to the one, the pastoral figure of the master. All the other relations with people beyond the pastor subsequently become irrelevant. A person becomes alone with the pastor. Second, a stray sheep is rescued by the shepherd and safely returns to the flock. By rejoining the flock, a person resumes his or her relations with other people, but the relationship with them is only ancillary. Only through the mediation of a dialogic relationship with the pastor can he or she resume or reenter relationships with ordinary members of the flock. In other words, a person belongs to the totality of the group by forming an exclusive relationship with the one who represents the whole. Individuation is the mise-en-scène of this setting in which a person is alone in his or her dialogic relationship with the figure of the master.

Only against the backdrop of this particular institutional setting that involves the operations of individuation and totalization can we appreciate the claims of equality because the idea of equality is metaphysical in the sense that it is a demand without the specific objective to be demanded. Let us briefly look back at the history of equality in which rights to equal treatment were implemented. For instance, it is only in the last few decades in some industrialized countries that unequal treatment of homosexuals has been questioned. Another example is the history of gender discrimination. Several decades ago it was assumed that female students were less capable in natural sciences and engineering in higher education, thereby making the number of female professors in these disciplines vastly smaller than that of male professors in virtually any country in the world. Since society consists of a variety of discriminations and differentiations, it would make no sense to claim that an objective to which the idea of equality is applied is either naturally given or self-evident. On the contrary, it is only through historical struggles that the actual content of equality can be determined. In this sense, the idea of equality is like a blank check; no content or target of equality is preestablished. Only through a social struggle to discover the sites of unjustifiable discrimination or inequality can we designate and identify the situation where the demand for equality is relevant. In this respect, equality is an idea rather than a concept, a potentiality rather than an actuality.

Let me restate my initial question: regardless of whether it is equality of outcome or of opportunity, of egalitarianism or of meritocracy, in order for it to be implemented, does the idea of equality not require a social imaginary such as "one gaze, one love" that represents a fantastic relationship between the whole and the individual? How can one conceptualize equality as a practical principle of social justice when one deliberately avoids such a figurative representation of the whole and the individual?

It is well known that Japan's defeat in World War II and the loss of the Japanese Empire came to determine the sentiment of nationality within designated areas on the basis of the so-called myth of the monoethnic society. The argument that the consciousness of "us Japanese" has existed since ancient times, so often found in Nihonjin-ron (the discourse of Japanese uniqueness) and previous to that in imperial history (*kôkokushikan* 皇国史観)—hence seeking the origins of their own communality within the past—had in fact been anticipated in Fukuzawa's (and in due course John Stuart Mill's) definition of "nationality." The myth that the consciousness of "us Japanese" has existed since ancient times is, in fact, the condition required for the sentiment of nationality to be invoked. Yet it was already predicted in the early years of the Meiji period that such a myth would be very useful in the construction of the nation and the sentiment of nationality. Nevertheless, there is one point that I must underline: Fukuzawa never assumed that there was a Japanese nation in the Japanese archipelago when he wrote his *Outline of a Theory of Civilization*, even though he was actively engaged in narrating Japanese history as "our history." He was passionately involved in the discussion about the sentiment of nationality, however, because he was convinced that a nation of the Japanese ought to be fabricated, invented, and manufactured. The Japanese nation had yet to come. This is to say that, whereas the multitude of people were living in the territories of the Japanese state, the Japanese as a nation had yet to exist in the early years of the Meiji period.

After the loss of the Japanese Empire in 1945, however, the situation was drastically different. Today you can scarcely find any intellectual who wants to build the Japanese nation since virtually every inhabitant of the Japanese archipelago believes the Japanese nation already exists. We understand that the Japanese nation was and is a historical construct, a social institution that had to be manufactured between the time of the publication of *An Outline of the Theory of Civilization* (1875) and the collapse of the Japanese Empire.

The Imagined Community and the Inward-Looking Society

What must be called into question is how fairness can be understood with regard to the figuration of the national community. As we have seen in the development of the Japanese nation for the last one and a half centuries, a portion of humanity has been segregated from humanity in general, and it forms a nation as the polity of the nation-state comes into existence. This is to say that the building of the national community signals the mise-en-scène of social formations in which the idea of equality is granted the status of their legitimacy.[24] It has been thought that only in a society whose solidarity is sustained by the sentiment of nationality would people be willing to accept the principle of formal equality in their everyday conduct. At the same time, as Fukuzawa Yukichi argued convincingly, nationality cannot be sustained unless the distinction of fellow countrymen from foreigners (自他之別) is observed. Only as long as foreigners are unambiguously discriminated against can people feel united as a nation. Whereas explicitly the nation is a society of sympathy within which strangers are bound together by imaginary ties, implicitly it is distinguished from other nations and upholds its totality through antipathy toward foreigners. The national community is a political premise for the idea of equality for a portion of humanity, but this community is sustained on the basis of discrimination against foreigners, against other portions of humanity. Accordingly it is argued that a community based upon nationality promises two things for its members: one is that we are all equal qua human beings as long as we are members of the national community. The other is that we must be distinguished from all those who are not members of the national community; the principle of equality must not be extended to the nonmembers of the national community. In other words, what John Stuart Mill called "the society of sympathy" among its members cannot be sustained unless it is also "a society of antipathy" against foreigners.[25]

It is no accident that individuals with no nationality or multiple nationalities are often regarded as abnormal in countries like Japan even today. After the independence of the United States of America and the French Revolution in the eighteenth century, the number of national states increased in the system of international law that initially emerged with the Treaty of Westphalia (1648). Since then, the international world, whose primary unit came to consist in territorial national state sovereignty, had acquired a tendency to regard individuals with no nationality or multiple nationalities as somewhat unfit for nationality.[26] This tendency still remains strong in present-day Japan.

Finally, I would like to give brief mention to the historical context that renders the question of social justice particularly relevant to many of the readers of this volume, who have been involved in the experience of immigration in one way or another. Initially I delivered the original version of this chapter as a speech in the city of Kyoto. Kyoto is known for its large resident population of immigrant (Zainichi 在日) and underclass residents (Buraku 部落).[27] Perhaps readers of this chapter are well aware of the racist movement called the Association of Citizens Who Denounce the Privileges Accorded to Resident Koreans and Chinese (在日特権を許さない市民の会), to my knowledge, the first openly racist movement in Japan since the end of the Asia-Pacific War.

Racial discrimination is nothing new in Japan. Many forms of racial discrimination were observed in prewar Japan, including the comparatively well-known cases of the genocide of Koreans and indigenous Taiwanese under Japanese colonial rule. During the Asia-Pacific War, a large number of racially motivated violent incidents involving Japanese military, state administrative, corporate, and citizenry personnel are reported to have taken place in China, Southeast Asia, and Okinawa, all over the Greater East Asia Co-prosperity Sphere. After that war, the patterns of racial discrimination changed because the Japanese Empire collapsed together with its integrationist policies of multiethnic imperial nationalism. As the Japanese state lost many of its overseas territories, the definition of Japanese nationality (national registry) underwent drastic changes, and more than 30 percent of its population became non-Japanese. In due course, the forms of racial discrimination and ideologies did not remain the same, but the most remarkable case of Japanese racism is that the intellectual and journalistic critique of racism, which involved quite a large number of scholars and intellectuals until the end of the war in 1945, disappeared as soon as Japan was defeated by the Allied Powers. Therefore, very little critique of racism has been propagated in mass media until recently. The Japanese public has very little awareness of the extent to which the Japanese nation is extremely insensitive to its own racist behaviors, speeches, and policies.

In this respect, the Association of Citizens Who Denounce the Privileges Accorded to Resident Koreans and Chinese (abbreviated Zaitokukai) is an almost inevitable consequence of racism in the postwar Japanese society. Nevertheless, I can discern nothing particularly Japanese about their propaganda, public demonstrations, and media presence. Their racism is mediocre and lacks originality. Precisely for this reason, this movement provides us with a good opportunity to explore the global features of today's racism in the international world.

The targets of exclusion for the Zaitokukai are resident Koreans, but the association's members also attack resident Chinese. I do not think they have carefully studied the histories of these ethnic groups in order to identify who is relevant in their rhetoric of exclusion, so their targets have shifted and changed. Frankly speaking, many observers of this movement have an overall impression that the Zaitokukai do not know what they are blaming or denouncing. They show very little interest in what they claim to denounce and abhor. In this respect, the Zaitokukai movement displays a weird resemblance to similar anti-immigrant racisms such as Donald Trump's in the United States. They are somewhat disconnected from the actuality of empirical reality.

What is immediately evident is that they want to exclude immigrants. What motivates the entire movement is their antipathy toward the fantasized figure of immigrants. Since they are not concerned with empirical facts concerning the objects of their hatred, one would have to conclude that the target of their antipathy could possibly exist only in their fantasy. It seems that the coherence of this movement is rooted in its members' common hatred of resident immigrants, those immigrants who supposedly refuse to return "home." In some way they intensely dislike the phenomenon of immigration. In this respect, theirs is manifestly an anti-immigrant racism. Nevertheless, the resident immigrants they supposedly abhor are of their imaginary world.

However, we must not rush to the conclusion that their anti-immigrant racism is illusionary or unreal simply because their movement is deployed in the realm of fantasy. Let us remind ourselves that, when Anderson introduced the notion of an imagined community four decades ago, it was not implied that the nation was illusionary or unreal because of its imaginary nature. In other words, the Zaitokukai's politics of fantasy discloses one aspect of the aesthetics of nationality, of the imaginary formation of the nation.

Their group title, the Association of Citizens Who Denounce the Privileges Accorded to Resident Koreans and Chinese (在日特権を許さない市民の会) includes a phrase composed of four Chinese characters, *zainichi tokken* (在日特権), the first combination "zainichi" (在日) meaning "staying in Japan," and the second combination "tokken" (特権) meaning privilege. It is important to note that this is a rather peculiar use of the combination "tokken" since the association is not referring to excessive benefits, favors, or advantages those immigrants enjoy in comparison to ordinary Japanese citizens. Normally in modern Japanese language, the word "tokken" implies that someone enjoys more benefits, favors, or advantages than an ordinary member of a community because of that person's special status. What the members of the Zaitokukai are outraged about is the matter of equality, but in their demonstration of anger, equality is understood in its reverse sense. The privilege that resident Koreans are allowed to enjoy is nothing but equality. They object to the inclusion of Korean immigrants among those who are equal. They argue that not only resident Koreans but also resident Chinese are allowed to enjoy the same rights to residence, employment, education, social welfare, and so forth as ordinary Japanese citizens; these immigrants are treated as if they are equal in the Japanese national community. Moreover, they say, these privileges are granted to them by law.[28]

Two statements are put forth in their accusation of resident Koreans, neither of which may we lose sight of. The first is their assertion that "we are equal qua human beings"; the members of the Zaitokukai demand that they too are fully entitled to be treated as equal. But this statement is accompanied by a second. By "we" they refer to Japanese citizens only. The second statement goes as follows: "We are equal as long as we are members of the Japanese national community." In other words, they deliberately adopt the stance of national humanism; they refuse to endow foreigners with the status of human beings. As discussed in chapter 1, since the end of the Asia-Pacific War, national humanism has been adopted as quite a popular political stance by a variety of groups, including some Marxists in Japan, even though the issues of Japanese responsibility had rarely been raised by non-Japanese before the 1980s.

How do they justify their argumentation? Since even the leaders of the Zaitokukai are not particularly concerned with the ideological coherence of their stance, I have so far not encountered any logically coherent argumentation to justify or rationalize their political claims. Nevertheless it is possible to imagine a plausible argument by which they could try to justify their stance. More importantly, since this movement is essentially an internet movement that solicits its audience online and recruits its followers through interconnected communication networks, it is important to discern possible arguments that the movement's supporters might well project onto the Zaitokukai's demonstrations, those both in the sense of street marches with placards and shouted political slogans that present demonstrators themselves as political agents and also in the sense of expressing their frustrations and staging social conflicts which their propaganda reflects.[29] In other words, what kind of demands and messages could these demonstrations possibly invoke among those who observe their street activism and the footage of their speeches against immigrants?

The first and second statements are important in this respect. Surprisingly enough, the members of the Zaitokukai, who are so vocal about justifying discrimination against resident immigrants, are seriously concerned with the issue of equality. One cannot overlook their thrust toward the universalism of fairness that is implied and emphasized in their demonstrations. They repeatedly try to defend the fact that "we are equal qua human beings" as long as they belong to the national community; they demand that they too are fully entitled to be treated as equal. This assertion seems to suggest that they—and their potential sympathizers—are extremely anxious about their own nationality with regard to the principle of equality. They are unsure whether or not they are actually regarded as equal, even though, at least by law, they are authentic members of the Japanese nation. What is indicated by the emotive and expressive shape of their demonstrations is that they are afraid of easily sliding down into the status of the non-Japanese because they feel they have been treated as if they were outsiders. In terms of employment opportunities, upward mobility in Japanese society, cultural capital (background in higher education, basic skills in intellectual communication in the national language as well as foreign languages, specialized expertise, professional training, familiarity with so-called national traditions, and so forth), and income levels, an increasing portion of the Japanese population are unsure whether or not they actually belong to the Japanese nation so as to be treated as equal.

The significance of the second statement is all the more obvious. It states that the members of the Zaitokukai belong to the Japanese national community. They are not non-Japanese, not foreigners who must be unambiguously distinguished from the Japanese. This is exactly what Fukuzawa Yukichi implied by the idiom "the distinction between fellow countrymen and foreigners" (「自他之別」), and, following the classical definition of nationality, they demand that citizens of the Japanese nation discriminate against resident Koreans and

Chinese, against immigrants who, they argue, are not entitled to enjoy the same status as the Japanese. The first statement is reinforced by the second statement to reproduce an aggressive form of national humanism, which expresses their deep-rooted ressentiment.

Many of the contentions of the members of the Association of Citizens Who Denounce the Privilege Accorded to Resident Koreans and Chinese are groundless, empirically faulty, or outright lies, but it is not difficult to detect in their demonstrations an aesthetics of nationality that is capable of invoking some sympathy among those Japanese who feel victimized in one way or another. Similarly, the anti-immigrant rhetoric put forth by Donald Trump is mostly groundless, faulty, and filled with lies, yet, under some circumstances, it may well persuade certain groups of people to endorse his incantation.

Of course, the point is not how well one can refute the Zaitokukai's contentions. That is too easy for us. But what do we do with the fact that their movement speaks for some repressed collective anxiety and is effective to mobilize certain portions of population? I suspect there is an astonishingly large number of Japanese who could potentially feel responsive to the rhetoric of the Zaitokukai. Already we have seen a similar movement of ressentiment that has invoked an aggressive populism in the United States and that successfully brought an anti-immigrant racist into the White House. Not unlike the people participating in Trumpian anti-immigrant racism in the United States, those actual or potential sympathizers of the Zaitokukai are most often so deprived of social capital that they have neither the basic will with which to objectivize their feelings of victimhood and to identify possible social causes for their misery so as to project some coherent social policies whereby to rescue themselves from their desolation, nor the emotional capacity to reflect upon the very process of projecting their own anxiety onto the fantastic figures of resident illegal immigrants.

In short, the Zaitokukai is an anti-immigrant racist movement that plays with the sentiment of nationality. In the last several years, similar tendencies have cropped up in many countries—in the United States, France, the Netherlands, Poland, Japan, Brazil, South Korea, the United Kingdom, and even Germany—and parliamentary democratic systems are now threatened by the presence of this inward-looking tendency in many parts of the world. This is why one cannot deny that this populist movement initiated by the Zaitokukai manifests some universal features of the nationalism of the modern international world. To the extent that the nation-state is the universal form of state sovereignty in the international world today, anti-immigrant racism like the Zaitokukai's can be present in any so-called modern national society.

The question I wanted to ask is related to this problem concerning how to conceptualize social justice that is not dependent upon one form or another of the aesthetics of nationality; how to conceptualize the idea of equality independently of the social imaginary of the national body (國體).

Equality beyond Nationality

With the formation of the nation-state, a new form of collectivity becomes representable as a particular class of human beings against the generality of humanity. The general class of human beings can now be divided into the particular sets called "nations," to which an individual must belong selectively and exclusively. This is truly significant, particularly today in the context of immigration; it is the reason why the modern nation-state cannot get rid of the tendency to regard individuals with no or multiple nationalities as abnormal even though an increasing number of states accept people of multinationality. Without this modern modality of identification, an individual would never be able to self-identify as a member of a nation, ethnicity, or race.

It is important to note that, in terms of identificatory poiesis or manufacture of the self, these different categories—nationality, ethnicity, and race—are homologous even though they designate entirely different sets of referents. And I could not agree more with Étienne Balibar that racism is neither contradictory to nor abnormal for the formation of the modern nation: racism is a necessary supplement to the nation form (1991, 1994).

In this respect, the history of the modern Japanese nation is not exceptional. To the extent that the overwhelming majority of individuals in Japan accept their national, ethnic, or racial identity as unequivocally Japanese, Confucianism has been overcome and is dead if what is meant by it is an assembly of discourses where one's conduct in the public sphere as well as in private affairs can be governed by the ethical imperatives of one's personal relations.

Confucianism is dead in the sense that our modality of identification is not uniformly dictated by the dogma of relational identity, and this is one of the decisive markers of contemporaneity in Northeast Asia. By the death of Confucianism, I do not imply either the end of Confucian scholarly practice or the disappearance of Confucian idioms. Neither do I suggest that people have given up Confucian ethics or rituals in places such as South Korea, China, and Taiwan. Nostalgia for Confucianism looms large among some social groups in these countries.

What I want thereby to suggest is that, in the contemporary modernity of general social formations in Northeast Asia, the principle of relational identification no longer covers the entirety of social relations, but instead must be restricted to the sphere of privacy. In the nation-state formation, neither relational identification nor specific identification predominates, and these two modalities of identification are distributed selectively between two spheres. And the sphere where relational identification is effective is usually called the family. Confucian virtues therefore retain normativity only in private family matters if they should ever be accepted, and when applied directly in the public realm, they no longer constitute a legitimacy but are regarded as indicative of nepotism, as illegitimate and corrupted forms of conduct betraying putative equality and fraternity, which are expected to prevail in a new communality called the nation.

Consequently, Confucianism is often regarded as an ideology for family matters, one that dominates the inner life of an individual just like any other modern religion. As I have analyzed, however, this characterization of Confucianism betrays its basic structure; it is important to keep in mind that the modern concept of the family, a sphere of private matters for the individual, did not exist in Confucianism. As has been asserted by an increasing number of scholars, we cannot overlook the narrowness of the category of religion in our discussion of Confucianism and Northeast Asian modernity. In similar fashion, we must also be cautious about the use of the word "family" and of "traditional family" in particular.

Of course, there have been many occasions on which the Japanese state has appropriated Confucian idioms and rhetoric into its policies and propaganda. Probably the most notable case is the Imperial Rescript on Education (1890), but even in this most Confucian-sounding ordinance neither the dogma of specific identity nor that of the pastoral governmentality of the emperor system was challenged at all.

The legitimacy of the nation-state is now based upon the governmentality of specific identification. Even though the dogma of relational identity survives in private matters, it must coexist with the dogma of specific identity; it is through this governmentality that national subjects are produced and reproduced. Even in the governance of its annexed territories, Japanese colonial governments implemented a number of policies to undermine the legacies of Confucianism and modernize their populations.

I do not think that the shared modernity of Northeast Asia is something we can simple-mindedly celebrate. It means that the modern social formations we live with in Northeast Asia are prone to racist and exclusionary violence. As many Japanese citizens have witnessed in discriminatory violence against resident Koreans in Japan in the last several decades, people share a similar modality of identification based upon the violent exclusion of those who do not belong to the nation, ethnicity, and race. We must be aware that this is an irreversible sign of modernity that is contemporary in Northeast Asia today. It is in this sense that we cannot afford to overlook the modernity of Asian societies even in such a derisory movement as that of the Association of Citizens Who Denounce the Privilege Accorded to Resident Koreans and Chinese.

At the same time, what concerns me more about the historical processes of modernization in Northeast Asia is how the dogma of relational identity survives in a variety of forms in spite of the overwhelming presence of the nation form. Where and how have the legacies of Confucian or premodern ethics undermined the aesthetics of nationality? How did immigrants manage to utilize the dogma of relational identity to fend off the demands of territorial national state sovereignty? In what instances did the legacies of Confucian ethics serve to promote the sense of equality outside the community of nationality, ethnicity, and race? What concerns me instead is not the destiny of Confucianism or its bastardized varieties: what matters is to discover an art of sociality dictated neither by the pastoral power nor by the aesthetics of the national body. We must seek the sense of community away from the aesthetics of nationality or familial authoritarianism. For it is impossible to leave behind racism without discarding the aesthetics of the nation form.

3. ASIAN THEORY AND EUROPEAN HUMANITY

On the Question of Anthropological Difference

A Civilizational Spell?

If not completely oxymoronic, the pairing of "theory" and "Asia," as in "Asian theory," for instance, may strike many readers, if not as an exoticizing curiosity such as "Zen theory," as a sort of quirk or a defamiliarizing trick. At best, it can have the effect of exposing the presumption often taken for granted in academic fields in dealing with some aspects of what we understand in the name of Asia, namely that theory is something we normally do not expect of Asia. Precisely because this sense of oddity invoked when theory is associated with Asia is no more than a certain presumptive or conditional reflex, neither theory nor Asia receives rigorous scrutiny; both remain mostly vague in conceptual articulation in this instance. Rarely have we asked ourselves why we are not unsettled about this feeling of incongruity, where this discomfort derives from, or how one could possibly explicate reasons for our taking this underlying presumption for granted. I suspect that, as long as it remains presumptive and refuses to be further examined conceptually, it turns into something one might well call a civilizational spell that will continue to cast a curse on us. In other words, we will remain haunted by this presumption about theory and Asia. In this chapter you will find a brief meditation on how we might disentangle ourselves from this spell.

So why do we feel odd about the unexpected combination of theory and Asia in the first place? Or, with more of an emphasis on our analytical attentiveness, how can we manage to evade a sense of oddity about the fact that we are accustomed to feeling strange about the combination of theory and Asia?

It must be said that there have been some attempts to explicate why theory and Asia do not go hand in hand; quite a few writers have attempted to offer some reasons or justifications for it, even though, since the end of World War II, only a comparatively small number of openly conservative or reactionary thinkers, who are ignorant of the history of Western or European thought, have dared to justify why Asians or non-Europeans are disqualified from speaking or conceptualizing theoretically. Yet, as the common sense prevalent in academic institutions in the North Atlantic as well as Asia holds, it has been widely supported that what is called theory is somewhat proper to Europe and later, as the United States assumed its global stature, also to the North Atlantic.

In the early twentieth century, a number of prominent intellectuals addressed the question of Europe's commitment to theory. Immediately, Paul Valéry and Edmund Husserl come to mind. For example, Husserl argued that Indian or Chinese philosophy could hardly be regarded as authentically "philosophical" because the life attitude that Indian and Chinese philosophers embodied was not genuinely "theoretical."[1] For him, Europe was not merely a geographic category. Unlike "empirical anthropological types" such as the Chinese, Indians, Eskimos, or even Gypsies roaming territorial Europe, he continued, Europe is a historical unity of peoples sharing a certain kinship or modality of being human, a European humanity, which distinguishes them from humanity in general. And it is absolutely impossible to conceive of this European "man" without his commitment to theory, which has been handed down in the name of philosophy from the ancient Greeks through the twentieth century. What one might detect in his insistence on the historical mission of European "man" is not only difference in terms of geopolitical origin and residence—geographic areas of Europe and those of non-Europe—in the international world but also somewhat more tangible perceptions of the familiar and the unfamiliar, the intimately human and the equally intimately nonhuman. As I argue in the following chapters as well, the teleology of reason that Husserl advocates does not make sense unless Europe is closely affiliated with the dichotomy of *humanitas* and *anthropos*, two distinct statuses in the general category of anthropos, that is, "man" or human being in general. Of course, here is an archetypical declaration of anthropological difference without which the idea of European humanity would be unintelligible.

For Valéry and Husserl, theory was unquestionably something that characterized the European spirit or the spiritual shape of Europe. They both referred to the crisis of theoretical or philosophical reason on the grounds that Europeans cannot fashion themselves as such without a commitment to theory. What they perceived in the 1920s and '30s was a crisis of the European man, the widespread reality all over Europe that Europeans were ceasing to be European in this specific regard.[2] In other words, they were horrified that Europeans were becoming less and less distinguishable spiritually from such anthropological types as Chinese and Indians.

To my knowledge, the statement that we normally do not expect theory from Asia has been put forth on a number of occasions, and some people—Valéry and Husserl included—have wanted to raise this issue as part of their critical assessment of the contemporary world.

Crisis of European Humanity

What is significant about the historical mission of European humanity for Husserl, for instance, is that, in his late works, notably his posthumous work collected and compiled under the title *The Crisis of European Sciences and Transcendental Phenomenology*, the entire venture of his phenomenology was reformulated as a historical movement of the European spirit, as a teleological project that is, at the same time, a recourse to the past origin of European humanity on the one hand as well as an infinite ecstatic self-overcoming in the future on the other. Clearly just before his death and under extreme political adversity, Husserl wanted to present his phenomenology as a historical embodiment of the mission for European humanity, and he attempted to speak as the ultimate representative of "the spiritual shape of Europe."[3] Yet his Eurocentric mission seems plagued with a number of political and philosophical contradictions that I would like to explore so as to indicate the issues involved in my larger project of dislocation of the West.

Let me start by offering a brief historical assessment of Husserl's ambiguity on racism and the international background of the early 1930s. We cannot overlook that he wrote about the crisis of European humanity in the political climate of fascism and anti-Semitism. It is more than probable that he offered his diagnosis of the crisis of European sciences as an implicit condemnation of anti-Semitic jingoisms in Europe.

As soon as the Nazi Party dominated the Reichstag of Germany in March 1933, it passed a number of pieces of legislation, including the Law for the Restoration of the Professional Civil Service. These were measures aimed at excluding anti-Nazi and non-Aryan elements from public institutions such as universities, schools, the judiciary, and the civil service. These Nazi policies were in accordance with the populist outcry for "Europe for the Europeans" that was spreading throughout Europe around that time. Indeed, the life of Husserl, an internationally renowned philosopher at Freiburg University, was severely affected, even though he was already in retirement as of 1928 from a position as professor of philosophy that was then inherited by his equally renowned student, Martin Heidegger, himself a Nazi Party member. Being a Jew born in Moravia in the Austro-Hungarian Empire, Husserl was no longer allowed to publish or give public lectures in Germany with the onset of these newly implemented Nazi policies.

In May and November 1935, Husserl was invited to give lectures in Vienna and Prague outside Germany. According to Ludwig Landgrebe, Walter Biemel, and others involved in the deciphering and compilation of stenographic manuscripts and notes left behind by Husserl—Husserl died in 1938—these lectures marked the beginning of the unfinished work we now know as *The Crisis of European Sciences and Transcendental Phenomenology*. One may well recognize in these writings a further elaboration of the themes that Husserl had already discussed in his previous works, including *Cartesian Meditations: An Introduction to Phenomenology*, which was based upon the lectures he delivered in Paris in 1929. What distinguished the Vienna and Prague lectures from those in Paris was his open confrontation with the political climate of the time. In *Cartesian Meditations*, Husserl addressed the question of modernity in philosophy while in *The Crisis of European Sciences and Transcendental Phenomenology* he reorganized his discussion of a set of topics on philosophy's historicity under a new directive or problematic he summarized as "the crisis of European humanity."

It is not hard to understand why Husserl had to shift his emphasis between the timing of his lectures in Paris and those in Vienna and Prague. The Vienna Lectures took place in the midst of the period of Austrofascism (1934–1938), a time when fascist fervor broke out not only in Italy and Germany but also in many parts of Europe—Portugal and Austria, then followed by Romania, Greece, Croatia, Spain, and France. Eventually Spain would be seized by what historians call clerical fascism. Countries such as Slovenia, Croatia, and Romania followed suit, and violent anti-Semitism spread all over Europe. On June 22, 1936, a month before the Spanish Civil War started, Moritz Schlick, known as the founding father of logical positivism and the Vienna Circle, was assassinated by a nationalist student due to Schlick's affiliation with Jewish intellectuals (see figure 3.1). This was a year after Husserl's lecture in that city. A Catholic national newspaper, *Schönere Zukunft*, responded to the Schlick assassination by insisting, "The Jews should be allowed their Jewish philosophy in their own Jewish cultural institute! But in the chairs of philosophy in the Viennese university in Christian-German Austria, there belong Christian philosophers" (Stadler 1995, 15; Mazower 2000).

The rise of National Socialism in Germany, or more generally of fascism in many European countries, Latin America, and Japan, provoked a widespread

FIGURE 3.1. Moritz Schlick assassination monument inside the University of Vienna. About one year after Husserl's lecture "Philosophy in the Crisis of European Mankind," delivered on May 7 and 10, 1935, in Vienna, Moritz Schlick, a leading philosopher of the German-speaking world, was assassinated by an anti-Semite/Nazi sympathizer on June 22, 1936. Even though Schlick was successful in organizing collaborative groups with many Jewish intellectuals, including Ludwig Wittgenstein, he was not a Jew himself. Neither would I claim that Schlick was particularly sympathetic toward Husserl's phenomenology. The assassin, Johann Nelböck, was released after the annexation of Austria into Nazi Germany in 1938. Photo by author.

fear, not only within Europe and the Americas, but also in Northeast Asia. As I have discussed elsewhere (Sakai 2009b), in Japan, for instance, a nationwide antifascist movement was organized against the dismissal of Takigawa Yukitoki (瀧川 幸辰), only two months after the Nazi ascendency to the national state. The minister of education, Hatoyama Ichirô (鳩山 一郎)—the grandfather of Hatoyama Yukio (鳩山 由紀夫), a recent prime minister of Japan (2009–2010)—dismissed Professor Takigawa Yukitoki from the Faculty of Law at Kyoto Imperial University for his alleged sympathy with Marxist scholarship and for his supposedly critical attitude toward family morality. In the same month that year—May 1933—Heidegger's *Rektoratsrede* (rector's address), was widely covered by Japanese mass media; leading intellectuals of the day, Tanabe Hajime (田邊 元), Miki Kiyoshi (三木 清), Tosaka Jun (戸坂 潤), Shinmei Masamichi (新明 正道), and others, wrote alarmingly about the rise of fascism in Europe. It is easy to detect the sense of urgency with which Japanese intellectuals received the news of a National Socialist insurgency—around this time *fassho* was first coined in the Japanese vernacular and began to be used to denote the contemporary global trends toward ultranationalism and doctrines of racial purity—and, for the rest of the 1930s, the topic of fascism continued to dominate Japanese mass media. The public debates about fascism endured until the Japanese state officially endorsed the leading regimes of fascist ideologies, Germany and Italy, on signing the Axis Pact in September 1940, and a few months later other countries including those of so-called clerical fascism—Hungary, Romania, Slovenia, Bulgaria, and Croatia—joined this pact, although the Japanese leadership was hesitant to openly endorse the ethnic nationalism and racist doctrines that were prevalent, especially in National Socialism. Even during the war, Japanese intellectuals and reform-minded bureaucrats—except for a few ethnic nationalists such as Watsuji Tetsurô (和辻 哲郎) and Nishitani Keiji (西谷 啓治), who played particularly significant roles in the intellectual scenes of postwar Japan—remained critical of the racial policies of Nazi Germany and the anti-Semitism of clerical fascism. Of course, the Nazis' outright disdain for the yellow race made it hard for the Japanese to accept Nazism. But, more importantly, many Japanese bureaucrats and intellectuals could not accept the basic tenets of National Socialism because they were concerned about the multiethnic imperial order that Japan was creating in East Asia; they advocated the ideas of the East Asian Community—and later the Greater East Asia Co-prosperity Sphere—by claiming it was Japan's mission to liberate Asian peoples from the shackles of white supremacy.

It was in such a political climate that Husserl delivered his lectures in Prague and Vienna. Husserl was a victim of the populist demand for "Europe for the Europeans," but he did not hesitate to endorse the rhetoric of Eurocentric exceptionalism when it was an issue of the spirit of European humanity. It is undeniable that Husserl insisted on the historical mission of European humanity to condemn the populist anti-Semitism that excluded Jews as non-European. By raising the issue of European sciences in crisis, he tacitly but unambiguously demonstrated that he was entitled to speak as a European genuinely committed to the historical mission of European humanity—all the achievements of transcendental phenomenology should serve as its testimonial; he may have advocated for the denunciation and correction of the typically anti-Semitic notion of Europe widely propagated in the campaign for "Europe for the Europeans," which not merely excluded but also targeted European Jewry as an intrusion from non-Europe, yet an explicit denunciation of anti-Semitism cannot be found in his *Crisis of European Sciences and Transcendental Phenomenology* or his lectures in Vienna and Plague. Perhaps he wanted to establish by perlocution that he could speak as an authentic European. He further argued that it was not sufficient to be born and raised and to reside in the geographic territory of Europe to be identified with Europe. For example, Gypsies were born, raised, and living in Europe, but they were not qualified as European, for being European required a certain historical resolution. What was expected of a European was nothing but a commitment to the teleological mission of European rationality. But, just like the Gypsies, did many others residing in Europe for generations and customarily assumed to have European identity in fact fail to satisfy this requirement?[4] As a matter of fact, did the vast majority of native Europeans fail to qualify as authentic Europeans?

Nevertheless, it is rather surprising that he seemed to have few qualms about identifying himself as an authentic European, not as a nomadic figure like Gypsies.[5] Was it not the most conventional tactic utilized by anti-Semitism to depict Jews as foreigners in the German land and as nomadic intruders into Europe? Did he not reproduce such a rhetoric of anti-Semitism by claiming that the project of phenomenology he had initiated and pursued for most of his professional career testified to his genuine European identity? What is his relationship to anti-Semitism as a version of anti-immigrant racism on the one hand and to the dichotomy of the West and the Rest for the sustenance of which anthropological difference is repeatedly invoked on the other?[6]

The Nation and Europe

There can be discerned two different demands in the racism advocated by National Socialism and many versions of fascism in Europe around that time. These were often confused with one another, and emphasis oscillated from one to the other. And this mix-up is observable in today's anti-immigrant racism as well. One is a demand based on the social imaginary of what Thongchai Winichakul (1994) called "the geo-body of a nation," a demand to expel intruders from the fantasized geographical sphere of the nation, which is supposedly clearly and unambiguously marked by national border. This demand serves as an operation in imagination by which the interiority of a national community is defined and constituted and the authentic members of a national community are recognized in distinction from illicit intruders from outside the national territory. An obsession with the border wall, for instance, illustrates the working of nationalism that advocates the expulsion of immigrants, thereby consolidating the fantasy of a national fraternity.

The other demand is closely associated with racial speciation. It is closely related to the classification of humanity according to the formula of classical logic, by which the general class of humanity at large is divided into the particular classes of race. This demand was powerfully promoted in National Socialism, which articulated what British liberalism called "the sentiment of nationality," the emotive-sentimental attachment to a national community, to scientific racism, and it insisted that a nation consists of human individuals living in the same land that share the same sort of biological and physiological constitution. The trope of "Blood and Soil" was adopted by the Nazi Party to promote the fantasy that the German nation, supposedly originating from the sedentary German peasantry, was constituted on the basis of two connotations of nature, in the geographical as well as hereditary senses, and distinguished from the nomadic population like Jewry. Therefore the demand to expel the intruders required their relocation away from the national territory, and the demand to purify the national blood required the strict genetic separation of races.

What is striking is the constant oscillation and confusion between the two distinct spaces, the national territory, such as Germany on the one hand and the larger and much less clearly delineated space of Europe on the other. Jews were imagined as nomadic intruders or eternal foreigners, and in some instances they were supposedly from outside the nation, but in other instances, they were regarded as non-European. No matter whether factually from outside the national territory or not, they remained foreign intruders. What is often neglected is that it was impossible to clearly identify the very outside from which foreign intruders came. Furthermore, intrusion does not always indicate violation of a spatial boundary; it can mean intrusion in a symbolic sense, such as the destruction of a social hierarchy and the contamination of homogeneity.

Therefore, the place from which intruders come is sometimes from outside the national territory, but at other times it is a remote place, on the periphery of Europe. Moreover, intruders often move in the symbolic space of nongeography. Just as in today's anti-immigrant racism, intruders may include people who have resided in the national territory for generations, in some cases much longer than the majority of the nation. The notion of intrusion is metaphoric par excellence; it symbolizes all sorts of undesirable qualities that cannot be accommodated harmoniously within the spatial structure of the modern international world. It is in this sense that anti-Semitism must be discussed as a version of anti-immigrant racism even though many Jews in Europe could hardly be regarded as immigrants.

This is one reason why we can overlook neither the investment of anthropological difference in the identity politics of Europe nor the spatial order sustaining the system of international law in terms of which the geopolitical space of Europe is distinguished from that of non-Europe in the modern international world.[7]

Until his death in 1938, Husserl was placed in an environment saturated by a number of anti-Semitic intellectuals such as Heidegger and Carl Schmitt. What must be noted is the ambivalent position that he must have occupied in the academic world of that time (Di Cesare 2018).[8] It is said that most Jewish intellectuals who lived in Germany after the devastation of World War I were caught by surprise by the rise of Nazism; many of them felt integrated into mainstream national society and Europe at large even though they were fully aware of the enduring legacies of anti-Semitism in Europe represented by a long series of thinkers such as Martin Luther, Voltaire, Immanuel Kant, and of course most recently Heidegger.

What is puzzling is that on occasion, particularly in the manuscript for *The Crisis of European Sciences and Transcendental Phenomenology* that he left behind, Husserl did not seem to thematically engage in the denunciation of the European intellectual climate of his day, specifically from the standpoint of the Jewish intellectuals who were expelled from German academia and the public sphere. There is hardly any acknowledgment that, essentially, he was treated as non-European, but he continued to speak as if he were a European. He appears to have been rather compelled to pursue an inquiry concerning the foundation of modern scientific knowledge in the lifeworld, an inquiry that is not entirely dissimilar to the Heideggerian critique of the metaphysical forgetting of Being. Whereas Heidegger denounced the entire history of Western metaphysics from its Greek beginnings to the twentieth century and beyond, Husserl attempted to reconfirm the mission of European humanity for the future to come through the idea of the teleology of reason. With recourse to the beginning of European reason in Greek antiquity, Husserl seemed to have taken upon himself the task of Europe's historical mission as a representative of European humanity.[9] Certainly he could not speak as a representative of the German nation, but in the *Crisis* book he seemed to present himself as an authentic European. Yet how did he reconcile his own status as an alienated member of the German nation with his status as an authentic European intellectual? Did National Socialism define German nationality in terms of Aryan blood? Did the imaginary racial category of the Aryan not serve to demarcate the blood and soil of the German peoplehood? Was the idea of European humanity free from the identity politics of the Aryan race? How could Husserl reconcile his philosophical attempt to establish modern European humanity with the anti-immigrant racism of the Aryan supremacy, which inevitably resulted in anti-Semitism?[10] Or is it possible to read Husserl's critique of the crisis of European sciences as an attempt to denounce such an essentialized identification of Europe?

It is possible that Husserl was required to be absolutely silent about contradictions between German nationality and European citizenship. Perhaps concerns for his safety, and that of his family, led him to publicly endorse the tenets of German jingoism, just as many Japanese Americans proclaimed their loyalty to the United States of America during World War II (Sakai 2004). What kinds of political strategies were in place for ethnic, racial, and sexual minorities with regard to their nationalisms in the decades leading up to and during World War II in Europe?

Above all, how was the hostility toward minorities on the grounds of national solidarity articulated to the imaginary unity of European humanity that was sometimes defined in terms of the spatial order of international law and at other times to the racial category of the Aryan by which the othering of Jewry was conducted? I do not think I can respond to these questions adequately in this chapter. They must be explored on other occasions. Instead, I will try to apprehend what Husserl implied by the phrase "European humanity."

The Identity Politics of Europe or the West: Anthropological Difference

Since Husserl did not pursue his argument concerning the historical mission of European humanity to its logical limits, let me illustrate two possible contentions already implied in his argumentation. First, it is very difficult to assume that the majority of people born, raised, and resident in Europe are somewhat more committed to the historical mission of European humanity than the Gypsies. They are interested neither in the pursuit of scientific knowledge nor in a theoretical reflection of it, for the vast majority of them are not intellectuals and are little concerned with the "spiritual shape of Europe." Admittedly even ordinary and nonintellectual Europeans produce a variety of knowledge, rely on it, and live with it in their everyday lives, but they do not regard knowledge production as either their profession or raison d'être. The criterion Husserl selected for the identification of Europeans seems significant only for a small minority of the population who are seriously concerned with issues of scientific knowledge. Their degree of involvement in the production, evaluation, and selection of knowledge varies, dependent upon profession, social status, educational background, and other social factors, but for the vast majority of European people, the critical esteem of knowledge is not a matter of serious concern. Then, can they still be called Europeans, according to Husserl's implicit criteria? As a matter of fact, do the vast majority of Europeans not fail to embody the historical mission of European humanity, unless it is claimed that the European spirit can be legitimately and exclusively represented by highly educated cultural and intellectual elites?[11]

Second, many Europeans travel around the world and have settled in many locations outside Europe. As Husserl pointed out, Europe is not merely a geographic designation. Europe may point to a geographic region, yet in fact the proper noun "Europe" is much more than a cartographic index. It designates some status, authority, or conviction beyond some paradigmatic configurations of social positions. Regardless of where one happens to reside, with whom one is affiliated, or in which activities one engages, it is presumed that, in the modern international world, a European person is somewhat distinct from the native or the indigenous such that Europeans are always mobile in a unique manner, never sedentary. In other words, Europeans are supposedly not bound to their native places.

This contrast between mobile and adventurous/enterprising Europeans and immobile and conservative non-Europeans has been symbolically highlighted by what Schmitt called "the spatial order of Eurocentric international law," whereby European and non-European states were expected to behave differently as far as the issues of new land appropriation were concerned. Europeans could "discover" previously unknown land as long as the land to be appropriated was located outside Europe (parts II and III in Schmitt 1950; 1976, 169–292; 2003, 140–212). The division of Europe and non-Europe was not merely a distinction assumed in the system of international law between the region where the new appropriation of territories was strictly regulated on the one hand and on the other the non-Europe world where new territories could be almost freely incorporated into the governmental and administrative system of a state recognized as a member of the international community, which is to say, the interstate community of Europe.[12] The division of Europe and non-Europe was metaphorically associated with the dynamics of the discoverer versus the discovered, of mobile travelers who looked for immobile residents versus the sedentary natives who were looked for, as if all Europeans were expected to behave as travelers. This one-sided privilege accorded to Europe's territorial sovereign states was most unambiguously pronounced during the Age of Discovery.

The distinction that privileges Europe over its outside is, first of all, demonstrably one of geography. But we cannot forget that in the sixteenth and seventeenth centuries geography gained a new significance, namely that of modern cartography or *fabrica mundi* by means of which the world was fabricated anew.[13] With the introduction of the new ways of representing the world, this distinction of

Europe and non-Europe is drawn not only on the land surface within the western rim of the Eurasian continent but also between the landmass of Europe and the rest of the globe. Furthermore, the very distinction of Europe and the rest of the world was not merely cartographic or spatial; it was reconstituted as an essential moment integrated into the constitution of the modern subject for whom the world is given. On this point, Husserl is explicit. In phenomenological inquiries, the world is characterized as a transcendental phenomenon and given as a correlative of subjective appearance (Husserl 1970a, 179ff.). What sustains this type of transcendental investigation is a paradox, according to which the subject to whom the world is given is also an object in the world. How is this transcendental differentiation between subjective and objective redefined as, or translated into, "anthropological difference" between European humanity and what Husserl called "empirical anthropological type"? Following the modern project of idealism, Husserl underlines two contrasting attitudes, the natural attitude of religious-mythological type whose task is to interpret beings encountered in the world and the theoretical attitude, which reflects on and criticizes the knowledge obtained out of practical concerns in the lifeworld by suspending or interrupting—in the attitude of epoché—naturalistic interests and desires. No doubt, Husserl ascribed the name "Europe" to the theoretical attitude of transcendental suspension.

However, it does not follow that Europe and non-Europe correspond to these "two spiritually unrelated cultural spheres," a sphere of the theoretical attitude on the one hand and the religious-mythical attitude on the other. In Europe, too, people live in the natural attitude out of practical concerns in their lifeworld.[14] For a third form of universal attitude is possible, that is, "the synthesis of the two interests accomplished in the transition from the theoretical to the practical attitude, such that the theoria (universal science), arising within a closed unity and under the epoché of all praxis, is called (and in theoretical insight itself exhibits its calling) to serve mankind in a new way, mankind which, in its existence, lives first and always in the natural sphere" (Husserl 1970c, 282–286).

For Husserl, therefore, Europe is not merely a geographic region located on the cartographic plane. European humanity is a new humanity to come, capable of bringing theoretical reflection into the sphere of the natural attitude, thereby continually transforming itself into a new humanity. In this sense, European humanity is a historical subject that never ceases to fabricate and create itself. Thus, there should appear "the distinction between world-representation and actual world, and the new question of truth arises: not tradition-bound, everyday truth, but an identical truth which is valid for all who are no longer blinded by traditions, a truth-in-itself." Thus, European humanity is distinct from the rest of humanity while, at the same time, being the representative of entire humanity. Husserl projected a sort of humanity whose attitude is characterized by "his constant and prior resolve to dedicate his future life always, and in the sense of a universal life, to the task of theoria, to build theoretical knowledge upon theoretical knowledge in infinitum"(286).

But can one possibly rely upon this distinction in order to demarcate Europe geographically, culturally, politically, and racially? As Europe is a peninsula attached to the Eurasian continent, where can a border be drawn between Europe and Asia? Does Europe include Eastern Europe, Greece, Turkey, or Russia? Was the West called for because of ambiguity inherent in the concept of Europe? Was it possible to assume some common cultural traits among societies and peoples in Europe? How could one escape the arbitrary use of civilization in classifying humanity?

We must indeed be skeptical of the distinction of Europe from the rest of the world, particularly when the ambiguity inherent in the geographic identity of Europe is amplified by adding cultural, linguistic, sociopolitical, religious, and racial dimensions to it. Instead of accepting the conventional identity of Europe, we must rather be attentive to its fictive and mythical functions, whereby European humanity is assumed to be distinguishable from the rest of humanity.

What is summarily called globalization is not merely an increasing mobility of people, commodities, and capital across national borders; it also suggests that the flows of immigration no longer follow the Eurocentric model of emanation, according to which immigrants, industrial products, ideas, and capital are expected to flow out of the presumed center of the world—Europe or the West—to its peripheries. Clearly, this modern fantasy of the incessant agility associated with the global migrants of Europe versus the stasis of the indigenous or native population in non-European localities is constantly betrayed; as a result, tremendous anxiety about immigrants in Euro-American societies arises.

After all, a simple question remains unanswered. Why must a philosopher genuinely dedicated to the universal mission of theoretical reason be European or a representative of European humanity? What is the status of transcendental phenomenology that claims itself to be the representative of European science? This much is obvious: the unity of Europe or the West is not empirically sustainable; it is, therefore, a putative unity, and the very distinction of European humanity and the rest of humanity is exactly what we call "anthropological difference," a fictive form of investment for an identity that cannot be sustained empirically.

Asia, the Orient, the East

Before undertaking a critique of Husserl's attempts to establish new modern European humanity, however, we ought to return to the initial statement about Asia and theory that I raised in the opening pages of this chapter in order to clarify the sense of oddity that radiates from the presumption contained within it.

The statement that one does not expect theory of a person if he or she is of Asia is in fact a negative corollary of another statement: theory is something that we normally expect of a person if he or she is of the West or Europe, and the relationship between the first and second statements is generally called a contraposition in logic.[15] Let us note that the first statement implied in this presumption is not thematically or primarily about Asia. Instead it is no more than a derivative of the general statement about the West or Europe.

As a matter of fact, the derivative character of the first statement in relation to the second is inherent in the designation of Asia itself.

As Takeuchi Yoshimi (竹内 好), a sinologist specializing in modern Chinese literature, observed more than half a century ago, the East—Tôyô (東洋), the Chinese compound for the Orient, as opposed to Seiyô (西洋), the Occident—which he more or less assumed to be representative of the rest of the world, arrived at its self-consciousness as a consequence of its defeat by the West or Europe.[16] During his college days in Japan in the 1930s, Takeuchi was immersed in the various available readings about Hegel; these ranged from the Marxian reading, arguably best represented by Lukacs, and the Kyoto School readings (Tanabe Hajime, Miki Kiyoshi, and philosophers of world history), through to modernization Hegelianism in Maruyama Masao (丸山 眞男). It is no surprise that he viewed the historical destiny of Asia in Hegelian terms.

Negativity, without which reflectivity—not reflex, which illustrates the lack of the reflectivity essential for self-consciousness to be accomplished—never originated in the East, and the absence of reflectivity was certainly implied in Takeuchi's word "defeat." He argued that Asia came to its self-consciousness through its defeat; the East could never be conscious of itself before it was invaded by Europe. Only through the acknowledgment of its lost autonomy, of its dependence upon and subjugation to the West—or only in the mirror of the West, so to speak (Takeuchi 2005, 149–165)—could the Rest reflectively acquire its civilizational, cultural, ethnic, or national selfhood. Historically, the moment of defeat was actualized in the colonization of Asia, and it is in this respect that modernity in Asia is unavoidably a colonial modernity. Takeuchi observed that only when Asia was defeated, invaded, penetrated, and subjugated could it emerge into modernity so that, in and for Asia, it is impossible to conceive of modernity without reference to colonial humiliation.

However, because of his uncompromising faith in the Enlightenment values of modernity, which could only be concretized in the institutions of the nation-state, Takeuchi could not envision the future of Asia—and by implication, the future of the Rest of the world—along a historical trajectory other than one of historicism. Like many intellectuals of Asia and Europe who had their formative years in the 1930s, Takeuchi had internalized modern historicism to such an extent that, for him, an effective struggle against the colonizing forces of the West could not bypass the creation of national subjectivity. His furtive loyalty to Hegel prevented him from conceiving any other historical trajectory than that of historicism in which the actualization and appropriation of modern values must first require a radical negation of external forces as well as of its internal heritage of a feudal past. Therefore, to be modern for Asia meant to appropriate the essence of Western modernity by resisting the West without and overcoming the reactionary heritage within. In other words, Asia must modernize itself by negating its own past as well as the West. Without any resistance to, or negation of, the West, there was no prospect of modernity for the Rest of the world. Where else, he would ask, if not in the midst of a struggle against colonial powers and the oppressive remnants of the past, could one possibly actualize the concrete and practical senses of liberty, equality, and fraternity?

He diagnosed Japan's modern history as a case with a genuine negativity absent. In contrast to Japan's modernity, he upheld an idealized image of China's modernity according to which negativity existed among Chinese people. He thought that, unlike Japan, which had imitated the West to the extent of reproducing its imperialism, China would actualize a truly authentic modernity by negating not only the West's intervention but also the remnants of its own past, such as Confucianism. Yet the dialectic, which he anticipated would lead historical conflicts forward, could not have made sense unless the externality of what Asia should resist had been postulated. So, for peoples in the Rest, modernity was considered a sort of historical movement that served to spatially consolidate the unity and substantiality of a political grouping called the nation, by negating external forces while at the same time temporally constituting itself as a subject, as an agent of self-determination, by continually overcoming its own past. This is why the dichotomy of "development from within" (*naihatsu* 内発) and "imposition from without" (*gaihatsu* 外発) was the ultimate criterion for Takeuchi's evaluation of modernity.[17]

In a schematization such as the one operating in his discussion of modernity, the unity of the nation depended upon the externality of what had to be resisted, which was more often than not mapped onto the cartographic plane. Just as with the Japanese invasion of China, that which must be resisted must come from outside the presumed integrity of the nation. A nation of Asia, such as China, was located within the reach of the West, but the West was external to it. The externality of what had to be resisted was thus comprehended in terms of the geographic distance between Western Europe and Asia. Thus, for Takeuchi, the West was postulated as an entity external to Asia, and the possibility that the West could be inherent in the Rest of the world was deliberately foreclosed. Perhaps, more importantly, we must note the other aspect of this foreclosure: deliberately excluded from consideration is the feasibility of the Rest being inherent in the West, the Third World immanent in the First World.

Takeuchi was determined to view the relationship between the West and the Rest of the world as one of geographic externality, of a border separating two entities; even though he acknowledged the designation of Asia as an instance of colonial defeat, he refused to comprehend the origin of Asia as a relation of mutual self-reflectivity or mirroring. What he was totally blind to was the truism, namely that so many of those self-fashioned Westerners could not discard their premodernity or pre-Enlightenment features. No Westerner is purely or wholly Western. One regarded as such is, after all, one who passes for a Westerner; one is only putatively of the West; only when one succeeds in being recognized as such is one a Westerner. In order to pass as Western, there must be observers, witnesses, or onlookers in whose views one is recognized as a Westerner. Thus, a desire to essentialize the Western identity is always accompanied by a desire to essentialize the identity of the Rest; the putative identity of the West is accompanied by the putative identity of the Rest.

In other words, it requires a particular configuration of positionalities to execute the identification of the West—and of the Rest as well.

The binary of the West and the Rest is often a matter of social class difference and of cultural capital. Precisely because of the inherent instability of civilizational identity, the supposedly unchanging characteristic of an individual's physiognomy, linguistic habits, or geographic place of origin is fixatedly sought in order to naturalize and essentialize an individual's position in the system of classification haunted by the desire for anthropological difference. This is the reason why, although very perceptive to the implications of

Eurocentricity in so many aspects of life in Asia, Takeuchi could not detect the workings of what elsewhere I have called "civilizational transference," a mutual constitution of desire between the West and the Rest, in nationalisms in Asia.[18]

Civilizational Transference

Although Takeuchi was unmistakably critical of the modernization theory promoted by American area experts, he could not avoid the cartographic imaginary that served as a substratum for knowledge production, namely, the postulate of the area upon which the modernization theory invariably relied. Therefore, his insight into colonial modernity could never go beyond a hierarchy that was premised upon the developmental teleology of modernization.

What Takeuchi somewhat shortchanged in his discussion of Asia was the dynamics of civilizational transference in the self-reflective postulation of Asia. He failed to acknowledge that, essentially, Asia exists for the West's self-recognition. For peoples living in Asia, there used to be no clear distinction between Asia and Europe. Asia had never been an immediate designation for the Asians, and therefore it could not have existed for them prior to the occasion of colonial defeat, an occasion that symbolized the very moment of negativity deliberately pinpointed by Takeuchi.

Since Greek antiquity, Asia always meant an ecstatic or outward orientation of Europe; it pointed to an area or people who were located east of the land inhabited by Hellenes so that it was not expected to designate a fixed geographic location, a closed land surface, or a determinate social group; instead it was meant to serve only as a directional index from the viewpoint of the Greeks, Romans, Europeans, or Westerners. However, it is important to remind ourselves that, in the genealogy of Western or European civilization, Asia played only a slight or no meaningful role from the end of the Roman Empire until the era of Eurocentric modernity simply because Europe was no more than a provincial periphery to the large metropolitan civilizations of Islam and Mongolia and the Chinese and Indian empires. Before the onset of what Schmitt (2006) called "the spatial order of Eurocentric international law," Asia was never designated as the Orient, eastern peripheries of the center of the earth. In short, there was no such thing as Europe, as we understand it today in reference to the region of sovereign states and the central figure of world history, prior to the explosion of the modern international world and the rise of global capitalism. The idea of the continuity of Western civilization from Greek antiquity to the present, as invented by European racists in the eighteenth century, is dubious since most of what

Western Europe claims today as its heritage from Greco-Roman antiquity was handed down from Islamic civilizations of premodern eras and many other non-European origins (see Bernal 1987).

In antiquity, Asia referred to the Greeks' geopolitical neighbors to the east in Asia Minor or along the Tigris and the Euphrates; next, those along the Indus and the Ganges were included, and eventually, as Europe expanded its system of Eurocentric international law through global capitalism and colonialism, the notion of Asia would extend to islands in the East Indies, peoples under the reign of the Central Kingdom—China—and even as far east as the Korean peninsula and the islands of Japan. This expansion of Asia and the term's versatility amply illustrate the directional character of Asia, that is, moving away—ex-static, meaning a movement beyond or away from the self—from the presumed locus of viewpoint.

Thus, Asia marks something reflectively social and cosmopolitan about how Europe could possibly be identified: is it ever possible to designate Europe without a reference to Africa, Asia, and the Americas? Asia is an open kind of reference; it indicates the directional relation of both the viewing subject and the viewed object, of the discovering subject and the discovered object. Of course, the West too is a directional designation, and, in this respect, the East—the polar opposite of the West—and Asia are often considered interchangeably, just as the West and Europe are interchangeable in so many instances. Thus, when all the historical nuances and accidents are reduced, Asia simply signifies the East of Europe. Asia's referential function was based upon Europe's self-referentiality in the sense that to refer to Asia is to indicate the position of Europe or the West self-reflectively.[19] It is the very ecstatic nature of the West that Asia reflects upon itself. Neither the West nor the East can be a determinate location; both are a relative designation so that what is determinate about this relation is the microphysics of power relations that makes the West and the East appear somewhat anchored, natural, or preordained. What makes the West or the East determinate is the very conduct that takes place in these power relations at the very locale where the West is bordered by the Rest. Nevertheless, neither of them is arbitrarily determined since, as Antonio Gramsci argued, these relations are hegemonic (Gramsci, 1996, 189–190; 2007, 175–176). However, instead of the Gramscian term, I want to consider them in terms of the microphysics of power relations.

Well into the nineteenth century many in Europe knew that there were numerous dynasties, theocracies, traditions, and peoples in Asia. Europeans called people in Asia "Asians," but they never expected Asians to refer to themselves as such. It was never assumed that the Asians themselves knew they were Asians. Court officials serving the Nguyên Dynasty, samurais of the Matsudaira clan, and merchants working in the port of Ningbo must have been aware that they were expected to recognize themselves as subjects of Emperor Gia Long, of the Tokugawa shoguns, and of the Qing emperors respectively, but it is unlikely that they were aware of being Asian. What Takeuchi called "defeat" happened in Asia from the nineteenth to the early twentieth centuries, as a result of which bureaucrats in Vietnam, soldiers in Japan, and schoolteachers in China came to acknowledge that they were all Asians. Defeat was not only a matter of competition or rivalry but also of self-recognition and identification. Their identity was nothing but the consequence of an "imposition from without" (「外発」). Furthermore, the defeat brought about a distinction between Europe and Asia, the mutually marked positionalities of Europeans and Asians. And the reign of these mutually defining positionalities is often called the colonial power relation. The defeat took place in a series of defeats in many parts of the globe, and it took a few centuries for the entirety of the earth's surface to be arranged or ordered with Europe as its center. The defeat thus came to signify global modernity according to which the entire world was reorganized with respect to the modalities of self-recognition.

I do not believe, however, that Takeuchi was entirely negligent of this truth about the dialectic of self-consciousness for the Asians. He wrote, "The Orient essentially lacks not only the ability to understand Europe but also to understand itself. What understands the Orient, and so brings it to realization, are those European elements within Europe. What makes the Orient possible is situated in Europe. Not only does Europe become possible in Europe, but the Orient also becomes possible there" (Takeuchi [1948] 2005). Nevertheless, Takeuchi stopped short of an ultimate cognition of the political reality in which the demarcation of Asia from Europe as a separate entity, region, people, or civilization is not only a consequence of defeat but also the very condition in which colonialism is preserved. An inscription of Asia as an entity distinct from Europe is far from innocent, and a people in Asia may not be able to dispel colonial power relations even if their national sovereignty is installed. On the one hand, Asia is a derivative of Europe's self-referentiality. On the other, the distinction of Asia from Europe is an effect of exclusionist and discriminatory bordering or border inscription. Accordingly, as soon as the Asians fashion themselves as such, the structure of heteronomous referentiality must manifest in their identity. For the Asians, paradoxically, the desire for autonomy requires that they be heteronomous.

In this context, it is absolutely imperative for us to guard against the typical mistake made by Husserl and many others: in the spatial configuration of Europe in relation to the Rest—Asia, Africa, and the Americas—Europe should never be postulated as a subject that evolves linearly along the chronological line from antiquity to the present, that transcends itself to form a successive life of its own from the past to the future, and that generates its own living tradition. The West is not an enduring entity; it is no more than an accidental assemblage of power relations that cannot be synthesized to form an organic unity either spatially or chronologically. In this respect, it is through Europe's mythological obsession with its ancient Greek origins that the spiritual shape of Europe came into focus as a living tradition and as an evolutionary teleology, with a historical mission to infinitely transcend itself by recourse to its archaic origin while at the same time distinguishing itself from its exterior. Husserl did not know how to protect himself against this mythological obsession most glaringly exemplified by National Socialism.

This mythological teleology of the West or Europe is imminent in what I suggest in reference to the derivative character of the statement "we normally do not expect theory of Asia." Just as Asia is indicated from the implicit and self-referential position of Europe or the West, the oddity experienced about theory as associated with Asia is a derivative effect of another statement, namely, "we normally expect theory of Europe." What we must call into question is nothing but this normalcy through which we expect theory to be of Europe or of a European origin.

So far, I have deliberately postponed the mention of two elementary questions; thanks to this reticence, my argument may appear persuasive up to this point. As a matter of fact, however, I am endorsing neither the autonomy of Asia as an active agent nor the victimization of Asia under Eurocentrism. What I am questioning is how the civilizational designations of the West, Asia, Europe, and so forth are still possible today. The two questions at issue are these:

Are "we" always and by definition ontologically prior to "you," so that the European priority hidden in the designation "Asia" is a consequence of some disastrous logical or philosophical mistake? Asia as an indexing function has nothing abnormal in its derivative and secondary nature; then what is not normal would be the modern system of geopolitical naming according to which the West has enjoyed the position of being the hub of the global standard. Does the West not illustrate the inevitable performativity of indexing, namely, that the center of the world could only be designated as the West of somewhere else? Is the West therefore distinguished from such previous global centers of civilization as the Central Kingdom that claimed to be the center without the regime of self-referentiality so that it could never have a positive outside, a realm outside the Central Kingdom? In this respect, the emperor of China was once literally the son of Heaven.

If positioned positively as the origin of spontaneity, can one possibly demarcate the distinction between the self and the alternate? Regardless of whether it is in dialectics or psychoanalysis, the self is always a secondary postulate, either to consciousness (in dialectics) or to specular image in the imaginary register (in psychoanalysis). In this respect, the designation "Asia" behaves normally, so to speak, and the problem of its derivative character, marked by the legacy of colonial defeat, derives not inherently from the postulation of Asia, but rather from the priority granted to Europe or the West. What is abnormal is the prior postulation of Europe in the self-recognition of Europe rather than the prior postulation of Europe in the self-recognition of Asia. The West is secondary, but it absurdly insists that it comes before the Americas, Asia, Africa, and the rest of the world. It is indisputable that the mutual determination of the West and the Rest involves power relations, but these should not be construed in terms of activity and passivity. Power relations that posit the West and Asia as designees are not governed by the causality of cause and effect, of spontaneity and receptivity; instead, they are organized by the logic of the middle voice.[20]

To manage the analysis concerning theory and Asian humanity, we must shift our focus from Asia to Europe, or to the West, in a sort of countermovement to that of Takeuchi Yoshimi. For this reason, the questions I want to entertain here are only reflectively and indirectly concerned with Asian humanity.

The questions at issue are the following: On what grounds was theory considered as being European in origin? What sort of argument attempted to justify the presumption that theory is something to be expected of Europe or the West? How has this presumption managed to remain uninterrogated until now? What would ensue if the conditions no longer existed in which we normally expect theory out of Europe or the West? In other words, how can we possibly assess the disappearance of this civilizational normalcy and disenchant ourselves from this civilizational spell?

Now in the scope of theory and Asian humanity, it is possible to view a number of eminent arguments that have attempted in one way or another to explicate why we somewhat presume that there ought to be some intimate link between theory—variously discussed under the headings of philosophy, modern rationality, scientific reason, commitment to the spirit of rigor whereby universal openness to knowledge production has been sustained, incessant return to the archê of the Greek origins—and Europe or the West: Max Weber's discussion on European modernity and the Protestant ethic, Valéry's insights into the crisis of the European spirit, Husserl's inquiries about the crisis of European humanity, and Heidegger's attempt to rescue the West from metaphysics by radically transforming it, along with many others.

I have drawn tentative examples from the first half of the twentieth century, during which the term "Europe" was gradually replaced by "the West." That period is significant in many respects because then, for the first time, the West or Europe became a topic of such intense debate. So it is in the element of crisis that Europe or the West was acknowledged globally as a domineering center of the world. But, as soon as it succeeded somewhat in receiving the legitimacy of global hegemony, it also began to suffer from a confusion inherent in its identity. Who are Europeans, after all? Where does the West end and the Rest of the world begin? What constitutes the very border by which the distinction of the West from the Rest can be drawn?

The West and the Rest: The Modern and the Premodern

Christopher GoGwilt notes that the term "Europe" was called into question early in the twentieth century, when the term "the West" gained a new rhetorical force. In reference to Heidegger's discussion of nihilism, he shows that, in Nietzsche's discussion of it, the word "Western" was never ascribed to it. Citing passages from Heidegger's *Nietzsche*, however, GoGwilt writes, "Heidegger here translates Nietzsche's term European (*europäish*) into the post-Nietzschean terminology 'Western history' (*abendländischen Geschichte*)" (GoGwilt 1995, 232). Heidegger was lecturing on Nietzsche in Germany under National Socialism, and consequently his terms were inflected in complex ways by the debates of the 1930s. Yet precisely the distance between the contested terms of Nietzsche's Europe and those of Heidegger's West indicates that the term "Western" acquired a rhetorical force between the 1890s and the 1930s (GoGwilt 1995).

GoGwilt argues that, after the emergence of this use of the term "the West," which originated from the Russian Slavophile–Westerner controversy over nihilism, Oswald Spengler could make the following claim about Europe and the West in his introduction to *The Decline of the West*: "The word 'Europe' ought to be struck out of history. There is historically no 'European' type. . . . It is thanks to this word 'Europe' alone, and the complex of ideas resulting from it, that our historical consciousness has come to link Russia with the West in an utterly baseless unity—a mere abstraction derived from the reading of books— that has led to immense real consequences" (Spengler 1991, 12n5).[21]

A half century after Nietzsche, Heidegger's focus was on Western metaphysics. During the interwar period there is no doubt that the problem of theory and the West was implicated in the widespread dread of the fantasized contamination of Europe by non-European elements, as I alluded to in the example of the populist outcry "Europe for the Europeans." Yet to discriminate Europeans from non-Europeans in Europe was a daunting task unless it was done in the sphere of collective fantasies. But it is also this task of fantasy that an increasing number of Europeans, or inhabitants of a geographic region called "Europe," want to engage in once again today, after a seventy-five-year hibernation. Whether "Europe for the Europeans" or "Europe exposed to radical Islam," we must never lose sight of the fact that the opposition of the West and the Rest is a trope whereby to project a substantive significance onto a demagoguery.

After World War II, both implicitly and explicitly, the presumed center of the West moved westward across the North Atlantic, as Americans began to claim this title. Given the tremendous elasticity with which this monstrous index has been determined cartographically, racially, ethnically, culturally, politically, or economically, it would be quite feasible for it to shift elsewhere once again in a few decades, for instance, to the eastern shore of the Eurasian continent facing the South China Sea.

However, the endless wandering and dissemination of this floating signifier named the West is not subject matter for my present argument. Instead we should concern ourselves with the question of theory and the West, with how theory can be presumed as the exclusive possession of the West.

By inquiring into the genealogy of colonial modernity we now begin to comprehend why theory had to be so intimately associated with the West. There is a figure of "man" or humanity implicated in the apprehension of theory, yet this humanity was not "man" in general. Instead it had to be modified by the adjectival "European" or "Western." Thus in modernity the genealogical analysis of colonial modernity exposes the participation of a certain humanism.

In what underlies the possibility of talking about the modern at all, it is essential to deal with an other to the modern, the premodern, with reference to which modernity has also been defined in a great many instances. Unless it is contrasted with the premodern, the modern cannot acquire any definitive sense as a periodic adjective. This pairing of the modern and the premodern may suggest a chronological order. Yet it must be remembered that this order has never been dissociated from the geopolitical configuration of the world. It is known very well by now that this essentially nineteenth-century historical scheme provides a prism through which to comprehend the locations and statuses of nations, cultures, traditions, and races schematically. The historico-geopolitical pairing of the premodern and the modern has been a major organizing apparatus of academic discourse in which modernity, modernization, and even modernism have been discussed. The emergence in the 1980s of the third and enigmatic term, the postmodern, possibly testified not so much to a transition from one period to another as to the shift or transformation of our discourse; as a result, the supposed indisputability of the historico-geopolitical pairing—modern and premodern—has become increasingly problematic and unsettling. Of course, it was not the first time that the validity of this differentiation has been challenged. Yet, surprisingly enough, the premodern-modern opposition has managed to survive many attacks, and it would be extremely optimistic to believe that it has finally become ineffectual. Nevertheless, those who still want to presume that this historico-geopolitical pairing is somewhat normal now suffer from a tremendous sense of insecurity. Particularly in disciplines that deal with Asia in the West or in countries accustomed to regarding themselves as modern, the level of anxiety has never been higher.

Either as a set of socioeconomic conditions or as an adherence of a society to selected values, the term "modernity" can never be understood without reference to this dichotomy of the premodern and the modern. In the historical context, modernity has primarily been opposed to its historical precedent; geopolitically it has been contrasted to the nonmodern or, more specifically, to the non-West. Thus this periodic dichotomy has served as a historico-geopolitical scheme according to which a historical predicate is translated into a geopolitical one and vice versa. A propositional subject is posited through the attribution of these predicates, and thanks to the cofigurative schematism of the West and the Rest, two kinds of areas are diacritically discerned: the modern West and the premodern non-West. As a matter of course, this neither means that the West was never at a premodern stage nor that the non-West can never be modernized: it simply excludes the possibility of the simultaneous coexistence of the premodern West and the modern non-West. This temporal differentiation is turned into a cartographic trope, so that the geographic expanse of the globe is dissected into stages of development, which in turn offer a spatial representation of a chronological series of world history.

European Man, or Empirico-Transcendental Doublet?

A cursory examination of the chronological-cartographic tropisms of modernity amply suggests a certain polarity or warp among the possible ways to conceive of the world both historically and geopolitically. For the West to exist, there must be a scheme of the world organized by a polarity that continually reproduces an imbalance or extraordinary one-sidedness between the West and the Rest, so that the West is regarded as the source of the global flow of commodities, ideas, and institutions. The classic vision of modernization has never questioned the reproducibility of this polarity, upon which not only the developmental teleology but also the disciplines of area studies have relied, whether wittingly or unwittingly. As some Asian intellectuals pointed out in the late nineteenth and early twentieth centuries, there is no inherent reason why the West/non-West opposition should determine the geographic perspective of modernity except for the fact that it definitely serves to establish the putative unity of the West, a nebulous but commanding positivity whose existence has been increasingly tainted with a sense of uncertainty in recent decades. After all, the West is a name for a positionality that is postulated in the microphysics of power relations and is also an object constituted discursively.

Evidently, the West is a name always associating itself with these regions, communities, and peoples that appear politically or economically superior to other regions, communities, and peoples. Basically, it is just like the name "Europe," which reputedly designates a geographic area, a tradition, a religion, a culture, an ethnos, a market, a population, and so on; yet, unlike all the other names associated with geographic particularities, it also implies the refusal of its self-delimitation or particularistic determination; it claims to be capable of sustaining, if not actually transcending, the impulse to transcend all the particularizations. Simply put, the West is never content with what others recognize it as; it always wants to approach others so as to ceaselessly transform its self-image; it continually seeks itself in the midst of interaction with other peoples, civilizations, and races; it wants to be always confident that it is never discovered by others but initiates discovery of them instead; it will never be satisfied with passively being recognized but also wishes to actively recognize others; it would rather be a supplier of recognition than a receiver thereof. In short, the West must represent the moment of the genus or generality, which subsumes the species or particularity. It is the source of spontaneity, whose initiative must be received by its subordinates. Thus, the West is supposed to assume the positionality of a universal (general) activity by assigning to the rest of the world the positionality of a particular passivity.

Indeed, the West is particular in itself, but it also constitutes the general point of reference in relation to which others recognize themselves as particularities. Empirically it is a particularity, but it always engages in the general—and by implication the universal—validity of how particular objects are identified. In this respect, it is transcendental.[22] The West is structured as a doublet with one side in the empirical and the other in the transcendental, straddling both the determinate and the indeterminate; it is fashioned after what an eighteenth-century neologism called the "subject." Unlike Asia, whose identity must depend upon the West's recognition, it does not seem to need the other to recognize it. Or, to put it slightly differently, it is claimed—a claim that must be questioned, as I have already hinted—that the West is capable of initiating its own self-recognition. Thus, as I have already elucidated above, whereas the prior postulation of Europe is assumed in the self-recognition of Asia, Europe refuses, or believes it possible to refuse, the prior postulation of Asia in the self-recognition of Europe. In this regard, the West considers itself ubiquitous and spontaneous; it is omnipresent and unique; it represents the universalism of the international world and is its unique and exceptional leader.

Normalcy, with the presumption of which an intimate association of theory and the West is taken for granted, comes from this peculiar status of the West. The historical complex in which this normalcy is embedded was once called "man" by Michel Foucault, namely a problematic of "an empirico-transcendental doublet" that has continued to motivate the sciences of man or the humanities in general for the last two centuries.[23]

Foucault deployed the Heideggerian problematic of finitude in his archaeological analysis of the "human being," and he thrived on illustrating the internal dynamic of humanism in the production of knowledge in the humanities. However, I do not think that he explored the significance of his own formula of the empirico-transcendental doublet in the context of colonial modernity. The modern positivity of man is characterized by man's mode of being or the mode of "repetition—of the identity and the difference between the positive and the fundamental . . . within the figure of the Same"(Foucault 1973, 315):

> Man became that upon which all knowledge could be constituted as immediate and non-problematized evidence; he became, a fortiori, that which justified the calling into question of all knowledge of man. Hence that double and inevitable contestation: that which lies at the root of the perpetual controversy between the sciences of man and the science proper—the first laying an invincible claim to be the foundation of the second, which are ceaselessly obliged in turn to seek their own foundation, the justification of their method, and the purification of their history, in the teeth of "psychologism," "sociologism," and "historicism." (345–346)

It is important to note that the politically and intellectually significant debates on the crisis of the European spirit or Western humanity in the first half of the twentieth century—of Weber, Valéry, Husserl, and Heidegger, to mention only representative figures—could not evade calling into question the foundation of scientific reason in specifically humanistic terms. Through discussions on theory, therefore, they had to address how it was ever possible to find human legitimacy for scientific rationality, but in this process, as we have witnessed in Husserl's investigation of the crisis of European sciences, they had to encounter the problem of European humanity. Precisely because of the humanistic problematic—the finitude of man—motivating the production of knowledge in the humanities, they had to doubt the destiny of European humanity. This explains why the crisis of scientific rationality was first construed in terms of the crisis of European humanity.

Foucault's analysis offers the most important insight into the presumed affiliation between theory and the West, or the teleology of reason and European humanity. However, let me note in passing that, despite his alluring analysis of "the empirico-transcendental doublet" called "man," the notion of Western culture or its unity is never doubted at any point in his career, and he never interrogated the putative unity of the West in relation to modern humanism. In other words, Foucault did not reach another point of contention about "man," namely the problem of anthropological difference in terms of which European humanity has been distinguished from the rest of humanity.

It is important to emphasize the dynamic character of anthropological difference here. It is a form of investment, of desire that can never be fulfilled. There are two aspects to be noted in anthropological difference. The first is that this difference never stabilizes itself since it manifests itself as a transition or tendency from difference in discontinuity to specific difference in continuity. It is an incentive or orientation that cannot be substantialized in the tactic of speciation (classifying into species, thereby establishing the hierarchical order of Aristotelian taxonomy: individual–species–genus). The second is its inherently oxymoronic nature, so to speak. Anthropological difference never escapes a perpetual oscillation; it can never be stabilized because it is internally overdetermined because it consists of two heterogeneous moments that contradict each other. The first moment, anthropological difference, appears only when two positions, "you" and "us" or "Asia" and "Europe," for instance, are in disjunction; only when there is no element in which two positions can be harmoniously accommodated. But, there is the second moment, an insatiable search for the conjunction of the two, a search for a stable paradigm wherein two positions can be systematically articulated to one another.

Anthropos and Humanitas

In the regime of knowledge production in the discourse of modern "man" since the eighteenth century, it has been assumed that there are two distinct relationships that man can have with knowledge. The suppliers of raw data and factual information are involved in the production of knowledge in the humanities. Certainly they are humans and, in that capacity, offer information concerning the particular cases of humanity and human nature. Presumably, they are found virtually everywhere in the world. This sort of knowledge serves no distinct role in distinguishing European humanity from humanity in general.

On the other hand, there is another sort of people who seek to know about humanity and human nature but who would never be content merely to be suppliers of information. They refuse to be satisfied with the accumulation of factual and empirical knowledge. Knowledge is not merely one of many aspects of their existence. For them, knowing is an essential part of their being in the world, so that their way of life will be affected as their relationship to knowledge production changes. They necessarily engage in the collection, evaluation, comparison, or analysis of raw data, but, more importantly, they are continually involved in a critical review of the existing means of knowing as well as the invention of new means. Their concern for their subjective conditions in knowing carries the weight of an almost moral imperative. For them, knowledge about humanity and human nature must not only consist of the variety of particular cases, but it must also entail a commitment both to a critical inspection of existing knowledge and to the project of changing and creating the means of knowing about humanity and human nature. They must constantly strive to exceed the limits of their own accomplishments. As we have already seen in Husserl's endorsement of the mission for European humanity, it has been taken for granted that the sort of humanity entrusted with this task for universal theory is to be found in Europe.

Thus, two different relationships to the production of knowledge presuppose two different conceptions of humanity in knowledge production. It is presumed that ultimately, by extracting what many peoples in the world have in common, knowledge about human nature will be attained. In such an instance, the notion of humanity as the guiding principle is that of general humanity, which inheres in every particular manifestation of human being. Yet a completely different relationship is also possible. It relates to the production of knowledge reflectively; it tries to set new conditions of knowing and thereby transforms both the constitution of the object for knowledge production and the subjective conditions of knowing. In this latter relationship to knowledge production, humanity is problematized not only as a generality that encompasses all particular cases but also in the aspect of subjective conditions: humanity manifests itself in self-reflective knowing about universal knowing and in the legislation of the new means of knowing to which "man" willingly subjects himself. The humanity that is sought in the second relationship is, therefore, not only epistemic but also practical: what is at issue here is not the general but rather the universal humanity, to use the Kantian distinction between generality and universality.

The difference between these two relationships to knowledge production in the humanities has been hinted at since the nineteenth century by the juxtaposition of two classical analogues, *humanitas* and *anthropos*.[24] As the historical evolution of the discipline of anthropology suggests, humanitas has meant people who could engage in knowledge production in both the first and the second relationships, while anthropos has gradually been reserved for peoples who participate in knowledge production only in the first. Thus, humanity in the sense of humanitas has come to designate Western or European humanity and is distinguished from the rest of humanity. This means that humanity in the sense of humanitas authorizes the very distinction of the West from what Stuart Hall (1996) incisively called "the Rest."

In due course, this disciplinary dichotomy of anthropos and humanitas must be articulated to anthropological difference without recognition of which the distinctive uniqueness of European humanity is unlikely to be authorized. It is assumed that Europeans (or Westerners) are those who are born, live, and grow up in Europe (or the West), but not all of those who reside in the geographic area called Europe are qualified for the second kind of people, as I have already suggested with regard to Husserl's discussion of Gypsies. In this instance, indeed, the index "European"—or "the West"—becomes thorny, to say the least. Beyond their residential place, the European must possess some property or trait that Husserl characterized in terms of "the spiritual shape of Europe." It was implicitly assumed that there were some Europeans who were neither intellectually nor spiritually European. It is suggested that it should be possible to tell authentic Europeans from inauthentic Europeans, from those who do not share "the spiritual shape of Europe" (Husserl 1970c); this differentiates those who participate in Europe's teleological mission from those who do not. Would the insistence on the authenticity of Europeans not have risked discriminatory violence in excluding the impure from the pure, in identifying those who authentically belonged to Europe from those who did not? It may appear that Husserl yielded to the populist demand of "Europe for the Europeans." Did he not offer a scheme by which to sift real Europeans from fraudulent ones, even though, admittedly, the spiritual shape of European humanity advocated by him could be immeasurably different from some racist stereotype of the true European fantasized by the populist demand? Did he not encourage the exposition of counterfeit Europeans from the vast population resident in whatever territory was designated by the word "Europe"? Gypsies were not the only case. Potentially there could have been many Europeans who could have failed to be Europeans even in the German context of the 1930s. Exactly the same can be said about the West today. Those who live and belong to the West are only putatively Westerners. In actuality, many can fail to qualify as such.[25]

By now it should be evident that the problem of two neologisms of "man" is not only about Gypsies or European Jewry. Anthropos and humanitas, both of which incidentally mean "man," are, in fact, inherent in the question of "man" in knowledge production as well as in the spatial order of the modern international world.

In *The Order of Things*, Foucault discussed the historical transformation of knowledge production in the modern disciplines of the humanities. It is evident by now that we cannot afford to dissociate Foucault's "man," the empirico-transcendental doublet, from the issues surrounding the dichotomy of humanitas and anthropos, and the West and the Rest.[26]

The End of Man

What is the West, after all? Let me first respond to this query from the standpoint of Asian studies: a collection of area studies fields left over from the days of the Cold War in American higher education and the surviving legacy of even older Oriental and African studies in European imperial centers.

Partly because of the consequences of what, for the last few decades, a number of people have referred to as "globalization" discernible almost everywhere on the globe, we are urged to acknowledge that the unity of the West is far from being unitarily determinable. What we believe we understand by the West is increasingly ambiguous and incongruous: the immoderately overdetermined nature of the West can no longer be ignored.

Until recently, the indigenous or local characteristic of a social and cultural construct found in places in Asia, Africa, and Latin America has routinely been earmarked in contrast to some generalized and euphemistic quality specified as being Western. It would be impossible to understand the initial formation of Asian studies as a set of academic disciplines in North American academia without this institutionalized gesture with which to identify what is unfamiliar or enigmatic to those who self-fashion themselves as Westerners in terms of the West-and-the-Rest binary opposition. Things Asiatic were first brought to scholarly attention by being recognized as different and therefore Asian. Thus, tacitly from the presumed vantage point of the West, "being different from us" and "being Asian" were taken to be synonymous in an anthropologizing gesture. The exoticization of Asia was demanded so as to implicitly and non-thematically postulate the positionality of "us." A similar operation could well be performed with Africa or Latin America so as to identify these places as belonging to the rest of the world, a Rest that remains when the humanity of the West is forcibly extracted.

Too often, therefore, the designation "Asia," a representative one of the Rest, has been accompanied by a sense of "being different from us" that in a reflective manner earmarks the ethnic or racial positionality of Asianists as Westerners. What is fundamental in the anthropological description of Asia is the primordial exposure of the observer to the look of the natives, what Rey Chow calls "the to-be-looked-at-ness"; this precedes the self-determination of the observer as a Westerner and the native as Asian and also discloses the positionality of the observer in ethnographic description, primarily as the observed rather than the observer (Chow 1995, 176–182). What is undeniably present in the postulating of the natives as anthropos is the gaze of local people to which the observed reacts and in which he or she attempts to pass for a Westerner. Yet, in the representation of anthropological description, the very relationship of the observed and the observer—for instance, a visiting anthropologist or area specialist who is exposed to the look of the natives and the villagers among whom anthropological fieldwork is conducted—is reversed. An anthropologist postulates himself or herself as an observer by disowning his or her initial status as the observed. It follows that the observer's anthropologizing self-fashioning as a Westerner is essentially a reactive self-posturing, reactive precisely because, in order to posture himself or herself as a Western observer, he or she has to disavow the initial moment of what Johannes Fabian (1983) called "coevalness."

As outlined in my critique of Takeuchi Yoshimi, the self-referentiality of the West is a consequence of this reversal, of a reactive self-posturing. Without this reversal, the West could never postulate itself as an active and spontaneous agent with an identity expected to be independent of an encounter with an other. It follows that what is decisive in the putative unity of the West is the postulation of separation, an operation of inscribing a border—"bordering," as conceptualized by Sandro Mezzadra and Brett Neilson—so as to make the world appear as if it has already and always been divided between the West and the Rest, to presume that, somewhat naturally and essentially, the separation of the West from the Rest or Asia had been preordained and prescribed. Therefore, in discussions of European humanity during the first half of the twentieth century, the anxiety about the crisis of the European spirit was accompanied by an essentialist insistence upon the unity of the West; this insistence had to seek the archê of what originally constituted the West—or Europe—as the Greek origin to which the Europeans returned so as to assert their future as Europeans.

In the fields of Asian studies, however, this level of commitment to theory can hardly be expected even though many of its specialists frequently appeal to the opposition of the West and the Rest. As a matter of fact, many of the experts in the fields of Asian studies are least interested in theory and, in some cases, are openly hostile toward it. Some of them go so far as to say that theory is no more than a fad. According to Husserl's teleology of reason, these anti-theoretical area experts do not embody the spiritual shape of Europe and are hardly qualified to call themselves Europeans or Westerners. Even though it is glaringly obvious that, because of their indifference to theory, the majority of them would fail to be eligible as humanitas, they have no misgivings about the very binary of humanitas and anthropos; rarely do they challenge the presumption that we normally do not expect theory of Asia.

Yet this peculiar situation exists beyond those who fashion themselves as Westerners. Notwithstanding the fact that the binary serves to figure out not only the non-Western or Asian other but also the Western self of North American and European Asianists in the regime of self-referentiality, we must not overlook the fact that it also operates in a practical way in the production and reproduction of knowledge in countries in Asia (and other sites believed to be in the Rest). In these places, the institutions of human and social sciences, such as the departments of sociology and English at universities, were established initially as local agents for the propagation and translation of knowledge produced in European or North American societies, of knowledge which is euphemistically labeled as "Western"; even today, most of these institutions are still trapped in the habit of regarding themselves as secondary or derivative, or as imitators or importers, of Western theory: it is somewhat held as a truism that theory cannot be generated in the Rest, so it must be imported from the West.

Please do not mistake me. I am not saying that scholars of the Rest must be original and resort to their own native traditions for their own theory; definitely I am not advocating some distinctly non-Western theory. Such an endeavor would do no more than reproduce a new version of anthropological difference.

What they have deliberately overlooked is that, in the West too, scholars imitate and import; in the West too, while some scholars are capable of critical reflection on their own knowledge production, many others are incapable of theory, obsessed with an endless collection of positivistic data. Many scholars in the "Orient" have so far failed to objectify the mythology of European humanity; they still uphold the exceptional character of Western rationality that has presumably been inherited continually from generation to generation since Greek antiquity. They have yet to rid themselves of their undue sense of indebtedness to the religious-mythical heritages of the West.

In fact, the sense of separation between the West and Asia is best exhibited among scholars in Asian countries who feel somewhat excluded or rejected by the West. The West-and-the-Rest opposition does not only designate the boundary of one civilization from another in a fantastical manner: it also dictates the aesthetic constitution of national community (Sakai 2013a, 285–312); it is also interwoven into the texture of the imaginary reality of the ethnic nation as it has been formulated in Asia. In other words, the national, civilizational, and racial identity of the nation in Asia requires the implicit and ubiquitous presence of the West. The aesthetics of the nation is inevitably implicated in the imperial aesthetics of the modern international world. The binary of humanitas and anthropos is indeed a matter of epistemic positionality, but it also serves as an aesthetic trope for other power relations. As the popular rhetoric of "Asian Values" amply demonstrated in the 1990s, many cultural nationalisms in the so-called non-West are shamelessly obsessed with the cultural traits of the West because the imagined integrity of their nations is representable only in contrast to some fantastic images of Western intrusion, domination, and influence. In these nationalisms, nationality can be rendered sensible to the general populace only as long as the West is felt to be the counterpoint.

In this instance, let me take a moment to note once more that the West thus disclosed is not a determinate position that exists prior to the anthropologizing gesture of equating "being different from us" to "being Asian." The distinction of the West and the Rest is always a retrospective inscription, a delayed projection onto "our" encounter with people of an unknown background, different linguistic heritage, or unfamiliar intellectual tradition. It is not because "you" belong to the West while "we" to the Rest that there is a gap, an irreducible distance between "you" and "us." In fact, the encounter occurs anterior to an articulation in terms of speciation in some primordial cultural difference that precedes species difference. In this encounter, we—in the sense of you and we—are together in discontinuity, exposed to one another in "compearance" (*comparusion*), so that it is hard to figure out what is going on between "you" and "us"; neither "you" nor "we" are apprehensive about what happens at the locus of the very encounter; "we" are at a loss at the locale of incommensurability; "we" might go through an experience of non-sense over what "you" and "we" are doing together.[27] By no means can this encounter be seen in terms of the dichotomy of the West and the Rest.

This is indeed the locale of translation. But the translation at stake here is not apprehended as a transfer of a message from one linguistic medium to another; it cannot be construed within the framework of communication model. What translation accomplishes is to open up a continuity in discontinuity; it creates a relation at the locale in which it is impossible to make sense. It is the surface of sociality on which personal relations can be inscribed anew.

The bordering of the West and the Rest never precedes this moment of translation, of making sense out of non-sense, of creating continuity in discontinuity. Consequently we would not recognize the presence of either a gap or border that prevents us from making sense together. On the contrary, in such an encounter we come across the experience of discontinuity. But, let me repeat, it cannot be represented by an image of cut, gap, barrier, or border. Discontinuity in this instance implies, above all, nonrepresentability in terms of spatial figures such as cut, gap, barrier, and border. By ascribing the distinct binary figures of the West and the Rest or Europe and Asia to "we" and "you," however, the sense of incomprehensibility is appropriated into the tropisms of anthropological difference, a difference already in the order of continuity. By locating the occasion of non-sense, incommensurability, or incomprehensibility within the binary configuration of the West and the Rest, the very difference of discontinuity is displaced by an anthropological difference, and it is apprehended as if bearing the order of continuity from the outset. As I have argued elsewhere with regard to translation, the regime of co-figuration operates in the element of continuity, and the experience of discontinuity disrupts the schematism of co-figuration (Sakai 1997b, 1–17, 40–71; 2009b).

What is overlooked in this insidious transition from discontinuity to continuity is that the former means something unrepresentable; incomprehensibility or incommensurability points to an experience—if the experience is strictly a constative statement describing a state of affairs empirically meaningful, then it should not be called "experience"—that cannot be rendered in representation. It is, therefore, impossible to represent it in terms of the figure of gap or border since those always imply some sort of break within the continuous space.

This binary of the West and the Rest is made to imply a lot more than a contrast of epistemic attitudes; condensed in this opposition of humanitas and anthropos are other social and personal features such as a discriminatory potential in wealth, profession, social class background, and the level of cultural capital, features which are most frequently appealed to in order to differentiate one individual from another, to classify people in such terms as race, social class, sexual orientation, and nationality within a social hierarchy.

The West comes into being precisely when "being different from us" is thus rendered analogous to "being Asian," "being African," and so forth. Similarly, from the viewpoint of those who fashion themselves as non-Westerners and as belonging to the Rest, the West is also postulated at the moment that, the positionalities of the West and the Rest being reversed, "being different from us" and "being Western" are taken as synonymous. Instead of being construed in view of many different social features, conversation and interaction about knowledge are figured out exclusively in terms of a schema—or a pair of schemata—that consists of the two poles of the West and the Rest. All the other social relations palpable in intellectual exchange are subordinated to this bipolar figuration; any cultural incommensurabilities one may encounter are all reduced to figures commensurate with the schematism of co-figuration (Sakai 1997b, 40–71). So, for the Westerners, the thematization of things Asiatic as "being different from us" is the first move toward negating or exorcising "them" from "us" in such a way as to prepare the very possibility of representing "them" as Asia and "us" as the West, according to the schematism of co-figuration. The Asiatic essence of things Asiatic is thematized and isolated, just like a figure separated against the background, so to speak. And one of the necessary conditions for the West to be perceived as real is to be recognized as such by its counterpart, the Rest, in a symmetrical and transferential manner. The West and Asia both serve in the structure of feeling for Westerners as well as for Asians and are thus implicated in the imperial aesthetics of co-figuration in the modern international world.

Dislocation of the West

Another disclaimer must be issued at this point. I have not so far offered a concise description of how theory has been conceived of or what it ought to be. Nor have I suggested by theory any specific protocol by which a formula in the form of a theorem can be applied to particular empirical cases so as to draw some conclusive generalized judgment. On occasion in this chapter, I have cited Husserl's discussions on the theoretical attitude, theoretical truth, and theoria, but by no means am I willing to endorse his conceptions of or prescriptions for theory wholeheartedly. First of all, let us not forget that the relationship that regulates theory and experience is not one of generality and particularity. So, by theory, I do not imply general formulas by which particular cases can be classified and subsumed under general patterns.

Yet at the same time, by "theory" I assume a certain openness to repetition and refutation. Unless it is able to be reproduced, reinscribed, or reinstated by any person or any group of people, I do not think it worthy of examination as such. Thus, theory is always concerned with the production of exoteric knowledge, but it is further involved in the reproduction and modification of the mode of that knowledge production. In this sense, theory is universal; theory must exist in the modality of universality. Theory is thus open to anybody; it must be institutionally guaranteed that the process of knowledge production not be confined to a closed circle of connoisseurs or apprentices; the type of knowledge that cannot withstand this open process of imitation, reproduction, reinscription and modification cannot qualify as theoretical.

After the devastation of World War I, Valéry concluded that Europe could only find its uniqueness in the essential openness and universality to which it was supposedly committed. Only through its continual self-transformation and self-innovation in the project of self-transcendence could it remain identical to what was then indicated by Europe. For Valéry, Europe emerged for the first time as internally unified only when its self-transcendence and coherence, or what he eventually capitulated to—in spite of himself—the Hegelian term "spirit," was fundamentally threatened. Europe came into being simultaneously with the crisis of its spirit. One may find a resolute expression of the project of transcendental and universalistic thinking in his adoption of this term "spirit" as well as his idiosyncratic notion of the method. Valéry emphasized that Europe is not a continent; this would imply that it was distinguished from the rest of the world not predominantly in terms of geographic markers, historical heritages, residential populations, or other historical continuities.[28] Instead what he recognized as the actuality of Europe consisted in an extraordinary imbalance and unequal distribution of resources and wealth in the world; beyond this one-sidedness, Europe could be defined only as a potentiality to reproduce this imbalance against the natural law of energy dispersion. Just as a drop of blood in the ocean spreads, dilutes, and eventually disappears, so does an artificially created imbalance gradually dissolve and move toward a sort of equilibrium in which blood is homogeneously diluted. Europe is a perversion of the law of equilibrium; it betrays the natural progression in which entropy is bound to increase; it has a miraculous capacity to reverse this process which nature dictates.

Valéry believed that Europe could only find its unity in the essential openness and universality to which it is committed. But, precisely because of its adherence to what makes it possible for Europe to exist, it could not help being exposed to the constant danger of its dilution, dispersal, and dissolution. In short, Europe was to express the two extremities inherent in capitalism: maximization of the unequal distribution of wealth and resources, on the one hand, and endless commodification and standardization, on the other. Europe was theory in the sense that, on one side, it thus meant a commitment to the mutually contradictory principles of the openness and the universality that work in accordance with the increase of entropy in the world system, and, on the other side, a miraculous reversal of nature that reproduces the imbalance against the law of thermodynamics.

Today, nearly one century later, what Valéry summarized as the essential feature of Europe can be seen in the emanation-vision of colonial modernity. In retrospect, we can see that, perhaps unwittingly, his diagnosis of the crisis of the European spirit disclosed an essential condition for the formation of European humanity, namely, modern colonialism.

Therefore, what was perceived as a crisis was an intimation of the age of decolonization, when the distinction between humanitas and anthropos can no longer be projected onto a cartographic plane. Perhaps the crisis of European humanity anticipated a situation in which Europe no longer commands a miraculous imbalance and where it is thoroughly provincialized—European humanity being reduced to anthropological types. In this situation, theory would not have to be ascribed to any geopolitically determined location.

By no means can I be certain that modern colonialism is finished today. Therefore, I hesitate to speak as if the two classical analogues of humanitas and anthropos have lost the relevance they once enjoyed. But this much seems certain. It is impossible to comprehend the differentiation of humanitas and anthropos in terms of geopolitical tropes. Two types of people cannot be differentiated from one another by geographic parameters. With this understanding, we can now see that a series of important questions remain unarticulated in the statement I referred to at the outset: "theory is something that we normally expect of Europe (or the West)." The questions we cannot evade today are these: Who is in Europe or the West? Who are Europeans or Westerners in the very distinction of humanitas and anthropos? Already Husserl has cautioned us, albeit in a questionable manner, by saying that European humanity was not a matter of territory. Today, it is no accident that some white nationalists and anti-immigrant racists compulsively insist upon the identity of Western civilization. Then, how could he somewhat imply that European humanity could be distinguished from such anthropological types as the Indians and Chinese? How could he differentiate Europeans from the mere residents in the European territory or area (Westerners from the residents of the West) without resorting to the naturalizing tactic of identifying Europeans in such terms irrelevant to historical imperatives as race and ethnicity? Is it feasible to insist that classifying Europeans by such mythical and fictive variables as race and ancient Greek heritage would not signify determining them essentially as an anthropological type? We know that the implicit inquietude invoked by these questions propelled many during the interwar period toward the problem of historicity and the Greek origins of European sciences. But, today, can we still cling to the lineage of Western civilization in order to know who Westerners are? Can we respond to this series of questions about how to distinguish Europeans from non-Europeans, Westerners from non-Westerners, without inquiring into the conducts and conflicts specific to the deployment of power relations? These positionalities are relational and contingent upon local conditions of power that frame up the contrasting positionalities of Europe and Asia/Africa/the Americas, the West and the Rest. Neither Europe nor the West is a long-lasting substance or an internally coherent organism. In extremely diverse situations, what should we understand is the microphysics of power relations in which Europe or the West—Asia or the Rest as well—appears substantialized and naturalized?

Through an examination of the microphysics of power relations, let us continue to hope we will eventually disentangle ourselves from the civilizational spell of theory and Asian humanity. Yet, it must be stated unambiguously that this analytic of the microphysics of power relations neither removes theory nor rejects the practical commitment to reflectively and critically engage in the transformation of disciplinary conditions of existent knowledge production. Rather, it is to demonstrate that theory does not require a civilizational self-fashioning on the part of the one who engages in it.

4. "YOU ASIANS"

On the Historical Role of the Binary of the West and Asia

Partly because of the consequences of accelerating globalization and the emergence of what for the last decade or two a number of people have referred to as the postmodern conditions discernible almost everywhere around the globe, we are urged to acknowledge that the unity of the West is far from being unitarily determinable. The West is a mythical construct, indeed, yet what we believe we understand by this mytheme is increasingly ambiguous and incongruous: its immoderately overdetermined nature can no longer be shrouded.[1]

"We Westerners"

Until recently, the indigenous or local characteristic of a social and cultural construct found in places in Asia, Africa, and sometimes Latin America has routinely been earmarked in contrast to some generalized and euphemistic quality specified as being Western. Without this institutionalized gesture by which to recognize and identify what is allegedly unfamiliar, enigmatic, or barbaric from the viewpoint of those fashioning themselves as Westerners, it would be impossible to understand the initial formation of Asian studies as a set of academic disciplines in North American academia. Things Asiatic were brought to scholarly attention by being acknowledged as "different and therefore Asian" within the framework of the Western/non-Western binary opposition. Then, tacitly from the putative positionality called the West, "being different from us" and "being Asian" were taken to be more or less synonymous through its anthropologizing gesture. A regimen was in effect according to which an acknowledgment of allegedly unfamiliar, enigmatic, or barbaric things was immediately a recognition of one's positionality as a Westerner. A similar operation could equally be performed with Africa or Latin America so as to identify them as belonging to the rest of the world, the rest that is left over when the humanity of the West is strenuously extracted from the world and somehow relocated somewhere above, beyond, or outside, in the transcendental positionality, vis-à-vis the world.

Let me begin this chapter with a brief meditation on the term "Asia" and the people who call themselves Asians. Instead of speaking from the usual viewpoint of "we Westerners"—a customary addresser stance when writing in English in the United States—let me address myself from the contrasting position of "we Asians." For those who fashion themselves as Asians, the word itself is implicitly "we Asians" and serves as a vocative of a first-person plural pronoun that self-reflectively designates a group of people whose primary commonality is supposed to consist of "being of Asia."

But who are the people who call themselves Asians? Or, more fundamentally, where is Asia? And what is it?

The population inhabiting the area called Asia is termed the Asians. From this, however, it does not necessarily follow that the people thus called Asians are able to gather together and build some solidarity among themselves through the act of their self-representation or autorepresentation by enunciating not only "we" but also "we Asians." Clearly there is a wide gap between the fact that the population is described as Asians by some observers standing outside the population—we will inquire into the conceptual specificity of this "outside" or a certain transcendence later—and the assertion by the people themselves in terms of the name attributed to them.

If one is confined within the group or located inside the enclosure, one would never recognize the totality of the group or the enclosure as a whole, for some viewpoint outside the group or perspective transcending the enclosure is necessary. One may not be able to locate oneself physically outside it, but at least in imagination one should be able to view one's group or geographic area as if located outside it. Cartographic location necessarily implies this imaginary transcendence, thanks to which one can view the place where one stands from somewhere else or from the position of somebody else. As far as geography is concerned, this imaginary viewpoint is often called a bird's-eye view, a transcendent position attributed to some flying bird high in the sky. Modern cartography necessarily incorporates this structure of a transcendent viewpoint.[2] The description of Asia is no exception to this rule.

This is to say that, in order to move from the state of being passively described as Asians by outside agents, some sort of leap is required into self-representation as a subject. This leap or self-assertion is accomplished when we announce that we are "we Asians." By declaring "we Asians," a group of people performatively assert that they constitute a collectivity of Asians and that each of them as a subject willfully belongs to it. And let us not be negligent of the historical verity that this leap could not have been made until the nineteenth century. Until then, generally speaking, there were objects designated as Asians, but there were no subjects who represented themselves as Asians. Only in the late nineteenth century did a few intellectuals begin to advocate the plausibility of constituting the transnational and regional subjectivity of Asia. In this respect, one can never overlook the particular genealogy of Asia, that the name "Asia" originated outside Asia, and that its heteronomous origin is inscribed indubitably in the name of Asia, even if it can by no means be taken simply as a geographic or cartographic locality.

In this juncture, however, it is important to remind ourselves that Europe did not exist before the sixteenth century. According to Michel Foucault and other historians, Europe emerged in the sixteenth century as a region devoid of imperial reign where no single state was strong enough to subjugate other states (Foucault 2004a, 2008). As Carl Schmitt stated succinctly, Europe emerged as a peculiar region where local polities competed with one another in such a way that there was hardly any reigning authority overseeing rivalries and disputes among them. Consequent to the decline of transregional authorities such as the papacy and the Holy Roman Empire, Europe emerged as a space managed by interstate relations without a reliance upon the imperial (Schmitt 2006). It is only in the eighteenth century that the whole mythology of European civilization accompanied by the modern myth of the white race was constructed to forge a continual existence of European civilization since its origin in ancient Greece. Martin Bernal argued that the European image of Greek antiquity was drastically transformed from the eighteenth century onward, and that this change promoted a subsequent denial by European academia of any significant African and Phoenician heritage in ancient Greek civilization (Bernal 1987). Thanks to his persistent and penetrating scholarship, we now know that one of the origins of the West is the eighteenth-century racist myth of whiteness. It is therefore worth noting that this change in the Western image of Greek antiquity was accompanied by the introduction of racism; this civilizational narrative served to reify whiteness as if it were a physiological fact, on the one hand, and to enact the disavowal of Islamic influence in the academic and cultural traditions of societies in Europe, on the other.[3]

It has been taken for granted for more than the last two hundred years that European civilization has continued to exist since classical antiquity, as if the European civilization has manifested and will continue to exhibit some traits that are transhistorically inherent in European humanity. As we have seen in Edmund Husserl's diagnosis of the crisis of European sciences and his ambivalent identification with European humanity, such an investment in the teleological mission of European civilization was a commonplace during the interwar period and even after World War II. Of course, such a teleology is thoroughly rejected in this book. Yet, for the sake of its analytical design, we cannot totally disregard the racist implications in the cultural essentialization of European civilization, for to inquire into the structure of this civilizational investment is part and parcel of our investigation into the racist structure of identity politics in the modern international world. Therefore let us trace the rhetoric that reinforces the teleological continuity of Europe for a while, so as to appreciate how Europe constitutes itself as both a transcendental exception and a centrality in the world.

It is well known and registered as historical fact that the word "Asia" did not originate in Asia. It is agreed that the word was coined by Europeans in order to distinguish Europe from its eastern others, in the protocol of constituting itself as a sort of regional unity. It was a term in the service of the constitution of Europe's self-representation as well as its distinctness. Asia was necessary for Europe because, without positing it, Europe could not have been marked as a unity distinct and distinguishable from its Eastern others. Yet as the putative unity of Europe is inherently unstable and constantly shifting, Asia has been defined and redefined according to contingent historical situations in which relationships between Europe and its others have undergone vicissitudes.

Since the nineteenth century, there has been an increasing number of occasions when "the West" was used almost as a synonym for Europe. The mytheme West came to assume a global currency in the late nineteenth and early twentieth centuries. Clearly the West neither signifies nor refers to the same thing as the word "Europe," not to mention the apparent linguistic diversity of terms that connote Europe or the West: "xiyan," "l'Occident," "seiyô," and so forth. Yet in its paradigmatic discriminatory function, the West began to behave like Europe. In other words, Asia was placed in a similar opposition to the West as it had been to Europe.

Today Asia is not necessarily subjugated to the domination of the West in terms of the system of international law. Most Asian countries are, at least in theory, independent of their former colonizers. Yet we are still not justified in overlooking the enduring historical truth that Asia arrived at its self-consciousness thanks to the West's or Europe's colonization practices, as Takeuchi Yoshimi (竹内 好) asserted more than a half-century ago (Takeuchi [1947] 1993; [1948] 2005; see also Sakai 1988). The historical colonization of

Asia by the West is not something accidental to the essence of Asia; it is essential to the possibility called Asia. As long as the "post" of postcoloniality is not confused with that which comes after the sovereign state's independence in chronology, Asia was a postcolonial entity from the outset. Takeuchi's insight was particularly poignant because he had to address the problem of modernity and modern subjectivity from the vantage point of a specific historical question: how could a Japanese intellectual, as an Asian person, still speak about modernity in Asia after Japan's defeat or after what the Japanese had done to peoples in Asia during the fifteen-year Asia-Pacific War (1931–1945)?

Against Takeuchi's diagnosis about Japanese modernity, Maruyama Masao (丸山 眞男) attempted to follow the tenets of Hegelian dialectic and to show that the moment of negativity could be discerned in Japanese thought in the seventeenth and eighteenth centuries, long before the Euro-American threats in diplomacy, best represented by the arrival in 1853 of the "Black Ships" led by U.S. Commodore Matthew Perry. Whereas the Chinese never succeeded in giving rise to their own negativity, Maruyama argued, a certain decomposition of the theological metaphysics characteristic of the premodern cosmology had already begun to occur in Japanese Confucianism (Maruyama 1952, 1974).[4] The disintegration of the unified view of the universe, almost comparable to the collapse of the Scholastic worldview that gave rise in Western Europe to the fragmentation of the world into three realms, epistemic, practical, and aesthetic, was taking place in Japanese thought. While in China the synthetic metaphysics of Cheng-Zhu Neo-Confucianism persisted well into the nineteenth century, the synthetic view of the world was severely doubted long before the eighteenth century in Japan. An intellectual possibility for something like Enlightenment, which prepared for modernity in scientific rationality, practical reason, and aesthetic judgment, was imminent in Japan. Precisely because of negativity inherent in Japanese thought, Maruyama claimed, Japan could be an exception in Asia. Implicit in his wartime historiography, which justified Japan's political leadership over China, was the old thesis of "flight from Asia, entry into Europe" (「脱亜入欧」), which meant that Japan should be capable of modernizing itself, while the rest of Asia must wait for the West's initiative and that, accordingly, Japan ought not to belong to Asia in this respect.

Unambiguously with respect to the invocation of "we Asians" in particular, Takeuchi's historicism was diametrically opposed to Maruyama's, yet it is necessary for us to acknowledge that both shared the foundational logic of historicism.

Asia could never be conscious of itself before it was invaded by the West, according to Takeuchi. Only through the acknowledgment of its lost autonomy, of its dependence on the West, or only in the mirror of the West, so to speak, could Asia reflectively acquire its civilizational, cultural, ethnic, or national self-consciousness. In other words, the defeat is registered in the genealogy of the name "Asia" itself.

Ostensibly Asia is a proper name; nevertheless, as a sign it would be too arbitrary unless it is paradigmatically opposed to the West (or Europe). Its putative identity depends on a very constitutive exclusivity so that Western and Asian properties/proprieties are not attributable to the same substance: it is preliminarily determined that the West is what Asia is not and that Asia is what the West is not; it follows that the same person or thing cannot be Western and Asian at the same time. Depending on the choice of paradigmatic axis, Asia could signify a vast set of concepts, and its reference is too rich, too varied, and too full to specify. Therefore, it does not possess any immanent principle with which to identify its internal unity, either. Except for the fact that it points to a certain assemblage of regions and peoples that have been objectified by and subjugated to the West, many parts of Asia have nothing in common. In other words, it is impossible to talk about Asia positively. Only as the negative of the West can one possibly address oneself as an Asian. Hence, to talk about Asia is invariably to talk about the West.

Takeuchi was typical of Asian and European intellectuals who had been exposed to European intellectual works in their college days in the 1930s in that he had internalized Hegelian and Marxian historicism to such an extent that he could not project historical trajectories beyond the historicist one in which the actualization and appropriation of modern values first requires the people's radical negation of both external forces and their internal heritage of a feudal past. He believed that Asian modernity could be accomplished only by appropriating the essence of what was believed to be Western modernity. But in order to appropriate the essence of Western modernity, there had to be a collective agent nation, and an Asian nation had to resist the West without as well as overcome the reactionary heritage within. In other words, Asia was to modernize itself by negating both the West outside and its own past inside. Where there was no resistance to or negation of the West, there was no prospect of modernity for Asia. For Asia as well as for the West, modernity meant a self-transcending project of struggle against the remnants of the past.

Takeuchi was undoubtedly a passionate nationalist in his emotive and affective constitution. Unlike Maruyama Masao, however, he diagnosed Japan's modern history as a telling case where genuine negativity was absent. Takeuchi was serious in his hope that China would actualize a truly authentic modernity by negating the West's domination as well as the feudal remnants of the past, in contradistinction to Japan, which had facilely accepted the West without resisting it, to the extent of imitating its colonialism and imperialism. The historical dialectic he anticipated could not have made sense unless the externality of what Asia was to resist had been posited. For him, Asia was, not only geographically but also politically, other to the West; from the point of view of Asia, accordingly, modernity was supposed to come from its outside. Takeuchi was most adamantly opposed to the large-scale attempt to construct a regional and transnational subjectivity, an imitative attempt to reproduce Western modernity, as embodied typically in the project of the Greater East Asia Co-prosperity Sphere, while he decisively approved the Chinese nationalist agenda that arose in the Chinese resistance to the Japanese invasion in Northeast Asia. His commitment to modernity would probably be misapprehended unless one senses his recondite shame about his own nation's imperialistic and dehumanizing maneuvers in Northeast and Southeast Asia in the 1930s and early 1940s as well as his intense rage in the late 1940s against U.S. imperialism, which was about to take over the Greater East Asia Co-prosperity Sphere. Then, for Asian peoples, modernity was considered a sort of historical movement that spatially consolidated the unity and substantiality of a political grouping called "the nation" by negating external forces while temporally constituting itself as a self-transcending subject, as an agent of self-determination, by continually overcoming its own past.

In Takeuchi's diagnosis of modernity, consequently, the unity of the nation depended on the externality of what had to be resisted, which was, more often than not, mapped onto a cartographic plane as the externality of one national sovereignty against another. What must be resisted must come from outside the presumed integrity of the nation, just like Japanese troops and capital entering Chinese territory in their invasion of China. A nation of Asia such as China was located within reach of the West, but the West itself was external to it. Or, more precisely, the territorial integrity and the imagined unity of the nation were constituted in the act of representing the West as an external threat. The externality of what had to be resisted thus had to be comprehended in terms of the geographic distance between the North Atlantic (Western Europe/North America) and Asia. This distance was further translated into the one between different political affiliations and, finally, between the friend and the enemy; it thereby came to mimicking, though perhaps inadvertently, the gesture of discriminatory distancing by means of which the West constitutes itself by distinguishing Asia and the rest of the world from itself. The feasibility that Asia could be inherent in the West was deliberately exonerated.

Takeuchi could not avoid the same cartographic imaginary of the globe upon which modernization theory is invariably dependent, although he was unequivocally critical of scholars who promoted modernization theory both in North America and Japan. A critique of Takeuchi's historical consciousness, an inherently historicist consciousness, therefore, should serve as our starting point for a new conception of modernity and subsequently a new conception of the relationship between the West and Asia.[5]

According to the conventional historical narrative, the large-scale social changes in Western Europe accompanied by the emergence of modern states, industries, and technologies are thought to mark the beginning of modern society. The origins of modern society are ascribed to a number of historical precedents: the development of representational government against the absolutist monarchy; the signs of industrialization in England in the eighteenth century; the formation of the bourgeois social milieu and the new ways of organizing everyday life according to the division of the public and the private; a series of political and social events that led to the establishment of a new polity that legitimizes itself in the name of the people or nation; the decline of mercantilism and the rise of industrial capitalism; the formation of the collective subject as the nation, which produces itself by self-representation or autorepresentation; and so forth.

All these precedents as well as the subsequent realization of modern societies are located in a cartographic area called the West. Inversely, it is believed appropriate to say that the West is postulated as the geographic area wherein all these modern things originated. Thereupon it is claimed that these events, which symbolize the coming of modernity, all took place within the West. Furthermore, modernity thus depicted is understood to be something that continually spreads; modernity emanates itself. Unlike an epidemic—arguably the most recent case of which is the Ebola virus epidemic—which is usually imagined to start in a peripheral site and gradually spread to the metropolis, modernity is fantasized as emanating in a reverse manner from the center to the hinterlands of the world.[6] The consequences, influences, and effects of this unitary process of social transformation that supposedly occurred strictly within the West, therefore, are said to be detected and observed in remote areas such as Africa, Latin America, Oceania, and, of course, Asia as a consequence of modernity's emanation.

Interestingly enough, it has been extremely hard for many intellectuals inhabiting Western Europe as well as the rest of the world to comprehend the notion of global contemporaneity unless the emanation model of modernity is presupposed. An art movement may be initiated by some artists in Korea, Brazil, or India. Yet, in order for it to be registered as a contemporary art, it must be positioned within the framework of synchronous chronology of the contemporary world in which an artistic project must be either explicitly or implicitly compared to those movements in the West. What used to guarantee the contemporary rather than traditional significance of an artistic innovation in locations outside the West was its implicit reference through the procedure of comparison to trends and movements recognized in the West. It goes without saying that this global structure of contemporaneity applies to many other domains such as literature, architecture, philosophy, and so forth. Thus, the notion of global contemporaneity has been complicit with the emanation model of modernity in the modern international world.

In due course, according to the Eurocentric chronology of global contemporaneity, modernity as a historical movement used to be represented as an emanative flow in the cartographic imaginary of the globe. Underlying the historicist apprehension of modernization was a certain vision of emanation without which the centricity of Europe could never have been sustained. Undoubtedly there is no room for a multiplicity of modernity in such a representation, but neither can the multiplicity inherent in modernity be adequately addressed by approaches commonly characterized as alternative modernities precisely because the very mytheme of the West, in contrast to which other modernities are asserted, has yet to be scrutinized in its functions and genealogy. Thus, what we have routinely comprehended in terms of modernity and the West must be called into question because the historicist schema of the world subordinates the divergent emergence of modernity to the single overarching process of homogenization. The West is given rise to because modernity has not been released from imprisonment inside the emanation model.

Nonetheless, a number of contemporary incidents do not conform to the emanation model of modernity; contemporaneity is definitely and increasingly being liberated from the Eurocentric structure of the modern international world. For instance, innovation in the fields of sciences, technology, and engineering is independent of the emanation model of modernity. Instead, it is increasingly dependent upon the availability of capital for research and industry on the one hand and the size of the pool of educated population on the other. Hence, we are no longer certain that the next generation of scientific and technological upheaval, comparable to the digital revolution of the 1990s, will originate in the North Atlantic.

Since the nineteenth century, the notion of an avant-garde had been associated with Western Europe and then North America in the plastic arts. But, nowadays, international art dealers do not look for the most radical and innovative works in North America or Western Europe. Instead they are exceptionally attentive to such places as Southeast Asia for avant-garde art. We are less and less guided by the presumption of old modernism, according to which new things are, almost by definition, invented in the North Atlantic and then spread to the rest of the world, not only in the fields of scientific and technological developments and visual arts but in other aspects of everyday life.[7]

One of the most important aspects of so-called globalization is the evaporation of this developmentalist fixation that the contemporaneity of the modern world is first set in the North Atlantic and that the rest is destined to follow the West's initiative and inevitably be delayed in development. While celebrated gullibly by advocates of neoliberal capitalism, we cannot afford to overlook that globalization gives rise to a widespread anxiety among certain sectors of the population in the so-called developed world.

Anthropological Difference

"The West" is a peculiar term; it is not adequately a proper noun capable of designating some referent in its singularity beyond the sum of its descriptions. Neither is it an ordinary noun since it is also adverbial. Its unity is somewhat suggested by the capital W, without which neither the conventional narrative of global positioning nor the geopolitical story of modernity could be sustained, for in essence every point on the surface of the earth is a west. What is overlooked in this narrative, above all, is the undeniable economic, social, cultural, ethnic, and religious heterogeneity that has continued to exist in the geographic areas imagined to constitute the West: Western Europe, mainly bourgeois Britain and France, in the nineteenth century, with the white bourgeois social class of North America being added later in the twentieth century. Examples of its heterogeneity are easy to find: the vast population of Eastern Europe, which is most often excluded from the West; African Americans who have lived generation after generation in the same places with the whites who fashion themselves as Westerners in the United States today; and the Asians in the United Kingdom who may have received a lot more traditional European education than the majority of working-class English, Scottish, and Irish people.[8] But more importantly, often overlooked is the fact that the contour of the West itself is drawn by this historico-geographic narrative of modernization. It is precisely because the West effectively disavows its diversity, as if its interior were congenitally homogeneous, that it is called for as a global mytheme in the first place. It is in this sense too that the West is a putative unity.

Today the West as an analytic concept is, if not totally bankrupt, unreliable and mostly useless to guide our observations about certain social formations and people's behavior in many loci of the world. It obscures our perception and misdirects our comparison, particularly in the cases of the social formations and cultural phenomena encountered in places such as Hong Kong, rural communities in the Deep South in the United States, Seoul, Leipzig, Singapore, and Shanghai.

The disciplinary formation of area studies is a case in point. Just as the West no longer serves as an effectual analytic concept, it is increasingly uncertain that the disciplinary disposition of area studies is still able to sustain its epistemic relevance. Some have already announced the death of this disciplinary disposition and claimed that it now lives in the modality of its afterlife. "What we mean by referring to the afterlife of area studies is a perspective that has surpassed the older global divisions inaugurated by World War II that informed the organization of knowledge and teaching of regions of the world outside Euro-America but considered essential in the Cold War struggle with the Soviet Union" (Miyoshi and Harootunian 2002, 14). Certainly the disposition of area studies that was constructed in response to the political conditions of the Cold War is anachronistic today, but a much broader historical perspective seems at stake.

It is not only the end of the Cold War that has rendered the entire disposition of area studies irrelevant. Its crisis is more profound. Whereas area studies sought to obtain knowledge about an object defined as an area, the pursuit of knowledge in area studies used to be couched in the dynamics of research agendas dictated by anthropological difference, a field subjected to what Stuart Hall (1996) called the discourse of the West and the Rest. Hence, we find it increasingly difficult to remain convinced that such research agendas as dictated by area studies continue to be viable; we are anxious that the very target area, which authenticates the very disciplinary disposition of area studies, may have ceased to be of significance. In short, area studies seems to be haunted by a misgiving, distrust, or skepticism summarily expressed by the idiom "the end of area."[9]

So as to elucidate how knowledge production used to be regulated by the practical imperatives by which anthropological difference is ascertained time and time again, let me take the exemplary case of area studies on Japan. With Japan being customarily located outside the West, one of the routine procedures has been to compare Japan with the West. It is immediately obvious that, unless what is referred to as the West is specified, comparing Japan with the West is too arbitrary and can hardly meet the standard of objective and academic knowledge. Neither can it be an academic and scientifically verifiable research unless Japan is specified.

Nevertheless, this bipolar setup in which an area called Japan has been studied has been exceptionally powerful and overbearing. As an academic institution, area studies on Japan justifies its existence by producing knowledge on its object, Japan. Yet, to the extent that it is institutionalized not in the humanities in general or social sciences but interdisciplinarily among the multiple disciplines of area studies at universities, the object must be registered as an area in the global configuration of the modern international world. In other words, it must enter a particular relationship with the West so as to be qualified and determined as an "area" (Walker and Sakai 2019). In contrast to as well as in separation from the West, the unique aspects of Japanese culture, history, and society as a whole can be identified and highlighted. To focus on Japan's uniqueness, one must examine as many contexts in which Japan and the West are different from one another and similar to one another as possible; one must compare Japan and the West in as many instances as possible. Yet Japanese society and its people are scarcely compared with other societies in the non-West, or, to put it more precisely, the West-and-Japan axis forms the main focal context or epistemological alignment to which all the other comparisons with the other non-Western areas are subordinated. This was possibly because only the comparison with the West would contribute to one's evaluation regarding Japan's modernization, and the degree of modernization has served as one of the classificatory criteria whereby the hierarchy among nations in the modern world has been ordered. Let us recall that anthropological difference is to be deployed not only spatially along the geographic parameter but also chronologically along the evolutionary parameter. On the one hand, Japan tended to be compared with the West. There used to be an obsessive concern with comparison of the West and the Rest. On the other hand, there used to be little or no desire to compare Japan with other societies, peoples, and traditions of the Rest.

Tellingly enough, two contradictory tendencies used to coexist among area experts on Japan in the 1950s and '60s. Quite frequently, a Japan expert could appeal to both at the same time. The advocates of modernization theory typically argued that the Japanese were most successful in appropriating Western institutions, knowledge, and values, which prepared Japanese society for capitalist development. This is, they argued, why it could be said that Japan was the only genuinely modernized society in all of Asia. At the same time, the leading figures in Japanese studies most often insisted that Western society—supposedly best represented by the highly developed state of U.S. society—is fundamentally different from Asian societies, and, invariably, Japan remains different no matter how much the Japanese have endeavored to appropriate Western culture, traditions, and values. Tirelessly and tediously, they seemed to repeat Kipling's refrain, "East is East, and West is West, and never the twain shall meet."

Possibly there is not much point in striving to find out retrospectively how relevant or inappropriate such contradictory assessments were on a factual basis. Nonetheless, it may be of some interest to uncover the politics of knowledge inherent in modernization theory since area studies were directly connected to the policy making of the United States during the Cold War. Moreover, the introduction of area studies in American higher education was actualized at the same time as the implementation of global policies as a result of which Pax Americana was proclaimed. Some good analyses have already been undertaken in this regard, and this is not an appropriate place for me to embark on such a task.[10] However, I might as well note one thing about the copresence of conflicting tendencies. Such contradictory assessments were necessary so as to accommodate the positionality of the area expert in the discourse of the West and the Rest. While area studies on Japan explicitly purported to accumulate objectal knowledge on Japan, such an enterprise was implicitly underlain by the desire that the area expert reside on the side of the West, occupy the positionality of a Westerner.[11] In this regard, the classical critique of anthropology's claim to power launched by Johannes Fabian (1983) is equally compelling in the case of area studies.

This is to say that, by fashioning the researcher himself or herself as a subject of knowing, describing, and evaluating, and as a subject who supposedly occupies the positionality of the West, the researcher's work is most frequently undertaken to study some aspect of Japan and the Japanese as a marker of the identity of Asia—the non-West or the Rest—without opposition to which the identity of the West can barely be postulated. Their study is designed to know more about its object. But, at the same time, it is driven by an area expert's identity politics. In other words, one cannot overlook the hidden or repressed side of area studies that is propelled by an urge to frame up the positionality of the researcher as a subject to know within the field of polarity structured by anthropological difference within a fantasized dichotomy of the West and the Rest. It follows that their obsession with Japanese uniqueness illuminates the underlying concern for anthropological difference between the West and the East, a difference in terms of which their identification with the West is carried out.

Therefore, this anthropological difference functions equivocally as a practical imperative on the one hand and as an epistemic or constative judgment on the other. It is a command, and in the sense of a practical norm to which one can choose to conform or not to conform, it is a law of practical imperative. But, at the same time, the anthropological difference is something essential or innate so that, thanks to one's original constitution such as some physiological feature or ethnolinguistic trait, it is assumed that one is predetermined as a Westerner or born into the West; it derives from the preestablished civilizational configuration according to which humanity is classified into the West and Asia (the East, the Orient, or the Rest). In this respect, it is also a law in the sense of empirical regularity whose constancy is beyond an observer's whim. One is objectively a Westerner or an Asian, an African, or what have you. For this reason, it is so important to discover how different, in terms of civilizational traits or characteristics, the social mores or cultural formations of the target people of observation are from those of area experts engaged in observation and to describe constatively how culturally different theirs are from ours.

Thus, many area experts investigate specific features of an exotic people and their social life both culturally and civilizationally. It is well known that, in the 1950s and '60s, many area experts on Japan undertook the project of so-called national character studies. They attempted to characterize Japanese attitudes toward authorities, behavior patterns, group dynamics, emotive-affective reactions to social conflicts, and so forth in terms of national characteristics of the Japanese people, as if the Japanese nation could have been viewed as some sort of archaic primitive society comparable to the tribal societies of Native Americans, which cultural anthropologists were expected to study. In other words, those Japan experts believed that they could construct a scientifically objective and policy-oriented study of Japan on the basis of Japanese national culture and character as though a single unified culture in the Japanese national community as a whole could be postulated. Even today, some seem obsessed with some national characteristic not exclusively of the Japanese, but more generally of Oriental peoples. Yet, notwithstanding an underlying exoticism in the expert's mindset, does Japanese anime, for instance, demonstrate some distinctively non-Western property or propriety more significant than the fact that what the individual researcher perceives to be non-Western indicates only that this particular person happens to be unfamiliar with it? Although the rhetoric of culturalism is not as popular nowadays as it used to be, the juxtaposition of the West and Asia cannot be abolished overnight. Certain people will insist on relying on the configuration consisting of these historical constructs because they have to fashion themselves in these terms and also by means of their distinction from each other. By positing Asia as "over there," away from the West "on this side," this voyeuristic optic somewhat engenders a fleeting sense of a distinction between the West and the Rest, an ephemeral extenuation not to submit things Western to the same analytical fields of scrutiny as things Asiatic. Consequently and ironically, the putative unity of the West is barely sustained because they deliberately avoid submitting Western and Asian things to the same field of analysis. How perspectives are organized according to this distinction thus prescribes and presages where the West is imagined to be located and who is entitled to feel modern.

The history of global modernization postulates that the comparison must be carried out only between the West and the Rest. In order to effectively interrupt the discourse of the West and the Rest, a different comparative strategy must be revised. Comparative operation must be conducted between the rest and the rest or between the West as a rest and the Rest. I do not know at this point where this strategy is declared, but the whole rhetoric of "we Asians" must be orchestrated with the issues of what Pedro Erber (2015) suggested in terms of contemporaneity.

I maintain that the time of modernity is never singular; it is always in multiplicity. Modernity always appears in multiple histories. Yet I totally disagree with the proponents of alternative modernities. The multiplicity of modernity must not be understood to mean that its plural origins exist side by side in a homogeneous geographic space of the globe. Neither should the multiplicity of histories be understood as a juxtaposition of the plural homogeneous empty temporalities of national and ethnic histories.

Although we are aware that modernization theory is hardly sustainable today, we are not entirely free of the binary structuring schemata that are constantly utilized within contemporary discussions of modernity by the geopolitics of modernization theory. Since such schemata reduce modernity to modernization, the representation of the world they prescribe is hierarchically organized into the West and the Rest, the developed and the underdeveloped, the white and the colored. Worse still, these binaries are supposed to overlap to form a fantastic coherence of the world vision in which capital, values, and knowledge emanate from its putative center to its peripheries.

Heterolingual Address

The emanation model of modernity stems from a fundamental misconception of the basic element of modernity. Modernity is inconceivable unless there are occasions when many people, many industries, and many polities are in contact with one another despite geographic distance or social incommensurability. Modernity, therefore, cannot be considered unless in reference to translation.

It is impossible to conceive of translation as an operation of transfer by which equivalence is established in the signification of the same message between two versions in two languages. We must never allow ourselves to be lured into the model of commodity exchange. In other words, translation cannot be conceptualized according to the model of communication upon which the emanation model of modernity, for instance, is based. Translation facilitates conversation between people in different geographical and social loci who would otherwise never converse, but it also provides them with a space where the appropriateness and validity of translation is constantly discussed and disputed. In this space, we misunderstand and mistranslate one another, but we also recognize the urgent need to strive to understand and translate one another so that we can repeatedly discover how we misunderstand and mistranslate. Translation is always enunciated with a view to its revision and correction. From the outset, a translation is performed as a correction of the previous one and is open to another translation of the same. In this respect, translation is always actualized in repetition.

This also teaches us how modernity takes place in many sites in the world. Modernity is always relational in the sense that it cannot be confined to one race, religion, tradition, or nation, for it always happens as translation. These identities of race, tradition, and nation are constituted through translation and discovered retrospectively after the enunciation of translation. Translation allows you and me to share, but in order to share, we must translate and transform the original and create something new. In this sense, translation can be construed as a modality of being-in-common, as a sharing of community, of community that is not a communion.[12] Sharing, therefore, is necessarily an experience of poietic work toward the other, of innovative endeavor by revising and renovating the means of communication. For this reason, pidginization, a local experience of creating a pidgin from multiple languages, points to something fundamental about modernity and its multiplicity in spite of the international constitution of the modern world. The nationalist demand for the archetype of an unmixed and original language occurs equally as a reaction to and a denial of such an ongoing pidginization and multitude. This is why, as I have argued elsewhere (Sakai 1997b), the origin of national or ethnic language cannot be found except in the modern regime of translation.

In this respect, modernity is, above all, a process in which people transcend distances of many kinds—geographic, social, political, religious, and so on—in order to be exposed to, and thereby in contact with, one another. Let me note that universality, not generality, is indissociably related to transcendence in this sense. The misunderstanding of the nature of modernity stems from the misconception of the event of being in contact with others. This misunderstanding parallels a confusion concerning translation and its representation.

Contact can never be construed as a one-way process of transmitting a doctrine or value from one party to another. Unless contact is a social relation for which, in the final analysis, there can be no overarching viewpoint, even the transmission of a doctrine or commodity exchange cannot occur. Thus, contact is inevitably an infection or contamination capable of transforming both parties involved in the transaction. If a social process of transforming, distorting, or destroying the way people are is called violence, modernity is indubitably a violent event to which both parties are equally exposed (but not equally hurt or traumatized). Modernity is not a stasis, the state of some societies that can be specified by a set of characteristics. It is, rather, a kind of violent transformative dynamic that arises from social encounters among heterogeneous people.

The notion of the subject that autonomously constitutes and transcends itself toward its future plays such an important role in the understanding of modern consciousness and in the history of the nation, precisely because modernity's inescapable heteronomy can be overlooked and erased so as to represent the past in the evolutionist formula of the national history or civilization history. Only under the erasure of its inevitable engagement with heterogeneity is history usurped by national narratology and turned into an evolutionary development. A defeat or humiliating subjugation of one party by another because of the other's economic, technological, or military superiority is, without exception, an experience involving both parties, however differently it may be experienced. Unless modernity is mistaken as development in various historicisms, unless it is thought to be a stage of evolution into which the nation as a subject grows, it is simply impossible to rank various social formations in the chronological hierarchy of advancement and retardation.

What are mapped onto the chronology of maturation and growth are consequences of a violent transformative dynamic: a military conquest, a religio-educational civilizing process, economic competition and rivalry, and political antagonism and struggle. There is no inherent reason why the prosperous should naturally be advanced on the evolutionary ladder or the conquered should necessarily be primitive.

Yet in the emanation model of modernity, an economy of distribution prevails by which the West is assumed to be active in affecting social transformation in Asia while the latter always remains passive. This economy would then postulate two contrasting but mutually supplementing presumptions: on the one hand, the West is capable of transforming itself on its own initiative from within while remaining unaffected by the rest of the world; on the other, Asia is incapable of transforming itself from within while being constantly affected by the West. Consequently, what may be regarded as the content of modernity, such as ideas, institutions, and the ways of life particular to the modern social formation, cannot be circulated other than in a one-way process of indoctrination. This is a vision of the civilizing mission that, in fantasy, satisfies the narcissistic wishes of those still trapped within the missionary positionality, and—as I discuss in chapter 6 with regard to the transferential complicity based on culturalism between the United States and Japan after World War II—such a vision respects the premises of culturalism and covertly posits the unity of the West as a transhistorical entity just like an essentialized national culture. The emanation model of modernity thus invites Asian intellectuals' reactionary response; it gives rise to their obsessive concerns with their own version of modernity and their own modernization initiatives.

The global emergence of modernities has been accompanied by a drastically increased frequency of social encounters and commodity exchanges across the world. While social encounter and commodity exchange give rise to demands for transparency in communication and equivalence in value, they inevitably evoke the incommensurable in our sociality and the excessive in equation. Yet the incommensurable and the excessive cannot be apprehended outside the contexts of contact. For this reason we must not lose sight of the fact that the particularistic insistence on the immutable ethnic and national cultures and traditions goes hand in hand with the universalism of historicism. The culturalist insistence on the integrity of an ethnic and national culture in Asia is always partnered with a covert obsession with the culturalist unity of the West. The rhetoric of "Asian values" or "the tradition of Oriental spirituality," for example, is nothing but a reactive and resentful reversal of Eurocentric culturalism.

Today it is increasingly difficult to overlook the fact that the emanation model of modernity is both politically dubious and intellectually inadequate. This prevailing view of the West is no longer acceptable, not only because its material fabric is in the process of being raveled but also because we ought to refuse to view the relationships among many locations in the world according to the developmental teleology of historicism.

Global modernity has accelerated cultural, economic, and political interchange between different regions and brought different forms of power-knowledge into a more intense interaction. What once appeared exclusively European no longer belongs uniquely to the Euro-American world; an increasing number of instances are occurring in which non-Euro-American loci are more Western than some aspects of North American and European life. This diversification of the West allows us to discover something fundamentally Asian,

African, and (Latin) American in those people who fashion themselves as Westerners as well as to conceive of relations among people in many locations of the world in an order other than the racialized hierarchy of the Eurocentric worldview. After all, is the West one of the most effective and affective culturalist imaginaries today? Can one still recognize a West that is authentically specific to European heritage and that can be unambiguously distinguished from the rest of the world? Can we be serious enough to subscribe to the white supremacist rhetoric of "the love of Western civilization" even today? Racism being the institutionalized form of desire to naturalize and dehistoricize social relations and identities, the mytheme of the West cannot be cleansed of its racist implications as long as culturalism is the most prevalent means of naturalizing and essentializing a person's social status and a social group's identity.

The Transpacific Politics of Anthropological Difference

By now it is self-evident, I hope, that the insistence on the propriety and native authenticity of "us Asians" would only reinforce the discriminatory and distinctive uniqueness of the West and prevent us from dismantling the colonial relationship that underlies the identities of both the West and Asia. In this specific context, the putative unity of the West, the dominant and universalistic position, is sustained by the insistence on the equally putative unity of Asia, the subordinate and particularistic position.

To further illustrate this point, let me draw an example from the history of postwar Japan and refer to what many people in Northeast and Southeast Asia have called the Japanese war responsibility amnesia. As amply suggested in an article by Takashi Fujitani on Edwin O. Reischauer's September 1942 "Memorandum on Policy towards Japan" (the latter reproduced as appendix 1 in this volume), which Fujitani discovered at the National Archives, the Japanese national tradition and the unity of Japanese culture were clearly conceived of as instruments for an American occupation of Japan (Fujitani 2000, 137–146; 2001). As early as ten months after the Japanese attack on Pearl Harbor, Reischauer proposed using the Showa emperor as a puppet for the U.S. Occupation Administration after Japan's surrender. This memorandum is extremely informative in depicting the overall design of postwar U.S. policies toward Japan, including the endorsement of "the national body." In retrospect, we realize not only that Reischauer (1947, 1955) was consistent in his subsequent publications, such as *Japan Past and Present* and *Wanted: An Asian Policy*, but also that almost all of his proposals were implemented in U.S. policies toward Japan and East Asia after the war. This fact is most uncannily indicated by the marker "@ Harvard University" at the end of the memorandum, as if he had intimated the historical destiny and political significance of area studies on Japan and East Asia at Harvard University in the U.S. domination of Japan; Japanese studies there played the eerie role of go-between in international politics by later training and producing a future Japanese empress for the third generation of "the puppet."[13]

From the late 1940s onward, there gradually emerged a certain bilateral international complex of academic and journalistic activities and collective fantasies that worked powerfully to justify and legitimate the postwar emperor system along with U.S. policies toward Japan and East Asia. This bilateral international complex can be summarized as pertaining to a discursive formation, and I would like to call it "the discourse of the postwar emperor system." This discourse should encompass not merely governmental publications and policies about the emperor and his family, academic justification and study of the emperor system, information generated by journalism, or images and fantastic scenarios produced by cinema, radio, and television broadcasting, and mass print cultures, but also the practices of direct and indirect censorship in many different contexts and levels of various media. Clearly delineated within this discourse are the United States' stance in the subject position of the West and the Japanese stance in the subject position of Asia. In this respect, the discourse of the postwar emperor system is a subset of the discourse of the West and the Rest. Yet while the figure of Japan serves as a representative of Asia in this discourse, the viewpoints of people from other Asian countries—not only former Japanese colonies such as Korea and Taiwan, but also China and Southeast Asian countries that were occupied by Japanese troops during the Asia-Pacific War—are entirely excluded. What is called "the bilateral narcissism of the United States and Japan" is clearly one of the regularities of this discourse.[14] In its unity as a discursive formation, it is neither American nor Japanese since it is bilateral. Hence one can consider the following as all pertaining to the same discourse: academic articles by Japanese conservative ideologues such as Ishii Ryôsuke (石井 良介) and Watsuji Tetsurô (和辻 哲郎); the public policy memoranda and journalistic publications by American ideologues and technocrats such as Edwin O. Reischauer, John W. Hall, and Faubion Bowers; a great number of films that allegorically depict the international relationships between the United States and Japan and other regions of East Asia in gendered terms; censorship imposed on the publishing industry, national press, and school textbooks by Occupation Administration personnel and the Japanese Ministry of Education; and self-regulation voluntarily practiced by the Japanese as well as the U.S. mass media (although the targets of censorship are not necessarily of the same kind). Within the discourse of the postwar emperor system, which involved as actors and spokespeople not only the U.S. Occupation Administration staff and Japanese collaborators and nationalists but also U.S. experts on Japanese studies and Japanese academicians in social sciences and the humanities, there are a few important commands that the design of the new emperor system clearly delineated and that the participants of this discourse were expected to tacitly observe.

First, Emperor Hirohito should not be held accountable for any wartime actions because otherwise he would be useless as a puppet leader of Japan to be manipulated by the U.S. Occupation Administration in order to rule Japan under U.S. hegemony. Reischauer claimed that Hirohito should be just like Pu Yi of Manchu-kuo under Japanese colonial rule. But Hirohito had the potential to be much more effective than Pu Yi as a puppet since the mystification of the emperor had already been deliberately accomplished by the prewar Japanese state. In other words, the arrangement of domestic hegemony was much more systematically and coherently prepared for the successful performance of the puppet in Japan proper in the late 1940s and afterward than in Manchu-kuo in the 1930s.

Second, the Japanese people should not be deprived of their sense of national tradition and cultural uniqueness. As Watsuji argued consistently, they should achieve cohesion as a nation in terms of the organic wholeness of their national culture and the continuity of national history. This is where the two schools of culturalism, the Japanese ethnic nationalists and the U.S. national character studies scholars, found common ground despite their diametrically opposed orientations. The emperor's political usefulness lay in his aesthetic function of making Japanese people feel unified, giving them a sense of togetherness without any concrete content. There was no need to define the emperor as an embodiment of the national will or to seek the political function of the emperor in his ability to direct state policies (Watsuji 1962). Hence he should be deprived of all legislative, administrative, and judicial authority. The underlying axiom of this emperor system was tautological: the Japanese should feel unified because they were Japanese, and because they were born in Japan and raised Japanese, they should feel destined to be Japanese. Unlike the imperial nationalism of prewar Japan, the Japanese nationalism of the postwar period did not rely upon the rhetoric of multi-ethnic unity; its emperorism stopped any pretense of inclusiveness; the Japanese emperor was no longer a symbol of multi-ethnic integrity. Rather, Japanese nationalism was now openly and unreservedly ethnocentric.

Third, as Takashi Fujitani has asserted, during World War II, U.S. policy makers had to take racial problems into account as part of their ideological warfare in U.S. domestic as well as international politics (2000, 143). It is important to keep in mind that, well into the 1960s, many American area specialists believed they had to continue to fight their ideological battle.[15] As a devoted patriot of the United States, Reischauer was afraid that the historically infamous treatment of residents of non-European ancestry, anti-Asian immigration legislation, and especially the internment of U.S. residents of Japanese ancestry in concentration camps could well bolster support for the Japanese cause in East Asia.[16] He thus confirmed the anxiety widely shared by the mainstream population in the United States at the beginning of the Pacific War. As George Lipsitz illustrated, during World War II in the United States, "racial segregation in industry and in the army kept qualified fighters and factory workers from positions where they were sorely needed, while the racialized nature of the war in Asia threatened to open up old wounds on the home front" (Lipsitz 1998, 193). As if responding to the reality of racial segregation during the war, Reischauer argued, "[the] point I wish to make has to do with the inter-racial aspects of the conflict in Asia. Japan is attempting to make her war against the United Nations into a holy crusade of the yellow and brown peoples for freedom from the white race."[17] The Japanese attack on white Americanism and white supremacy could well invoke a universal sympathy with the Japanese justification for their policies in Asia and the Pacific. Therefore, he concluded that the United States must appear universalistic and open to all races in order to win the ideological war against Japan. Here it is worth remembering that, almost simultaneously, the ideologues of the Japanese Empire put forth exactly the same argument for racial and ethnic equality among the peoples under Japanese colonial rule. Here, too, let me note the truism that imperialism without universalism is a contradiction. To emphasize the empire's commitment to the universalistic and multiethnic principle, the Japanese government's condemnation of racist policies, and "the integration of ethnic groups according to the Imperial Way" (Murayama 1943), the ideologues of the Greater East Asia Co-prosperity Sphere repeatedly issued and regurgitated old statements and idioms. These included "Emperor's equal mercy to every subject without the slightest discrimination among different ethnic groups within the Empire" and "Every person who wishes to reside on a permanent basis in the territory of this new nation is equal and should be able to enjoy the right to be treated as equal, regardless of whether of Han, Manchu, Mongolian, Japanese, Korean or any other ethnicity" (Ito 1932). A number of publications, such as Shinmei Masamichi's (新明 正道) 『人種と社会』 (*Race and Society*) and Kôsaka Masaaki's (高坂 正顕) 『民族の哲学』 (*Philosophy of Nationality*), offered philosophical and social scientific critiques of racism and ethnic nationalism as part of the state's "ideological warfare" (「思想戦」) against Anglo-American colonialism, Soviet communism, and Chinese ethnic particularism (Shinmei 1940; Kôsaka 1942). (It is significant that Watsuji Tetsurô, who repeatedly made racist statements against Jews and Chinese, in spite of Japanese state policies against overt racism from the late 1920s until the defeat, produced the most lasting cultural nationalist justification of U.S. policy concerning the new emperor system.[18]) Yet it is obvious that the critique of racism was called for out of a number of political necessities: the Japanese government and the military had to compete with the United States, Britain, France, and other old colonial powers for popularity among peoples in Asia, and therefore it had to appeal to Asian peoples' abhorrence of Euro-American white supremacy. Due to the shortage of labor for industry and increasing casualties in the military, a large number of young people had to be recruited and drafted from the colonized population in Korea and Taiwan to serve in the Japanese military and industry. It is important to remember that, just as U.S. Secretary of War Henry L. Stimson was afraid of imagined black rebellions being instigated by the Japanese and the communists, Japanese leaders too were haunted by an anxiety over possible mutinies by the colonized.[19]

Just as Reischauer's patriotism was genuine in its careful consideration of how the American racist attitude would appear to the Asian gaze, the unequivocally racist aspect of U.S. nationalism was all the more evident in his overtures on the strategic need to disavow racism in the United States. This aspect of American imperial nationalism (as well as the Japanese version) is perhaps best captured by Takashi Fujitani's idiom "polite racism."[20] The disavowal of racism, without which transpacific hegemony cannot be established, was actually built into the United States' nationalism (also into Japan's, at least until the end of World War II), so that, even after the Asia-Pacific War, it continues to present itself as in the integrationist rhetoric of American nationalism. Regardless of how polite it may appear to be, however, it serves to preserve the racial hierarchy of American society. Depending upon contingent social conditions, its contrary tendency, "vulgar racism," rears up every now and then. Just as we have observed the rise of vulgar racism in the last few years, American social formations never seem to escape from repeated oscillations between polite and vulgar racisms.[21]

Reischauer's speculations were not about what policies and procedures were required to eliminate racial discrimination in the social reality of the United States of America; instead, he was devoted to strategic considerations for how to prevent Asians from perceiving Americans as outright racists. In short, what he was compelled to consider was how to make America appear nonracist. He could clearly see that the Japanese policy makers intended to take advantage of the racist orientation of American society, of which many intellectuals in Asia were fully cognizant. Being relatively familiar with Asian reactions to American racism, Reischauer did not fail to acknowledge that racism had become an undeniable variable in international diplomacy. Accordingly, he recommended that the U.S. administration ought to carefully consider how the American racist attitude would look to Asian peoples so as to effectively compete with Japan in the Pacific theater. Of course, it does not mean that either Reischauer or his Japanese counterparts were primarily concerned with the abolition of racial discrimination within their respective imperial nations. What they clearly shared was a recognition that the governmental acceptance of racism and ethnic nationalism was absolutely counterproductive to the management of global diplomacy and ideological warfare. They insisted, therefore, that their policies had to be cloaked under the aura of universalism, regardless of how unreal or contradictory such a universalism may have been in concrete historical situations. It must also be noted, however, that the antiracist rhetoric as such could eventually result in the removal of certain racist institutions. Even Reischauer's antiracist rhetoric cannot be treated merely as a case of false consciousness.

Finally, the consequent transformation of Japanese racism should not be overlooked. The installment of the new emperor system actually marked the end of the antiracist argument in Japan. It seems that the Occupation Administration deliberately censored not racist, but antiracist utterances and publications in postwar Japan since the denunciation of Anglo-American imperialism and Dutch colonialism was almost always premised on the general critique of white supremacy during the war. It is not surprising, therefore, that the administrative headquarters of the supreme commander for the Allied Powers would have been most afraid of antiracism being directed at their governance of the occupied territories in Northeast Asia. Apparently, such an oppression of the critique of racism was also a very convenient measure for the Japanese government that had to discard the population of its former colonies and the minority population inside Japan proper, such as the resident Koreans and Taiwanese.[22] The majority of the newly redefined Japanese nation did not object to the censorship of the critique of racism either. Since the atrocities committed by the Japanese during the war were very often racist in nature, the censorship could in fact help them overlook their own colonial guilt and war responsibility. Instead of prosecuting suspected war criminals for their racist violence, an international division of labor was established between the United States and Japan according to which the United States continued to be in charge of uniting various ethnic and racial groups under the banner of universalism while the Japanese gave up an active role in the business of such multiethnic integration. This is one reason why the followers of modernization theory persistently characterized Japanese society as particularistic while believing that American society was somewhat innately universalistic. In other words, the Japanese were supposed to be content with their naturalized status, passively internalizing the description given by outside observers, whereas the Americans would seek to transcend and transform the racial and ethnic particularities so as to create a new subjectivity within the premises of their imperial nationalism. This international division of political and intellectual labor was appropriated by both parties so readily that the American rhetoric of universalism has been supplemented by the Japanese rhetoric of particularism. As I have already hinted at in the discussion of national character studies and Japanese cultural nationalism, the pursuit of Japanese national character studies invoked its counterpart, Nihonjin-ron (日本人論 or the discourse of Japanese uniqueness), as if some miraculous channel of transference and countertransference had been built across the Pacific. It goes without saying that this transpacific division of intellectual labor conforms to the very tenets of anthropological difference.

Postwar Responsibility

The Meiji Constitution unambiguously defined the emperor as the supreme commander of the Japanese military forces, and in his name the Asia-Pacific War was fought and many atrocities committed. To redefine the status of the emperor as the symbol of the unity of the Japanese nation and its culture while overlooking his war accountability was to relieve the entire Japanese nation of that accountability, as many analysts have already noted.[23] Under the Meiji Constitution, all soldiers and bureaucrats were supposed to act under the command of their superiors, and those superiors would surely claim that they acted under the command of their superiors, and ultimately every important policy including the declaration of war was legislated and implemented as an order of their commander in chief, the emperor. Furthermore, an aesthetic apparatus of modern governmentality was powerfully at work: every subject was supposed to be under the gaze of the emperor, and his or her belonging to the totality of the nation was guaranteed by the individual's unmediated loyalty to the emperor. Since the Meiji Restoration, the integrity of the national community was symbolically defined by the singularity of the figure of the sovereign, the emperor, under whose imaginary gaze every subject was individualized as an infant under the emperor's care (天皇之赤子). Under the gaze of the emperor, every subject was equal and entitled to receive his love (一視同仁); through the symbolic figure of the emperor, every subject was integrated into the whole of the nation regardless of ethnic, religious, linguistic, or social class background (一視同仁四海兄弟).

In the transition to the postwar emperor system, I do not believe that this aesthetic apparatus of governmentality was dismantled. Stripped of its legislative, administrative, and judiciary capacities, the emperor system would continue to work as an extremely efficient aesthetic system of government. In the final analysis, this is why U.S. policy makers preferred the preservation of the emperor system to its abolishment. This is one of the reasons why they anticipated that, through the careful manipulation of the emperor, an effective and less apparently oppressive colonial rule could be established in Japan.

When Emperor Hirohito (the Showa emperor) was pardoned, how could one possibly prosecute his subjects, who at least in theory followed his command even in their brutality and inhumane acts? What the U.S. Occupation Administration sought instead was a few scapegoats, such as Tôjô Hideki (東条 英機) and a very small number of militarists, and no doubt Japanese conservatives and many wartime leaders wholeheartedly welcomed such a decision. From the viewpoint of the Occupation Administration, the International Military Tribunal for the Far East (the so-called Tokyo War Crimes Tribunal) was held as a public procedure to officially legitimate the exemption of the emperor and the overwhelming majority of the Japanese from further investigation into their war responsibility. The Tokyo War Crimes Tribunal was a complete failure in its historical significance because the prosecutors would not deal with the racist and sexist atrocities committed under colonial and imperialist policies in East Asia. In short, it did not pursue the possibilities inherent in the idea of crimes against humanity for fear that the accusation against the Japanese leadership for their crimes against humanity could easily boomerang back to the Showa emperor and the puppeteers who manipulated him backstage, namely the Allied Powers and in particular the United States.

Fifty years later, such a political settlement has produced a situation in which an increasing number of Japanese are shameless about Japanese imperialist maneuvers in Asia in the 1930s and early 1940s while they are blindly happy with the new U.S. strategic arrangement in East Asia.[24] It is true that a more overt anti-American rhetoric flourishes in Japan today among populist nationalists as well as those self-proclaimed realist nationalists who boast of their technocratic capacity for rationality in politics, but they can never take issue with postwar U.S. occupation policies that dispensed the Japanese from their war accountability and colonial guilt.[25]

The preservation of national history and of the putative unity of national culture was thus an exceedingly effective means of keeping the occupied population, first, under direct American rule and then indirectly complicit in U.S. hegemony. The most ironic and interesting aspect of the postwar relationship between the United States and Japan can perhaps be found in the fact that the United States effectively continued to dominate Japan by endowing the Japanese with a sense of Japanese tradition and with grounds for their own nationalism. It is through the apparent sense of national uniqueness and cultural distinctiveness that these people were subordinated to U.S. hegemony in Northeast Asia.

Even today, Japanese nationalists are incapable of confronting the complicity between their nationalism and American hegemony. As long as the Japanese were allowed to secure a sense of national cohesion in their cultural tradition and an organic unity of their culture, they would never be able to engage in serious negotiation with peoples in Northeast and Southeast Asia who were directly victimized by or related to the victims of Japanese imperial nationalism. These people may well be generous and forgiving to individual Japanese nationals but would never forget the past deeds of Japanese imperial nationalism.

However, despite such a complicity of postwar Japanese nationalism, which has insisted on its particularistic exclusionism, with the United States' imperial nationalism that has tried to appear universalistic, the anthropological difference between the West and the Rest has been rigorously pursued throughout the postwar period in Japanese cultural nationalism as well as in U.S. area studies on Japan. Furthermore, the rhetoric of Japanese culturalism has been predominantly obsessed with the image of Japanese distinctiveness, but such a rhetoric was only produced in contrast to some fantastic image of Western culture against the backdrop of the cartographic imaginary of the globe. The Japanese cultural identity was formed with a view to some imaginary observer positioned outside the organic whole of the Japanese nation. And this imaginary observer is habitually referred to as the West and often symbolizes the reign of Pax Americana.

"You Asians"

I do not think that the assessment I present here is limited to the case of Japan after its defeat in the Asia-Pacific War or World War II. This is just one instance in which the sense of ethnic and national identity is invoked in the foreground of the binary scheme of the West and the Rest. It might appear strange that the United States and Japan, the largest and second largest—now third largest—national economies of the world and two prominent imperial nations, still recognize each other in such a colonialist manner. But this instance only demonstrates how relentlessly the discourse of the West and the Rest persists and how captivating the lure of anthropological difference remains.

Given the aforementioned understanding of the West and its discriminatory constitution, how can "we" possibly address ourselves as Asians? What practice should we resort to in order to disrupt the apparatus of anthropological difference? The final question I would like to pose, then, is: how can we possibly prevent our self-referential address, "we Asians," from being caught in this binarism or from reproducing something like Japanese culturalism? I do not dare to say I am able to offer a perfect solution here. My response is a proposal at best, and it is brief, at the risk of oversimplification.

First, let me issue a warning disclaimer that neither the West nor Asia is a mere illusion that one can dispel by adjusting one's mental attitude. They are both social realities even if of an imaginary kind. However, if the distinction between the West and Asia is increasingly independent of geography, physiognomy, ethnic culture, or nationality but is instead a matter of cultural capital shaping the individual's socioeconomic status, one can be attentive to the biopolitical formation of the qualifications in terms of which the West and Asia are distinctively and performatively presented as well as to how people invest in the acquisition of such qualifications. In this respect, the West is a sort of "fictive ethnicity," to use Étienne Balibar's terminology.[26] In some social contexts, an increasing number of people fail to qualify either as Westerners or as Asians. We come across more and more instances that may appear to be oxymorons: a Chinese with superb taste in classical European music; a black American with upper-middle-class mannerisms; a poor white American whose faith is utterly incompatible with scientific rationality or Enlightenment secularism; an Indonesian preoccupied with Christian ethics; a European gentleman who is superhumanly meticulous and patient with his handwork in the fine details of his craftsmanship but absolutely hopeless in mathematical reasoning; and so forth. When examined carefully, none of these instances illustrates an inherent quality that determines the natural endowment of a person either as a Westerner or as an Asian. What makes such an instance appear as a cultural or civilizational oxymoron, and potentially as an excuse for social discrimination, is our prejudice, our pre-predictive judgment to be made in accordance with the anthropological difference of the West and Asia, or the West and the Rest. It is our prescribed investment in a certain distinction, in a justification for exclusion, and in our own positionality. It is probably impossible to rid ourselves of these prejudices altogether in one clean sweep. Yet we may be able to invent a number of strategies whereby to avoid reproducing such a discriminatory gesture. For, at any cost, we have to avoid shaping Asia as a mirror image of the West at its worst.

Instead of naturalizing the category of the Asian, of grounding Asian identity in some presumably immutable properties of a person or a group, we should treat it as a consequence of constantly changing socioeconomic conditions. We should call a person Asian whenever we find in that person some effect of social adversity or a trait of some quality that has been regarded as uncivilized, underdeveloped, or even barbaric from the Eurocentric perspective, regardless of his or her physiognomy, linguistic heritage, claimed ethnicity, or habitual characteristics. We should use the word "Asian" in such a way as to emphasize the fluidity of the very distinction between the West and Asia rather than its persistence. We must dislodge the index "Asia" from the dichotomous configuration of the West and the Rest.

Even though we would face an outright rejection in this action by those who fail to qualify as, but adamantly insist upon, being natively Westerners, we should seek occasions to call those who customarily fashion themselves as Westerners "you Asians." Asians must be a vocative for invitation. Asians are new barbarians. It is in order to break through the putative exclusiveness of our cultural, civilizational, and racial identity that we must address ourselves to others by saying "you Asians." As long as you are not afraid of admitting that you are free from the command of anthropological difference, you are fully qualified to be an Asian.

5. ADDRESSING THE MULTITUDE OF FOREIGNERS, ECHOING FOUCAULT

NAOKI SAKAI AND JON SOLOMON

Let us take the point of departure from a dialogue between Michel Foucault and Zen monks in Japan that highlights the problematic relation between anthropological and epistemological regions at the heart of Foucault's Occidentalism (Foucault 2001a, 618–624).[1] Launching a critical evaluation of the Occidentalism of an important thinker who has remained an inspiration throughout much of this volume, we are not concerned with delimiting his work within the fatigued framework of debates over Western theory and non-Western cultures. Quite the opposite; the critique of Occidentalism itself is a theoretical enterprise whose effects must always be seen in relation to the praxis of social relations and the politics of knowledge. This chapter mounts a critical intervention into the link between regionality and thought (specifically, the construction of respective Western and Eastern regions with their corresponding ways of thought) that constitutes Foucault's dialogic construction of "the West" and "Western thought" and the conjunctural formation of the two as "crisis."

On the occasion of his second trip to Japan in 1978, Foucault paid a visit to Seionji, where an ensuing brief dialogue between himself and several Japanese monks was recorded and published in two different versions, Japanese and French.[2] The main points of the dialogue have been excellently summarized in a penetrating—and ultimately disappointing—analysis by François Jullien, a philosopher and sinologue. Foucault's posture in the dialogue appears incredibly naive, and there is certainly a strong part of his positions—the conventionalized oppositions between East and West that orient his discourse—that would easily fall under a postcolonial critique today. The dialogue itself is painfully aware of this limit, as Foucault identifies Western thought with crisis and crisis specifically with the historicity of imperialism and its project of universalism.

Unfortunately, there is today, as far as we know, no extant version of this dialogue in its original form. Neither published version amounts to a simple transcription. We know that Foucault did not speak Japanese, and we assume that his interlocutors, monks, did not speak French. Presumably, the dialogue itself was conducted in both French and Japanese, alternately, with the aid of on-site, consecutive translation. In addition, it is highly probable that further refinements in the on-site translation were made in the process of transcription for the published version. In any case, both versions share what they erase: the practice of translation itself.

Jullien, commenting (significantly, also in the form of a dialogue) at length on Foucault's Zen dialogue, finds in it "everything . . . not only the confrontation, as fleeting as it may be, with a thought from outside, but also at the same time the areas of understanding and misunderstanding" (Jullien 2000, 17). Outside, failure, and everything: While Jullien's astute reading of the dialogue grasps its global significance beyond Foucault, accounting for what would be called, outside France, the postcolonial aspects of Foucault's Occidentalism, Jullien's "everything" implicitly includes, like Foucault, the crucial element of translation, yet misses its significance for the praxis of social relations.[3] Our task here is not to refute Jullien's reading, but rather to follow his lead, adopt the same posture, and tease out of the Foucauldian dialogue more of this elusive "everything"—in this case, the social praxis of translation, a point of departure that would ultimately necessitate a radical reformulation of both Foucault's Occidentalism and Jullien's corresponding "outside."

The dialogue counts a total of three instances in which translation is mentioned. These three instances cover what may be considered to be the multiplicity of translational practices and representations: the metaphorical, the spatio-communicational, and the practico-addressive. When Foucault speaks, at the close of the dialogue, of the way in which philosophy has always been "translated" into disastrous political programs, he appeals to a notion of "translation" as a generalized mode of transposition in relations across the social field. "Philosophy" is translated into "politics": translation names the process that would relate two discretely separate spheres or realms of experience. "Translation" in this sense becomes the metaphor of metaphor, the very principle of its own operation. Our question would be to know to what extent a certain determination of philosophy itself has been based on a particular metaphysics of translation as meta-metaphor. Is not metaphor itself a "metaphor" for translation? Before we even begin to answer these questions, let us at least observe that they will inevitably extend across different fields of both knowledge and social formation. In effect, we will be asked to attend to the intersections between, on the one hand, the role of national language and disciplinary specialization in the institutional formation of the modern, national-imperial university and, on the other hand, the division of the world into geopolitical units based on a supplementary relation between sovereignty and civilizational difference.

Leaving aside these more or less acquired Derridean considerations (Derrida 1990, 2004, particularly part II), let us return now to the beginning of the dialogue, where we once again find, in the second question posed by the monks to Foucault, the issue of translation: "I am told," says one monk, "that almost all of your works are translated into Japanese. Do you think that your thoughts are understood enough?" (Foucault 1999, 111; 2001a, 619). Foucault dodges the very terms of the question by repeating his well-known critique of authorial intention. In Foucault's response, we can also detect a nascent moment in which one reader of the French "original" and another of the Japanese "copy" both implicitly occupy the same position in relation to the socially produced meaning of the text. All readers, including the author, operate within the same scope of (de)legitimation, and the meaning of the text can only be the product of endless rereadings of readings among these variable positions. What both Foucault and his Japanese interlocutor seem to miss, however, is the potentiality that the Japanese translations may well in fact pose questions of understanding back to the "original" French text in a way that requires us to ask French readers exactly the same question. Indeed, we must call into question the assumption of immanence in the monk's query that implicitly links French readers to the French text. The fact that one can suture French language to French community does not in itself guarantee the success of communication. This radical exteriority of social relationships to the production of meaning is precisely that point to which we want to draw attention, in our ensuing discussion of translation, with the distinction between address and communication. Whereas "address" names a social relation (that between addresser and addressee) that is primarily practical and performative in nature, hence still to come, "communication" names the imaginary representation of that relation in terms of pronominal identities, informational content, and receptive destinations: who we are supposed to be and what we were supposed to mean. Theories of communication regularly obscure the fact of address in communication, whereupon they are derived from the assumption that supposedly we should be able to communicate among ourselves if "we" are a linguistic community. To confuse address with communication is thus a classic hallmark of what we call "the regime of homolingual address" (Sakai 1997b, 6).

The institution of homolingual address is a form of homosociality based on a model of community abstracted from the notion of communion or fusion, what Jean-Luc Nancy calls "immanentism" (Nancy 1991; Solomon 2003c), among its members.[4] What is precisely excluded from such homosociality is the fact of failure in communication, a failure that does not occur simply because of presumed gaps between linguistic communities but also because to try to communicate is to expose oneself to exteriority, to a certain exteriority that cannot be reduced to the externality of a referent to a signification (Sakai 1997b, 7).

Jullien's strategy in reading Foucault, which incidentally forms the introduction to his strategy for reading China through the notion of "outside thought," pivots upon a conception of "outside" that is essentially hermeneutic—and arguably quite different, in its idealist spatiality, from the meaning Foucault (1966a, 2003) first ascribed to that phrase. "Chinese" texts in their foreignness allow the insertion of a heterogeneous element into the constitution of "our" everyday, thus allowing "us" a critical distance upon "our" temporality and identity. Certainly, we would not want to underestimate the critical potential inherent in such moves. Nevertheless, at the same moment that hermeneutics reveals the historicity of our position, it can also be used to institute a certain economy that regulates the distribution of the foreign—typically through spatialized representations of separate linguistic spheres. Naturally, in order to delineate an outside and locate the foreign within the hermeneutic economy of the anticipated meaning against the horizon of prejudice and tradition, it is imperative to disqualify forms or instances that obscure or simply do not adhere to the boundary between inside and outside.[5] In order for the merger of horizons to take place, each horizon must be first sanitized of foreign contamination and homogenized so that the foreign may come only from without. In terms of linguistic activity, translation is precisely one such form to be disqualified, in both its formal and practical aspects, including notably the exceptional position of the translator, the plurality of language forms among the addressee(s), and the figure or regulative idea that substitutes for the impossibility of making the unity of language an object of experience. Forms of address that take such exteriority into account in the very formation of an impossible interiority are what we call heterolingual forms of address. The social relationships denoted by such forms do not add up to anything—they form what can be called a nonaggregate community. "In this respect, you are always confronted, so to speak, with foreigners in your enunciation when your attitude is that of the heterolingual address. Precisely because you wish to communicate with her, him, or them, so the first, and perhaps most fundamental, determination of your addressee, is that of the one who might not comprehend your language, that is, of the foreigner" (Sakai 1997b, 9). Clearly, the distinction between homolingual and heterolingual address thus goes far beyond the question of communication as raised by Foucault in terms of authorial intention. Indeed, our work on translation is designed to illustrate that translation names primarily a social relationship whose form permeates linguistic activity as a whole rather than simply constituting a secondary or exceptional situation.

In Jullien's case, it would be quite easy to show that the constitution of the outside is based instead upon the confusion and mobility enabled by the ambiguities inherent in the word "Chinese," which becomes a site of immanence that nevertheless transcendentally sutures an immense plethora of different enunciative positions, historical periods, and social identities. Ultimately, this transcendental suturing enables a notion that particular readers immanently embody the ideas of a certain corpus of texts on account of their putative linguistico-ethnic identity: in other words, the presupposition that Westerners understand Western texts in a primary, authentic manner—in short, better than non-Westerners. It may be worthwhile to point out, once again, that the most powerful historical form to date of this hermeneutic notion has certainly been found in the construction of an idealized Western readership that is posited as someone who identifies with a position continuous with "Western thought"; Western readership is supposedly capable of comprehending, from within the horizon of Western prejudice, the entirety of Western thought from Heraclitus to Eriugena, from Leibniz to James, down to Whitehead and Sartre. It is precisely the figure of Western readership that implicitly underlies the Japanese Zen monk's query about Foucault's work in translation. In a move that demonstrates the way in which this figure is always complicit, that is, co-figured, with another figure, Thierry Marchaisse, Jullien's interlocutor, poses exactly the same problem of immanently embodied transcendental understanding, with the terms simply reversed: "If there is one thing that Foucault effectively cannot do," asserts Marchaisse, "it is to understand Zen as it is understood by the monks around him." This statement formally is not any different from saying, "If there is one thing the Japanese readers of Foucault cannot do, it is to understand Foucault as the French (or the Westerners) do." Significantly, Marchaisse and the Japanese Zen monk do not ask whether the Zen monks, or the Westerners, themselves understand things in the same way among each other— much less how Zen or the Foucauldian text and the sets of heterogeneous practices within each attempt to manage such distinctions. Jullien, in order to explain this difference or more precisely, in order to capitalize upon this difference as an unassimilable supplement exterior to the expressions of our thought, exclaims, "That's the place where it all becomes Chinese" (2000, 26).

Hence, it is only the foreign outside "our" tradition that is incomprehensible. In fact, Jullien, before turning to Foucault, begins his dialogue with Marchaisse by theorizing his own personal experience of presenting Chinese philosophy to those for whom it is so unfamiliar that they can only understand it through misrecognition and ignorance. It is an experience of incomprehension so acute that, he says, "it is extremely difficult for me to *begin* to make myself heard" (Jullien 2000, 9, emphasis in original). Of course, "to begin to make [oneself] heard" is precisely the situation of address that inheres in or precedes—more precisely, we should say "ex-poses"—every instance of communication.[6] Yet Jullien's entire focus falls exclusively upon the communicational aspect of the situation, upon the effect of misrecognition that address produces upon his auditors (including, differentially, even himself). It is precisely at this point that the instantiation of "we" in address becomes a presupposed site of interior identity in communication. "Now, this is exactly one of the principal difficulties to which my work exposes me: when I try to present it, I do not *at the outset* 'meet' anyone, I have no designated partner" (Jullien 2000, 14, emphasis in original). In fact, Jullien's difficulty is itself an incredibly fecund clue: identity does not precede communication, but is rather abstracted from it after the instance of enunciation. The fact that there is no "designated partner" is in fact the essential situation of address, in each and every instance, since address does not require the presupposition of relation (codified through designation) to be effective. Yet according to the communicational model of encounter to which Jullien turns, this constitutive indecision is obscured through representations based on the mutual recognition of designated positions. From such a perspective, the situation of "no designated partner" becomes an obstacle. What is being obstructed? Certainly not the form of address itself. Obstruction, were there any, would occur only when the work of address becomes reified into a thing. Hence, the relation of address becomes identified with the interiority of a given position designated as Chinese. The spatialization of relationships and their codification through a given designation is a key feature of communicational representation. Needless to say, this or that designation in particular is not the only one possible; in the case of "Chinese," it is neither the only one that has been used in the past to describe some of the texts in question, and quite probably not the only one that will be invented by future social formations to come. However, when the given designation of positions is assumed, or represented, to be prior to the act of address in communication, the positions themselves become effectively identified with a thing that is supposed to be outside of the social relations that produce them rather than the social relations themselves—what Foucault calls, at the end of the Zen dialogue (in a moment referring to the new role assigned to intellectuals), "what is going on at the present" (2001a, 624). If to speak of knowledge at the exclusion of this relation were the only choice left to us, we would surely join Jullien in experiencing the enormous frustration brought upon us by the ineluctable division between "Chinese" and its outside. Yet Jullien's negative assessment of the actual situation he encounters in the situation of address should not prevent us from recognizing the immense opportunity that awaits us in the midst of his experience. Seen from the perspective of communication ex-posed in address rather than communication abstracted from address, the undesignated partner who might listen to me presents both of us (and others) with the moment at which social relations can occur—precisely because they remain open.

Sadly, the incredible opportunity that lies behind Jullien's frustrated hopes for a designated partner are buried beneath a mountain of specific difference between languages, nations, civilizations, traditions, and races. Predictably, both Jullien and Marchaisse repeatedly appeal to a certain "we" that is not only a relation in address but also a hermeneutic site of sedimented historical experience and the putative totality of a particular language. "We" thus have a long historical experience of encountering "them," whence "our" experience is immediately communicable among "us"; "their" experience, by contrast, requires translation. Neither Jullien nor Marchaisse problematize their own dialogue in terms of... dialogue—the potential failure of communication that inheres in every linguistic exchange. Hence, as Jullien remarks just shortly before the ineluctable moment when "it all turns into [incomprehensible] Chinese," dialogue becomes an "impossibility." This impossibility, however, is conveniently contained by "Chinese," thereby excluding it from "French." In this series of equivalencies and surprisingly monologic dialogues, Jullien and Marchaisse thus confuse the pronominal invocation "we" with a group of those who are inherently capable of communicating the same information with each other. Such communication is conceived of solely in terms of accurate repetition.

Now of course, Jullien's partner in dialogue, Marchaisse, does not speak or read Chinese, hence Jullien speaks to him also as a translator, a role to which he appeals shortly after this comment by highlighting the problems of "a dialogue that does not communicate" and leads to Zen "satori—which is ordinarily translated," Jullien reminds his auditor, "by 'illumination' ['Enlightenment']." It is impossible for us, in the context of a discussion about and inspired by Foucault—the thinker whose work was in large part devoted to redefining the meaning of the Enlightenment—not to dwell upon the possibilities inherent in this (mis)translation. Jullien, for his part, bypasses the opportunity and proceeds directly to the way in which practice, repetition, becomes a technique leading up to the realization of virtuosity. An integral part of Jullien's argument is that Chinese thought has always been concerned with a discontinuous process of "laborious maturation" and "instantaneous realization." Centuries before Zen appeared in China, the Mencius text had already charted out the essential ground later assumed by Zen. This historical narrative, which is not of Jullien's invention and to which the Japanese monk in dialogue with Foucault also refers ("It seems that most Chinese specialists believe that Zen Buddhism came from China rather than India"), is a typical object and product of culturalist hermeneutics: we all know the story according to which Zen is presented as an original sinification of Indian dhyana and in this way supposedly provides a model for an original and originary Chinese mimeticism—an impossibly contradictory formula—that will serve the cultural analytic of promoting particularity through mimetic reference to the universalism of the West. In this way, cultural interiority is posited as being anterior to the introduction of the foreign. In this limited space, we would simply like to draw attention to what this narrative structure excludes: that the conditions of possibility for identifying the subject of sinification may themselves be posterior to an essential hybridity.

Other points on which to argue with Jullien's position would similarly require far more elaboration than we can mount here, but they are certainly worth mentioning. Alternate interpretations of the texts and schools to which Jullien refers are possible. We note that Jullien's reading of Mencius is strikingly similar to the core concern of Cheng-Zhu Neo-Confucianism, which itself bears the inscription of a historically formulated response to Zen.[7] Needless to say, the practice of Zen itself may also include significant resources for undoing the opposition between "laborious maturation" and the pure form of "instantaneous realization." After all, Huineng's appearance (637–713) as Sixth Patriarch of the Zen lineage, his rejection of the gradualist Northern School, was aimed precisely at this distinction.

Inevitably, notions of labor as repetition bear within themselves implicit theories of language. The contrast drawn between Jullien and our own position explodes here into a full-fledged parting of the ways when we consider how the very same elements deployed by Jullien (repetition, labor, virtuosity, pure form, Neo-Confucianism, Zen, cultural difference, exteriority, materiality, and the constitution of national language) can be all present yet in a radically different configuration. Inversely, once we admit the extent to which disciplines of knowledge based on the unities of national language and national community intrinsically accord importance to translation—only to conceal it through naturalizing representations that effectively spatialize anterior systematicity—we may begin to see how the role of the translator has significant implications for a typical Foucauldian concern: the role of the intellectual in general. In Jullien's case, it is quite clear that his comments about the esoteric impenetrability of "Chinese" parallels the way in which he draws scrutiny upon the inadequacy of the conventional translation of "satori" as "illumination" in French—a word that carries connotations of "Enlightenment," much like the standard English translation of satori as "Enlightenment." Here we must remind ourselves that the positing of the untranslatable and the incommensurable is possible only retrospectively, after the enunciation of translation opens up a space of communication and commensurability. The practice of translation itself remains radically heterogeneous to the representation of translation. Such heterogeneity itself sprouts from the fact that the unity of language cannot be an object of experience in the Kantian sense. Yet Jullien's dialogue with Marchaisse consistently returns to the notion of a systematic unity that underlies and separates the respective Chinese and Western language worlds. Hence, the role of the sinologue-translator, as seen in Jullien's dialogue with Marchaisse, becomes that of an active agent in the regulation and distribution of the heterogeneous/foreign. In other words, what we are given to see is the way in which the transferential desire to see oneself from another's position is actually created after the process of translation. The positions themselves are not prior to the translational exchange, but are rather constructed out of it, in posterior fashion, by substituting the spatiality of representation for the temporality of praxis. Hence, the desire to recuperate the authentic meaning of satori, now corrupted by an inadequate translation entangled by "illumination," is inseparable from the desire for self-referentiality as a means of regulating the hybridity and heterogeneity that precedes delineations of self and other.

An alternate, genealogical approach to the undeniable inadequacy of translation might instead turn the surplus of "illumination," with its modern connotations of Enlightenment, back onto satori, and vice versa—not as a hermeneutic means of discovering who we have become through a process of laborious maturation, the creation of an accumulated historicity called "our tradition," but rather as the initial and perhaps instantaneous ex-posing of who we really have been becoming for quite some time under the migratory regimes unleashed and policed by capital. At this point in history, the political project of Enlightenment and the spiritual project of anatman or selflessness talk to each other, or remain silent, not in an abstract body of knowledge but in the concrete action of knowledgeable bodies.

Significantly, Foucault's otherwise platitudinous call for a "confrontation" between Eastern and Western thought, the means of overcoming the crisis presented by the end of imperialism, is focused on the figure of the philosopher. "This crisis has produced no supreme philosopher who excels in signifying that crisis.... There is no philosopher who marks out this period" (Foucault 1999, 113–114; 2001a, 622–623). If the crisis cannot be signified, the reason is certainly because the crisis concerns the very possibility of signification, as such, what Nancy identifies as the problem of "the sense of the world" in a historical age when "meaning," "world," and "being" can no longer be distinguished.[8] Foucault's interest here falls squarely on the future: "if philosophy of the future exists, it must be born outside of Europe or equally born in consequence of meetings and impacts between Europe and non-Europe" (Foucualt, 1999, 113–114; 2001a, 622–623). Foucault, like all of us, does not know what the future holds, yet he senses its topographic contours. But where would "outside Europe" be in an age when "Europe" is synonymous, as Foucault asserts, with the universal? Clues to this enigma can be pieced together by placing Foucault's interest in the ninth-century monk Rinzai (Linji in Chinese), whom he finds to be a "great Zen philosopher," alongside his experience of Zen. Significantly, Foucault remarks that Rinzai was "neither a translator nor a founder." Hence, we arrive at the third instance of translation mentioned in the Zen dialogue, the one we have called practico-addressive. In virtually the same breath, Foucault also cites the example of Rinzai to demonstrate that Zen itself is not wholly Japanese and, by implication, not wholly Chinese either. In other words, Rinzai, in Foucault's lexicon, stands as a figure for a philosopher who refuses the tasks of school building and of translation inasmuch as they both relate to the project of national construction. Are we not faced here, in a nutshell, with the entirety of anthropological difference since it entered the national-imperial university system with Hegel and Humboldt in the nineteenth century? Schools of philosophy in the modern period have invariably been typed as national schools; such constructions are intrinsically built upon a specific regime of translation—it is how "national language" comes to be recognized as such—that provides a metaphysical principle for positing an organic alliance between a particular school or style of thought and a specific geographically defined community.[9] Significantly, after Foucault advances his admiration for Rinzai as a radical philosopher, he immediately retreats, as a show of deference to his interlocutor, back to the default position of national institutions of translation: "I read the French translation by Professor Demiéville, who is an excellent French specialist on Buddhism"—French translations and French specialists, to which we must also add French philosophers, the universalism of which (and critiques thereof) relies upon a division of labor thoroughly supervised by the regime of homolingual translation. It is in response to this remark that one of the Japanese monks facing Foucault advances the thesis, held by "Chinese specialists," that Zen is thoroughly Chinese. With this exchange, the suturing of enunciative positions and communicational totalities is complete, thereby erasing the moment of address. This moment is emblematic of the entire modern regime of translation spanning the difference between colonial and imperial modernities. What is lost is the fact that the generality of address itself, the very capability of address as such, precedes the assignation of enunciative positions. Perhaps this is the reason why Rinzai is especially well known, within the Zen school, for his practice of striking the befuddled student: striking is to aiming as communication is to address. For "addressing does not guarantee the message's arrival at the destination. Thus, 'we' as a pronominal invocation in address designates a relation, which is performative in nature, independent of whether or not 'we' actually communicate the same information" (Sakai 1997b, 4–5).

In the figure of Demiéville, the French specialist of Oriental thought, we have the typical sort of body favored by the modern disciplines of the human sciences: this is the body of knowledge, a system of regularized dispersion, precisely the sort of power-knowledge configuration at which Foucault aimed. The study of these figures and their historicity is precisely what Gilles Deleuze and Félix Guattari call "noology"—the way in which the "image" or figure of the body of knowledge, as an instance of the state-form in thought, is marked by a historical transition from the philosopher to the sociologist (1980, 466; 1987, 376).[10] We are interested here in the way these figures are in fact featured with other figures, with the way the idealized Western reader is paired with the area studies specialist, and distributed spatially. It is well known that knowledge in the human sciences has been deeply intertwined with national sovereignty and language in the modern period. Just as social divisions created by uneven global development have been encoded in very specific and profound ways into the structure of knowledge, in terms of disciplinary divisions as well as in terms of the legitimate objects, methods, and theses that compose each discipline, so the meanings of these divisions have been further refracted by the crystallization of nationalized language that has governed the production, dissemination, and reception of knowledge—indeed, the very criteria of truth—in the age of the single world. In short, the human sciences as they have developed bear within them—structurally, ideologically, linguistically, and philosophically—the pre-suppositions of "world history" configured through both sovereignty and co-lonialism (Solomon 2004a).

BY NOW IT IS clear why we had to take our point of departure from an an-alytic of Foucault's Occidentalism. Not only Foucault himself but also Zen monks and an area specialist commentator, François Jullien, all operate in the regime of cofiguration that inevitably erases the moments of social rela-tion and construes the dialogue exclusively in communication between fixed subject positions ordered by the homolingual address and localized by spatial representation. Supposedly most sensitive to the perils of reified self-hood, the participants of this dialogue nonetheless are content to fashion themselves as national and civilizational subjects. In accordance with their retrospectively constituted identities, they produce a neat configuration of power-knowledge, according to which the West and the Rest, France and Japan, and white and nonwhite appear to continue to map the world and the disciplinary classifica-tion of knowledge (Solomon 2003b).

The metaphysics of translation evinced in Foucault's Zen dialogue by the figure of the area studies specialist marries geopolitical regions of the globe to disciplinary divisions in the construction of knowledge. Our name for this joint matrix, the recursive admixtures of world and thought, is the amphibo-logical region, a name inspired by François Laruelle's nonphilosophy.[11] Typical modernist formulations such as German Romanticism, Chinese Confucian-ism, and American pragmatism would all be examples of the amphibological region, as would the personalities populating it, such as French specialists of Oriental works (or, quite simply, French specialists of French works in a world system organized around geopolitical divisions of work). In Foucault's Zen dialogue, the amphibological region is at all times present, no moment being clearer than at the closing section of the interview in which Foucault describes Europe both as a definite geographical region and as a universal category of thought through which categories themselves appear. As such, the amphibo-logical region corresponds exactly to what Foucault, in *The Order of Things* (*Les mots et les choses*), calls the "transcendental-empirico doublet" that character-izes the emergence of man as both subject and object of (self-)knowledge in the modern period. The amphibological region is, thus, precisely the quintessen-tial biopolitical habitat corresponding to Foucault's modern man.[12]

The philosopher who is neither a school builder nor a translator is thus the "philosopher"—if that term is still appropriate—who is no longer concerned with regulating the heterogeneity of world and text through the regime of homolingual translation. In the Zen dialogue, Foucault finds a hint of this precisely in the experience of Zen, which is for him, in this instance, largely concerned with a new set of relationships concerning the body, or again, the body as an ex-posed site of relationship. Jullien, a reader whose compelling attentiveness is matched only by a propensity to squander the transformative opportunities that lie therein, seizes upon the ineluctable meaning of this experience, particularly as Foucault's account of it stimulates only a response of silence from Zen monk Omori. Yet the depth of Jullien's observations fall short of calling our attention to the potential significance of Foucault's inscription of the body as an alternative to "philosophy" understood as schools of national translation.[13]

Let us echo Foucault's concern for a philosophy of the future, which we might as well call "the dislocation of the West," by outlining a project that aims to develop a comprehensive theory of translation that would simultaneously address both: (a) a notion of democratic translational practice that replaces the sovereignty of "bodies of knowledge" (typically codified as different regions/ nations of the world and their corresponding area studies) with the sociality of "knowledgeable bodies"; and (b) a corresponding reorganization of the human sciences based upon a democratic notion of humanity as a transcendental multitude of foreigners-without-the-foreign.[14] Here, it is important to note, we are advocating neither the rise or decline of the West nor the universalization or provincialization of it; neither does our project amount to the disowning of heritage from the past. At the demise of the regime of national translation and under the heterolingual address, it would be very obvious that the West cannot be referred to even in the trope of an organic unity that grows or languishes. Ours is to dislodge the West from the racist logic of homosociality and relocate identity in a nonrelational form (Me and the Foreigner are identical in the last instance) that would enable the immense diversity of minor politics and syncretic knowledge. Yet our task of the dislocation of the West is not easy at all.

INSTEAD OF "TRANSLATION, BIOPOLITICS, Colonial Difference," we might as well have titled our introduction to the 2006 special issue of *Traces* from which this chapter is drawn "States of Complicity." It will come as no surprise to many that we associate the theme of complicity first and foremost with the role played by the nation-states in their world system as it has been developing over the past four centuries (Solomon 2004b). While the rise of contemporary technologies of "securidentity" certainly trace their roots to techniques of government advanced by the metropolitan imperial nations—what Foucault calls "governmentality"—there is great need to reread that history, like the history of liberalism itself, through the experience of the populations in the colonies. In this respect, we cannot afford to continue to indulge ourselves in Occidentalism. Just as the canonization of English literature as a colonial measure in British India was imported back into England in order to mask an ideology of class, the roots of governmentality will, we can expect, one day be found to lie in the exceptional practices of colonial administration (vis-à-vis the normative position accorded to civil society within the framework of imperialism).[15] The United States of America has undoubtedly embarked on a course that can only further aggravate this history. The unilateral violence of U.S. imperial nationalism is certainly a grave threat to people around the globe (including, of course, people in the United States), yet we would deny ourselves the chance of finding a real identity for the multitude of foreigners if we let the explosions of U.S. unilateralism blind us to noticing how the nation-states together codify a profound form of unilateral power (now exemplified by the apparatus of securidentity) across the social field. The unilateralism inherent in governmentality as such, only apparently less urgent than that currently exercised by the United States, cannot simply be described through the model of coercion, unless we redefine "coercion" to include the competition instituted by the world-systemic form itself. Indeed, the entire problem of governmentality begins, for Foucault, in the liberal critique of state intervention.[16] Behind the humanist faces of national independence, self-determination, resistance to cultural homogenization, rights, and law, we must see how the nation-state itself is intrinsically designed as a transcendental form of quasi-permanent unilateralism in which all nation-states are complicit. From this perspective, the challenge ahead of us is to bring the issue of coercion back into a broader analytic that tries to explain why such institutions and states of domination are such an attractive place for foreigners in the first place.

The global analytic of complicity we propose does not mean that we close our eyes to the actual and highly fluid differences of power between the obviously unequal nation-states and the various populations circuiting through them (Sakai 2003). This is the Foucauldian perspective of biopolitics, which distinguishes states of domination and the techniques of government that institutionalize and sustain those states from the ebb and flow of power and play in everyday life that Foucault calls strategic relations. The imperative to national subjective formation, the imperative to form a majoritarian project, to appropriate the minority positions in a state of domination sustained by the communicational techniques of a unitary "voice of the people" and an authoritative "body of knowledge"—this sort of unilateralism has proven to be far more durable than the national social projects of any single nation.

In order to understand why democratic nations repeatedly move, in a relatively short space of time, in and out of quasi-fascistic political formations, we need to start accounting for the recursive circuits cycling between three very different series, or subsets, of the problem. The divisions are well known; let us simply summarize them here. First, of course, there is the structural or national series (gender difference, labor difference, and linguistico-ethnic difference); then the systemic series (sovereignty, the West and the Rest, and empire); and finally the political economy series (labor, value, and time). The fascinating debates now raging within the fields of sociology and international relations over the role played by the United States in the current conjuncture generally advance their arguments—a kind of moral posturing—by opening up the contingency of elements in one series only to reify elements in another series. They cannot adequately deal—that is, in relational fashion—with the fluidity of and between the basic categories such as gender, class, ethnicity, race, geographic region, and civilization. This kind of disciplinary short-circuiting is not only a good sign that entirely new categories of analysis aiming at multiple levels are needed; it also serves as an important clue to understanding how fascist formations, be they colonial or imperial, repeatedly arise. Between the three major subsets of the political problem that creates the conditions for fascism lies a hidden, recursive circuit.

In spite of the attention given to the innumerable forms of hybridity and difference that preexist the contemporary circuits of migration, exchange, and cooperative networking, we continue to see a majoritarian consolidation of culture as a kind of fossilized artifact. Needless to say, nationalization is not just a process of "reduction" (as it was termed by the nineteenth-century Spanish colonial administration in the Philippines) conducted upon disparate elements of territory, market, and ethnicity; it also retroactively creates knowledge, bodies, and life. The archive, the language, the culture, and the history—in short, the modern fetishization of "communicable experience"—are as much sites of primitive accumulation for the construction of majoritarian subjects of domination as are the modes of production and labor for capital. Would the usage of terms such as "accumulation" and "exchange" thus suggest their meaning be extended to a metaphorical, or perhaps even literary, sense? Evidently not. The benefits of such accumulation (what Jason Read [2003] calls "the real subsumption of subjectivity by Capital") exclusively accrue to actual, authoritative bodies of knowledge. These bodies are the ones that speak the unitary language. Such authoritative bodies could be either people or institutions; in either case, they are the forms of relation regularized according to the apparently natural boundaries of the individual and its corollary, the collective. So much has already been written about the process of extreme abstraction required to sustain the premise of the individual that one might think it unnecessary to repeat it here: the real site of metaphorical excess, when it comes to the authoritative body, is actually to be found in abstractions such as the individual speaking subject and the nationalization of the speaker's language.

Nothing sustains and typifies the transcendental representations managed by these authorities, these majoritarian bodies of knowledge, more than the tandem notions of the West as a normative value and of modernity as an unfinished project. Taken together, these two axes form a grid of global proportions along which the microgradient of majority/minority relations is continually plotted. Undoubtedly, herein lies the key to a minoritarian analytic and a new interdisciplinary syncretism on a global scale. But can we really assume the consistency and indexical veracity of the map onto which such positions are plotted?

We all know the story of anti-Eurocentrism, according to which the minoritarian critique of Western hegemony in the context of the (post)colonial nation sustains the critical shock to the Western majority formation. By transposing it into a local register, the critique of Eurocentrism becomes a good rhetoric for the elite, whose subjectivity is partly formed in their systemic competition with the West through the structural (class) accumulation of value by the labor of their social inferiors. Similarly, the majoritarian dispensation of respect for minoritarian difference short-circuits the possibility of recoding relations on a completely different terrain. The dialectical form of this relation is well known: apparently free, the position coded "Master" suffers from its actual bondage to the labor of the Slave; the position coded "Slave," however, dreams of nothing if not the chance of assuming, finally for itself, the magisterial height of the Master—without realizing that the Master position is always already deprived from the very outset of the possibility of being simply for itself. Certainly the first step out of this aporia is to admit that the very split between the two distinct forms of modernity—the imperial modernity and the colonial modernity—is itself the very definition of something like modernity in general in the constitution of the hierarchical, nondemocratic world of capital. Even in their very opposition, both the colonial modernity and the imperial modernity are bound to a common index, the normative value of the West, the supposed naturalness of which obfuscates a state of domination. This sleight of hand is accomplished, as always, by the form of an exception. Indeed, as deconstruction has never tired of showing, the dialectical subject of history excepts itself from history (without taking exception to history), thereby eliding the continual presence, or trace, of third-term exteriorities (supplements, exclusions, and displacements).

It is precisely because we look at what we are calling, in an inevitable moment of pure jargon, traces or exteriorities that we avoid falling into the either/ or formalisms of signifying chains and political economy. Instead, we want to draw links between exteriority in the sense described above and the notion of externality utilized by economists. "Externality" names any situation in which the action of two parties (be they friends or enemies) to an exchange (verbal, economic, military, etc.) affects, either positively or negatively, a third party not directly participating in the exchange of the other two. Clearly, this notion of externality could also be applied to the position of the translator as it has been described in the modern, homosocial regime of translation. In the intercourse between nation-states, we will want to know who are the third parties affected by their complicity. Will these third parties be easily recognizable in the same way as the talking subjects and juridical persons taken to be constitutive of the nation? Evidently, the answer is negative. Just as the border between two physically adjacent countries does not in itself form a positive space but is the negative condition for the creation of the national interiorities on both sides of the line, we would expect that these third parties would also be found in the silent, stuttering, and/or interrupted interstices between the talking subjects and authoritative bodies typically supported by the nation-states.

The attempt to regularize the status of these interstitial spaces, even when propelled by good intentions, inevitably has profound implications across the social field—including, of course, the talking subjects provisionally sustained by the nation-state. It is a truism to say that we are living in a time when the previous forms of exteriority and externality are in crisis or have collapsed completely while new forms proliferate. The development of the systemic integration now culminating in globalization is one of the most visible effects of this massive reorganization of exteriority. With the implosion of unexplored space, the extension of the comity of nations across the face of the globe, the supplement of exteriority known as civilizational difference (the economy of spatialized lawlessness that defined the West by separating its competitive rule of law from a non-West available for lawless, infinite violence) has reached a point of crisis. Elements associated with Western modernity can now be found in places that have conventionally been excluded from the West—often in forms that are more authentic than what is found in the West itself. At the moment when the global expansion of the two universal forms of capitalism—the commodity and the nation-state—is finally complete, such civilizational distinctions appear, historically for the first time, as what they essentially are: void of any specific content and thus absolutely ideological. No longer is there any ground whatsoever to substantiate the distinction between the West and the Rest. Or, to put it differently, it is no longer possible to continue to disavow that the West is floating and dispersing (with the tides of domination); but it is equally important to note that the West is not declining. Hence, our project of the dislocation of the West. No wonder we have seen, in the supposed age of the decline of sovereignty, a call by right-wing thinkers to reinstitute the axis of civilizational difference at the heart of global security management. Since the sovereign nation-state system was initially developed with the Treaty of West-phalia (1648), at the inaugural period of the imperial-colonial era when the world was divided into two realms, one governed by international laws (the West) and one exposed to the discretion of colonial powers (the Rest), it is no wonder that a breakdown in the apparatus of sovereignty would produce shock waves in the lines of civilizational difference and vice versa.[17] Civilizational difference has from the outset performed the role of a necessary supplement required by sovereignty's impossible quotient of interior consistency.

It is crucial to understand that the apparatus of sovereignty does not initially concern the national space, which is primarily structured by the markers of social distinctions such as class, but concerns first and foremost the international space of a world system. Hence, the relative erosion of sovereignty seen in the transnational flows of global cities does not indicate that the system of sovereignty has diminished; it has simply mutated. It is for this reason that the sovereignty of the nation-state seeks its legitimacy in the discrete imposition of exclusionary rules upon migrants entering its territory and into xenophobia.

We are witness to an age when the toxic waste of sovereignty's implosion is leaching into the very ground on which sovereignty was supposedly constructed—the idea of the nation as a form of organic life. Even as the transnational flows of capital erode the juridico-institutional form of the nation-state, it continues to be progressively consolidated at a biopolitical level.[18] The nation-state has become a complex form of life-support system. While it positively manages the life of the population concerned, it also simultaneously exercises fundamental constraints upon the bodies passing through it, inciting some theorists to ask whether the modern nation-state (and sovereignty) ought not to be understood in relation to the political experience of the camp (Chao 2001; Gang 2005). Needless to say, these life-support systems serve to manage labor—the one commodity that capital, until now, has been unable to produce—yet in so doing, they also engender the formation of specific kinds of subjectivity.

In order to understand this change, we will have to chart out the new itineraries and new forms of exteriority being posited today, against which life is supposed to be a natural given. The title of our introduction to the 2006 special issue of *Traces*, "Translation, Biopolitics, Colonial Difference," which joins the reason of state (sovereignty) to the state of police, is an ambiguous formula that describes the oscillating form of biopower deployed by the modern nation-state. In a series of public lectures in the late 1970s on the birth of biopolitics, Foucault distinguishes the biopolitical problematic that emerges in the eighteenth century from the problems of government in the preceding period. The term "sovereign police," first coined by Giorgio Agamben, an astute philosopher of biopolitics, is of course a combination joining the two forms of state reason that preceded the biopolitical project. As a form of juridical discourse on legitimacy, sovereignty was originally theorized as a form of external limitation upon the power of the monarch. As the obverse complement to this external power, the state deployed a police authority that was naturally external to the people who were its object. In both instances, the composition of state power was conceived or enabled through the application of limitations that were extrinsic by design. With the advent of modern theories of political economy in the context of liberalism, however, a new series of objects and techniques were enabled, the aim of which was to render the principle of governance completely intrinsic and self-contained. This intrinsic principle was that of a maximal-minimal quotient of efficiency (or intensity) extending, eventually, far beyond the classical concerns of labor and capital to include all aspects of the social and private body. It displaced the previous forms of sovereign law and police state without, however, eliminating them.

Even as liberalism's seemingly inexorable expansion has freed more and more spaces from subservience to sovereign power, the productive power of life itself has become more and more the focus of governmental activity such that the forms of sovereignty and police can now be found in a micropolitics of life. Foucault implicitly warns against optimism (induced, for instance, by the transformation of sovereignty) when he speaks of an "indispensable hypoderm" complementing the face of power. Foucault is certainly not calling for a metaphysics of the deep, of underlying essence here. The entire style he developed, first archaeological and then genealogical, was motivated, as he continually emphasized, not by an interest in "the way things were," but rather out of concern for "our immediate and concrete actuality" (Foucault 2004a, 25; 2008, 22). In other words, Foucault was interested in how the praxis of knowing creates not objects of knowledge, but new subjectivities (which might not be simply subjects of knowledge).

Although "the life" is supposed to be given as an inalienable right at an absolute remove from the purchase of sovereign power, it paradoxically has become invested with sovereign forms. Today, nationalized forms of life (notably culture and language) are still proposed as the "hypoderm" of which Foucault spoke, a substratum or accumulation that supposedly underlies or undergirds the massive variations in the actual forms of life disclosed by the globalization of capital. What if the hypoderm were not the internal wellspring of national culture, but rather the effect of capital's increasing penetration? In marked contrast to the great triptych of contemporary social analysis—gender, race, and class—culture and language are completely occult in their hypodermic status. Nothing exemplifies this situation better than the global index of whiteness today. Formerly one of the world's most highly mobile, diasporic populations, the white population around the globe today has entered a period of amazing fixity on the one hand and of fluidity on the other: a period of fixity in which white bodies are regarded as the most stationary and least capable of transforming themselves; it is, however, also a period of fluidity in which whiteness constantly shifts and transforms depending on the conditions of the social formation. But, precisely because of this apparent fluidity, the obsessive insistence upon whiteness and the efforts to naturalize it have never been more prevalent than today, and whiteness is more frequently than before fantasized by the white themselves as immobile fixity—much like that formerly ascribed, by white colonists, to the Indigenous. Is this not what the current notion of homeland security aims for? Yet how can one not see such native preserves as a kind of biopolitical camp into which precarious labor herds itself in the meager hopes of survival?

In order to bring what may be the most compelling and ubiquitous forms of nationalization left today—those concerning life—into the realm of a creative minoritarian resistance that does not aim to take power through civil war or balance power through sovereign complicity, but rather aims for an entirely different form of social organization, we need to begin by charting out the ways in which forms such as culture and language typical of nationalized life have been formed in the crucible that joins the commodity to the national subject. Communication surely is the ideology of capital, but this alliance of commodification and subjectivation rests on a biopolitics. Even as life stripped of any qualifications other than existence has become the paramount, universal form of the humanitarian rejection of violence, it paradoxically continues to function as a strategic, necessary tool in the unlimited extension of that violent power. Through the category of life, the sovereign police try to manage, now quite violently, a series of strategic externalities that amount, finally, to the institution of a highly mobile gradient of majoritarian authority all around the globe. This majoritarian authority should undoubtedly be called "the West." Yet in the familiar series of equal signs that describe its tautological movement (e.g., white = male = Christian = European language = white, etc.), the meaning of "the West" in all historical specificity must be measured against an actual constitutive process that reveals it to be, time and again, so highly arbitrary that it is in fact actually void of any specific content. This is why there is no hope for finding any ground to substantiate the difference of the West and the Rest. The only thing it really names, in the end, is what might be called, paraphrasing Hegel, the bad infinity (of a relation ill conceived).

Global complicity is obviously, thus, first and foremost, a form of bad cooperation, a form through which capital appropriates the very solidarities and networks that determine its madly rational mutations. For this very reason, it is incumbent upon us to stress, from the outset, that we are not the least bit interested in an analytic of complicity that could be used, in the style of a political correctness inquisition, to absolve our friends and damn our enemies. Quite the opposite; what we are aiming to problematize here are the specific forms of exteriority and externality inhabiting the widest possible variety of subjective practices. Ultimately, the minoritarian analytic is not at all concerned with codifications and classifications in the order of knowledge. Although these are necessary, and cannot be compromised, their sole purpose is in the constitution of new human subjects.

Far too many of the figures proffered today to populations around the globe as the objects of collective dream and desire—or simply as the form of recognition that has become a prerequisite to such dreams—are nothing but rehashed versions of yesterday's imperial identities, many of which exist only as the spectral others of modernity (i.e., the premodern). This is the form of subjectivity that is really but a state of domination rather than an active participation in the guidance and development of strategic relations. If contemporary sociology thinks of nothing but an analytic of risk, this is surely the indication, as Maurizio Lazzarato points out, of a massive inability to conceive of invention at the level of the subject.[19] It is only when the possibility of creating something new as a form of becoming has been denied (or has been itself absorbed into a predetermined set of targets or destinations) that the question of agency becomes reduced to a calculus of loss and gain. Needless to say, the very notion of a society of risk thus formulated would necessarily be unable to avoid complete penetration by the apparatus of governmentality.

We originally proposed the idea of bringing translation squarely into a politically informed discussion about the production of social relations in much the same way that labor has occupied a central place for theorists since Hegel and Marx. The modern regime of translation is a concrete form of "systemic complicity." In other words, it is a globally applicable technique of domination aimed at managing social relationships by forcing them to pass through circuits on the systemic level (such as national sovereignty). In our research on the transnational discursive structure of both Japanese studies and the institution of the Japanese emperor system, or again in the relation between imperial nationalism and the maintenance of ethnic minorities, we were persuaded that the geography of national sovereignty and civilizational difference indicates an important kind of subjective technology or governmental technique that has, until recently, been thoroughly naturalized by an anthropological discourse of culture.[20] It is only today that we can begin to see how a multiplicity of disciplinary arrangements forming an economy of translation (in place since the colonial era but far outliving colonialism's demise) actually produces differentially coded subjects, typically national ones, whose constitution is interdependent and, at specific intervals, actually complicit in a single, yet extremely hierarchical, state of domination. Our aim was thus to trace a series of genealogies within which translation is no longer seen as simply an operation of transfer, relay, and equivalency, but rather assumes a vital historical role akin to that played by labor in the constitution of the social.

Like labor, language is a potentially totalizing category that concerns not just a specific activity, but a form of social praxis that produces, or at least binds, the production of the world and the self. Like labor, language could easily be seen as something that is not the exclusive purchase of the individual, but an essential part of humanity in general (without which any notion of humanity in general would necessarily presuppose a sort of global final solution leading up to the last man). Finally, like labor, language appears to call into question the meaning of repetition and singularity.

Our research into the position of the translator within the modern regime of co-figured, nationalized language shows a precise parallel to the logic of sovereignty itself. Just as Agamben has shown how the logic of sovereignty is based on the form of exception (embodied by the figure of the sovereign), the position of the translator has been represented in a similarly exceptional fashion. Our work has turned this relationship inside out, demonstrating that the regularity of the national language as a formation in which the (hybrid) position of the translator has been deemed irrelevant is in fact produced only after the subjective encounter of social difference in translation (or in any social situation in which communication might fail). By proposing to look at the formation of national language through the exceptional position of the translator, we have been able to show that it is indeed a systemic, or transnational, technique of domination. This discovery parallels the growing awareness, largely advanced by Yann Moulier Boutang (1998), of the crucial role in capitalist expansion played by the various forms of slave labor rather than the regularized forms of wage labor. Hence, our proposal to displace the state of domination managed by the dual normalizing technologies of wage labor and nationalized speaking subjects with the inventive subjectivities seen in the exodus from wage labor and national language.

The similarities between the logic of slave labor upon which wage labor secretly rests and the regime of translation upon which national language is secretly built are profound. In both instances, the action of a subject (translation or labor) expresses itself in an object (the work) that is thought to define the generic form of human activity itself. As such, both have potentially political implications yet are most often associated with the pure economy of exchange. How we propose to look at this exchange, of course, determines the space we accord to individual autonomy and agency. Yet, according to an all-too-familiar reification, the creative potential of human activity is admitted in the constructivist account of social formation only to be turned into an objectivized thing, a series of institutions or objective realities that recursively constrain the way subjects actually work, limiting the power of invention to specific disciplinary rules. Just as the Marxian critique of the commodity fetish proposed to remind us that the fruits of labor, now reified, actually bear within them the trace of a social relation (and hence the possibility of creative transformation), we advance the thesis that translation can also be understood as a form of social relation requiring similar critique. In effect, translation appears to us as the social relation from which the critique of communication as the ideology of capital is most directly linked to a politics of life or, again, the politics in which life becomes invested by capital.

6. THE LOSS OF EMPIRE AND INWARD-LOOKING SOCIETY

Part 1: Area Studies and Transpacific Complicity

Every so often in the last two decades or so, I have wondered about what sort of future the end of Pax Americana—global peace under the hegemony of the United States—will bring to peoples in East Asia. What political possibilities will peoples there be allowed to pursue when the political, economic, and military restrictions imposed on them by the global dominance of the United States of America are loosened? It goes without saying that, by the end of Pax Americana, I do not suggest some fantastic scenario such as a swift disappearance of American military bases in Okinawa, South Korea, Japan, and elsewhere in East Asia or the replacement within a few years of the U.S. Pacific Seventh Fleet by Chinese naval forces in the protection of maritime trade routes in the Western Pacific. Such scenarios are unlikely, since, realistically speaking, one can neither predict the emergence of a superpower equivalent to the United States of the late twentieth century nor the continuation of the age of imperial nationalism, a nationalism characterized by extraterritorial domination by such countries as Britain, France, Japan, and then the United States in the first half of the twentieth century.[1] With the demise of Pax Americana, a new iteration of imperialism may well be emerging, but it will no longer be sustained by the territorial national sovereignty of a nation-state (cf. Sakai 2007, 2008; Sakai and Yoo 2012, 279–322).

By Pax Americana, I mean to suggest a set of historical conditions under which the domestic politics and economy in each of the U.S. satellite states in East Asia have been restrained as well as promoted; the international relations within which these states subordinate to the American empire—Japan, Taiwan,

South Korea, the Philippines, and so forth—have consolidated their foreign policies and American military bases in each territory under the protocols of a U.S.-centered collective security system; the vicissitudes of the definitions of state sovereignty thanks to which American policy makers could claim and pretend that, despite apparent imperialist prerogatives they have enjoyed for more than a half century all over the world, the United States was essentially opposed to old colonialism and that its domination was of a different type from that of the colonial powers of Britain, France, the Netherlands, and Japan. In short, the idiom "Pax Americana" summarily signifies the overwhelming preeminence of U.S. military, economic, and political forces in the world since the end of World War II as well as the international management of media outlets and knowledge production, thanks to which the United States of America has been continually presented as the mecca of the West.

In due course, this idiom also indicates the historical reality of post–World War II Northeast Asia in which such institutions as Japan's emperor system (天皇制) were formulated and legitimated. It is not only the so-called postwar constitution of Japan but also the symbolic emperor of Japan that must be apprehended as part and parcel of Pax Americana.

In this chapter I want to situate the probable end of Pax Americana in Northeast Asia's history since the end of the Asia-Pacific War or World War II. Inevitably I will reiterate the well-known postwar history of this region; I do not pretend that I can introduce new insights or perspectives to the narrative that is already familiar to many of my readers. But, instead, I would like to emphasize the need to retrospectively examine what we have assumed about the postwar history of Northeast Asia as well as review our history from the perspective of the end of Pax Americana.

Inward-Looking Tendency in Japan

After the collapse of the Japanese empire in August 1945, a transpacific order emerged across the vast expanse of the Pacific Ocean. This order found its political expression in what is customarily referred to as the "San Francisco System," sanctioned by the Treaty of Peace with Japan (and the U.S.-Japan Security Treaty) signed by the United States of America, Japan, and some of the Allied Powers in September 1951. Unlike the organization of the United Nations, the San Francisco System was not sanctioned universally. India, Yugoslavia, the Republic of China, or the People's Republic of China, for instance, did not participate in the conference, and although the Soviet Union did, it did not sign the treaty. Thanks to the inauguration of this San Francisco System, Japan was officially reintroduced into the international world, and then the Allied occupation of Japan ended in 1952. But, of course, this did not signal a universal recognition of Japan as an independent sovereign state; subsequently it also ended its state of warfare with the Soviet Union in 1956, with the Republic of Korea in 1965, and with the People's Republic of China in 1978.[2] Under the San Francisco System, Japan recovered from war devastation, reestablished its governmental bureaucracy and social institutions under what is generally referred to as the postwar constitution, and subsequently from the mid-1950s enjoyed high economic growth for more than three decades; this period of high economic growth is somewhat comparable to the Chinese economic expansion since the 1990s. Japan accomplished one of the most meticulous modernizations, and achieved one of the highest standards of living, one of the most competitive educational systems, and one of the most comprehensive welfare systems in the world. The international order under which Japan flourished was extended step by step to cover the entire globe and was called Pax Americana. This not only meant the basic political, economic, and social conditions under which societies in Northeast Asia have transformed themselves; it also came to signify the transpacific hegemony that governed not only the political, economic, diplomatic, and military policies of client states subordinate to the United States of America in East Asia but also the emotive and ethical lives of peoples in many regions from the western coast of North America to the eastern shore of the Euro-Asian continent.

It was in the 1970s, when the United States was defeated both militarily and politically in Vietnam, that Pax Americana began to show its first signs of exhaustion. Since the end of the Vietnam War, some people in East Asia have clandestinely speculated on the probability of an alternative order to that of Pax Americana. In due course, the Japanese, who undoubtedly have benefited most among all Asians from this American hegemony in the political climate of the Cold War, have to face a more uncertain future because now they cannot take for granted either their prestigious position or their tremendous wealth accrued as a result of American favoritism. They do not know how long they can continue to enjoy a high standard of living comparable to that of a few reputedly advanced societies in North America and Western Europe.

One should expect that the Japanese will both prepare for the prospect of hardship and look for new attitudes to adapt themselves to forthcoming adversities in which they must compete and struggle among themselves and also with international neighbors without the guaranteed protection of Pax Americana. Yet, ever since the economic bubble burst in the early 1990s, Japanese society seems to have indulged in a collective nostalgia for the good old days of its postwar high-growth economy. What has been revealed about this society in the last two "lost decades" is that many Japanese people have somewhat lost their entrepreneurial spirit, their attitude of moving forward and opening outward. What is noticeable in Japan in recent years is a social tendency conspicuous in the everyday life of individuals, mass media, national politics, and popular culture; it leans in a reactionary and isolationist direction, an inclination toward an introverted and reclusive withdrawal from the international world. In recent decades, we have witnessed such an inward-looking tendency in many countries in Western Europe and in the United States, but this predisposition is more conspicuous in Japan.[3]

Of the three major questions I would first like to pose in this chapter, the first is preliminarily twofold: how did Pax Americana come to play such an important role, not only in the spheres of diplomacy, military affairs, international trade, and national politics but also in the domains of everyday life, collective fantasy, and individuals' sensation-emotions? Also, how and why were the Japanese so efficiently captured in the hegemonic lure of Pax Americana? In short, the first question I would like to entertain is, how was Japanese imperial nationalism reconstituted after the war in accordance with the political, economic, and military order of the Western Pacific? This question prompts a corollary inquiry. Apparently the Japanese Empire collapsed when it was defeated in 1945 in the Asia-Pacific War. Subsequently more than 30 percent of the Japanese population, in annexed territories such as Korea, Taiwan, Sakhalin, northeast China, and the Pacific Islands, ceased to be of Japanese nationality within several years of Japan's surrender. But, as far as those Japanese who continued to identify themselves with the Japanese national state after the war—legally those Japanese whose family registers (戸籍) were recorded with permanent addresses within Japan proper—were concerned, did they not continue to regard themselves as subjects of an empire? Did they manage to reject the mindset of the colonizer who had customarily looked down upon the second-class citizens of the Japanese Empire? If many of them in fact failed to get rid of their imperialist hubris, what allowed them to disavow the loss of their empire?

The next question I pursue in this chapter correlates with the first in a number of contexts. Given the persistence of the colonial mindset among Japanese people, how does the anticipated end of Pax Americana affect their attitude? How can their inward-looking tendency possibly be articulated to Japan's postcoloniality and the end of Pax Americana?

Finally and most importantly, in addition to these two key questions, we must not overlook a third one whose importance has been hinted at not only in this chapter but also throughout this volume. The inward-looking tendency

I focus on with regard to hikikomori (reclusive withdrawal) is manifest in the social formation normally marked as the nation of the Japanese, and indeed it cannot be dissociated from Japanese nationalism. Yet it is misleading to assume that Japanese postcoloniality of this kind will be adequately comprehended within the framework of a national history. It is of course a Japanese phenomenon, but it is much more than that. What must be called into question is the historical transformation of the nation form itself; though the Japanese nation may appear to be an issue for a national history, the constitution of the Japanese nation as such cannot be problematized within the scope of a national history; the nation as a community with particular internal structures is an occurrence in the modern international world; only against the general problematic of internationality, without reference to which Japanese collectivity cannot be identified as a nation, can the nation form of the Japanese nation be understood.

To the extent that the nation form is intelligible only against the backdrop of the international world and that the modern international world consists of a series of microgradients, an inward-looking society cannot be investigated without reference to the innate fluidity of anthropological difference—difference between the West and the Rest, between the modern and the premodern, between the universal and the particular, between European humanity and non-European humanity, and so on—as well as the overdetermined articulation of gender difference, labor difference, and linguistico-ethnic difference to national subjectivity.

What is of decisive importance is that these differences cannot be conceptually determined as forming a stable systematicity; they are overdetermined and, therefore, haunted by an innate fluidity. These are so inherently unfixed in mutual determination that they cannot be securely accommodated within the given disciplinary formation of knowledge. Perhaps the best example of this fluidity innate in anthropological difference can be found in what Michel Foucault succinctly referred to as the indeterminate position in human sciences of "man," "an empirico-transcendental doublet" (1966b, 314–354; 1973, 303–343).

It cannot be overemphasized that the anti-immigrant racism of the Zaitokukai in Japan is coterminous, for example, with the resurgence of white nationalism in the United States. For the urge to discriminate against immigrants originates in the Japanese—and in the white American in the case of white nationalism in the United States—desire to establish an individual as well as a collectivity in terms of nationality, but to do so requires determination of the very difference in terms of which Japanese are constituted as distinct from non-Japanese. Likewise, the white man must appeal to the category of race in order to assert his position in contrast to both the nonwhite and the nonmale. Yet the very distinctions that sustain whiteness on the one hand and masculinity on the other are always articulated to one another in reference to other microgradients, including other variables of social positionalities such as ethnolinguistic capacity, degree of cultural capital, social class, labor configuration, and familial affiliations. Even if one is assured of Japanese legal status in a family registry, one is not securely guaranteed Japanese positionality in the microgradient of the majority-minority relation. An affirmation of his Japanese majoritarian positionality is brought about only when he is distinguished from or contrasted to a minority positionality that is overtly non-Japanese. One may be a Japanese as far as legal status is concerned, yet one cannot be certain of not being excluded from Japanese nationality or the national body (國體). Similarly, while someone may well be recognized as white according to the premise of scientific racism, that person could be disqualified as a Westerner— of course, being white is often confused with being of the West here—when judged for his cultural capital as a progeny of Western civilization. The anxiety that originates in the innate fluidity of anthropological difference is probably best exemplified in white nationalists' fixation on Western civilization in the phrase "the love of Western civilization."

What is revealed in these instances of racial, civilizational, or national identification is that a social positionality must be articulated to a series of majority-minority differences—Japanese and non-Japanese, white and nonwhite, the West and the Rest, male and female, and so on—of microgradients constituted as part of an inclined plane. Therefore, these differences are neither neutral nor devoid of power orientation but are necessarily projected as an incline from majoritarian to minoritarian positionalities. Although womanhood is statistically majoritarian in many social collectivities, the female often occupies the minoritarian positionality in contrast to the majoritarian positionality of the male. Thus, gender difference is not a static opposition between two species of gender, but rather a social relation infatuated with an urge for domination. Accordingly, the contrast between majority and minority means much more than the numerical sizes of two compared groups; it illustrates an orientation, a tendency or value judgment in potentiality about the binary opposition in the difference. This is to say that each of these differences is located in the field with a power orientation or an incline from a majoritarian positionality to a minoritarian one. This is why we have borrowed from mathematics the term "gradient," a multivariable function of the derivative, that indicates a polarity in the field of social interaction, from which sociopolitical identities or positionalities—the West, white, male, civilized, and so on, in contrast to the Rest, nonwhite, female, barbaric, and so on—are articulated to one another.

We must never forget that the West or whiteness, for instance, is no more than a positionality that is indeterminate outside the majoritarian-minoritarian gradients; only in fields saturated with polarities can these positionalities appear determinate and guaranteed. Nevertheless, the global configuration of majority-minority gradients, a configuration that elsewhere I call "anthropological difference," has been eroding in the last several decades, particularly in the age of globalization. In due course, those who used to believe they were firmly located in the West can no longer be assured of that Western positionality. This explains why, in search of their secure positionality, those who used to believe they were securely in some majoritarian positionality have to chase after their self-assured majoritarian distinction in the series of differences in the configuration of anthropological difference. When their racial positionality of whiteness appears uncertain, for instance, they seek a warranty for their self-assured positionality in the mythical history of Western civilization; when their Western positionality is visibly shaken, they look for their majoritarian status in an authentic nationality against recent immigrants, as if the rejection of immigration could possibly authenticate their majority status. Thus, they meander along the series of anthropological differences only to find that they can never be assured of the majoritarian positionality they desperately crave. Thus, the endless search for majoritarian security prompts an equally endless translation of one difference to another.

In this chapter our focus is the Japanese nationalism of hikikomori and the recession of Pax Americana. Yet I would like readers to keep in mind that a concern for identitarian anxiety, generated by the rapidly changing configuration of anthropological difference, is never absent in my inquiry. In other words, underlying my analysis of Japan's loss of empire is the problematics of racism in its multidimensionality. Thus, the recession of Pax Americana is not discussed exclusively in reference to the vicissitudes of the imperial nationalism of the United States; it is understood as an integral part of the reconfiguration of the modern international world.

Hikikomori

No doubt, there are historical conditions without which the Japanese could not have maintained their imperialist mindset in the face of Japan's unconditional surrender to the Allied Powers as well as their loss of colonies and of the subordinate populations of annexed territories. In view of the fact that the set of problems that I discuss in this chapter all surfaced during the two lost decades of economic stagnation—the 1990s and early 2000s—in Japan, I cannot evade a question of a methodological nature. Are these problems subsumed under the general problematic of postcoloniality? And to what extent is post-coloniality implicated in the inward-looking tendencies manifest not only in Japanese society but also in many postindustrial societies in Western Europe and North America?

The term "postcoloniality" suggests a state of affairs characterized by anach-ronism or by a perverse refusal to change, with the prefix "post" connoting not "after" or "posterior to" an event, but rather the persistence or endurance of something that should have perished. It implies some ghostly presence of the past that refuses to dissipate in the present. By postcoloniality, therefore, I mean the state of affairs particularly noticeable among former colonizers or within an ex-imperial society in which the people's mindset and the modality of their identification remain distinctly imperialist or colonial while colonial-ism, as embodied in the institutions of state sovereignty and exercised in the administrative and economic order of colonial discrimination, is over. In order to discard the old colonial mindset and to form different relations with people of former colonies, members of an ex-suzerain nation must undergo processes of self-reform and must learn how to fashion themselves differently in relation to the people of these former colonies, those of minority status on whom they used to feel entitled to look down.

Let us keep in mind that, for ex-colonizers, usually the processes of self-reform as well as the acquisition of new subjective technology do not come without pain. Former colonizer nations have to undergo the experience of col-lective shame; these processes can even be traumatic. Whereas the process of subjugating the inhabitants of a colonized territory under colonial adminis-trative government is usually experienced as a trauma for colonized people, the experience of independence, of liberation from the constraints of colonial gov-ernance, forming a new nation and constituting a new sovereign state of their own can be equally drastic. It is almost impossible to imagine that the process of withdrawal from a colony and abandoning all the privileges associated with colonizer status can be easily compared to the traumatic experience undergone by the colonized populace. Yet, in different and more insidious ways, the loss of empire can be traumatic for the ex-colonizer population.

Additionally, I must emphasize that the loss of empire can entail positive experiences. These are not only essential steps in decolonization but also cre-ative opportunities in which people of both the ex-colonial suzerain nation and the ex-colonized areas can produce new selves; they can dispose of the old subjective technology by which they were formed as colonizers and colonized respectively in co-figuration. Then they can invent new technologies by which to liberate themselves from the old majoritarian-minoritarian gradient and so build themselves into different personalities; ultimately they can thereby overcome the residue of old colonialism and so decolonize themselves.

The steps demanded for decolonization are complex and varied. By no means am I able to discuss this phenomenon in general here. Instead of analyzing decolonization in its complexity and historical diversity, I choose to approach the problematic of postcoloniality with a specific topic in mind, namely, the end of Pax Americana. Moreover, allow me to delimit my scope to a particular perspective from which to view this problematic; I would like to adhere to the perspective of shame. I offer my analysis of the feeling (情) of shame first because it is a communal feeling not wholly internalized into the individual's psyche and second because it is through the experience of shame that steps can be envisioned to overcome the remnants of old colonialism and thus decolonize.

Shame is a feeling that occurs in an individual's relation to somebody else, that testifies to an individual's openness to other human beings; it is a feeling of community, of being-in-common par excellence. For instance, when you are alone in a bathroom, you do not feel ashamed when you are totally naked. In order for you to have the feeling of shame, you must be under the gaze of some other human; you must be exposed to others. You do not feel ashamed when your naked body is looked at by a cat or dog there. Accordingly, there are two conditions in which you can feel ashamed or have the feeling of shame. The first is where you must be aware or know of the presence of another human being or other people. Between you and another human being, or other people whose presence you are aware of, there must be the polarity of "I" and "you," a relationality that Émile Benveniste calls "personal."[4] In this respect, the feeling of shame does not originate in me; it originates in my relation to you. The second is that the other being or beings in whose presence you feel ashamed must be human or some personal being. It must be noted here that the category of "human" is problematic to say the least, a point I return to later. In this respect, the feeling of shame bears witness to our fundamental—humanistic—sociality so that it is always possible to say that shame is a feeling evoked by the presence of some other human being or other some respectable beings.[5]

In observing Japanese society in recent years, one might be struck by a sense of oddity. Now that so many of Japan's neighboring countries have gained prosperity and international recognition, as a result both of political changes in Northeast Asia brought about by the end of the Cold War and of the greater economic growth they have enjoyed in the last half century, the Japanese attitude toward neighboring countries seems to have somewhat regressed rather than progressed with respect to the decolonization of East Asia. In the last several years it has been hinted that an increasingly large number of Japanese loathe the prospect of a shameful encounter with their Asian neighbors rather than welcome the opportunities that came with decolonization. In contrast to the publicly accepted predicament in which Japan's future will depend all the more upon the peoples of Northeast Asia as business partners, a majority of the Japanese nation does not hesitate to disavow the shameful histories of Japan's past in East Asia; as right-wing journalism—most typically represented by the *Sankei* and *Yomiuri* newspapers, although *Asahi* and *Mainichi* are now following suit—deliberately publishes articles that are blatantly condescending and colonialist toward the People's Republic of China and the Republic of Korea, the Japanese public seems to condone ignoring the history of Japanese colonialism and war crimes and instead prefers to repeat the narcissistic accounts of Japan's successful modernization. It is very difficult to elude a general impression that many in Japanese society are ready to repress any critical reflection on Japan's past and instead choose to be "shameless." The Abe Shinzô (安倍 晋三) administration capitalized on these trends and on the platform of the denial of collective shame; it tried to create a national consensus on matters ranging from education to Japan's rearmament and foreign policies. What has become glaringly obvious is the lack of a collective will in the Japanese nation to decolonize itself. Instead of opening up the national community to new and challenging relations with peoples in Northeast Asia, Japan seems to prefer the predictable and familiar configuration of international politics under Pax Americana, as if the Japanese wanted to return to the golden days when Japan's position was unambiguously defined within the Cold War confinement strategy.

Tentatively, I would like to call this nationalism that refuses to decolonize itself the nationalism of hikikomori. "Hikikomori" is a Japanese term that signifies a comparatively recent social phenomenon of reclusive withdrawal. The term connotes a group of adolescents or adults who literally withdraw from social life into the confines of their bedrooms seeking isolation, while it also signifies a social problem caused by these individuals.

It is important here, however, to clearly distinguish hikikomori individuals with this social problem from what I call the nationalism of hikikomori. These two uses of hikikomori must not be confused either in conception or in terms of their referents. It is impossible to hold that hikikomori individuals normally and regularly embrace the nationalism of hikikomori or participate in it. It is important to keep in mind that the social problem of hikikomori includes elements of critical awareness about the nature of modern society and the logic of the market that are based upon the neoliberal principles of competition and meritocracy. Hikikomori individuals are most often alienated from such a social environment and refuse to live according to neoliberal ideals. In contradistinction to hikikomori individuals, the nationalism of hikikomori does not show any such critical awareness; it does not intend to help or support hikikomori individuals at all; as a matter of fact, it is indifferent to the social conditions in which some individuals are forced to adopt this tactic of reclusive withdrawal, often at enormous cost to themselves and to their families; to my knowledge, the nationalists of hikikomori have rarely shown any critical interest in the social conditions promoted by neoliberalism and the rhetoric of market fundamentalism; instead, with a set of collective fantasies of communion, they endorse neoliberal ideologues and employ an ideological maneuver to displace critical knowledge of the very social conditions that force hikikomori individuals to withdraw from social life. In short, the nationalism of hikikomori seeks to substitute a fantasy of national camaraderie for a critical assessment of contemporary capitalism and the nation-state.

Through an analysis of the nationalism of hikikomori from the perspective of the experience of shame, I would like to ponder the steps demanded for decolonization, the practical decisions that must be made for that purpose, and the aesthetics of postcoloniality, without reference to which we can hardly comprehend the range of emotive-sensational conundrums that decolonization possibly entails. In discussing the experience of shame, the central concept to be mobilized is the concept of the feeling—情 or *qing*—that was widely discussed in Confucian metaphysics in the early part of the modern period. In the tradition of Cheng-Zhu rationalism—also called Cheng-Zhu Neo-Confucianism—the feeling was conceptualized as the actualization of human nature—性 or *xing*—but, of course, I have no intention of making theoretical recourse to the authoritarian metaphysics of premodern Confucianism. What interests me is the revision or critique of Cheng-Zhu rationalism achieved by some philosophers in the seventeenth and eighteenth centuries. Of particular importance is the radical de-ontologization of Cheng-Zhu metaphysics accomplished by Ito Jinsai (伊藤 仁斎) through his meticulous reading of the Confucian classics. He attempted to flip Zhu Xi's ontology of *li* (理 or rational principle) and *qi* (気 or existential force) on its head, so to speak, thereby prioritizing an existential actuality over the ideal possibility. One of the theoretical consequences I draw from Ito's intervention is that feeling is not a secondary manifestation of what underlies the world of appearance. The feeling of affection (愛), for example, is not a derivative of the universal human nature of benevolence (仁); on the contrary, since a feeling cannot actualize itself unless it is also embodied in other registers so that it is inseparable from an action at large, the feeling of affection and its accompanying conduct establish or produce the human nature of benevolence that may appear to be institutionally precedent to the feeling of affection. In other words, through his devastating critique of the legacies of Cheng-Zhu Neo-Confucianism, Ito inaugurated a poietics of feeling, a study of the productive function of feeling.[6]

Pax Americana and Japan's Emperor System

Now we must shift our attention to the historical circumstances under which the social formation, of which the phenomenon of hikikomori was one of the consequences, came into being. Both the postwar recovery of the Japanese economy (from the late 1940s through the 1980s) and its subsequent stagnation (the 1990s and early 2000s) occurred under the general condition of Pax Americana.

The series of U.S. foreign policy initiatives and their drastic failure since September 11, 2001, have offered us a good opportunity to highlight what we had suspected but could not explicitly conceptualize about the status of the United States of America in the world. During the First Gulf War in 1990–1991, the U.S. government refrained from directly invading Iraq partly because it could foresee the mounting difficulties of reestablishing the government there; however, in 2003, the George W. Bush administration and its allies falsified intelligence information for the sake of belligerent propaganda and declared that the Iraqi government was developing weapons of mass destruction; this tactic justified their invasion of Iraq. They swiftly succeeded in occupying Iraqi territory and subsequently demolished the Ba'ath Party administration under Saddam Hussein, even though it was clear that the United States had no long-term plans for occupying Iraq or for eventually withdrawing their military troops from it.

Surely this incident reminds us of a number of previous imperialist maneuvers including Japan's Manchurian Incident (1931) and the United States' Gulf of Tonkin Incident (1964), in which both the Japanese military and the U.S. National Security Agency deliberately lied to the public in order to start military attacks against local warlords and the Chinese Communist Party in northern China and against North Vietnamese naval vessels in the Gulf of Tonkin, respectively. The comparison with the Manchurian Incident is particularly telling since it demonstrates a striking similarity to the failures of American policy toward Iraq under the George W. Bush administration. Just as in the Japanese occupation of north China, which marked a new stage in the long and disastrous political fragmentation of China from which Japan could never disentangle itself until its defeat in 1945, the American occupation of Iraq gave rise to a civil war and unwittingly nurtured the Islamic State of Iraq and the Levant (ISIL) movement. One can see a somewhat comparable development in Afghanistan; in not having studied its history and geopolitical conditions or the long-term consequences of American political and military maneuvers, in the 1980s the United States' anticommunist dogmatism sowed the seeds for an antimodern fanaticism in order to reduce the USSR's influence there. Once the USSR retreated, the indigenous religious fundamentalists that had been aided by the United States turned Afghanistan into a hotbed of anti-American global movements. Just as Japan wanted to create puppet governments in Manchukuo as well as in the territories occupied by the Japanese army in northern China in the 1920s and '30s, the U.S. government attempted to establish puppet governments in both Iraq and Afghanistan; however, remarkably, Iraqi leaders then insisted on the total recovery of their sovereignty and the end to a humiliating occupation.[7]

To demonstrate how Pax Americana has internally and gradually been undermined, one should compare U.S. military and political strategy concerning the occupation of Japan immediately after the Asia-Pacific War—in the late 1940s and the 1950s—with its recent policy toward Iraq. In this comparison of two instances of American occupation, we can see the changing circumstances under which the global status of the United States has been decomposing.

During the 1980s, just as in today's China, Japan was one of the most popular topics in English-language mass media due to its economic success. Since its economic bubble burst at the beginning of the 1990s, however, Japan has been much less frequently mentioned in English print and television journalism. Yet, after the September 11 incident in 2001 and the American invasion of Iraq, Japanese popularity resurged in global mass media. For one thing, the 9/11 incident reminded the global audience of stereotypical Japanese images: the suicidal attacks of Al-Qaeda fighters no doubt invoked the wartime memory of kamikaze attacks by Japanese pilots against Allied war vessels in the Pacific.

Furthermore, in order to justify its military occupation of Iraq, the George W. Bush administration frequently referred to Japan as an exemplary case of successful occupation that, it claimed, laid the foundation for today's democratic Japan as a model of obedience to the United States of America. Time and time again, President Bush boasted of his confidence that Iraq could analogously be turned into a subservient satellite of Pax Americana. He stated that Japan had once launched a total war against America, but through skillful occupation it had now become a democratic nation-state, accepting any demand from the United States. "Iraq is capable of becoming another Japan," Bush seemed to be saying: "For this historical mission, we are now fighting on Iraqi soil." Now many of us are fully aware of how empty and ridiculous his rhetoric was. The series of policies undertaken in Iraq have obviously undermined the conditions that sustained Pax Americana.

Unlike the Truman and Eisenhower administrations in charge of the occupation of Japan in the late 1940s and 1950s, apparently the George W. Bush administration never succeeded in its occupation of Iraq and Afghanistan. Not surprisingly, both the Iraqi and the Afghanistan governments rejected the type of Status of Forces Agreement (SOFA) that the Japanese government had willingly accepted in the 1950s, the acceptance of which could give long-lasting extraterritorial privileges to U.S. military personnel. Instead, the Bush administration was forced to sign entirely different SOFAs with Iraq and Afghanistan that guaranteed the complete withdrawal of American troops to prevent the United States from continuing to expand its global and imperial network of military bases there. It follows that neither of these countries will serve as a satellite state subservient to the United States in the future in the way that Japan, Britain, Germany, and South Korea have played the role of satellite states in Pax Americana for the last seven decades.

Although George W. Bush emphasized the similarities between the U.S. occupation of Japan and that of Iraq, one can hardly overlook some decisive differences between the two. Whereas the Bush administration was reluctant to consult area experts about the region, the Franklin Roosevelt administration made deliberate preparations during the war to build expertise on Japan— these efforts to create a field of specialized knowledge marked the beginning of area studies on Japan—prior to its occupation: as soon as the Japanese attacked U.S. naval facilities at Pearl Harbor in Hawai'i, the U.S. government organized training programs for Japan experts with Japanese language skills and knowledge of Japanese society, culture, and history; some Japan experts and policy makers began to study the dangers and difficulties involved in a probable occupation of Japan to facilitate a discussion of political forms under which Japan would be governed during the period of Allied occupation.

From the outset of the Pacific War, U.S. leadership never doubted that they would be victorious over Japan. The ultimate question for them was not how to secure a military victory there, but rather how to occupy and govern it. In the 1930s they had been closely observing the Japanese invasion of China as well as how they Japanese failed to contain civil wars in the territories they had conquered. Thus, American policy makers were aware that the Japanese military could occupy some territories in China by military force but that Japan could not govern the regions and populations thus conquered.

From this observation, the Roosevelt administration seemed to have learned an important lesson: it is comparatively easy to conquer a country militarily, but the most difficult task of any occupying force is to establish a peaceful order and to govern without the use of military violence. As a matter of fact, already in the early years of World War II, American policy makers serving the Franklin Roosevelt presidency understood that the essential problematic of Japan's occupation was that of a colonial governmentality. Yet they also understood that they must colonize Japan while deliberately concealing any intentions or tactics of colonialism.

It seems to me that the answer to this problem also came from their study of Japanese tactics and failures: the policy makers of the Roosevelt administration studied the way that the Japanese attempted to solve the problems of colonial governance in the territories they occupied such as Manchuria, Mongolia, and northern and central China. It is noteworthy, particularly in view of developments after the collapse of the Japanese Empire in 1945, that some Japan experts in the U.S. government had proposed the idea of a puppet emperor by whom Japan would be governed during American occupation long before Japan's defeat. They carefully studied Japan's attempts to govern its occupied territories in China, most notably its attempts to build puppet regimes such as the Manchu-kuo (1931–1945) and the Regional National Government in Nanjing (or the Wang Jingwei [汪精衛] regime, 1940–1945) and subsequently elaborated upon these policies for their own strategy toward Japan. In other words, what I suggest here is a genealogical continuity between the Japanese colonial strategy in the occupation of China and what I have elsewhere called "the discourse of the Emperor System in postwar Japan" (Sakai 2000b).

Part 2: Empire under Subcontract

In September 1942, Edwin O. Reischauer, a young professor at Harvard University who would later be known as one of the founding fathers of area studies on East Asia in the United States and who would serve as U.S. ambassador to Japan in the 1960s, wrote a letter to the U.S. War Department titled "Memorandum on Policy towards Japan." It was only four pages long, but retrospectively it can be demonstrated that it concisely summarized the nature of the transpacific alliance that would build between the United States and Japan after the collapse of the Japanese Empire. The document was rediscovered at the National Archive in Maryland by Takashi Fujitani of the University of Toronto more than a half century after it was composed (Fujitani 2000, 2001). Even though his accomplishments in scholarship on Japan and East Asia in general as well as in the domain of U.S. foreign policy are well recognized, I believe it implausible that young Reischauer could determine the future of American policies toward Japan and the Far East singlehandedly at a comparatively early stage of the Pacific War—only nine months after the Japanese attack on U.S. naval facilities at Pearl Harbor. I am not inclined to attribute too much genius to his impressive diagnosis of the times and this farsightedness about the U.S. governance of Japan. Frankly speaking, however, I can hardly suppress a sense of awe at his missive's astute assessment of the international situation in the Pacific as well as his policy proposals: first, as to how the United States should organize its propaganda warfare against the Japanese ideological campaign and, second, as to its strategic considerations for the occupation of Japan.

In this respect, I believe that Reischauer's "Memorandum on Policy towards Japan" (the text is reproduced in its entirety in appendix 1, this volume) can be regarded as an entry point into the general discussion on the political, diplomatic, socioeconomic, and theoretical aspects of Pax Americana to come in the Western Pacific in the post–World War II world.

"Memorandum on Policy towards Japan"

Let me begin my discussion of this U.S.-Japan complicity by elucidating the historical significance of this document with a view to the transpacific alliance that would form as the platform for the future system of American collective security in East Asia.

Reischauer's letter is a testimony powerful enough to dispel the prevailing myth that has continued to obscure the nature of the U.S.-Japan alliance since the Treaty of Peace with Japan was signed in San Francisco in 1951 in the midst of the Korean War. This so-called San Francisco Peace Treaty clearly expressed the new strategic configuration in the Pacific on the basis of which postwar American foreign policies toward the Far East would be systematically developed. No doubt the Cold War was the predominant concern for American policy makers at that time, and, strategically speaking, Japan was to occupy the most important position to block the potential onslaught of communism against American satellite regimes and its economic and political interests in the Western Pacific. In this configuration, it is important to remember that the stability of the Japanese state was absolutely essential; the U.S. Occupation Administration of Japan manipulated the legitimacy of Emperor Hirohito so as to sustain the national integration of the Japanese population and to facilitate the U.S. domination of Northeast Asia.

Among the public in Japan, including political scientists and historians until recently, and in mass media even today, the prevailing narrative about the survival of the emperor system at the end of the war claims that the United States seriously entertained the idea of prosecuting Emperor Hirohito after Japan's surrender to the Allied Powers but that General Douglas MacArthur, as supreme commander of the Allied Powers, decided to pardon him and preserve the emperor system under the new constitution despite the opposition of some member countries of the Allied Powers. It has been routinely explained that the U.S. decision not to prosecute Hirohito was reached as a result of negotiations between the U.S. Occupation Administration and Japan's conservative forces. Along with a famous photograph of MacArthur, tall and casually clothed, standing next to Hirohito, short and in formal morning coat, the Occupation Administration released a sentimental anecdote describing how deeply MacArthur was moved by the personal character of Emperor Hirohito when he was summoned to the Allied Powers' general headquarters in Tokyo for the first time (see figure 6.1).[8] Relying upon this narrative, right-wing commentators in Japan—today they are in the mainstream—used to argue that Japan did not actually surrender to the Allied Powers unconditionally because the Japanese never gave up the essence of their nationality or national body (*kokutai* 國體), the emperor system.[9]

Reischauer's memorandum shattered this very reassuring myth, comforting for Japanese nationalists who want to continue to see the ongoing legitimacy of the Japanese imperial lineage in the figure of the emperor.[10] The letter unambiguously shows that the American decision to preserve the Japanese emperor system had absolutely nothing to do with Japanese conservative groups' maneuvers to preserve the nation's nationality (kokutai); it finally disclosed the truth that has been vehemently denied by some Japanese ideologues; it illustrates that those Japanese conservative figures have been repeating the fantastic scenario that the preservation of the Japanese emperor system was a consequence of efforts by Japanese diplomats and politicians around the time of Japan's surrender. As a matter of fact those Japanese ideologues, claiming to be ardent nationalists, served to fulfill the desire of the colonial masters; they acted as the most subservient retainers for the American empire. The memorandum proves that the policy option to save Emperor Hirohito had already been contemplated as part of the American occupation of Japan three years before the Japanese government accepted the Potsdam Declaration on August 14, 1945, and thereby surrendered to the Allied Powers.

FIGURE 6.1. MacArthur and Hirohito. After Japan's surrender to the Allied Powers, the Showa Emperor (Hirohito) paid his first visit to General Douglas MacArthur, the supreme commander for the Allied Powers (SCAP), in the U.S. Embassy in Tokyo on September 27, 1945. This photograph was taken then and publicly released by SCAP with the story that MacArthur was tremendously moved by the character of Hirohito, who was said to have volunteered to sacrifice himself for sins committed by the Japanese, Hirohito's subjects. MacArthur and his staff were already and implicitly advocating the manipulation of Hirohito along the lines suggested by Edwin O. Reischauer three years before. Photo by Gaetano Faillace. Courtesy of U.S. Army.

Reischauer was an instructor who had just started his teaching career at Harvard, but he was also serving in the U.S. intelligence service when his letter was sent to the War Department. Not surprisingly, he had been studying Japanese attempts to create puppet regimes in China. In the memorandum he wrote, "Japan had used the strategem [sic] of puppet governments extensively but with no great success because of the inadequacy of the puppets" (Reischauer 1942; see appendix 1). What was made glaringly obvious is that, in the minds of American strategists, postwar Japan was comparable to Manchu-kuo, a colonial regime that was under the control of the suzerain state but was expected to be independent. It is astonishing to me that, until now, not only American experts but also Japanese intellectuals have refrained from comparing postwar Japan to Manchu-kuo; this collective disavowal was made conspicuous by the disclosure of the Reischauer memorandum. The silence of America's Japan experts on this topic is easier to predict, for there was no need on their part to disclose the rationale behind their maneuvers. But the question is rather about how to comprehend the peculiar muteness of Japanese mass media on this point. Why did they have to collaborate with the strategists of the occupation to enhance the American colonization of the Japanese? Why were they, or why are they still, keen to endorse the very myth that facilitates and validates Japan's subjugation to the United States? Why are they willing to embrace their own subjugation to this colonizing hegemon?

In Manchuria, Japanese imperialists wanted to create an independent state that they would govern but where the people believed they held national sovereignty. Even though I do not think they succeeded in installing this kind of oxymoronic polity that was both colonized and independent at the same time, without question Japanese policy makers were experimenting with a new type of sovereignty; they were trying to redefine the concept of state sovereignty. The Japanese had to invent such a strategy mainly because they had to implement measures to alleviate anticolonial struggles and evade confrontation with rising Chinese nationalism. They were aware that the old rhetoric of European colonial governance could no longer be sufficiently effective to persuade the subjugated inhabitants of Europe's colonies in Latin America, South Asia, Africa, Southeast Asia, the Middle East, and even in Northeast Asia; the Japanese imperialists had to seek policies with which to continue to govern the territories they occupied militarily while at the same time making the people in these occupied areas believe they were independent and free from colonial subjugation. Despite their repeated attempts, however, the Japanese imperialists could not succeed in this task because of what Reischauer called "the inadequacy of the puppets."

Even as early as September 1942, Reischauer was convinced that American policy makers were able to accomplish the task of inventing an anti-anticolonial governance better than the Japanese; he considered the Americans to be more clever and competent imperialists than the Japanese. His confidence was buttressed by the fact that "Japan itself has created the best possible puppet for our purposes, a puppet who not only could be won over to our side but who would carry with him a tremendous weight of authority, which Japan's puppets in China have always lacked. I mean, of course, the Japanese Emperor"

(Reischauer 1942; see appendix 1). What was crucial for the success of this task was that the colonized people had to believe they were independent, just as, in modern societies, a new type of power, biopower, works most effectively over people who believe themselves to be free. When people believe they are independent, they can be most realistically and thoroughly subjugated in the element of biopolitics. This insight was exactly what the Japanese did not have in their attempts to create their puppet regimes in China. Some intellectuals were already arguing for the need to support Chinese nationalism in the 1930s for the sake of Japanese governance over China, but the Japanese government could never implement a policy toward China that is comparable to the American policy toward postwar Japan.[11]

As though under the same sort of state sovereignty as that of Manchu-kuo, after the Asia-Pacific War the Japanese people had to be encouraged to believe that they were independent, even under the hegemonic and global reign of the American empire, that is, a sort of colonial subjugation under the authority of U.S. collective security. For this feeling of independence to be actually shared among the Japanese people, they should not be deprived of their nationality (國體), their sense of national solidarity; regardless of changes in the form of the government, in the territory of their state, or the composition of the national population, the people were destined to be together as a nation due to their shared history.[12] This explains why postwar Japan has not been able to dispel the myth or collective self-deception that Japanese politicians and bureaucrats fought for the continuation of the emperor system at the time of Japan's surrender. The myth effectively and successfully functioned to conceal the American strategic maneuver to nurture Japanese nationality and thereby pacify and subjugate the occupied people. This strategy served two objectives: the purpose of the United States' successful occupation of Japan, on the one hand and the purpose of protecting pro-American conservative forces from the accusation of succumbing to the newly arriving conquerors, on the other. The U.S. policy makers and the Japanese conservatives needed this myth precisely because Americans valued and respected the Japanese feeling of nationality for the sake of their successful colonization of Japan. Rather than serve the will of Japan's nation, the Japanese national body (nationality), symbolically embodied in the figure of the emperor, actually served the U.S. Occupation Administration by making it possible to turn Japanese nationalism into an instrument for the United States' colonization of Japan. In order for the American strategy concerning the occupation of Japan to work meritoriously, therefore, the truth of the Japanese nationality symbolized by the emperor should never be disclosed. This is the truth—U.S. policy makers originally inherited the idea from Japanese imperialists in the 1930s and early 1940s—about the mutual dependence of nationalism and colonial governmentality, around which U.S. policies toward East Asia were designed and implemented after the Asia-Pacific War.

Having learned much from the quagmire of guerrilla warfare that the Japanese created in China, Reischauer stressed the need to think ahead, three years prior to Japan's unconditional surrender to the Allies, and to lay out a plan for the American occupation of Japan along the lines of the following strategy:

> The possible role of the Japanese Emperor in the post-war rehabilitation of the Japanese mentality has definite bearing upon the present situation. To keep the Emperor available as a valuable ally or puppet in the post-war ideological battle we must keep him unsullied by the present war.
>
> ... It is not improbable that he could be won over to a policy of cooperation with the United Nations far more easily than the vast majority of his subjects. He, and possibly, he alone, could influence his people to repudiate their present military leadership. If he proves to have the potentialities of a real leader like his grandfather, so much the better. If he proves to be no more able than his half-demented father, his value as a symbol of cooperation and good will can still be extremely valuable. (Reischauer 1942)

Toward the end of the Asia-Pacific War, the crucial issue with which Japanese leaders were primarily concerned in their negotiations with the Allied Powers about the conditions of Japan's surrender was neither the welfare of the population of the Japanese Empire nor the integrity of its territories. Instead, their focus was on the preservation of kokutai, which one might translate as "nationality," "national sovereignty," or "national body." In the language of the prewar Japanese state in the 1920s and '30s, the national body (kokutai) was defined in terms of a combination of private property rights and the sacred lineage of the imperial family. So to violate the national body meant either socialist and communist activism that denied the unlimited validity of private property rights or the critique or rejection of the emperor as the sole legitimate national sovereign. In the late nineteenth century, when the institution of the emperor was first installed, this institution was a most illuminating case of "the invention of tradition."

As the Japanese Empire expanded territorially in the late nineteenth and early twentieth centuries, annexing Hokkaido, Okinawa, Taiwan, Korea, the Pacific Islands, and, finally, in the late 1930s and early 1940s, large parts of Northeast and Southeast Asia under the umbrella of the Greater East Asia Co-prosperity Sphere, the emperor was increasingly associated with the universalistic principle of Japanese reign under which people of different ethnic backgrounds, different languages and cultures, and different residences were entitled to be integrated into the imperial nation and treated as equal subjects. In this light, Japan being an imperial nation, the prewar emperor was rarely made to represent overtly the unity of a particular racial or ethnolinguistic community. No doubt there were extremists who insisted upon the purity of blood, such as Watsuji Tetsurô (和辻 哲郎; Sakai 1997b, 110–114), but the intellectuals who participated in the policy making of the Japanese state could not afford to indulge openly in ethnic narcissism. They had to concern themselves with how to prevent the fragmentation of a multiethnic nation into ethnic and class rivalries.

In the years subsequent to Japan's defeat and the disintegration of the empire, the legal status of the emperor underwent a drastic change. The prewar emperor system was replaced by a judicially different one that was also called *ten'nôsei* (the emperor system 天皇制). While the emperor was defined as the sovereign of the Japanese state and the commander in chief of all Japanese military forces under the Meiji Constitution, the new constitution implemented by the U.S. Occupation Administration defined the emperor as "the symbol of the unity of the Japanese nation." After Japan's defeat, the word "kokutai" was eliminated from the official vocabulary of the Japanese government, but its original signification—nationality—continued to be preserved in the figure of the emperor.

In retrospect from the viewpoint of the twenty-first century, it appears that the implementation of the new emperor system coincided with the culturalist discussions of Japanese national unity in Japan as well as in the United States. From the late 1940s onward and well into the 1980s, it became fashionable to explain the historical features of Japanese society in terms of Japanese national character, Japanese culture, and Japanese uniqueness. Thus after the loss of the empire, the emperor was made to symbolize the continuity of Japanese tradition and the unity of Japanese national culture. Some reactionary intellectuals, like Watsuji Tetsurô, positively valued the new definition of the Japanese emperor and, implicitly or even unwittingly, volunteered as ideologues for the U.S. Occupation Administration and produced an argument that justified the new emperor system on the basis of cultural nationalism.

War over Racism

Before moving on to what is implied in this structural complicity of nationalism and colonial governmentality for transpacific politics in the early twenty-first century, let me highlight the other topic of Reischauer's memorandum: ideological warfare over racism in the Pacific.

Reischauer tried to draw the attention of the staff of the War Department to what he called "the inter-racial aspect of the conflict in Asia." He was concerned with the general success of Japan's propaganda campaign at that time: "Japan is attempting to make her war against the United Nations into a holy crusade of the yellow and brown peoples for freedom from the white race. China's courageous stand has prevented Japan from exploiting this type of propaganda too much, but it has apparently met with a certain degree of success in Siam and the colonial lands of southeastern Asia and even in a few circles in China" (Reischauer 1942). Reischauer was worried that the Japanese were winning in this ideological warfare in the Pacific and Asia and that, even if the United States could win the war militarily, it would be extremely difficult to fabricate the legitimacy of U.S. domination over Asia. He had to remind the staff of the U.S. federal government about the actuality of the world beyond Western Europe and North America, where the assumption of white supremacy, on the basis of which European and American colonial governments ruled over local populations, had been publicly challenged by Japan.

Today we know that, even on the American domestic front during the 1930s, Japan had earned some support against the Anglo-American domination of the world. A number of prominent African American intellectuals such as W. E. B. Du Bois expressed their support of Japanese maneuvers in East Asia even though Japan's policies were indisputably colonialist and undeniably motivated by imperialist ambition. It was, therefore, absolutely necessary for the United States to counteract the Japanese propaganda against Eurocentric racism and then to eliminate the public space where racism was to be explicitly debated. Furthermore, U.S. post–World War II policies, international as well as domestic, may well be characterized as a reactionary response to emerging antiracism all around the world. The idea of Pax Americana was so dependent upon the management of antiracist rhetoric that the U.S. government had to remove or hide obvious signs of racism on the domestic front in order to sustain its commanding position in the United Nations, even though it was virtually impossible to conceal so many symptoms of domestic racial discrimination in the United States.

Two important points must be underlined in this regard. Even before the United States entered World War II, a number of liberal intellectuals had warned the public that, without improvements in domestic race relations, racial minorities might well refuse to collaborate with the U.S. government's war efforts in a war with Japan (Buck 1942, 11–21). Marc Gallicchio demonstrates that domestic politics could not be completely insulated from the consequences of the imperialist policies of the United States. He cited the survey report conducted by the Office of Facts and Figures (reorganized into the Office of War

Information in June 1942): "The striking fact revealed by these figures is that one-half of the Negroes interviewed in New York city expressed to *interviewers of their own race* a belief that they would be better off, or at least no worse off, under Japanese rule" (Gallicchio 2000, 142, emphasis added). Liberal intellectuals like Pearl Buck had to acknowledge that black Americans were frustrated with American society, and that their apathy could easily undermine the government's war efforts. Furthermore, it was obvious that international politics could not be insulated from racism at home. Gallicchio argues, "The problem of black American apathy and Asian passivity or outright support for Japan could not be treated separately because the same forces that defended America's caste system would insist on white supremacy abroad" (2000, 142). Perhaps for the first time in U.S. history, white elites were forced to acknowledge that white supremacy itself could be a factor that gravely threatened the national security of the United States of America.

Reflecting on the widespread panic felt by liberals and policy makers of the United States in the aftermath of Japan's surprise attack, Reischauer (1942) issued a warning: "We have also unwittingly contributed to Japan's dangerous propaganda campaign." The American track record on racism was notorious not only among the Japanese but also among the Chinese and other Asians due to a series of racist immigration laws since the nineteenth century, not to mention the treatment of African Americans and Native Americans on the domestic level. The most recent threat to the justification for U.S. involvement in warfare in the Pacific was the confinement of Japanese Americans in internment camps, thereby "affording the Japanese in Asia with a trump propaganda card." Reischauer's memorandum continues, "The removal from the West Coast of the American citizen of Japanese ancestry along with the Japanese aliens was no doubt a move made necessary by immediate military considerations, but it provided the Japanese with a powerful argument in their attempt to win the Asiatic peoples to the view that the white race is not prepared to recognize them as equals and even now continues to discriminate against them." Therefore, he recommended:

We should reverse this situation and make of these American citizens a major asset in our ideological war in Asia. Their sincere and enthusiastic support of the United States at this time would be the best possible proof that this is not a racial war to preserve white supremacy in Asia, but a war to establish a better world order for all, regardless of race, and, when the military victory is achieved, these American citizens of Japanese ancestry could serve as an opening wedge into the minds and hearts of the Japanese people. (Reischauer 1942; see appendix 1)

It is, however, entirely misleading to believe that only Americans should be concerned with racism within their nation. We must never lose sight of the fact that racism is not a problem particular to the United States. In the Japanese Empire too, a number of anticolonial uprisings—from the March First Movement in Korea in 1919 to the Wushe massacre in Taiwan in 1930, not to mention the racial hierarchy within the system of Comfort Stations all around East Asia and mass killings of migrant workers and civilians in the Tokyo area at the time of the Kantô Earthquake in 1923—in China, Singapore, and other places occupied by the Japanese military unambiguously testified to Japanese racism and peoples' struggles against it. The antiracism campaign by the Japanese government was not simply for the sake of disqualifying American claims to racial equality in the eyes of Asians. However, the campaign for the management of antiracism was absolutely necessary for the Japanese state to maintain their hegemony in East Asia and to integrate multiethnic elements into their imperial nation. Japanese policy makers and liberal intellectuals—some of whom were former Marxists—had to revise the rhetoric of antiracism and universalist ideology for that precise reason. Such governmental publications as *Daitôa kensetsu-ron* (大東亜建設論, The construction of greater East Asia) illustrated the presence of a very strong concern about racism within the bureaucracy of the Japanese government. The document was published in the name of Murayama Michio (村山道雄), a representative of the Planning Agency (企画院) in the Cabinet Secretariat; it attempted to explicate the governing principles adhered to by the Tôjô Hideki (東条英機) administration. Despite the fact that Japan had just signed the pact with Germany and Italy, neither scientific racism as a social theory nor German National Socialism's anti-Semitic policy was endorsed within the Planning Agency (Murayama 1943).[13]

Surprisingly, white liberals and policy makers in the United States as well as Japanese progressive intellectuals and reformist bureaucrats—*kakushin kanryô* (革新官僚) in Japanese—shared a similar perspective about the war in the Pacific. Perhaps the Japanese were first sensitized to the international significance of racism and then Americans followed. Regardless of vastly different positions they occupied in international politics, however, it seems that they had to come to the same sort of understanding about the ideological character of the war in the Pacific in that neither the United States nor Japan could hope to succeed in establishing or maintaining a hegemony in East Asia unless an imperial nationalist government engaged in the warfare announced policies against racism and racial discrimination, both at home and in areas it wanted to rule (Fujitani 2011).[14] As far as racist policies were concerned, American and Japanese imperial nationalisms were compelled to enter a competition in which the disavowal of their respective racisms became such an important public policy goal. In the Pacific theater, unlike the Atlantic theater, the war could not be won by an imperial nationalism that openly endorsed racist policies. No matter how nominal its denunciation may have been, imperial nationalists had to appeal to the rhetoric of antiracism. Whether policies against racism were actually implemented or not is another matter requiring careful examination, but at the very least the need for such policies had to be acknowledged. Thus policy makers were forced to appreciate the common ground in the ideological warfare in which both Japan and the United States were engaged.

America's Manchu-kuo

What is most impressive in Reischauer's 1942 memorandum is his foresight about the two strategic directives on which the regional hegemony of the United States was later built. No doubt this letter was composed by an outstanding imperialist whose patriotism was beyond question.

In considering the underlying structure of transpacific politics that gradually took shape in the decades subsequent to the collapse of Japanese imperial nationalism, we cannot overlook two features—not unrelated to the two directives mentioned above—by which American policies toward East Asia were distinguished from those of previous imperial powers: British, French, Dutch, and Japanese. The first feature concerns the fact that, already in the 1930s, it was increasingly difficult to overlook nonwhite people's rage about white supremacy and colonized peoples' struggles against colonial injustice.

The decade following the end of World War II, during which the seminal plan for area studies programs was introduced and then implemented in American higher education, coincided with the beginning of the Cold War; this was marked by the U.S. foreign policy initiative known as the Truman Doctrine. As a new hegemon of global colonialism, the United States inherited the imperialist legacies of Britain, France, Japan, and so forth and tried to resurrect the global order of internationality, of the bipolar structure of the West and the Rest, that had been shattered by the devastation of industrial facilities in Europe, Russia, and Northeast Asia during the World War II. In this process the putative unity of the West was refashioned, and the symbolic center of the international order now represented by the United Nations had to move from the eastern shore of the Atlantic to its western shore.[15]

As previously noted with regard to Reischauer's 1942 memorandum, the topic of white supremacy, already the key issue in imperialist competition in the Pacific theater during World War II, could no longer be overlooked in the Atlantic theater either after the war. The world war gave rise to global conditions under which anticolonial struggles in South and Southeast Asia, Africa, and Northeast Asia could not be easily overpowered. Furthermore, it was almost impossible to imagine a critique of colonialism that was not also a critique of racism. The survival of the bipolar structure of the West and the Rest now depended upon how the critique of white supremacy was to be responded to, dispersed, and contained. The Truman Doctrine was obviously designed to "colonize such anticolonialisms" as proliferated during World War II and its aftermath (Estava, 2010, 6–8).[16] Of course, one cannot overlook the contemporaneity of the onset of the Cold War with the inauguration of area studies as academic disciplines.

It is evident that one of the most important missions undertaken by postwar area studies experts at American universities was to protect the United States from charges of racism. It is no accident, as students of American ethnic studies observed in the 1960s and '70s, that area studies experts were deliberately insensitive and indifferent to issues of racial discrimination and colonial cruelty. The repression of concerns for racial justice was baked into the very disciplinary construction of area studies. Let us keep in mind that the systematic training of Japan experts, who would constitute the core of area studies programs on Japan after the war, was begun under the directive of the Office of War Information (previously the Office of Facts and Figures) mentioned above. Before an engagement in ideological warfare against communism, those experts could not afford to be lenient toward the Asian rhetoric of antiracism; they could not help but be concerned with how to relieve America from its stereotypical image of white supremacy. Therefore, the U.S. Occupation Administration was particularly sensitive to imminent antiracist rhetoric that might arise in the criticism of American authority within Japan. It is known that, rather than Nazi followers and Japanese ethnic nationalists, many of the prominent critics of racism in academia and journalism who advocated for antiracist rhetoric during the war were purged soon after Japan's surrender. A thorough but informal censorship of antiracist arguments—let me underline that censorship was not against propagandas promoting racial discriminations or against racists themselves—was imposed upon mass media as soon as the U.S. Occupation Administration was established. It is quite remarkable that the discussion of racism and the liberation of colored peoples from white supremacy was effectively silenced within a few years after Japan's surrender, and that most liberal intellectuals in Japan, who wrote critically about racism during the war, did not dare continue to argue against it. This inhibition was not only about Japanese racism, plentiful evidence of which was readily available through accounts of atrocities committed by the Japanese military, but also about Euro-American racism. What characterizes postwar Japanese academic and journalistic media in both the East and the West is its utter silence on issues of racism.

The second feature is directly related to the second directive concerning how to occupy Japan, and it is best expressed in Reischauer's proposal about the treatment of the Japanese emperor. Except for the People's Republic of China, the Democratic People's Republic of Korea, and later the Democratic Republic of Vietnam, the countries in the Western Pacific—South Korea, Taiwan, Japan, and the Philippines—became satellite states under the control of the United States after the Asia-Pacific War. Nationalism in each of these American satellite states was carefully managed, and, among these countries, Japan is perhaps the most successful case from the viewpoint of the maintenance of U.S. collective security.

As I suggested earlier, one might find in Manchu-kuo a precedent model to Japan under Pax Americana. Manchu-kuo (満州國, the state of Manchuria [1932–1934] and the Empire of Manchuria [1934–1945]) was crowned with a nominal head of state, Pu Yi (溥儀), who was deprived of virtually all administrative, legislative, and judicial powers, while postwar Japan was headed by "the symbol of national unity," who was equally stripped of all powers by the constitution. Manchu-kuo was still a monarchy under the auspices of the General Affairs State Council, and the state of Manchu-kuo retained the framework of a colonial protectorate, which could never legislate or administer any policy counter to the opinion of the colonial military, the Kantô Army (関東軍), because the Japanese army held veto power over any decision reached by the Manchu emperor.

Regardless of whether or not any policy has actually been implemented counter to the opinion of the U.S. government in the last seven decades, the Japanese state has had the right to behave as an independent sovereignty under the system of collective security since the end of Allied occupation in 1952. Legally it is bound by the Treaty of Mutual Cooperation and Security between the United States and Japan, and this treaty includes the Status of Forces Agreement (SOFA) which gives U.S. military stationed in Japanese territories the privileges of extraterritoriality. Just as the Japanese military could remain in Manchu-kuo, the United States maintains its military bases and personnel in Japanese territory, most visibly in Okinawa but also in many places all over the territories of the Japanese state, and still enjoys certain special rights that colonizers used to hold. The U.S. military presence may not be openly visible in Japan proper, but the relationship between the United States and Japan can hardly be described as equal between independent sovereign states, as implied by the classical notion of international law. This is one reason why, for the last seventy years, so much publicity has been produced to convince the Japanese public that the relationship between the United States and Japan ought to be described as an equal partnership. Precisely because of the semicolonial subjugation Japan still experiences, it is necessary to constantly mention "equal partnership."

The greatest significance of Reischauer's assessment of Emperor Hirohito lies here. The Japanese never succeeded in giving as many trappings of national independence to Manchu-kuo as the United States did to Japan after the war. And this returns us to the question of nationality, or kokutai (national body), as discussed in chapter 2. One has to return to the old liberal notion of nationality or kokutai precisely because its narrow legalistic definitions have obscured rather than elucidated its political significance with regard to the vicissitudes of Japan's sovereignty. By obscuring nationality or kokutai, literally translated as "the body of the nation," the Japanese state has succeeded in concealing the contingent and poietic nature of the nation itself. The state deliberately displaced the topos of debate from the historical formation of national unity to the nation as an instrument of state legitimacy. Insulated by many layers of censorship, deification, and national rituals, the institution of the emperor was mystified, reified, and naturalized in prewar Japan. For this reason, the public was led to believe in the eternal presence of the emperor system from the first emperor, Jinmu (神武), twenty-six centuries before the Asia-Pacific War, whereas, in fact, the emperor system was apprehended among most of the educated public as the symbol of modernization in the early years of the Meiji period. The mythological narrative attributed to the emperor system, which the public came to embrace as a result of national education and strict censorship along with high treason legislation since the inauguration of modern state sovereignty, was not only about the fable of an uninterrupted lineage of imperial succession but also the transhistorical presence of the Japanese nation. The state bureaucracy appreciated the emperor system because it offered them an extremely effective means of defining and reconstituting the nation. So as to disguise the truism that the nation was something manufactured in modernity, policy makers have to find ways to invent, transform, and control the figure of the nation in terms of which national unity was imagined. Reischauer understood this crucial point very well with a view to the American governance of Japan. The American colonization of Japan had to be accomplished under the presumption of the Japanese nation's autonomy. In other words, it was expected that Japanese people would will to be colonized out of their own free will.

By deliberately preserving the emperor system, the United States managed to encourage the Japanese to preserve their feeling of nationality. Even under conditions of colonial subjugation, the Japanese could feel united with an intact national unity.

Before Japan's defeat by the Allies at the end of the Asia-Pacific War, some Japanese intellectuals sought strategic options by which to both nurture Chinese nationalism and subdue the Chinese nation under the broader regional hegemony in the East Asian Community (Miki [1939] 1968). But the Japanese state could neither formulate nor implement any coherent strategy to simultaneously accomplish these two apparently contradictory goals. What U.S. policy makers envisioned was not extraordinarily innovative; instead, they pursued the idea of a puppet government to its logical limit: to turn Japanese nationalism into an instrument for colonial governmentality. And Reischauer clearly envisioned this possibility in the figure of Emperor Hirohito.

According to the postwar constitution introduced into Japan by the U.S. Occupation Administration, the emperor was newly defined as the symbol of the unity of the Japanese nation. American policy makers could predict that the most difficult task to confront Americans was how to govern the Japanese population under occupation. So, predicting Japan's surrender, Reischauer (1942) wrote, "Military victory is, of course, the essential prerequisite for any war objective, but certain of the more fundamental problems of winning the peace cannot be overlooked in the meantime." Japanese nationalism might be a menace as long as Japan continued to fight against the United States, but once it was defeated, the fragmentation of the local population would be an even more serious threat to American rule. The Japanese won military battles in China, but they found it almost impossible to govern the Chinese during the Asia-Pacific War. Observing Japan's failure in the occupation of China, Reischauer advised the War Department staff for fear that Americans might dare to duplicate this mistake.

One can appreciate his vigilance all the more if we look at the history of American military engagements in Asia in the last seven decades. One could refer to the recent lesson of the American invasion of Iraq. They gained a quick military victory there, but did they win the peace?

It is no surprise to find this caution in Reischauer's 1942 memorandum: "It will be an extremely difficult task after the war to win over to a policy of sincere cooperation with us sufficient numbers of Japanese to bring Japan back into the family of friendly and cooperating nations" (Reischauer 1942). This insight of his reminds us of the significance of nationality as the essential moment of governmentality in the nation-state. Therefore, his question about how to win the

Japanese over to cooperation with the U.S. administration can be paraphrased this way: nationality as embraced by the colonized people is essentially ambiguous from the viewpoint of colonial administration. It can be mobilized to build a people's solidarity against colonizers, but it can also be utilized to pacify the nation and urge the Japanese to endure tremendous hardship under occupation. Moreover, it is imperative to keep in mind that nationality is always something that must be manufactured and reproduced. It never exists naturally, just as the nation—in the sense of both kokumin (国民, political nation) and minzoku (民族, ethnos or cultural nation)—is not a natural condition. This point cannot be emphasized too strongly despite—or precisely because of—the fact that the naturalization of nationality is most often adopted by nationalists as a strategy with which to invent the feeling of nationality.

Nationality is most effective when it is accepted by the people as if it were a given and inescapable destiny. In this respect, nationality is a sort of collective facticity (*Faktizität*) in the Heideggerian sense in that the people understand themselves as destined to live interwoven with things in the world in a determinate way. Adhering for the time being to Heidegger's perspective—in *Being and Time*, in which facticity is introduced as *Dasein*'s modality of being in the world that is prior to knowing (Heidegger 1996, 52ff.)—one might as well express it slightly differently: nationality is encountered by Dasein in the facticity of its being-with-others (*Mitdasein*; Heidegger 1996, 112). When the conditions are fulfilled so that nationality is accepted as a collective facticity, therefore, the feeling of nationality can work on each individual member of the nation so powerfully that he or she is induced to feel destined to belong to that nation.

One's belonging to the nation, then, would be entirely naturalized so that one's nationality could hardly be distinguished from the naturalized determination of one's existence. Nationality could no longer be differentiated, for instance, from the ethnicity symbolized by the fact of a shared mother tongue, as if the mother tongue were something inherited transhistorically.[17] And, in extreme cases, nationality could be confused with the physiological determination of one's existence.[18] When nationality is naturalized, it is in fact indistinguishable from ethnicity or race. The national body (kokutai) in the sense of the monarchical sovereignty defined in the Meiji Constitution was dismantled and replaced by the popular sovereignty of the postwar constitution under U.S. occupation; however, the national body in the sense of nationality was further naturalized after the collapse of the Japanese Empire. It is no surprise that, even today, almost eight decades after Japan's defeat and seven decades after Japan's independence, many Japanese refute the fact that they were either raised as

Japanese or became Japanese; they refuse to admit that their Japanese identity is a consequence of contingent social conditions; instead, they claim that they were just born Japanese. For them, nationality, ethnicity, and race are indiscriminately confused. But this is exactly the state of affairs that is achievable when nationality is thoroughly naturalized.

In the long run and with the benefit of hindsight from the early years of the twenty-first century, the preservation of the national body (nationality) worked as a remedy for two paramount annoyances in one fell swoop, that is, as an answer to the two problems confronting policy makers in charge of the U.S. occupation of Japan. It helped prevent Japanese nationalism from developing into an aggressive anticolonial type, and also induced it to turn into a national solidarity, a particular kind of national solidarity that is subservient to colonial administration.

Thanks to the prevalent sense of national unity among the Japanese public, MacArthur's administration could manage to prevent a widespread fragmentation of the Japanese nation, despite the fact that a sizable portion of its population turned into what was then called *sangokujin* (三国人, the third-country person or people), meaning people who were neither Japanese nor foreigners, that is, a surplus population resident within the newly defined Japanese territory who could not be classified by the rules of the international world.[19] The third-country people or sangokujin were a portion of the renewed Japanese nation that could remain totally indifferent to intensified nationality; they were not explicitly foreigners, but they would not share the feeling of nationality. In short, they were of an ethnic minority just like the stereotypical figure of the Jews—uprooted cosmopolitans who never truly belonged to the German nation—as promoted by many anti-Semitic nationalists in Germany and in Europe at large in the 1930s. Therefore, the U.S. Occupation Administration as well as the Japanese state regarded these third-country people as potentially the most dangerous segment of the population resident within the newly defined national territory. Beyond the third-country people, the naturalization of nationality advanced and was thoroughly accepted. But to the extent that new nationality was consolidated, this kind of minority population was ostracized from it.

Consequently, as nationality was naturalized, the third-country people— notably resident Koreans for a number of historical reasons—would be turned into the target of the most intensified discriminatory violence of Japanese racism.[20] Until the loss of the empire, the Japanese state had to engage in the integration of its multiethnic population and suppress both racist rhetoric and practice for fear that it would bring about the splintering of the nation. In other words, the wartime Japanese state had to embrace what Takashi Fujitani (2011) calls "polite racism." For the same reason, ethnic nationalism was thoroughly denounced and censored, particularly during the interwar period and the war years. As I argued previously, the Japanese government had to adopt the rhetoric of universalism and antiracism in order to prevent any portion of the national population from undertaking separatist struggles against the colonial state. With the preservation of the national body within the shrunken population and the subsequent naturalization of nationality, there ceased to be the need on the part of the Japanese government to sustain antiracism propaganda. It is remarkable how fast Japanese nationality transformed from a sense of solidarity encompassing a universalistic multiethnic nation to one of a particularistic monoethnic nation after the disintegration of the empire. After the Asia-Pacific War, censorship of ethnic nationalism was lifted, and the Japanese public began to appropriate the rhetoric of ethnic and cultural nationalism openly. The rhetoric of antiracism, which was, among its multifaceted functions, undoubtedly a defense against anticolonial nationalism, lost momentum. Consequently the Japanese public has been deprived of one important preventive measure against the propagation of racist nationalism. They are kept ignorant of antiracism to such an extent that even such obviously racist behaviors and speeches as the infamous public speech referring to sangokujin given by the governor of Tokyo, Ishihara Shintarô, were not denounced in mass media.

Thus, U.S. policy to preserve and naturalize the national body, kokutai, in the liberal sense of nationality solved both major problems at once. It created a stalwart sense of the unity of the ethnic nation, which disallowed fissures inherent in the national community from developing both along social class lines and in regional and professional differences. It reduced the danger of sectarian violence tearing the nation apart, which could have made Japanese society ungovernable. It prevented socialist reforms, of which the U.S. Occupation Administration and Japanese conservatives were most afraid, from being demanded by its citizens. Furthermore, it succeeded in appeasing the nation so that it could be governed most effectively from the viewpoint of colonial administration. The naturalization of nationality proved to be the most successful and pragmatic policy in governing Japan under Pax Americana.

But it also solved another problem, that of antiracism. The U.S. Occupation Administration was most afraid of the antiracist argument, which could easily undermine the legitimacy of American governance, not only in Japan but also in East Asia at large. This was precisely the development that Reischauer's memorandum warned against. However, as nationality was naturalized and appropriated by Japanese opinion leaders, the antiracist rhetoric that the Japanese state and its elite intellectuals had so vehemently deployed to disqualify the legitimacy of American domination in the Pacific and East Asia during the war virtually diminished after the war.

Of course, the U.S. Occupation Administration utilized some measures of censorship to crush antiracism and thereby desensitized the Japanese public to issues of racial discrimination. The most important factor, however, lay in the transformation of Japanese domestic politics; the Japanese willingly forfeited the rhetoric of antiracism and became disinterested in issues of racism in favor of their reified national, ethnic, and racial identity. They wholeheartedly welcomed the naturalization of their nationality, but in return they disinvested from the problem of racism. They were allowed to behave as ethnic and cultural nationalists but at the cost of dodging antiracism.

Transpacific Complicity

Please allow me to skip chronologically across seven decades from 1942, the date of Reischauer's memorandum, to August 2010. I want to introduce two summary observations about the sociopolitical climate in the conservative shift that took place in Japan in the two decades up to the Liberal Democratic Party's (LDP's) defeat in the national election for the Chamber of Representatives in August 2009. For nearly two decades in the 1990s and early 2000s, Japan's national politics drifted to the right and manifested its jingoistic tendency for the first time since the disintegration of the empire.

Since the end of the economic boom in the early 1990s, Japanese mass media have often broadcast statistics indicating the alarming trends in Japanese demography: its rapidly aging composition (27.4 percent of the population were sixty-five years of age or older in 2017, compared with 7.1 percent in 1970); arguably the highest life expectancies in the world (86.99 years among females and 80.75 among males in 2015); the declining population (128 million in 2010, estimated to decline by 30 percent in the next half century); a very low total fertility rate (1.26 children on average born to a woman over her lifetime in 2006). These figures indicate that Japanese society reflects projected patterns of a postindustrial society. Interestingly enough, however, the same figures are often used to predict how increasingly hard it will be, in a matter of a decade or two, to maintain the systems of everyday life that help sustain the stability of family life, work environment, medical welfare, and social services in general. With a shrinking work force, more people will be dependent upon fewer in the national budget; insurance of many sorts (life insurance, property insurance, and so forth) will become too expensive for an average citizen to afford; social welfare (national health insurance, national pension, nursing home care, and so forth) will be cut back drastically. In short, it seems that fewer and fewer Japanese will be able to take for granted the image of a middle-class family life—a nuclear family with two children living in a house in the suburbs with an annual income of some 60,000 U.S. dollars or more—that they thought the majority of the nation could achieve in their lifetime only two decades ago. Instead of the dream of a middle-class society—until the 1980s, sociologists used to estimate, something like 90 percent of Japanese regarded themselves as belonging to the middle class—in the last decade or so, the return of old concerns over class differences, as well as new ones about the loss of hope, have been ubiquitous. I do not think these demographic figures need necessarily be read as predicting a doomsday for Japan, but what is absolutely certain is that they have reinforced the prevalent perception that the Japanese as a nation have lost optimism about their future. Consequently, one of the most popular research areas in the social sciences in Japan today is "the study of hope"; a new field of academic discipline, kibô-gaku (希望学), has emerged. One might be reminded that it was against the backdrop of demographic decline—low birth rates and shrinking population—that the political climate of fascism was nurtured in many countries in Europe during the interwar period.

Let us note that Japanese nationalism has gained its peculiar belligerence against a background of the loss of hope. Without doubt, this pessimism reflects many aspects of Japanese society today, two of which are an increasing income disparity and a weakening of upward social mobility.

In order to elucidate the historical dimension of Japan's current jingoism, let me refer to the family lineage of Abe Shinzô (安倍晋三), who served as prime minister from 2006 to 2007, and again from 2012 to 2020, before Fukuda Yasuo (福田 康夫, 2007–2008). Generally speaking, I do not believe that the knowledge of family lineage explains much in modern politics, even though admittedly we sometimes appeal to monarchical tropes such as the Bush dynasty. Apart from the fact that an increasing number of Japanese parliamentarians come from families of well-established political heritage—the previous Democratic Party prime minister, Hatoyama Yukio (鳩山 由紀夫), is a grandson of Hatoyama Ichirô (鳩山 一郎), the fifty-first, fifty-second, and fifty-third prime minister of Japan (1954–1956); and Asô Tarô (麻生 太郎), the last LDP prime minister (2008–2009) before the LDP defeat, is a grandson of Yoshida Shigeru (吉田 茂), who served as prime minister from 1946 to 1948 and again from 1948 to 1954; Fukuda Yasuo, the prime minister prior to Asô, is a son of Fukuda Takeo (福田 赳夫), who was prime minister from 1976 to 1978—it must be said that Abe Shinzô is symptomatic in more ways than one. But it is probably necessary to keep in mind a few features of Japan's parliamentary politics before we return to the topic of the transpacific complicity of the postwar period.

Abe Shinzô is a son of Abe Shintarô (安倍 晋太郎), who was married to the daughter of Kishi Nobusuke (岸 信介). Hence, Abe Shinzô is a grandson of Kishi Nobusuke. One might say that the specter of the Greater East Asia Co-prosperity Sphere returned with the inauguration of the Abe Shinzô cabinet in 2006, when once again the East Asian Community—the initial name for the Greater East Asia Co-prosperity Sphere—was a fashionable topic of conversation in Northeast Asia. Kishi was one of the political leaders to establish the LDP in 1955, and Abe Shintarô was involved in conservative politics as a core member of the LDP until his death in 1991. It can be argued that Abe Shinzô is a symbolic representation of the complicity of the U.S. imperial presence with the remnants of prewar Japanese imperialism, an eerie echo of the Cold War that has haunted Japan's postwar democracy.

While Abe Shinzô does not seem to demonstrate an acute awareness of the sinister aspects of his family's past, Kishi's grandson has inherited the legacies of Kishi Nobusuke and Abe Shintarô in Japan's conservative politics. It is significant that his grandfather, Kishi Nobusuke, a brilliant bureaucrat of the prewar Ministry of Commerce and Industry, contributed much to the economic and political design of the Greater East Asia Co-prosperity Sphere. Kishi was one of the leading technocrats who organized the Five-Year Industrial Development Plan in Manchu-kuo in the late 1930s before joining the Tôjô Hideki administration in 1941. Undoubtedly he was one of the most important policy makers in industrial logistics for the Japanese Empire. It is said that he laid the foundation for Manchu-kuo's industries and turned Manchuria into an experimental ground for Japan's wartime New Deal. He served as minister of commerce and industry in the Tôjô Hideki cabinet and organized the supply system for the entire region of the Greater East Asia Co-prosperity Sphere.

After Japan's defeat, Kishi was arrested as a Class A war criminal and spent three years in Sugamo Prison in Tokyo, where other Class A war criminals, such as Tôjô Hideki, Sasakawa Ryôichi (笹川 良一), Shiina Etsujirô (椎名 悦二郎), Shôriki Matsutarô (正力 松太郎), and Kodama Yoshio (児玉 誉士夫), were held. While some of the Class A war criminals were executed or died in prison, Kishi, Sasakawa, Shiina, Shoriki, and Kodama were among those who escaped execution. Waiting for his war crime trial, Kishi seems to have established connections with the American occupation authority, and, as American policies took the "return course" under the mandate of the Truman Doctrine, he emerged as the representative of U.S. interests in Japan.

In 1994, the *New York Times* reported that in the 1950s Kishi and his brother, Satô Eisaku (佐藤 栄作), who served as prime minister from 1964 until 1972, demanded that the U.S. Central Intelligence Agency finance them (Weiner 1994). Now we know that at least two of Japan's prime ministers in the postwar period were CIA agents. Kishi's connection to prewar fascist and Class A criminal Sasakawa Ryôichi, who originally founded today's Nippon Foundation, is well known, and with Sasakawa he assisted the activities of the Holy Spirit Association for the Unification of Christianity—the so-called Unification Church, whose followers are derogatorily called "Moonies" in the United States—led by Sun-Myung Moon, and he founded the International Federation of Victory over Communism (勝共連合). Kishi was in charge of many U.S. anticommunist propaganda campaigns in Japan, South Korea, and Taiwan. He was perhaps the most notorious among those politicians of post-war Japan who survived after the disintegration of the empire. It goes without saying that Kishi was very well connected, not only to Japanese colonial bureaucracy but also to the remains of the Japanese colonial system in Korea, Taiwan, and Southeast Asia.

As prime minister, Kishi attempted to consolidate the United States' collective security arrangement by having the U.S.-Japan Security Treaty ratified by the Japanese parliament; however, intellectuals, students, socialists, labor unions, and groups of citizens organized a massive anti–security treaty movement in 1960, as a result of which he was forced to resign as prime minister. Public outrage against Kishi Nobusuke as an opportunist representing continuity from the Japanese Empire to the U.S. empire in East Asia was arguably the most explicit expression against the legacy of wartime authoritarianism on the one hand and in favor of the Japanese people's commitment to democracy on the other hand.

Mutô Ichiyô (武藤 一羊), a sociologist and well-known activist of the transnational people's network, argues that, after the Asia-Pacific War, the Japanese state stood for and continued to legitimate itself upon three constitutional principles that are essentially antinominal to one another.[21] The postwar Japanese state could promote no policy involving foreign affairs and military arrangements that could simultaneously satisfy all three of these constitutional principles. These principles are (1) an anticommunist free world promoted by the United States; (2) an absolute pacifism embodied in the constitution; and (3) an imperialist heritage from the prewar Japanese Empire (Mutô 1999, 16–17). What Abe Shinzô earnestly appealed to was the third principle; he assumed that the first and the third principles could be harmoniously synthesized to the exclusion of the second. As a matter of fact, the United States has made deliberate efforts to accommodate the third principle within the first since the onset of the Cold War in the late 1940s; this explains why prewar imperialists like Kishi were recycled in order to help build the system of U.S. military dominance in post–World War II East Asia.

In the transpacific complicity between the United States and Japan, the topos of negotiation between U.S. policy makers and Japanese conservatives was not over the preservation of the emperor system, but rather the extent to which the third principle of imperial heritage could be implemented. As I have already shown in relation to Reischauer's memorandum, the preservation of the emperor system was anticipated unilaterally by the United States long before the end of the war and was not negotiable. But the principle of imperialist heritage was an entirely different matter since American policy makers came to realize that they had to rely upon the legacies of Japanese colonialism as they learned more about the task of managing the areas of East Asia after the war. The scientifically organized knowledge of local commerce, kinship structures, migration patterns, religious customs, political histories, and judicial systems in the regions, which was absolutely essential for the management of those areas, was all in the hands of the former colonial masters, and the new masters had to find ways to oblige them to hand over the archive of accumulated research on Japanese colonies in East Asia along with the know-how on colonial governance. It is not at all surprising that the U.S. Occupation Administration began to pay particular attention to some officials like KishiNobusuke when the second principle of absolute pacifism embodied in the constitution became more and more counterproductive from the viewpoint of American foreign policies toward the Far East.

What I would like to emphasize here is that the Kishi–Abe (father)–Abe (son) lineage represents the part of the conservative bloc in Japanese politics in which you can find a marriage of prewar Japanese imperial nationalism and postwar U.S. imperial domination. From this perspective, it is understandable that a series of Japanese LDP politicians want to visit the Yasukuni Shrine (靖国神社), the symbolic embodiment of that imperialist heritage.[22] In spite of their rhetoric against the constitution that they claim was imposed upon Japan by Americans, their visit to the shrine constitutes a confirmation of this United States–Japan complicity, from which postwar conservative politics was born in Japan.

Until the 1980s, Japanese conservatives could expect that the first and third principles could easily be accommodated if the second principle (the postwar constitution) could be effectively neutralized. In other words, they believed that U.S. policy makers would not object to their pledge to the principle of Japanese imperialist heritage as long as they agreed to dismantle the constitution. However, it seems to me that a new situation is emerging in East Asia. Let me suggest some of the major transformations that I observe taking place there today.

The Paradox of Postwar Japanese Nationalism

As the new constitution came into effect in 1947, a number of reforms were carried out by the U.S. Occupation Administration, and most of them, including the constitution, have remained unchanged for over seven decades. It may appear that the Japanese government and some important aspects of Japanese national society were fundamentally transformed under American occupation, and that these changes took root in the new nation. Nonetheless, it is still possible to discern a strong nostalgia among the Japanese public for the prewar colonial empire; this has seemed to wax rather than wane in recent decades. Japan lost some of its old colonies or annexed territories, and in losing them, Japan's population was undoubtedly decolonized in the sense of being deprived of colonial territories and prestige. Yet we cannot evade this question: Have the Japanese undergone the process of decolonization?

It goes without saying that, for the majority of residents in the colonies, the effects of decolonization were immediate, and that they ceased to be Japanese when they were deprived of their Japanese nationality. But the majority population of the Japanese Empire, whose family registers were found in Japan proper, managed to insulate themselves from the effects of decolonization except for the presence of what was called sangokujin (third-country people) immediately after the disintegration of their empire. The third-country people were a surplus of the nation, an excess to the national community whose members were supposed to be bound together through sympathy.

In order to confront these questions concerning the failure of decolonization in Japan, I believe we have to return to the problem of transpacific complicity, thanks to which the Japanese nation managed to disavow the loss of its empire while subordinating itself to the American collective security system of Northeast Asia. This is to ask how the Japanese public could reconcile two contradictory attitudes: the one marked by the sense of cultural and racial superiority over peoples of East Asia and the other marked by the sense of colonial subordination and racial inferiority to the United States. What is at issue here is how to conduct a comparative analysis of transpacific complicity, of a political arrangement in which the Japanese imperialist heritage was accommodated in tandem with the anticommunist collective security system promoted by the United States in the 1950s and '60s in Northeast Asia.

By now it should be obvious that a comparative analysis of transpacific complicity prompts us to examine the discipline of area studies in North America and that of Japanese history during the post–World War II era in Japan. It is no accident that I started my analysis of transpacific complicity with Reischauer's 1942 "Memorandum on Policy towards Japan." It is thanks to the mutually reinforcing conditions of transpacific parallelism that area studies in North America and national history in Japan can be treated as one common disciplinary formation in spite of innumerable disparities, dissimilar methodologies, and different readerships. Both academic genres share a number of presumptions that have been held sacrosanct in academic and journalistic discussions of Japanese national character, Japanese colonialism, and Japanese fascism. What is implied in this presumption is that there is no need to examine what constitutes Japan as an area and as a historical unity. Instead of exploring what regimes and social relations allow Japan to be posited as a unity, the disciplinary formation of area studies simply obliges an academic inquiry to begin with the postulation of Japan as an area.

Since the inauguration of the Koizumi Jun'ichirō (小泉純一郎) administration—prior to the Abe administration—the controlling LDP has openly sought a number of pieces of legislation to promote the status of the Self-Defense Agency to that of the Ministry of Defense. Here it is important to note that, although the constitution was originally prepared and legislated by the U.S. Occupation Administration, the official policy of the U.S. government, which succeeded the Truman Doctrine when the U.S. presidency changed from Harry S. Truman to Dwight D. Eisenhower in January 1953, has consistently advocated for changes, particularly, to Article 9, which proscribes Japan's use of military forces to solve international conflicts. In delivering a letter from President Eisenhower to Prime Minister Yoshida Shigeru and Emperor Hirohito in November 1953 in Tokyo, Richard Nixon, then vice president of the United States, publicly declared, "Now if disarmament was right in 1946, why is it wrong in 1953? And if it was right in 1946 and wrong in 1953, why doesn't the United States admit for once that it made a mistake? And I am going to do something that I think perhaps ought to be done by people in public life. I'm going to admit right here that the United States did make a mistake in 1946" (cited in Dower 1979, 464–465; and Schaller 1997, 69). Therefore, there has never been a reason for Japanese nationalists' demand for a change in the constitution to be perceived as anti-American, either by the United States or by the Japanese government. Even in their demand for the change of the constitution imposed upon the Japanese nation by the United States of America, the Japanese conservatives are dutifully following the American prerogative. It is no more than an endorsement of the American initiative and leadership; it is nothing but a confirmation by a party occupying the positionality of the subordinate, of the intention of one occupying the positionality of the dominant. In other words, the attempt to change the postwar constitution amounts to no more than a transferential appropriation of the desire of the colonizer by the colonized. Under the current constitution, the Japanese Supreme Court offered a juridical interpretation that the existing Japanese military force, although one of the largest in annual expenditure and one of the most technologically sophisticated in the world, is a self-defense force that supposedly is more like a police force.

What has been deliberately withdrawn from public debates on constitutional change is the question of national sovereignty with regard to the existing Self-Defense Forces (自衛隊) in Japan. A peculiar and unexamined assumption has prevailed, according to which, in the wake of the implementation of a new constitution without pacifist articles, the Japanese state would somewhat automatically regain its sovereignty so that its military forces would be under the command of the Japanese government and its commanding official, the prime minister. However, it is glaringly obvious that this is merely a fantastic scenario. Ever since its initial establishment in 1950 as the Supplementary Police Force (警察予備隊) under the U.S. Occupation Administration, Japanese Self-Defense Forces have been designed and organized as subordinate organs within the American global command network in the postwar collective security system. Unless the SOFA that dictates Japan's semicolonial status and U.S. extraterritoriality in detail is thoroughly rewritten, it is highly unlikely that this constitutional change will allow for Japan's military independence from American domination and its extensive network of military bases and intelligence in the world.[23] Instead it will only deprive the Japanese government of the grounds for the policy choice to refuse to send troops overseas to solve international conflicts as mercenary troops under American command, just like the case of South Korean troops who were sent to Southeast Asia under U.S. command during the war in Vietnam (Park 2003, 80–120). In other words, it seems much more probable that a constitutional change would accelerate Japan's military subordination to the global system of unilateral military control by the United States when Pax Americana is receding.

Consequently, what I want to call "the paradox of Japanese nationalism" encourages the Japanese to develop two seemingly contradictory attitudes. While they insist on separation from and even indifference toward people of neighboring countries in East and Southeast Asia, they perversely welcome

U.S. domination and tend to find their own desires within the scenario of Pax Americana.

To understand this paradox of Japanese nationalism, we should probe the history of postwar Japan and refer to what has been known in Northeast and Southeast Asia as Japan's amnesia toward its colonial and war responsibilities. But most importantly, we have to look at the paradox of Japanese nationalism, not within the framework of linear national history, but rather through a comparative transnational perspective.

A comparative analysis of transpacific complicity will reveal to us the formation of a new governmentality, the emergence of which did not necessarily lead to the disappearance of the nation-state. Virtually speaking, this new governmentality reduces humanity to nationality and is most violently effectual through national humanism, as I described in chapter 1. What I want to suggest is a historical transition from the American occupation of Japan to the recent violent manifestation of national humanism. Therefore, the scope cannot be limited to the transpacific complicity of the United States and Japan. More broadly, it attests to the general transformation of state sovereignty in the late twentieth and early twenty-first centuries. It enhances the relationship of complicity with each nation-state and thereby deprives the nation-state of sovereignty. The fate of the postwar Japanese constitution is probably the best testimony to the fact that the complicity of the United States and Japan has followed the embryonic logic of this new emerging governmentality.

In this volume, I have dealt with the issues of race and racism from multiple perspectives. Evidently the spatial structure of the West and the Rest, anthropological difference, the speciation of humanity, and other issues are all relevant to my inquiry into how race is constituted, how racism is practiced, or how racial identity is performatively installed. Furthermore, an analysis of transpacific complicity between the United States and Japan sheds light on how the critique of racism has been managed and displaced in the disciplines of area studies in the United States on the one hand and in national studies—national literature, national history, national ethnology, and so on—in Japan on the other in order to enhance a particular type of essentialization of ethnonational identity and put forth a particular type of cultural nationalism that could be accommodated in Pax Americana.

Seven decades later, such a political settlement has produced a situation where an increasing number of the Japanese have become shameless about Japanese imperialist maneuvers in Asia in the 1930s and early 1940s (Ukai 2000) while being amnesiatically happy with the new U.S. strategic arrangement in East Asia, except when occasionally jarred by incidents like an English-language book on the Rape of Nanjing (Chang 1997; on the historical significance of Chang's book, see Gluck 2002, 191–234) and the U.S. congressional resolution to condemn the Abe Shinzô administration's attitude on the Comfort Women (wartime sex slavery) issue. It is true that an overtly anti-American rhetoric may sometimes be used by these populist nationalists, not to mention those self-declared realist nationalists who boast of their technocratic rationality. However, they will never take issue with postwar U.S. occupation policies since, thanks to these policies, the Japanese were exempted from war responsibility and colonial guilt. While claiming to be victims of American domination, they scarcely pay attention to the victims of Japanese aggression. In leading the movement to censor the topic of the Comfort Women in Japanese high school history textbooks and public television broadcasting, Abe Shinzô was well known for his open dismissal of Japanese war responsibility and sex slavery (Yoshimi and Yoneyama 2006). As later in this chapter I offer my assessment of how Abe's aberrant behavior during his official visit to the District of Columbia was conditioned by the double structure of U.S.-Japan complicity, he seemed to believe his jingoistic stance was implicitly endorsed by the United States.

Given the structure of transpacific complicity between the United States and Japan, within the framework of which the LDP has been dominant in Japanese politics for more than half a century, the Japanese public, although not all of it, of course, expected Abe, the LDP president, to act the way he did, and they endorsed him to a considerable extent. Hence, the key question here is, how should we understand the structure of transpacific complicity?

What has been postponed and impeded in this structure of complicity is the very process of decolonization, the process in which individuals would gradually learn how to form new social relations not premised upon the legacies and vanities of colonialisms. Yet are either the Americans or the Japanese capable of discarding their national pride, that is, their colonialist conceit? Let me emphasize in passing that one of the core questions in decolonization is how to liberate ourselves from racism. In this sense, decolonization cannot be dissociated from knowledge production for the sake of antiracism at large.

In this analysis of the structure of the transpacific complicity, let me issue two cautionary disclaimers:

1 No doubt what I have described as transpacific complicity is a sort of colonial relationship reproduced over the last several decades between the United States and Japan. Nevertheless, this apparently one-sided relationship should never be comprehended as merely an

extension of classical colonial domination, according to which one territory that has failed to constitute itself as a territorial state sovereignty is conquered and ruled by a fully fledged nation-state. Through this complicity, on the contrary, national sovereignty itself has been transformed and reconstituted so that the international world of the late twentieth and early twenty-first centuries cannot be construed in the vocabulary of nineteenth-century liberalism. It is, therefore, pointless to criticize this transpacific complicity from the viewpoint of a nationalist emancipation from colonial domination. After all, this complicity was a product of arduous intellectual, political, and administrative maneuvers—colonizers' hard work, one might say— that came out of Japanese and American efforts to neutralize and domesticate anticolonial nationalisms. No doubt it was a consequence of the bilateral endeavor to "colonize anticolonialism."[24]

2 Discussing the transpacific complicity between the United States and Japan, I have not limited myself to the diplomatic and colonial relationship between these two countries. By transpacific complicity, I am also concerned with the historical trajectory of successive projects of the East Asian Community (the Greater East Asia Co-prosperity Sphere) and the United States' collective security system in East Asia. In comprehending transpacific complicity, I sought the continuity of the agenda of imperial nationalism rather than a disruption between two imperial nationalisms. Even though Japan apparently occupied a subordinate position in its relationship to the United States after the Asia-Pacific War, until recently it could continue to behave as if it were an empire in its relationship to other countries in East Asia. It is for this reason that I call this peculiar international status of Japan "an empire under subcontract."

This means that I want to know to what extent the futures of imperial nationalisms can be extrapolated from our knowledge of the past and the present. I am by no means sure that nationalisms of the region (South Korea, Taiwan, the Philippines, and those in Southeast Asia) will evade a similar complicity, even though my knowledge of these national formations is limited. Chinese nationalism is a different case, but it is important to see how it can give rise to a different scenario of internationality and regional hegemony. Nevertheless, the question of nationality cannot be overlooked in Northeast Asia either. More importantly, this analysis of transpacific complicity must be articulated on the one hand to our concern with racism as a naturalized form of nationalism and on the other to a general inquiry into the emerging transnationality beyond the horizon of colonial modernity.

The Coming of the End of Pax Americana

At the end of the Asia-Pacific War/World War II, U.S. policy makers sought to find ways to appropriate Japan's jingoist ethos into their colonial governance of Japan. Arguably, the American governance of postwar Japan is, as a colonial rule, the most successful in the span of human history, to such an extent that the people in Japan do not reflect on how they are dominated by the United States. In contrast to the occupation of Japan, the occupation of Iraq by the United States and its allies could not give rise to cooperation with the ruling forces by the people of the occupied territories. The George W. Bush administration destroyed Saddam Hussein's government, broke up the state bureaucracy, and executed its dictator as soon as American troops defeated the Iraqi military. Its executioners seemed to believe that a system of government could be built anew based upon the consensus of the Iraqi nation after first destroying the institutions of state governance.

What characterized this reckless strategy toward the Iraqi population was a lack of elementary knowledge of modern politics: allegedly Bush's lieutenants did not understand that the national community or ethnic nation of Iraq does not exist independently of the Iraqi state. A nation does not exist naturally; it must be artificially manufactured. In modern times, the modern state takes the historically specific form of the nation-state. It is generally presumed that the polity called the nation-state is composed of the nation and the state in a peculiar synthesis, two entities each of which purportedly exists independently of the other. But, above all else, it cannot be overlooked that the element of the nation is of the imagination and that it is actualized as an imaginary aesthetic construct. It is supposed to be existent only insofar as certain of the state institutions are working; in the absence of the reproductive apparatuses of the state, the nation cannot be reproduced either. The policy makers of the Roosevelt and Truman administrations fully understood this point: if the state apparatuses for national integrity in Japan were missing, the unity of its people would be lost; if the unity of the nation were lost, the American occupation of Japan would be extremely difficult, if not outright impossible. The situation in Japan could easily follow the fate of China under Japanese occupation. It would easily be dragged into a quagmire of civil war.

To evade this uncontrollable situation, the most effective solution readily at hand for the supreme commander of the Allied Powers was the preservation of the emperor system. A graduate student in my seminar once exclaimed about the American governance of Iraq: "You should not have killed Saddam Hussein! You should have saved him and conferred on him the status of symbolic dictator if you wished to repeat the example of Japan!"

To a great degree, international politics has been shaped by the global vision outlined by the policy makers of the United States of America ever since the Asia-Pacific War/World War II ended with the defeat of the Axis Alliance of Germany, Italy, and Japan. As the post–World War II era was marked by the subsequent decline of the colonial empires of Britain, France, the Netherlands, and so forth, these old colonial orders were gradually appropriated into Pax Americana. Of course, we cannot forget about the period of the Cold War from 1947 through 1991, the traces of which are still visible in the divided Korean Peninsula and in the presence of two Chinas across the Taiwan Strait. Under the polarization of the liberal bloc against the Soviet bloc, the United States and its allies encircled the Soviet Union, the People's Republic of China, and their satellite countries and attempted to isolate them in international politics and world trade. As a result, in the Western Pacific there was only limited communication and trade between the so-called socialist alliance of China, North Korea, and North Vietnam and the countries under the U.S. system of collective security, South Korea, Japan, Taiwan, the Philippines, Indonesia, and so on. Although the People's Republic of China and North Korea largely remained outside the sphere of American influence until the 1980s, it is undeniable that the international order of East Asia has evolved within the framework of Pax Americana due to the exceptionally powerful military and economic presence of the United States. Toward the end of the twentieth century, Northeast Asia was increasingly noted for its rapid growth in consumer capitalism and digitalized mass media, but it is indisputable that the modernization of these countries was initially stimulated by the United States.

It was during the 1970s, when the United States was defeated in the Vietnam War, that the first symptom of exhaustion in Pax Americana could be detected. Further, the series of misconceived policies undertaken by the George W. Bush administration after the 9/11 attack has alerted us to the extent to which the global authority associated with American hegemony has already been hollowed out. Now that its military withdrawal from Iraq and Afghanistan seems inevitable, the United States cannot continue to rely upon what Chalmers Johnson (2004) called "the Empire of Bases." Neither can it return to the old Cold War policy of containment. As a result, it is not surprising that the U.S. government has indicated its willingness to consider a new Pacific order based upon a collaboration between the United States and China; this illustrates the advent of a new historical era in which, even Americans have to acknowledge, Pax Americana has been eclipsed.[25]

In the seventy-four years since the defeat of Japanese imperial nationalism, Japanese intellectuals have never encountered a more important problematic in regard to Japan's future relationships with its neighboring countries than that of the end of Pax Americana. To my astonishment, as I have already noted a few times, Japanese domestic politics seems to remain totally indifferent to this changing international environment; I continue to be bewildered by the campaign pledges and policy speeches offered by the Abe Shinzô administration of the LDP after they returned to power in the Japanese House of Representatives election in December 2012. Not only the governing alliance of the LDP and the New Kômeito but also Japanese mass media at large have managed to ignore the historical circumstances in which Japan has been situated for the last two decades or so. They deliberately ignore Japan's semicolonial status in relation to the United States; they continue to overlook the emerging economic reality of Northeast Asia in which Japan no longer enjoys special status as "the only genuinely modernized country in Asia," a label bestowed on it by the worshippers of modernization theory. In the 1960s and '70s, when, within Cold War geopolitics, Japan was the most important satellite state/ ally of the United States in the Western Pacific, it used to enjoy a relatively high standard of living and an exceptionally modern social system, perceived as vastly superior to any in neighboring countries. The per capita average income, for example, was more than five times that of South Korea or Taiwan and perhaps nearly twenty times that of China; an increasing number of Japanese people could benefit from the system of social welfare, initially designed during the Asia-Pacific War and evolved after the war, to eventually become almost equivalent to those systems in West European social democracies; Japan became notorious for its "examination hell" but produced a highly educated working population, and the ratio of Japanese people who received higher education was incomparable in Asia or Europe (although not in North America); consequently, Japanese industry could rely upon a very skilled and highly trained labor force for the continuing growth of its economy; values particular to the polity of liberal democracy were adopted in Japanese society to such an extent that basic human rights such as freedom of speech appeared to be socially accepted. In comparison to Japan, South Korea and Taiwan appeared underdeveloped and were still plagued with the remnants of premodernity and antidemocratic dictatorships. Few would have objected to the observation that Japan was the most advanced or developed society in Asia, partly because people still believed in the simplistic notion of progress and the developmental history of modernization, not only in Japan but also in the so-called Third World at large.

Accordingly, in spite of a brief hiatus immediately after the collapse of the Japanese Empire at the end of the Asia-Pacific War, it seemed as if Japan could continue to maintain its status as a colonial empire as the leader of the Greater East Asia Co-prosperity Sphere in East Asia. Of course, this is a matter of collective fantasy, but at least during the period of Japan's high economic growth—from the mid-1950s through the 1980s—there used to be objective historical conditions that contributed to the collective delusion of Japan as an empire.

However, in the late 1970s, just as the eclipse of Pax Americana was first visible, the relative position of Japan in relation to its neighbors began to change. First, a small number of people began to notice that economies were growing at incredible rates in countries such as Singapore and Hong Kong. Then, industries in Taiwan and South Korea began to expand rapidly on their paths to modernization. In the 1980s, the People's Republic of China joined these new dragons and began to attract foreign capital. And now, after more than three decades, the economic configuration of Northeast Asia has completely changed, and it is on the cusp of becoming the largest economic region in the world.

It is evident that not only Japan's relative position vis-à-vis its Asian neighbors but also the relationship of Japanese individuals to peoples in East Asia have been redefined as a result of the drastic changes of the last several decades. Apparently it is simply ridiculous to believe that Japan still maintains the status of an old colonial empire in the Western Pacific today. It is equally outlandish for the Japanese to behave as if they are the only modernized people in Northeast Asia and are entitled to advance the mission of civilizing their less advanced neighbors.

Nevertheless, the extreme rightists who dominate the LDP and the Japan Restoration Party (日本維新の会) still seem to be committed to this old fantasy of an imperialist Japan. How could these political forces gain sufficient votes to occupy center stage in Japan's national politics when they dare to ignore the actuality of the international circumstances in which Japan is situated in the twenty-first century? What sort of strategy do they mobilize to persuade the Japanese nation to persist in embracing such an anachronistic vision of imperial Japan against the torrent of counterevidence of objective historical conditions that surround the people of Japan today?

If the Japanese seriously wish to coexist with their Asian neighbors, the first question they must pose is this: how and why has such a delusional lack of recognition of the historical situation gained such broad acceptance in Japan, when it only confines the Japanese nation to hikikomori or a reclusive withdrawal (ひきこもり) and traps them in a melancholy of collective self-pity?

State Sovereignty under Pax Americana

As has been made clear, Japan has been a satellite state under the hegemony of the United States of America ever since the defeat of the Japanese Empire in 1945. Since its independence in 1952 with the end of the Allied occupation, Japan cannot be portrayed as a colony in the classical sense of the term. It cannot be subsumed under any of the categories of non-self-governing territories listed by the United Nations: it is not an overseas territory like Bermuda or the Falkland Islands administered by Britain, or an unincorporated organized territory like the U.S. Virgin Islands or Guam, or an overseas collectivity like French New Caledonia. Rather, it holds a peculiar form of state sovereignty according to which Japan is at the same time colonized and independent. This new form of state sovereignty must be analyzed and conceptualized so as to appreciate the system of international governance we have customarily called "Pax Americana."

According to international law, Japan is a fully fledged sovereign state, so it is supposed to behave as an independent state in international politics. Yet in the domains of diplomatic and military affairs, it is subordinated in an obviously asymmetrical relationship with the United States. The Japanese government has disavowed and concealed this semicolonial relationship, but its colonial subordination became glaringly obvious when the two countries had to negotiate the status of American military forces in Japan's territories such as Okinawa. Unlike the U.S.-Iraq Status of Forces Agreement (SOFA), the U.S.-Japan SOFA, initially signed under the San Francisco Peace Treaty and still valid today after many modifications, continues to give extraterritorial privileges to American military personnel stationed in Japan.

A few years after the end of World War II, the supreme commander of the Allied Powers was forced to redefine the policy goals for the Allied occupation of Japan and Northeast Asia. The United States had to drastically change its policy toward East Asia, which resulted in a policy shift from the democratization and demilitarization of Japan to the rehabilitation of Japan as a cordon sanitaire against communism. Until 1949, when the Chinese Nationalist Party was expelled from mainland China and the People's Republic of China was inaugurated, American policy makers envisioned the postwar order of East Asia with China as the pivot; the United States was going to dominate the vast areas and peoples of the former Greater East Asia Co-prosperity Sphere by encouraging and overseeing the economic and social development of China. Yet, with the victory of the Chinese Communist Party, America's entire vision of East Asia had to be reconfigured. As is well known, what prompted this drastic alteration of American policy toward East Asia was called "the Loss of China."

The expression strikes us as somewhat outlandish, but it discloses very well what was occurring in the minds of American diplomats, bureaucrats, statesmen, and the public around that time. In order to lose something, you must first own it. Unless you own a wallet, you can neither claim it as yours nor lose it. So you cannot lose somebody else's property before you take it from that person. Then what does the expression "the Loss of China" imply? In order to blame somebody for the Loss of China, you must first own China. There must have been the presumption that China was already in America's possession. But, at that moment, did the United States already own China? Did it not belong to the people in China? Evidently, the American public assumed that they were granted two prerogatives in their imagination: first, just as the Japanese assumed it before the Americans, people in China were incapable of owning their own land—an entitlement assumed by sovereign states in the classical system of Eurocentric international law—and, second, China was already a promised land in the sense that the United States was ordained to redeem the old China in its Manifest Destiny. In a sense, the Loss of China tells us about the imperialist birthright that American leaders had assumed about East Asia. At that time, it was taken for granted that, after the defeat of the Japanese Empire, China already belonged to the United States of America.

What happened in response to the Loss of China was the so-called Reverse Course, which began around 1948 and lasted until 1952. The U.S. government reconsidered its long-term strategy toward East Asia and began to envision its emerging order with Japan as the pivotal center of American hegemony. As was illustrated by Richard Nixon's public statement in his 1953 visit to Japan, the U.S. government undertook a threefold attempt in place of the policies of democratization and demilitarization of Japan: to rehabilitate Japanese heavy industry, to reestablish Japanese capacities for rearmament, and to assign the role of an empire under subcontract to Japan. A totally different role was then expected of Japan: it began to be regarded as a bridgehead against the onslaught of communism for the American colonial order in East Asia. As already discussed above, as Japan resumed the status of an empire under subcontract, a number of Class A war criminals who had managed warfare during the Asia-Pacific War were rehabilitated onto the stage of Japanese national politics. In East Asia, the United States thus inherited the Greater East Asia Co-prosperity

Sphere by reassigning the agents of Japanese imperial nationalism to the service of American imperial nationalism.

Along the lines of the Reverse Course, the attitude of the U.S. government toward the constitution of Japan, which was essentially written and introduced by the U.S. Occupation Administration in 1946, took a 180-degree turn. In 1950, soon after the outbreak of war in the Korean Peninsula, the National Police Reserve, which would evolve into the National Safety Forces in 1952 and eventually the Japan Self-Defense Forces in 1954, was established by dictate of the supreme commander of the Allied Powers. Let me restate once again that since that time the U.S. government has been consistently hostile toward the postwar constitution, so in its anticonstitution campaign the Abe Shinzô administration took advantage of this American hostility toward the so-called Peace Constitution.

As a matter of fact, in the 1960s and '70s, conservative politicians with liberal leanings within the LDP organized an orchestrated resistance against American pressure to change the constitution. But conversely, there were some LDP politicians like Kishi Nobusuke who positioned themselves as agents of the United States in Japan.[26] One might as well call these political actors "war criminal conservatives" precisely because they did not have any other option but to become lackeys for American interests in East Asia for fear that U.S. intelligence agents would take advantage of their war criminal records to blackmail them.[27] Undoubtedly, in Japanese society, this group of war criminal conservatives benefited most from the American Cold War policy of containment.

In the 1950s and '60s, it was politically staged that the principles of Japan's imperialist heritage and the anticommunist liberalism of the United States could be somewhat accommodated within each other through under-the-table negotiations between political brokers of the two countries. Particularly for those war criminal conservatives who wanted to boast of the glory of the Japanese Empire, the years during and soon after the Reverse Course were almost a honeymoon period. The right-wing politicians who dominate the LDP today have inherited the legacies of the war criminal conservatives. It is not surprising, therefore, that these extremist politicians want to depict the Cold War era of U.S. containment policies as if it were a rosy era of an extended Japanese Empire.

But, as I have suggested above, the international conditions that allowed for the empire under subcontract to enjoy its exceptional status vis-à-vis neighboring countries are no longer present. Today, it is getting more and more difficult for the United States to shoulder the economic burden of the collective security system globally, and in Northeast Asia in particular, so the costs of

American peace in Northeast Asia must be redistributed among the countries in the Western Pacific.

It is important to keep in mind that Japan was an exceptionally important factor in U.S. policies toward East Asia in the 1950s and '60s. During the Meiji Restoration, the Japanese state, which adopted many institutions for a modern nation-state ahead of any other country in Asia, pursued the policies of capitalist modernization and emerged as one of the colonial powers by the beginning of the twentieth century. The development of industrial capitalism radically transformed many aspects of life in the Japanese archipelago; the Japanese assumed the position of a colonial empire in East Asia that would supposedly guide other peoples in neighboring countries toward modernization through the implementation of Japan's civilizing mission. This sense of civilizing mission was inevitably discredited when the Japanese Empire surrendered unconditionally to the Allied Powers in 1945. One would have expected the Japanese nation to give up its imperial ambition once and for all during the Allied occupation immediately after their defeat.

At the onset of the Cold War, however, the geopolitical conditions of Northeast Asia changed once again, around the time of the Loss of China and the Korean War. Thanks to its comparatively early modernization in the late nineteenth and early twentieth centuries, Japanese society could enjoy a number of exceptional conditions that did not exist elsewhere in East Asia: the modern bureaucracy created by the Meiji state; a highly developed system of national education that produced a highly educated and literate population; an accumulation of scientific and technological knowledge, not only among the social elites but also among the masses; a thoroughly secularized public culture in which no religious organization—except for the authority of the emperor—could compete with the national government in its spiritual and political influence; and accumulated capital in the form of technical know-how, management skills, and organized labor of large corporations. While the industrial facilities and urban housing had been decimated by American bombing during the war, human resources remained almost intact in the decades after Japan's surrender.

By the 1960s, as the followers of modernization theory used to say, Japan was supposedly the model for modernization that all the underdeveloped countries should emulate. From the viewpoint of American policy makers, in other words, Japan was an exceptionally vital element in the design of the United States' collective defense strategy in East Asia. In terms of economic output, the per capita standard of living, the industrial capacity to adopt new technology and to produce high-technology products including the most sophisticated weaponry, Japan was an unmistakably valuable asset not to be co-opted by America's enemies. From the strategic vantage point of the United States, it was so obvious that the success of their containment policy was to a large extent dependent upon whether or not Japan could be persuaded to distance itself from either the communist bloc or the Third World nonaligned countries and instead to ally itself with the so-called free world. Therefore, American policy makers understood very well that what was at stake in their approach to Japan was how to both nurture hatred among the Japanese public for the Chinese and maintain a sense of disdain toward other Asians; this would strike a wedge between the People's Republic of China and Japan. As the Reverse Course became the official directive of American global strategy, the United States began to look for ways to impose on the Japanese public the image of the ideal Japanese, a sort of ego ideal that was expected of the Japanese (期待される人間像).[28] It is most interesting that, in consideration of the long ideological disputes between the United States of America and Japan over issues of racism during the interwar period, what the American policy makers expected of the Japanese was precisely that they should not hesitate to hide their sense of racial superiority over the Chinese and Koreans. What becomes apparent in this analysis of U.S.-Japan transpacific complicity is the mutuality of desire between Americans and Japanese in the postwar period, the very structure that I have elsewhere called "civilizational transference," in which one party's desire for the other party is transferred from it to the other and so reproduced in the manner that is generally called transference in psychoanalysis.[29] As we outlined in chapter 5, this psychoanalytical formula must be modified and redefined in terms of a power differential between majoritarian and minoritarian positionalities. Civilizational difference occurs in the social field oriented by polarity of a microgradient in which the majoritarian positionality is constituted in tandem with the minoritarian positionality. It is expected that the Japanese, occupying the positionality of the colonized in this case, should desire to fashion themselves according to an image imposed upon them, but it is the very desire that the (white) Americans, occupying the positionality of the colonizers in this dialectic game of mutual recognition, have of the Japanese. Simply put, the Americans wanted the Japanese to be unambiguously racist, and for American policy makers, the image of the Japanese striving to discard their own racism toward other Asians of underdeveloped countries was nothing but a nightmare.

John Foster Dulles, who supervised the San Francisco Peace Treaty before he was appointed secretary of state by President Eisenhower, envisioned Japan's future relationships with other Asian countries. Probably recalling his personal experience as a legal counsel for the U.S. delegation at the Versailles

Peace Conference, Dulles took into consideration in his overall comprehension of George Kennan's proposed containment policy his discernment that the Japanese attitude toward Chinese and Koreans was very much dictated by their own sentiment of racial superiority. Of course, Dulles did not hesitate to integrate his observation into U.S. policy toward Japan; neither did he fail to build persuasive rhetoric for the Japanese people's sense of their own standing in the hierarchy of races in the world. Thus, in the U.S. policy of containment it is not difficult to witness Dulles's prescience, which can be interpreted either as his observation or as his anticipation, that the Japanese ought to be racists. Of course, the temporality of this prescience is ambiguous. Is it a prediction of the state of affairs in the future based on factual knowledge? Or is it sheer wishful thinking for actualizing in the future? Conceivably it is both, and we must not lose sight of this ambiguous temporality in our analysis of Pax Americana.

Dulles believed that the Western Alliance, which forms the core of the free world, was a sort of elite club exclusive to Anglo-Saxons and that the Japanese were desperate to join it. Frederick S. Dunn, a diplomatic historian, once summarized the historical records left behind by Dulles as follows: "It might be possible to capitalize on the Japanese feeling of racial and social superiority to the Chinese, Koreans, and Russians, and to convince them that as part of the free world they would be in equal fellowship which is superior to the members of the Communist world" (Dunn 1963, 100).

Observing the recent controversies among the governments of Japan, the People's Republic of China, and the Republic of Korea over the issues of the prime minister's visit to the Yasukuni Shrine, the Comfort Women problem, and historical revisionism, one cannot help but admit the farsightedness of Dulles. The Abe Shinzô administration maintained a demonstratively condescending attitude toward China and South Korea, but it is immediately apparent that the scenario for its conduct duplicated the one prepared for the sake of the policy of containment by American policy makers more than a half century ago. It appears that what Abe Shinzô and his cabinet wanted to achieve in the sphere of international diplomacy was a belated revival of the containment policy, of the design for international order initially put forward in the Truman Doctrine and further pursued by the secretary of state in the Eisenhower administration. Speaking from the present moment in history, we must concede to Dulles's astute and accurate observation of Japanese statesmen and bureaucrats. But it is also imperative for us not to overlook the fact that his prescience gave rise to the necessary institutional conditions for the Japanese racial consciousness to be shaped in certain ways in postwar Japanese society. It is under Pax Americana that the Japanese have been encouraged to nurture and maintain their sense of racial superiority to the Chinese and the Koreans. In our analysis of the discourses of Pax Americana, therefore, we must strive to accurately and objectively describe conditions in Northeast Asia under the mounting hegemony of the United States of America; but we must also not forget the prescriptive and productive aspects of this arrangement, of how things were expected to be under Pax Americana.

Except for a few important incidents, such as the citizens' nationwide protest movement against the U.S. collective security system that occurred a few years after Dulles's death, the Japanese government as well as the majority of the Japanese people have behaved just as he predicted and anticipated they would. And we must remind ourselves that we still live in this international hegemonic arrangement called Pax Americana. Without analyzing Pax Americana in its descriptive as well as prescriptive aspects, we cannot arrive at an adequate historical comprehension of both the Japanese racism that poses incorrigible obstacles in relationships with neighboring countries and how American policy makers succeeded in building a wedge between Japanese and Chinese or Korean nations.

Japanese Nationalism and the New Definition of Territorial State Sovereignty

The U.S. secretary of state, his staff, and many experts in area studies on Northeast Asia thus made concerted efforts to find effective ways to make the Japanese want to stay on the side of the Anglo-Saxon elite club since Japan presented such a strategically important role in American foreign policies. Retrospectively speaking, there were two main strategic reasons why Japan was so important for the United States of America toward the end of the 1940s and into the early 1950s.

First, as a result of the Allied occupation and the redefinition of state sovereignty, Japan was given the status of a satellite state subordinated to the global hegemony of the United States. As was disclosed in the citizens' movement against the ratification of the U.S.-Japan Security Treaty in 1960, however, Japanese nationalism could potentially have been anti-American and anticolonial. Should this potential have been actualized, it would have been predicted that the Japanese government would get closer to the People's Republic of China and slip from the policy of containment. Of course, this was what U.S. policy makers most feared.

By then, through the implementation of the postwar emperor system, however, the United States of America had successfully turned Japanese nationalism into an instrument of colonial governance. This was most evident in the behavior of right-wing nationalists (国粋主義者) after Japan's defeat. The political motto they displayed in their street demonstrations was "Support the United States and oppose the Soviet Union" (「親米反ソ」); this implied that these ultranationalists wanted to embrace the American forces occupying Japan while loathing peoples of socialist countries, none of whom participated in the occupation of Japan. Their nationalism embraced the very colonizers who were in control of Japanese land and people at that time, yet they did not hesitate to call themselves patriots. Their political doctrine was not merely blatantly ludicrous but also somewhat self-contradictory. What sort of nationalists were they to embrace the foreign forces who ruled their land? As a matter of fact, authentically patriotic nationalism had effectively perished in Japan after the Asia-Pacific War, except among leftists with socialist and communist orientations. The only viable versions of nationalism in postwar Japan were among those on the left, among the groups of Japanese citizens who aspired to socialist ideals and remained critical of the United States' hegemony in East Asia. Nonetheless, it is important to keep in mind that the ludicrousness that characterized the postwar right-wingers has remained up to the present day. The nationalism of the Abe Shinzô administration was distinct from the classical version that insists on the principle of national autonomy and national camaraderie for the society of sympathy; today it is no more than an anticommunist movement that promotes itself in the name of patriotism, exemplified by such organizations as the International Association for Victory over Communism that was initially sponsored by the U.S. Central Intelligence Agency.[30]

The second reason for Japan's extraordinary importance to the United States is that Japanese statesmen, bureaucrats, business executives, and academics retained the know-how of colonial governance over territories that Japan used to occupy and govern. After inheriting the Greater East Asia Co-prosperity Sphere from the Japanese Empire, U.S. policy makers found themselves with neither a sufficient number of experts on the societies involved nor prerequisite colonial expertise whereby to rule them. It is in this context that the Class A war criminal Kishi Nobusuke emerged as an exceptionally convenient asset for the U.S. government. As previously stated, Kishi was well known as a kakushin kanryô (reform bureaucrat) who served in the Tôjô Hideki cabinet during the war as minister of greater East Asia in charge of logistics throughout the region of the Greater East Asia Co-prosperity Sphere. In this respect, Kishi was an ideal person for American policy makers to assign the business of an empire under subcontract.

In national politics after the Allied occupation of Japan, a number of prominent politicians emerged who implicitly or explicitly represented American interests in Japan and East Asia at large. Who were these politicians with such dubious backgrounds who played such important roles in what is customarily referred to as the regime change of postwar Japan? Who were these war-criminal conservatives who dominated Japanese national politics behind the scenes? Included among Kishi Nobusuke's fellow prisoners at the Sugamo Prison are Sasakawa Ryôichi, Shôriki Matsutarô, and Kodama Yoshio, who played significant roles in the postwar establishment of U.S. hegemony in Japan and Northeast Asia.[31]

Soon after Japan's defeat, Kishi Nobusuke was arrested as a Class A war criminal by the U.S. Occupation Administration. After his release from Sugamo Prison and as American policies toward Japan took a 180-degree turn (the Reverse Course) in the late 1940s and the early 1950s, he was given financial support and assigned to prominent roles in Japanese politics in the 1950s by the U.S. government. In 1956, he served as the minister of foreign affairs in the Ishibashi Tanzan (石橋 湛山) cabinet. In 1957, he became prime minister and led the Japanese government for two successive terms until he was forced to resign in the midst of the turmoil of the Anpo Tôsô—the citizens' movement against the ratification of the U.S.-Japan Security Treaty—in 1960.

Kishi Nobusuke, Sasakawa Ryôichi, Shôriki Matsutarô, and Kodama Yoshio worked in different fields and helped to consolidate the United States' domination of Japan. In this respect, the multiple roles Shôriki played for the CIA illustrate how the transpacific complicity between the United States and Japan was consolidated in the first few decades after Japan's defeat. Shôriki engaged in a number of different industries as well as the publication of newspapers: the newly introduced television broadcasting, professional sports, and mass entertainment, including the business of game parks. What interconnects these different fields is the theme of propaganda: how to produce, censor, manage, and distribute information for mass consumption. Much to our astonishment, he could quite accurately predict the general directions in which postwar Japanese society would be transformed, the directions in which Japan would become one of the most advanced societies in terms of consumerism and mass media. In this sense, Shôriki was the most useful instrument of the CIA in Japan; he was one of the most effective components of Pax Americana, thanks to which the Japanese public still remains under the spell of American occupation. He served the Japanese Empire until its collapse, but after the war he served as a CIA agent for the American empire and played an important role in the reconstruction of Japan under Pax Americana.

Perhaps Shôriki Matsutarô's most symbolic postwar accomplishment lies in his role as the first chair of Japan's Atomic Energy Commission. After the *Lucky Dragon Five* incident in 1954, the Japanese public learned, possibly for the first time—the radio-biological effects caused by the atomic bombs at Hiroshima and Nagasaki had been strictly censored, first by the Japanese government and then by the U.S. Occupation Administration—of the potential danger of nuclear energy and radioactivity through citizen protest demonstrations as well as commercial films like *Godzilla* that depicted nuclear catastrophes. Fearful of the global propagation of antinuclear sentiment, the U.S. government acknowledged the need to organize public campaigns against citizen antinuclear movements, and President Eisenhower delivered a speech on atomic safety at the United Nations. The person selected for the job of launching this propaganda campaign against citizen antinuclear movements, and the Japanese allergy to nuclear energy, was Shôriki Matsutarô. The Atomic Energy Commission introduced the idea of the peaceful use of nuclear energy to the Japanese public so effectively that the majority of Japanese did not question the concept of the peaceful use of nuclear energy and its inherent contradiction until the disaster at the Fukushima Dai'ichi nuclear plant occurred on March 11, 2011. Under a directive from the U.S. government, Shôriki executed his mission so successfully in the areas of censorship, public opinion, and propaganda that many citizens of Japan have constituted themselves as subjects operating productively within Pax Americana.

What is undeniably manifest in Japanese society after the Allied occupation is the metamorphosis of Japan's nationalism. In this respect, Kodama Yoshio embodied a new type of nationalism that may sound oxymoronic: he advocated a sort of jingoism that accommodates colonial subjugation. In more senses than one, Kodama Yoshio represented the transformation of nationalist activism from the prewar to postwar periods in Japan.

In effect, prewar nationalism was replaced by an anticommunist or antisocialist jingoism. Therefore, the kind of nationalism advocated by figures such as Sasakawa Ryôichi and Kodama Yoshio could not even be considered nationalism by the old standard. It would rather be characterized by some distinct features of fascism. It is true that, usually, fascism retains a very strong and almost perverse abhorrence of socialism and communism, but in the absence of the desire for national autonomy and national independence, such an abhorrence alone cannot constitute the sort of fascism we know of from the interwar period. The kind of nationalism found in postwar Japan would be a joke should we not take into account the redefinition of the concept of state sovereignty.

Now the common ground among the war criminal conservatives is clear. They were the political agents who were exposed to possible blackmail by the American authority due to their war crimes. Let us not forget that those crimes were neither cleared nor forgiven. They were released from Sugamo Prison in exchange for a pledge to collaborate with the intelligence agency of the U.S. government. Therefore, they were not capable of standing against the United States and its allies—China and all the other Asian countries invaded by the Japanese military were excluded from their elite club—or of arguing for their political legitimacy. As a matter of fact, when they were thus pardoned, they permanently forfeited the ideological ground of their own political pursuits. As far as their national pride as nationalists is concerned, therefore, they were twice defeated.

From the viewpoint of the interface of international and domestic politics, it is evident why the United States valued Japan so highly. Now we must inquire into the second reason why Japan was far more important to American policy makers than other countries in East Asia. In Japan there was an accumulation of practical knowledge concerning the management of colonies in East Asia, of academic expertise on local traditions, ethnographic data, and language skills, and of intimate connections with local capitalists and elites. Accordingly, it is through Japan's old network of colonial expertise and personal connections that the U.S. government decided to rule regions that they inherited from the Greater East Asia Co-prosperity Sphere. The Class A war criminal Kishi Nobusuke became a highly important figure for Americans in this context. Let us recall that Kishi and his younger brother, Satô Eisaku (1901–1975), were on the CIA payroll.[32] As I have already mentioned, Kishi was a famous reform bureaucrat who drafted a planned economy in Manchu-kuo and who, during the war, served as a minister in charge of supply and distribution of goods for the entirety of the Greater East Asia Co-prosperity Sphere. In East Asia, from the perspective of the United States, probably no person was a better fit than Kishi for the job description of subsidiary imperialist or an imperialist under subcontract to the American empire in East Asia. Furthermore, he was a safe bet because of his criminal past, for which the United States could blackmail him were he to disobey American prerogative. Kishi thus constituted the core of the U.S. project of regime change in Japan; he was an ideally compromised figure from the perspective of American imperial nationalism.

War criminal conservatives thus attempted to preserve the legacies of the Japanese Empire by willingly collaborating with U.S. colonialism in East Asia. Since Japan was a satellite state within the system of U.S. neocolonialism, the

Japanese could continue to enjoy the status of colonizer in relation to the other peoples of Northeast and Southeast Asia. Japan was defeated in war, yet its people were allowed to maintain the colonizer mindset precisely because Japan was given the status of an empire under subcontract.

In spite of the historical fact that Japan was defeated in the Asia-Pacific War and/or World War II and lost most of its colonies, it is thanks to the double structure of this newly emerging colonial system in East Asia that the Japanese could evade the direct impact of the disintegration of empire during the 1950s. In this respect, although he appeared on the national political stage two generations later, as a politician, Abe Shinzô internalized most typically—and most ingeniously—the Cold War ideology of the 1950s and '60s that justifies the double structure inherent in Pax Americana. Wittingly or unwittingly, he best represents the continuity of postwar politics in Japan under Pax Americana.[33]

Not so much out of political calculation for accommodating reactionary populism that has steadily gained ground in Japanese national politics since the 1980s, Abe Shinzô disavowed the very notion of Japanese historical responsibility for its colonial past out of the fear that it would jeopardize the political legitimacy of the postwar emperor system and conservatism represented by the LDP. Postwar Japan was built upon nothing but the legacy of war criminal conservatism best represented by the lineage of his family, and blindly he tried to silence any voice that might well call into question the empire under subcontract. In due course, Abe Shinzô dared to exhibit condescending attitudes toward Chinese and Koreans while taking a subservient attitude toward white Americans.

His visit to Washington, D.C., in 2007 was an occasion when the double structure of the empire under subcontract revealed itself unmistakably. Rejecting repeated requests from former Comfort Women, he flatly refused to either meet with them or discuss their problems before his departure for the U.S. capital. But, outside Japan, an increasing number of people found the attitude of the Japanese government unacceptable, and his firm conviction seemed to be shaken. As the U.S. Congress unanimously passed a resolution to condemn the Japanese government's refusal of the Comfort Women's requests, and the EU parliament and other governments were condemning the Japanese government, he was at a loss.[34] Finally, he conveyed his regret personally, not to the former Comfort Women themselves, but instead to George W. Bush, even though the president of the United States had neither accused Abe nor his government over the issue of the Comfort Women nor raised the problem directly. Because this incident was broadcast all over the world, some readers might still remember Abe's wacky behavior in Washington. His conduct was truly discomforting for his countrymen and ludicrous for most people in the world. Yet what cannot be overlooked about this incident is that his strange behavior illustrated the double structure of Japan's position in Pax Americana, the simultaneous dual positionality of colonizer and colonized. In fact, this was an exemplary case of what I called "civilizational transference" above.

When people of South Korea, China, the Philippines, and Indonesia have asked about responsibility for Japanese colonialism, Abe Shinzô was able to remain aloof and indifferent to them; in fact, he dared to commit semicriminal acts to intervene in the public broadcasting of a program on sexual slavery and wartime violence against women and to impose censorship on it.[35] He behaved extremely pompously, as if colonial regimes still existed in the relationship between Japan and other countries that it had occupied. And he seemed to believe that such a colonial regime and the wide gap between developed and underdeveloped countries could be maintained by censoring information concerning the reality of Japanese colonialism in the past and the Japanese colonial mindset in the present.

It is clear that many Japanese voters respond to such a condescending attitude favorably, mistaking Abe's arrogance for Japan's strength. However, he could not adopt such an attitude toward Americans. His pompousness switched to subservience as soon as he met the president of the United States in person. Whereas George W. Bush had never asked him to say anything about the Comfort Women before the presidential audience, Abe volunteered to confess his regret to the president in the White House. For Abe Shinzô, the president of the United States of America was the fantastic father figure whose moral authority propelled him to personally confess his feeling of guilt. He projected his fear and guilt onto the figure of George Bush in this textbook case of transference. He could not help regarding Bush as the figure of moral authority, and he figuratively threw himself at his feet. I cannot think of a better illustration of transpacific civilizational transference between the United States and Japan than this groveling conduct by Abe Shinzô. Is this not exactly what Dulles planned to implant in the minds of the Japanese more than a half century earlier? Just as Dulles was perceptive enough to observe in the Japanese in general, Abe too was suffering from a tremendous sense of inferiority to white people.

If Abe Shinzô's peculiar behavior were no more than his personal idiosyncrasy, we would not need to ponder long over his strange conduct in Washington, for I am not particularly interested in his psychology or biography. What appears to characterize his attitudes toward the Asian and American peoples, however, is also present in the political unconscious that still restricts

Japanese politics today. The Japanese nation shares a lot with Abe Shinzô, and he enjoys a certain popularity among Japanese voters precisely because they too are trapped in the imperial unconscious that is an integral part of Pax Americana. In other words, unless we explicitly inquire into the hegemonic nature of Pax Americana and its implications with regard to racism, we will not be able to effectively analyze this double structure that is routinized in the empire under subcontract.

It has been reported that Abe relishes a certain popularity among the younger generation in Japan today. Statistically speaking, the younger the voters, the more support he received in recent national elections. No doubt younger voters and college students did not grow up under the Allied occupation of Japan; neither did they experience the debates over the U.S.-Japan Security Treaty or the Cold War policy of anticommunist confinement. Yet it seems that Japanese in their twenties and thirties have been equally locked in the double structure of imperial unconscious. This is one reason why they are still incapable of directly facing the questions of the Comfort Women or war and colonial responsibility. Precisely because it is unconscious, this double structure, as manifested in Abe's groveling behavior, does not fade or vanish.

This double structure was already discernible in the behavior of his grandfather in the 1950s. Kishi's attitudes toward the leaders of the former satellite countries of the Greater East Asia Co-prosperity Sphere on the one hand and toward American leaders such as Dulles and Eisenhower during his visit to Washington, D.C., on the other have been well investigated, and these accounts are available.[36] Moreover, it is not too difficult to understand the double structure of Japanese (post)colonialism that was apparent in Kishi's behavior. This structure could be interpreted as a consequence of a rational choice that Kishi had carefully considered and deliberately adopted in view of the fact that he was a war criminal who could be eliminated by U.S. authority at any time. As a matter of fact, the American policy of containment saved him and granted him an incredible opportunity to take charge of an empire, even if the empire he was in charge of was under subcontract and hence his role was that of a subcontractor.

The civilizational transference that is evident in Abe Shinzô's behavior was somewhat different from the double structure of Japanese (post)colonialism to which his grandfather was committed. Unlike in Kishi's case, it was not buttressed by cynical rationality; it was simply accepted because Abe had grown up accepting the reality of Pax Americana, a routinized reality in which Japanese society was regarded as an exceptional success case in modernization, namely "Japan as Number One."

What is very obvious about this dual structure observable in Abe and in his contemporary supporters' conduct is that it is not a vision for the future but a fait accompli, a sort of accomplished achievement of the present perfect, which many Japanese are afraid to lose. Therefore, the more readily one takes the premises of Pax Americana for granted, the more comforting and reassuring one may find the political statements put forth by the extreme right of the LD P. The gradual disintegration of Pax Americana gives rise to a tremendous anxiety and a sense of uncertainty among those victimized by globalization and neoliberal reforms; those victims seek nostalgic messages to reassure them of the old glory and past success in the political rhetoric of the extreme right rather than in the disclosure of factors that accelerate the precarious conditions among the victims and increase the unevenness among the working population.

Today, it is not only old-fashioned but also utterly anachronistic to behave within the confine of the double structure of Japanese (post)colonialism, to believe that Pax Americana will last forever. In the 1950s, it was under construction and not yet an established actuality in East Asia. To commit to the global policy of containment was a kind of gamble based upon a careful calculation, an aleatory decision on the part of Kishi Nobusuke. Seventy years later, Abe did not appear to be either careful or rational in his condescending rhetoric toward Asians and his subservient tone with Americans. What is of decisive importance is not the long-term future vision or rational reckoning that Abe and his staff entertained in formulating their policies, but instead the reason why this type of anachronism was welcomed by a large portion of the Japanese population.

Nationalism and Colonialism: The Question of Imperial-Colonial Order

So far in this chapter we have investigated the historically specific characteristics of postwar Japanese nationalism in conjunction with American policies, in what MacArthur called "the Anglo-Saxon's Lake," namely, the Pacific Ocean. Undoubtedly Japan's subordination to American hegemony is particular to the political situation of Northeast Asia and the western shore of the Pacific. But, at the same time, the bilateral relationship that the United States established with Japan exemplifies a general feature of Pax Americana, the global reign of the United States that came into being in the latter half of the twentieth century.

Already during World War II the United States executed and justified its international policies in the name of the United Nations. Pax Americana was supposedly a restoration of the system of international law, a system whose origin could be traced to the Treaty of Westphalia (1648) and which had been destroyed twice in the twentieth century. As historians including Carl Schmitt (2006) have pointed out, the system of international law was built on the spatial structure of binarism, Europe and non-Europe. Hence, international law was also called *Jus Publicum Europaeum* (Eurocentric public law), according to which European powers' colonization of the rest of the world was sanctioned.

Interestingly enough, while reconstructing the system of international law, the United States rather hesitated either to sanction European colonial empires' sovereignty over their prewar colonies or to directly oppress anticolonial nationalist movements in Asia and Africa. With the establishment of the United Nations, a redefinition of the international world seems to have taken place: the space of international law used to be limited to Europe, but after World War II it was expanded to include all the land surface of the earth. After that war, many former colonies including Taiwan and North and South Korea became independent, and it may appear that the international world was enlarged and its meaning completely altered under Pax Americana by the auspices of the United Nations.

The history of postwar Japanese nationalism offers an ideal opportunity to examine a series of questions. Does Pax Americana mark a fundamental transition from the old structure of the modern international world that continually insists on discriminatory differentiation between Europe and non-Europe or the West and the Rest? Does it inaugurate the end of the imperial-colonial order by which European humanity is distinguished from the rest of humanity? Or did America's global hegemony help to restore the system of international law to the degree that Schmitt wished the United States to preserve its Eurocentric structure in 1950, when he published the German original of *The Nomos of the Earth in the International Law of the Jus Publicum Europaeum* after the defeat of the Third Reich by the Allied Powers?[37]

The double structure of Japanese nationalism explains how to accommodate two almost contradictory demands: on the one hand, every territorial state must be allowed to maintain its sovereignty and autonomy, and on the other hand, the old Eurocentric imperial-colonial order (or we must say West-centric" since the center of domination moved from Western Europe to North America) must be preserved. What I have found so far is that postwar Japanese nationalism is a magnum opus in the accommodation of the imperial-colonial order in the midst of a newly defined internationality.

Thus, Pax Americana resurrected the system of Eurocentric public law, but, in this system, nationalism and colonialism were no longer in disjunction. For decades, a number of Asian, African, and Latin American intellectuals have sought ways to resist, undermine, and disrupt American imperialism, but it has almost always been taken for granted that non-Western nationalisms were naturally and automatically opposed to American imperial-colonial domination. Now at the end of Pax Americana, however, what must be called into question is this unwarranted presumption that nationalism and colonialism contradict one another. So far I believe I have succeeded in demonstrating that postwar Japanese nationalism accommodated two contradictory demands, one for the nationalist autonomy of a nation-state and the other for a national population willing to subject itself to the authority of an outside power, within the framework of the imperial-colonial order initially, as created by Eurocentric international law.

What is at stake in this chapter as well as in this volume as a whole is not only an elucidation of the transpacific complicity between the United States and Japan but also the historical significance of the end of Pax Americana. In other words, I understand the end of Pax Americana will mark a historical moment in the structural transformation of the modern international world. Underlying my inquiry into the reconfiguration of the imperial-colonial order is a concern for the problematic generally referred to as the loss of empire, an inevitable process that requires an appreciation of the structural transformation of the imperial-colonial order so that the spatial structure of the international world can be comprehended adequately. I am convinced that nationalisms under Pax Americana can be investigated far beyond the case of postwar nationalism in Japan.

I have so far postponed the discussion of another empire under subcontract in Pax Americana. Indeed, it is the United Kingdom to which I direct attention in the final part of this chapter.

Part 3: Inward-Looking Society

Already in many places in Asia, the Abe Shinzô administration has been criticized for its anachronistic attitude. What is implied by this idiom, "anachronism in historical cognizance" (「歴史認識の錯誤」), pertains to both sides of the double structure of Japanese (post)colonialism: racist condescension toward Asian neighbors on the one hand and subservience toward Americans on the other in the mindset of subsidiary imperialists. The Abe administration was criticized for its historical fallacy even in the United Nations.

So as to understand how to escape this double structure and the postcolonial situation in which Japanese people are trapped today, from this point on I would like to consider the experience of shame and the nationalism of hikikomori (reclusive withdrawal). What is announced in their refusal to face the problem of the Comfort Women is their abhorrence of the experience of shame. Because they abhor the predicted experience of shame, they try to evade encountering people from other Asian countries since an encounter with Asian people would surely evoke the feeling of shame. Yet it is important to keep in mind that this whole scenario of shame about Japan's past and abhorrence of encountering other Asians is played out in the realm of collective imagination. Under this perspective, I have tried to comprehend the behaviors characteristic of Abe Shinzō and the discourse of Pax Americana at large.

The Japanese knowledge to be shared with Asian neighbors must include that which will allow an extrication from this double structure of Japanese (post)colonialism, a double structure necessarily imposed on those who want to continue to fashion themselves as imperialists by the need to sustain the empire under subcontract. This knowledge addresses a question concerning decolonization, a question of how to free the former colonizers of the old habit of recognizing themselves and the former colonized within the majoritarian-minoritarian gradient of colonizer and colonized.

In the last few years I have come across many intellectuals from Asia who offer diagnoses of contemporary Japanese society. Perhaps these varied diagnoses can be summarized this way: The Japanese are trying to solve the problems of the twenty-first century with a method distinctly from the twentieth century.

Loss of Empire

Postcolonial studies invented the idiom "loss of empire." It signifies the state of affairs in which the process of decolonization is prevented from proceeding even after the politico-judicial system of colonialism has been dismantled. The term "postcolonial" has often been misconstrued to mean the study of a colonized society after the removal of colonial governance. I do not believe that the main object of postcolonial studies is a society once colonized and then transformed as it becomes independent, with the term "postcolonial" meaning what comes after colonialism or what happens after the liberation from colonialism. Instead, postcoloniality is most distinctly manifest in a nation or national society whose state used to govern colonies and whose population used to serve the state as colonizers in relation to the governed populations of the colonies. In other words, the kind of population that postcolonial studies thematically investigate are not people who inhabit the regions once governed by another state sovereignty, but rather people who used to rule colonized people and continue to regard themselves as somewhat superior to those natives or indigenous populations.

In the case of the Japanese Empire, postcolonial studies do not thematically investigate the people of previously annexed territories such as Okinawa, Taiwan, South and North Korea, the southern part of Sakhalin, Manchuria, some territories in northern China, islands off the northeastern shore of Hokkaido, the Pacific islands in Micronesia, some territories in mainland China, and so on; rather, they investigate those people whose family registers were kept at addresses in Japan proper, those who remained Japanese according to Japanese laws of nationality after the liberation of the colonies. Of course, the identity of people cannot be solely reduced to original addresses in family registers. What is significant and often ignored is that the main focus of postcolonial studies ought to be on those Japanese with family registers in Japan proper who continued to identify themselves with the Japanese nation after the collapse of the Japanese Empire in 1945.

Thereupon, first of all, what I would like to ask in relation to the Japanese nation is this: Can the Japanese endure the political actuality of the Western Pacific without Pax Americana? Do they seriously want to live with people from neighboring Asian countries? Are they ready to share their lives with people from those neighboring Asian countries? Seemingly so many Japanese today want to distance themselves from people from those countries, to evade dialogue or even an encounter with them. Why are they so reluctant to socialize with foreigners, and other East Asians in particular?

The phenomenon generally referred to as the loss of empire indicates the typical reaction of those who previously enjoyed colonial privileges, their reaction to the reality of postcolonial conditions. Many subjects of the former suzerain state refuse to accept the collapse of the political, sociological, judiciary, and economic institutions that once sustained the colonial hierarchy and the explicit or implicit practices of social discrimination. All these institutions used to help the people of the colonizing state to routinely look down upon the people in the colonized territories or those from there; colonialism is a synoptic term by which the colonizing people are allowed to denigrate the colonized people thanks to these institutions. When the colonized are removed and no longer effectual, the colonizing people come to face a void in their self-esteem or the loss of their pride. This is essentially what the idiom "loss of empire" signifies in the first place.

Here it is important to distinguish the acceptance of the collapse of colonialism from the mere acknowledgment of such a collapse. What is at stake is a postcolonial anxiety induced by the changing conditions of a national society because of which one who used to occupy a majoritarian positionality can no longer assume it in the colonial gradient of majority-minority difference.

Belonging to the rank of colonizer, one receives a number of advantages denied to the colonized. Whereas there are always a number of social privileges independent of the colonial distinction of the colonizer and the colonized, there are certain features of social distinction that are not directly dependent upon the colonial distinction but that are indirect derivatives of it. Regardless of the fact that every aspect of everyday life in colonies is not singlehandedly determined by the colonizer-versus-colonized hierarchy, the colonial distinctions serve to differentiate between individuals belonging to the colonizer social class and those subsumed under the colonized social class. Therefore, it is completely inadequate to appeal only to the social functions of colonial distinctions in order to understand how people are classified according to the set of social categories, positioned hierarchically in relation to one another, and discriminated against in certain groups within the population of the colonies as well as in the suzerain nation.

What plays an exceedingly important role in persuading individuals to position themselves within the social formation of colonial societies is the framework of the collective imaginary in which various scenarios are circulated to make these individuals customarily imagine their status in relation to others. While identifying themselves with the larger whole of the nation, with the totality of Japanese population subjected to Japanese national and territorial state sovereignty, they also discover their enclaves and racial, professional, class, and gender positions within that nation. In the nation of the United States, for instance, all Americans are supposedly equal as far as their nationality is concerned, but every one of them knows that some are more equal than others. The knowledge of one's American nationality is always accompanied by another understanding of where he or she belongs in terms of race, social class, ethnicity, and/or educational level within the entirety of the national population. Similarly, in the multiethnic empire of Japan, the colonial distinction between the Japanese from Japan proper and the Japanese of annexed territories was never totally overlooked, even in the official emphasis on Naisen Ittai (Japan Proper and Korea in One Body). While policies of interethnic marriage were promoted by the government, the Japanese from Japan proper would never cease to distinguish themselves from local Taiwanese or Koreans in terms of cultural heritage, fluency in the national language (国語), political rights such as the right to vote, and many other features.

When the colonized region and its inhabitants acquire state sovereignty and gain independence, the colonial government, together with a number of sociopolitical institutions, collapses and liberates the colonized from the constraints of many discriminatory rules and customs. The majority of the colonizer population resident in the colony lose their privileges and political rights, are deprived of their assets—land they used to own, houses they used to live in, corporations they used to run, and so forth—and are forced to return to the former suzerain country. Just as the colonized acquire a new citizenship in their newly independent country, the colonizers no longer occupy the social positionalities they used to take for granted or enjoy the higher standard of living to which they were accustomed. The impact of decolonization is drastic; the consequences of the loss of colony seem immediate and unambiguous, particularly for those who have lived in the colony and have grown accustomed to its distinctly colonial hierarchy.

Therefore, one may assume that the end of colonialism is witnessed, experienced, and acknowledged once and for all by those who undergo the process of independence, liberation, and decolonization. The postcolonial society should be clearly and unambiguously marked by the "post" of postcoloniality, in the sense of "posterior to colonialism," that one has left behind the reality of colonialism and lives in an era chronologically posterior to one in which people were ruled by various colonial institutions. However, I have strong reservations about this use of either term, "postcolonial" or "postcoloniality" in the sense of "coming after colonialism" or "chronological posteriority to colonialism."

A set of phenomena generally summarized by the idiom "loss of empire" points to the mindset of people, mainly people of a former suzerain nation, who refuse to discard the view of the world organized by an old colonial hierarchy or to adopt new identities within the new social relationships that emerge after the collapse of colonialism. In their fantastic world, colonial distinctions persist. They cannot feel at ease in new social arrangements after the independence of a former colony; they are incapable of discovering comfort in the social relations that become established in decolonization. Instead they seek the comfort of the old world still regulated by colonial fantasies. As their old empire is lost, the socioeconomic advantages that previously guaranteed the colonizers' social prestige and their sense of superiority and pride are also lost. They can no longer assume the old majoritarian-minoritarian gradient thanks to which certain positionalities are marked distinctly superior to certain others. It is important to keep in mind that these socioeconomic advantages are not only apprehended at face value but also regarded as manifestations of the colonizers' inner quality so that they most often hold what we might call a "precritical conviction" that they are innately and essentially better in their intelligence, constitution, wealth, and cultural capital than the colonized. Usually advantages endowed by colonial hierarchy are translated into innate superior qualities in the colonizers. In other words, they can only find comfort in a world racially segregated and hierarchically organized.

Such a vision of the world of colonial comfort that is ordered according to colonial and racial ranks is not limited to some privileged and exceptional social groups. Those of the suzerain nation who have never been to the colonies also have learned how to identify themselves in the collective fantasies about the subjects of the suzerain state and the inhabitants of the colonies. We cannot overlook the dynamic aspects of hegemony that are largely motivated by scenarios stored in the collective imaginary of nations.

After its defeat at the end of the Asia-Pacific War, Japan lost most of its overseas territories, and, as previously stated, more than 30 percent of its population ceased to identify with the totality of the Japanese nation. Similar processes of decolonization took place in these old colonial empires within a couple of decades after the end of World War II. This is how the peoples of the former suzerain empires had to face problems associated with the loss of empire.

How can they sustain the self-esteem nurtured in colonial fantasies when they lose their colonies and their own imperial status? Let us note that, even when the empire, which has supported the integrity of its territory and the colonial advantages for the colonizer social class, is disintegrated overnight, the old collective imaginary cannot dissipate easily. The people of the former suzerain state must undergo a certain, almost traumatic, experience so as to realize that the old colonial world is gone, to appreciate that their old fantasies are irrelevant, and to transform the structure of their self-esteem.

Generally speaking, the majority of old colonizers who have been nurtured in colonial fantasies tend to take for granted an unrealistic sense of their self-esteem after the colony's independence even after the loss of their empire. Particularly when the empire is lost gradually or when the illusion of an empire is created to replace the old colonial government, as is the case in postwar Japan, it is very difficult for former colonizers to reflect on their own assumed identity, to see their self-esteem objectively from the perspective of a third party. The viewpoint of the third party is indispensable precisely because, in occupying the positionality of neither colonizer nor colonized, the third party in the colonial relationship is usually not implicated in their collective fantasies. Accordingly, people who stand outside the majoritarian-minoritarian gradient of colonial relationship manage to see how ridiculous the sense of self-esteem that the former colonizers carry is.

However, it is very difficult for the former colonizers to come to terms with the actuality of the loss of their empire. Most often they end up in denial. The more obvious the former colonizers' perception of the abrogation of colonial institutions, the more they insist on holding on to the sense of their superiority over the former colonized. Despite their insistence on a colonial hierarchy, however, any objective social conditions that used to support the social distinctions between the colonizer and the colonized can no longer be found. If they continue to insist on their old self-esteem, they will have to disavow the loss of their empire, to evade any third party who would destroy their world of fantasies, and to withdraw into a reclusive communality in which every member continues to live in the old world.

The nationalism of hikikomori (reclusive withdrawal) may include people of younger generations, born into a world in which the empire had already been lost. Yet those who have failed in upward mobility in the present-day world, who have to live under precarious conditions, or who suffer from a situation of uncertain employment may well join this group of reality deniers. Instead of trying to adapt themselves to the new social conditions of a decolonized world, they would rather cling to the anachronistic world of colonial order and what Abe Shinzô (2006) called "the beautiful Japan." These are the people who want to solve the problems of the twenty-first century with the methods of the twentieth century.

Setting Sun or *The Remains of the Day*

Thereupon, let us shift our focus from the macrostatistics of the social formation in the political, economic, and sociological conditions we face today toward the microphysics of individual aesthetics—the domains of feeling, sentiment, and emotion.

An excellent diagnosis of the loss of empire that I would like to mention first is provided in the literary work *The Remains of the Day* (1989), a novel by Kazuo Ishiguro, a Japanese-born writer working in the United Kingdom. With remarkable subtlety and precision, this masterpiece describes what the loss of empire brings upon individuals in everyday life. Indeed, it is a fiction, so it does not tell us on a factual basis how the loss of empire is perceived by former colonizers. As a literary text, it articulates the large-scale historical transformation to the individual's emotive and sentimental reactions to it in symbolic terms. As a piece of fiction, it narrates a typical story of an individual who cannot cope with the tremendous weight of historical change. The novel takes the form of a personal account narrated by Stevens, a butler, who manages an old mansion called Darlington Hall. Darlington Hall consists of two worlds, the people upstairs, represented by Lord Darlington, who has socialized widely both nationally and internationally, and the people downstairs, cooks, maids, chauffeur, gardener, and other servants, who work to maintain this large residence. Stevens occupies a bridging position between the upstairs and the downstairs in this anachronistic world.

No overt reference is made to the destiny of the British Empire in this novel, yet it is apparent that the fate of Darlington Hall symbolizes the vicissitudes of the empire, from the interwar era when the glory of Great Britain was recognized globally to the postwar era when, just like Japan, the United Kingdom was another empire under subcontract. This butler is one who secures the continuity of this institution in spite of many and fundamental changes that occurred between the era when Darlington Hall was actually owned by its namesake and the subsequent era, when it was bought by Mr. Farraday, an American millionaire who decided to retain Stevens as manager at Darlington Hall after World War II. Lord Darlington's sympathy with the Germans during the interwar period leads to his downfall; he is eliminated from national politics for his apparent collaborative relationship with the Nazis. In other words, the novel tells of the span of history in a nation from its glorious past to a present in which Darlington Hall is maintained and managed by a butler as if nothing had changed, as if the complete façade of an empire were kept intact by order of an American diplomat who used to work with Lord Darlington. Thus, the butler is allowed to behave as if actually in charge of this aristocratic mansion, as if he were a member of the upstairs. No doubt the figure of the butler serves as a mediator between the two tiers of upstairs and downstairs, of two social classes from the former suzerain nation. Thanks to his social role, the butler is allegorically equivalent to the political leadership of the empire under subcontract. As a subcontractor, Stevens is allowed to behave as if he represents the authority of the nation as a whole, as if he acts in place of Mr. Farraday, who is in fact the real master.

Undoubtedly the figure of Darlington Hall works as an allegory of national society. In due course, Ishiguro meticulously portrays the behavior and sentiment of the British upper middle class by describing the character Stevens the butler in terms of the stylistic features of his speech, his confession, reportage, and reasoning in general. The narrative style itself reveals what sort of person

Stevens is supposed to be. Moreover, Ishiguro's scrupulous attention to the stylistic variation of characters in the novel succeeds in presenting the rich variety of people in English society three-dimensionally.

For instance, Stevens's first name remains unknown throughout the novel since the people upstairs customarily call him "Stevens" with no honorific title. Of course, they never feel close enough to him to call him by his first name. On the other hand, the people downstairs never feel close to him either and always greet him as "Mr. Stevens." In a peculiar way, Stevens is isolated from all the other characters of the novel. This feeling of alienation is brilliantly captured by the author and contributes much to the outstanding portrayal of this character. In short, Stevens is polite, believes in the value of moderation, holds a strong sense of responsibility, reveres tradition and social convention, looks down at those with no self-control, is devoted to his profession, and is modest enough to hesitate to exhibit his personal feelings. In other words, Stevens appears to be the embodiment of all upper-middle-class virtues. Many readers who are fond of *The Remains of the Day* find a typical English man in Stevens; some venture to say that this novel is dedicated to an authentic depiction of the English national character.

Ishiguro's portrayal is, as a matter of fact, much more ironic. Let us examine the style of Stevens's narration. His writing may appear cultured and classic at first glance, but everything he says and writes is, so to speak, borrowed and stereotypical. With amazing skill, Kazuo Ishiguro invents a manner of speech that shows the fundamental lack of self-confidence in this character. Routinely Stevens interacts with his master and people of aristocratic background and of the upper class and has adopted their vocabulary, idioms, sentence structure, and manner of speech through mimicry. But he never dares to say or express his own ideas or feelings; he never ventures to voice what he is not supposed to; he never allows himself to show his raw feelings, of rage or exhilaration, which would risk disturbing the atmosphere of the occasion. Precisely because he does not examine censoriously either the social roles he is expected to play or the social positions he is allowed to occupy, he cannot distance himself from the rules of conduct expected of him. What is absent in this character is the capacity for critical knowledge of the social conventions he is bound by. It is demonstrated that Stevens is a character incapable of expressing any honest opinion or genuine feeling that might embarrass his interlocutor. In this way, Ishiguro successfully concretizes a character who is equipped with borrowed ideas, borrowed mannerisms, and borrowed feelings but who never shows direct expressivity, a character symbolically representing the conditions of upper-middle-class life in the empire under subcontract.

For Stevens, his pride is indistinguishable from the reputation of Darlington Hall, as though his fate were inseparable from that of the house he is expected to serve. Yet the house is more like a ghost from the past, not a representation of a family consisting of living human beings. Thanks to Mr. Farraday, Darlington Hall maintains its appearance and tradition, but it no longer radiates its past grandeur. Here derives the title of the novel, *The Remains of the Day*. It suggests fading light and a leftover warmth of the day in the twilight hours of the setting sun. The novel thus depicts the loss of self-confidence of those who obsessively identify with the lost empire and their desperate clinging to the splendor of the past.

For a long time, Britain has been known for its conspicuous social class system. One cannot fail to see that the almost stereotypical and anachronistic image of English society is projected as a backdrop to the story in *The Remains of the Day*. Darlington Hall is unambiguously divided into two contrasting worlds, the tier of the upper class and that of the working class. In this respect, perhaps deliberately, Ishiguro chose an apparently antiquated setting for a character who lives in a bygone world. Yet, as a matter of fact, the protagonist Stevens, supposedly a caricature of this outdated world, suffers from a certain double consciousness, which indeed reflects the double structure of the heyday of Darlington Hall. Interestingly enough, he is not unaware of this double consciousness.

Stevens speaks and behaves like a gentleman of the upper middle class, as if he were segregated from the working class to which he belongs. Yet he is fully aware that he can never truly belong to the upper class. The scenes with his father, who was also a butler, illustrate his working-class roots; he has no intention of hiding his upbringing from his coworkers. Of course, both Lord Darlington—and his family as well, I assume—and then his new employer would never mistake him for an upper- or upper-middle-class gentleman. Neither are the servants at this aristocratic mansion ever deceived into thinking so. Nevertheless, outside Darlington Hall, Stevens can pass for a member of the English upper class. Accordingly, ordinary people who are not used to the upper-class social world, like the landlady of a guest house in Salisbury, can easily be deceived by his appearance, manner of speech, and the luxury car he drives. She recognizes him as an upper-class gentleman whom she feels obligated to treat with distinction. Only a fairly well-educated local doctor called Dr. Carlisle can understand Stevens's peculiar status. Puzzled over where to locate Stevens in the social hierarchy, he finally asks, "But you aren't a manservant of some sort, are you?" (Ishiguro 1989, 207). For those who take the class hierarchy of a social formation for granted, Stevens passes as belonging to a higher social status, yet for those knowledgeable enough about social hierarchy, his double standing cannot be overlooked.

Stevens's double consciousness is clearly articulated to the theme of the loss of empire. We must note, however, that this articulation, too, is twofold. First of all, Darlington Hall represents a social space in which his double consciousness is accepted and even legitimated, given that both the upstairs and the downstairs accept the fact that he belongs to the working class, even though he dresses up and behaves as if he belongs upstairs. His dual stance is accepted by both masters and servants alike because it is justified as part of his profession. Of course his obsession with professionalism is directly related to this. In this regard, Darlington Hall is a space of imperial order in which social classes are clearly and unambiguously delineated. After the collapse of the British Empire, therefore, this outdated estate, Darlington Hall, symbolizes the remains of the good old glorious days. It is an enclave insulated from the general changes in society. It is in this sense that this place represents the loss of empire.

Yet, even outside Darlington Hall, the loss of empire prevails. Even though Britain is no longer an empire ruling the seven seas, both Stevens's mannerisms and speech idiosyncrasies are immediately recognized by "unsophisticated folks" as signs of superiority, as markers of colonial order in which he is supposed to be endowed with a number of privileges that are denied to those people who cannot behave or speak thus. In this respect, social class affiliation is immediately translated into social classification of a colonial world. Of course, it is according not only to British imperialism but also to all other imperial orders of the modern international world that the colonial hierarchy is associated with social class affiliation. This is one reason why, from the Meiji period on, the Japanese public adopted and internalized so many English bourgeois customs—the morning coat, English-style etiquette, the black funeral outfit, English afternoon tea, and so on—to such an extent that they practice these old habits even when they are no longer practiced in their country of origin. In the late nineteenth century, the adoption of English customs was regarded as a sign of upward social mobility; the acceptance of English habits was recognized as a marker of membership in the upper social class.

Misrecognition of Stevens by unsophisticated people reminds us of the colonial prestige that colonizers used to enjoy outside their countries and in the rest of the world. Even those from a humble social background could enjoy the status of the upper class and be treated as if belonging to it. Stevens did not travel internationally. His journey depicted in *The Remains of the Day* extends from Darlington Hall, fictionally located near Oxford, to the West Country in the southwestern part of England. Nevertheless, what he encounters in this quite provincial journey reminds many of us of the sort of colonial prestige the British and citizens of other colonizing states used to enjoy as well as the anxiety that comes with the insecurity they have to undergo in the loss of empire. At any time some fairly educated person could appear and say, "But you aren't a manservant of some sort, are you?" The aura of empire may make one look like a gentleman of the bourgeoisie, but, in the next instance, all of that conceit could be shattered.

There is no question that *The Remains of the Day* is a brilliant parody of English society in the latter half of the twentieth century. In many respects, Stevens is a representative of the English upper middle class and middle class who wants to live under Pax Americana, as if their empire were still actual.

The novel points out two symptoms of the loss of empire. The first is the character of Stevens, who is portrayed as a sort of hikikomori (withdrawn recluse). Yet in his role as butler, he shows no sign of reclusive withdrawal. He knows how to handle various social relations and to interact with the guests of the hall; he is recognized as a proficient manager, both by his employer whom he obeys and by his staff whom he oversees. By no means is he characterized as what is referred to as hikikomori in contemporary Japan, a person withdrawn from society. In his status as a butler, he is perceptive of others' intentions and desires, can make sound judgments about human dynamics, and is able to read the feelings of his companions. Nonetheless, his ability to read the atmosphere of the situation is completely dictated by his professional identity. Beyond the context of his profession as a butler, he is not perceptive or responsive to the demands of others. Outside the hierarchical order of the empire symbolically expressed in the configuration of Darlington Hall, he is not able to react to the needs of any situation spontaneously. He cannot communicate with one whose stature is not determined within the hierarchical order of the house; he cannot respond to others outside the context of his butlership. Unless he is given a social role in advance, he cannot act. Consequently he is pathetically lonely.

The first symptom is not unrelated to the second. The second symptom might be summarized as a crisis of masculinity. Stevens is expected to have a number of interpersonal skills without which he would not be able to serve as a butler. He must be able to prepare the dinner table so that invited guests may enjoy their visit to Darlington Hall; to evaluate the social ranks of guests and assign them appropriate rooms; to adjust his attitude dependent upon the social occasion and the social status of his interlocutors; and so on. Not included in these social skills are how to express his own emotion in conversation, how to enter an intimate and sexual relationship with another person, and how to create new social relations with people whose social status and rank are unknown to him. Stevens is utterly helpless outside his professional context because all of his social skills are functional only within prescribed situations. In other words, he is not capable of encountering other people beyond stipulated social roles. What he is incapable of doing is to encounter the other as a stranger.

Miss Kenton, the housekeeper at Darlington Hall, is favorably disposed to Stevens. She insinuates her willingness to have a lasting relationship, but her signals to him are repeatedly frustrated, for he is incapable of responding to her personally. As a matter of fact, he is at a loss as to how to engage emotionally with another, irrespective of his professional qualification as a house manager to an aristocratic household; he does not know how to act in a situation in which he is not expected to behave according to the set protocols of Darlington Hall; he cannot liberate himself from his assigned role as butler or become independent of the given configuration of social positions; he is utterly helpless when deprived of a prescribed scenario for his role appropriate to his social position. It is in this respect that Stevens is socially impotent, and in the novel *The Remains of the Day* his helplessness is most provocatively but truthfully portrayed. Yet here we must keep in mind that his impotence cannot be reduced merely to his inability to enter a sexual relationship with another but connotes much more. What prevents Stevens from opening up to others, from liberating himself from his obsessive concern for social propriety?

Persona and the Crisis of Masculinity

In order to appreciate what Stevens's "impotence" alludes to in this novel, let me offer a brief analysis of the concept of personhood.

In everyday life, one apprehends what social role one is expected to play and, under normal circumstances, identifies with that assigned position. In the configuration of a family situation, for instance, one behaves as a father in relation to another person occupying the position of a child. One knows what one is expected to do as a father vis-à-vis his child, and one expects that child to behave according to the positions assigned in the configuration of a family. Or one identifies with the social position of a student and behaves in relation to other social positions, such as teachers and fellow students, according to what is expected of that social position as a student.

Thus, a combination of these relational positions and the ethical norms associated with them constitutes a paradigm of power. And this paradigmatic configuration is perhaps comparable to a dramaturgic stage in the sense that characters occupying particular positions are expected to follow certain ethical imperatives specific to their relational positions. Moreover, this paradigmatic configuration is in the order of a social imaginary precisely because a character is expected or imagined to behave in ways that fulfill the assigned role in the scenario to be presented on this stage. It is fantastic because it is equally probable that the character may not behave as expected. Of course, the character on this dramaturgic stage has been given the name "person" since Greco-Roman antiquity.

As the classical etymology of the word "person" suggests, the concept of personhood derives its connotation from Greek *prosopon* and Latin *persona*, which means a theatrical mask. In other words, we cannot deprive personhood of its dramaturgic connotation. Sakabe Megumi (坂部 恵) explored the social ontology of personhood in his *Poetics of Persona* and *Hermeneutics of the Mask*, which I rely on here as a *fil conducteur* (Sakabe 1989, 2009). A mask is effective only in a configuration involving other masks, and it indicates a particular social role or character in paradigmatic relations to other masks in a scenario in which a character is in action with others. Accordingly, a person signifies a human being insofar as the human is marked by a mask or its equivalent representing a particular social role or status. For an actor to wear a mask is to be assigned to a specific character on a particular stage in the deployment of a story, that is, a scenario (or a postulated sequence of events). A mask is displayed on the stage, which is structured in terms of a network of characters. Yet it must be noted that what is indicated by "stage" is ambiguous. First, it is possible to differentiate onstage from offstage: a stage, as distinguished from offstage, is a segregated space of imagination where a mask worn by an actor is real and is supposed to be taken seriously. But, just as an actor can remove his mask, the reality of a character symbolically represented by the mask is unreal or merely fantastic off the stage such that the actor assumes the role of a character on stage but can switch it off away from it. Thus actors can move from onstage to offstage or vice versa; accordingly, they are aware that the reality of the social role is dependent upon a whim. Nevertheless it does not make their personhood or others' personalities arbitrary. On the contrary, only insofar as it is coordinated in the configuration of a dramaturgical paradigm involving other characters or positions can it be real or seriously considered. In short, this dramaturgic paradigm is essentially fantastic.

Therefore, a stage means a physical space into and out of which an actor can move. But, at the same time, as the verb "to stage" amply suggests, a stage is a fantastic state of affairs in which characters played by actors wearing masks behave and fashion themselves as if they were actual embodiments of these characters. Thus, a stage is a visible scene for an audience, whereas offstage is invisible; onstage, a person wearing a mask is being looked at, while offstage a person is not involved in an acting performance for an audience. What is suggested by this ambiguity of the stage is nothing but the fact of personhood as a social construct: whereas the stage is a physical space on which actors interact, it is also a fantastic projection that can be switched on and off. Then what is suggested by this shift from onstage to offstage or vice versa?

We live in an infinite number of configurations of the dramaturgical paradigm. We may move out of one, but it does not mean that we are totally or absolutely off the stage at all. Offstage for one such configuration may well mean onstage for another. Even though admittedly one cannot concurrently locate oneself in multiple configurations of the dramaturgic paradigm, there is no guarantee that one can ever find oneself outside of any configuration or that one can be off the stage totally. In this sense, "stage" functions in a manner similar to "situation." This is why one can hardly dissociate the word "situation" from its theatrical connotations. Situation is a dramaturgic space in which a human or nonhuman actor is positioned within a surrounding; with regard to the conditions of the agent's location, his, her, or its status is defined so that it is not merely a physical location of the agent but also a situation; according to what narrative is attributed to it or how it is contextualized in a scenario, a situation can be defined and redefined infinite times.

One can behave in a situation to fashion oneself as a father in the configuration of familial positions. But one can enter an entirely different configuration of clinical medicine in which social roles are defined by a different set of paradigmatic positions such as medical doctor, patient, or nurse. The same individual constantly moves from one scene to another, from one configuration to another. Accordingly, a situation is articulated and rearticulated. In principle, the number of such dramaturgic configurations is infinite.

When moving from one stage to another, the new configuration into which one moves may well be insufficiently determinate, and in it a character to be supposedly acted can be undefined or poorly scripted. One can be thrown into a new situation where one cannot figure out how to be positioned in relation to others. In moving into a new situation, one cannot expect that the new social role to be played is always prescribed adequately or without ambiguity. One can never evade the element of unpredictability in entering into a new configuration, even if one's prescribed role is meticulously described in advance. And, more fundamentally, it is impossible to eliminate the element of wager in one's conduct in any situation since all social conduct is in essence aleatory (Nancy 1986, 1991).[38]

Let us be careful not to confuse two separate issues here. When shifting from one configuration of dramaturgic paradigm to another, the new configuration may or may not be familiar or predictable. Even if one has never played the character of a newly married bridegroom, one can somewhat predict how to behave in the company of the new bride's parents and her siblings. But one may be totally at a loss when entering the new configuration of corporate executives among whom seniority based upon managerial specialization and professional expertise is rigidly observed. A change from one configuration of dramaturgic paradigm to another presents unpredictability. This is a type of unpredictability that cannot be evaded in everyday life since one necessarily moves around in many different situations.

There is, however, a different kind of unpredictability. Even though you know very well what is expected in relation to your teacher, and what social role you are supposed to play in the situation of a classroom, an inevitable disparity always exists between your prescribed role in a particular configuration and what you are compelled to do in your actual performance; this is a discrepancy between your conduct insofar as it is figured out or prescribed in your imagination and your conduct in its material exteriority. Before you act, you can predict what you are going to do, figure out what you are expected to do. Yet this does not mean that you are capable of carrying out what you are supposed to perform. Actual conduct is not only posterior to prediction, prescription, and expectation in time; action that has been actualized is also necessarily exterior to a performer's expectation and intention. As Hegelian dialectics teaches us, action must be externalized and alienated from the sovereignty of the performing subject in such a way as to be much more than what you are expected to accomplish. Your actual conduct is necessarily excessive beyond what you mean to do. It is thanks to this externality or alienation inherent in action that your conduct or performance is open to excess beyond your intention; it is precisely due to an exposure to unpredictability that your action is social and that you are being-in-common with others.

Regardless of whether or not you know how to fashion yourself in a new configuration, you may well fail to fulfill the rules of conduct expected of the social role to be acted out, for a situation that is not at all aleatory does not exist. Even if you presume you are well versed in a configuration, you may well fail in the prescribed role expected of you. You may well be laughed at, scorned, or totally ignored. You may be hurt or injured physically or mentally. Thus, shifting from a prescribed position into an indeterminate one inevitably presents a risk of being humiliated. Despite tremendous risk and danger, however, people neither give up the aleatory task of seeking a new configuration yet to be prescribed nor stop attempting to perform a familiar role anew in such a way as to renew the significance of an old configuration or of encountering other people anew. Normally people never cease to look for new social relations or new configurations of the dramaturgic paradigm because it is only in seeking to transform a prescribed configuration that you can change the reality in which you live and the personhood you have been confined to.

Stevens's impotence consists in his inability to risk the security of his prescribed identity. He is afraid of an aleatory encounter's potential to expose him to a lot of shame and to unpredictable risk. What he most fears is to feel ashamed as a result of discarding his familiar and prescribed social role. He is incapable of opening himself to new possibilities, of inviting others into his life, and of transforming himself through the experience of shame. Not knowing how to evade unpredictability, he hesitates to go forward and instead retreats back into the sphere of security.

The choice of the word "impotence" could be somewhat problematic since it usually symbolizes a crisis of the paternalistic and conventional notion of masculinity, implying a lack of sexual capacity in the heterosexual setting. Here, too, I must be cautious. Masculinity pertains to a category of sexual difference in contrast to femininity. However, just as there is no fixed or predetermined nature in human beings, neither are masculinity or femininity naturally endowed. It follows that masculinity is without exception a historical construct, and, with respect to social formation, it is arbitrary and can manifest itself in a plethora of forms. Nevertheless, in modern social formations for nation-states, masculinity has been apprehended in a certain commonplace manner since a number of distinctly modern institutions such as the dichotomy of the public and the private, the registration of the modern monogamous family, national conscription, and the ideal of romantic love have been imposed upon populations subjugated to territorial state sovereignty. In modernity, the characteristic male has often been apprehended as a figure who manages and dominates social relations within the unit of the modern family on the one hand and as a warrior willing to kill and sacrifice himself for the national community on the other. With the emergence of the modern family and the national population and residential census, the population of all subjects beholden to territorial state sovereignty is reconstituted as a homogeneous object of constant surveillance, discipline, and registration. Consequent to the formation of territorial national state sovereignty, the totality of the inhabitants within the territory bounded by national borders has been expected to constitute itself as a homogeneous population under that sovereignty and is divided into the two genders, male and female. Thus, masculinity acquires some universal and unambiguous connotations which can be found in almost every country that has been modernized (Nishikawa 2000, 7–93).[39]

Evidently the notion of masculinity was profoundly affected by the emergence of homosexuality, which marked the establishment of a certain and very strict gender classification particular to the modern family.[40] It is important to note, therefore, that the crisis of masculinity should not be immediately confused with homosexuality, transsexuality, or a crisis of heterosexuality. Even though Stevens is incapable of responding to Miss Kenton's interest, it is not because of a homosexual orientation that he is insulated from a heterosexual encounter. In some sense, his impotence is more contemporaneous.

Nationalism of *Hikikomori* and the Experience of Shame

At the beginning of this chapter, I forewarned that I would use the word "hikikomori" in two distinct ways since I did not want readers to immediately ascribe adverse overtones to it. I have no intention of attributing a morally negative denotation to this word itself. However, it must be evident by now that the idiom "nationalism of hikikomori" does unambiguously carry a negative connotation since this type of nationalism implies the substantialization of nation, ethnos, or race, and easily lends itself to the dynamics of racist exclusionism.

As I stated previously, hikikomori refers to a sociological phenomenon in which adult individuals (mainly male) refuse to go out into the public realm and instead confine themselves to their bedrooms and homes. This behavior was first noticed in the 1980s in Japan. Since these hikikomori individuals persistently refuse to participate in personal relations necessary to perform professional, pedagogical, and other social activities, they end up alienating themselves from society at large. It is true that, generally speaking, people with mental disorders find it difficult to engage in social activities, but it is not believed that hikikomori victims fall into this category.

On rare occasions, hikikomori manifests itself in symptoms that resemble those of Asperger's syndrome or autism, but sociologists and psychopathologists insist instead that it originates under certain social conditions. In this respect, hikikomori people find themselves incapable of adjusting to the rules of cooperativeness and competition in places of education, work, and so on. They are maladjusted to a society governed by neoliberal norms, where one is envisaged to be flexible enough to operate by the rule of friendly cooperation on the one hand and by the tenet of ruthless competition on the other. In other words, one is supposed to be facile enough to be both competitive and cooperative concurrently. Neoliberalism demands that every successful person should work in the atmosphere of cooperation while competing mercilessly with coworkers. Perhaps hikikomori people take such a modern society too seriously, and their withdrawal from the social sphere must be understood as a rejection of such a workplace dominated by neoliberal norms or a protest against it. This suggests that hikikomori is not dissimilar to what in psychoanalysis used to be called "hysteria": a state of emotional excess beyond the patient's control, an excess that cannot be governed according to given social expectations.

When hikikomori takes place, it is said that two features can be identified. One is a discrepancy between a patient's way of life and the general norms of society that he is expected to fulfill. Because a hikikomori person adheres to ethical norms that are rather unique or unconventional, he cannot function in an ordinary social environment. The second moment to be found in a hikikomori person is a feature that Freud (1991) once called "ego-syntonic." The patient would insist on the ego ideal he adheres to so that no contradiction could be perceived between the patient's way of life and his ego ideal. This means that, by withdrawing from the outside world, the patient struggles to defend the image of his ideal self against society's conventional norms and expectations. Instead of conforming to society's conventions, he tries to protect his unconventional ego ideal.

In contrast, in the nationalism of hikikomori one can hardly find any element of protest or refusal of the ideas of competition or market fundamentalism as celebrated in today's capitalism and neoliberalism. Neither does a sympathizer with the nationalism of hikikomori attempt to defend his ego ideal against the conventional logic of self-responsibility or ruthless competition at the expense of his professional or educational career. Instead of risking his own career, he is always willing to conform to whatever norms modern society expects of him. What he seeks to conserve through the nationalism of hikikomori is not his loyalty to an idealized ego, but rather a sense of inclusion, of the guarantee that he is not ostracized from the imagined totality of the national community. The nationalism of hikikomori allows him to imagine that he continues to occupy the positionality of the majority in the majoritarian-minoritarian gradient. What he is most afraid of is exclusion from the fantasized communion of the national community. Consequently someone sympathetic to the nationalism of hikikomori would not hesitate to sacrifice his own moral integrity for fear of isolation. We must never overlook the potential fragility of interiority in talking about the inward-looking tendencies that can easily be observed in the United States as well as other so-called postindustrial societies in Europe and Japan. Far from feeling securely included in whatever nation they imagine to belong to, those who are most easily seduced by the rhetoric of exclusionist nationalism are also those who feel most insecure in their insider status to their respective national communities.

Thus, whereas the incident of hikikomori happens to rather independent and principled individuals, in contrast, the nationalism of hikikomori seems to appeal to conformist personalities who do not stand against social conventions and who are afraid of being isolated or ostracized. The nationalism of hikikomori prevails among those who wish to be safely inside the national community, securely insulated from immigrants or foreigners coming from the outside by a fantasized national border, among those who desire to be located inside the nation by erecting an imaginary barrier to prevent foreigners from entering their space.

Thus, at stake here is the violence of exclusion that seems inherent in the nationalism of hikikomori. Since violence is exerted by the nationalism of hikikomori out of the desire to protect communion and fantasized togetherness in the national community from foreign intrusion, we must now understand how the national community is constituted in imagination, how this community is supposed to consolidate the togetherness of its authentic members, and finally how hikikomori (reclusive withdrawal) is imagined to guarantee the insularity of this national community.[41] For, as far as the nationalism of hikikomori is concerned, as we have seen in the case of Stevens in *The Remains of the Day*, individual membership in the national community is a matter of collective fantasy rather than of nationality warranted in the legal sense by the sovereign state.

Another issue that cannot be overlooked in our analysis is anxiety, for which the nationalism of hikikomori is supposedly a remedy in fantasy. Let us corroborate again that what is commonly shared among the followers of hikikomori nationalism is a tremendous fear of potential expulsion from the community or deprivation of its membership. Yet they do not want to be specific about the concrete agenda or particular relations that make them feel uncertain or insecure, and, most often, their anxiety remains rather amorphous. Or one could claim that their anxiety is of an existential kind. Therefore, their fear is best described in negative terms: the nationalists of hikikomori are afraid that they are going to lose what they supposedly have taken for granted for a long time. Their anxiety is essentially reactive; their nationalism is defensive and self-protective against fantasized intruders who are going to steal their happiness and security; adherents to the nationalism of hikikomori are concerned about how to safeguard what they feel entitled to, since they are going to lose what they have long assumed themselves to be endowed with.

Characteristically, the trope that dominates their sentiments and emotions is a spatial one, that of inside and outside of what Thongchai Winichakul calls a "geo-body."[42] This trope operates in polysemy and multiple fantasies and empirically is rarely specified. Is it the inside or outside of a geographic territory? Is it of legal qualification for resident registration? Or is it ethnolinguistic capacity to speak the national or ethnic language? In fact, this trope alludes to all these plural sememes or multiple contexts of different denotations and connotations.[43] Hence many such followers are obsessed with the image of a border or wall that supposedly protects the insularity of the national territory at the national border. And this is why hikikomori nationalist violence takes as its target the immigrant who supposedly invades the national community across the national border or the alien inside who disturbs the supposed homogeneity of the interior space of the national community.

With regard to this trope of inside and outside, how is the sense of belonging to the nation constituted? How is the individual's national identity fantasized? Here we should remind ourselves once again, as I elaborated in chapter 2, that the national community is a modern invention, a social formation particular to modernity, because it is formed according to social norms and a dynamism distinct from those dictates of relational identification. Whereas in premodern social formations communities were formed on the basis of kinship, professional connections, caste networks, and so on, the modern community of the nation is constituted on the basis of a social organization that rejects the principle of relational identity. In premodern social formations, individuals were connected to one another through the relations of kinship, neighborhood, professional division of labor, clan affiliations, and so on. The family of premodernity did not institute the private sphere of the modern family from which distant kin and domestic servants were excluded. Hence, it was very hard or nearly impossible to draw a clear-cut boundary between the inside of a family and the outside. The network of familial affiliations formed an extended family in which the division between its members and nonmembers was elastic. Since, in similar fashion, the community was formed in terms of a network of kinship, caste, clan affiliations, and professional connections, it was very difficult to conceive of a clear partition between its interior and its exterior. It follows that an individual belonging to the community was identified within the network of social relations or ranks—kinship, caste, professional hierarchy, clan lineages, and so forth—so that the relationship between the individual and the whole of the community had to be mediated by a number of layers, of webs of affiliation.

CONCLUSION
Shame and Decolonization

The historical process by which the modern nation came into existence was indeed gradual, and the formation of the national community was not accomplished overnight, even though the new form of community, "peoplehood"— "we the people"—was announced at times of revolutionary upheaval in the American Declaration of Independence and the French Declaration of the Rights of Man and of the Citizen, both of which inaugurated the instantaneous implementation of a human as a citizen of the nation. With respect to the structure of belonging, the emergence of the new community of the nation brought about a new power formation whose features can be summarized by the two dynamics of individuation on the one hand and of totalization on the other.

Under the dynamics of individuation, a member of the community is abstracted from various social relations in which he or she is engaged in everyday life and thus is grasped as an indivisible substance. Let me again briefly summarize what I attempt to elucidate in chapter 2. In the web of familial affiliations, a person occupies a specific position in relation to other members of the same kinship. A person is a daughter in relation to her mother but an aunt in relation to her niece; a person is a brother in relation to his siblings but a grandson in relation to his grandparents; a person is a servant in relation to her master but a wife in relation to her husband. In the configuration of a pedagogical institution, she is a teacher in relation to her pupils; in that of clinical medicine, a patient in relation to her medical doctor. A person acquires identity in a particular configuration of the social network and, depending upon a particular context of social conduct, shifts from one configuration to another. Hence, she is never singularly determined in and of herself as a substance independent of other people occupying different positions in social formations, but her identity is always relational, situational, and multiple as far as the principle of relational identity is concerned. Thus, she is never detached from the present instance of discourse in which she performs and enunciates her conduct in relation to a particular person—or persons—who also occupies a specific position in the same configuration.

In the national community, however, the principle of relational identity is strictly confined to the domain of privacy, and a person is stripped of these relational identities and regarded as an individual, as if a person's personality were immanent in individual personhood irrespective of his or her relations to others.[1] This manner of grasping personhood is typically dictated by what is called individualism, according to which the character and status of a person that derive from relations to other people are regarded as accidental. And all the essential properties of a person are purportedly immanent in her personhood as an individual. Individualism is thus an essential ingredient of the nation as long as the nation is projected as a form of communion.

According to the dynamics of individualism, therefore, a person belongs to a national community without the mediation of the network of personal relationships, such as kinship. This leads to the second dynamic of totalization. And this is probably one of the reasons why Benedict Anderson (1983), for example, characterized the modern nation as an imagined community. The principle of relational identity presumes that a person is acquainted with other members of the community when she or he claims to belong to it. In this context, it is worth referring to Émile Benveniste's discussion about the discursive function of personhood.

It is well known that Benveniste refused to admit personhood to the so-called third-person pronouns—"he," "she," and "they" in the case of English, for instance. For, otherwise, a person would never be situated in the present instance of discourse in which she can have a personal relation of "I" and "you" with another person (Benveniste 1971, 223–230).[2] Only when a speaker is in a relation of "I" (addresser in the present instance of discourse) and "you" (addressee in the present instance of discourse) can he or she be a person. In other words, unless one is in the situation of an enunciation, that is, in the present instance of discourse, as either an addresser or addressee, one cannot be designated by a personal pronoun. The principle of relational identity operates in a personal relation according to Benveniste's definition of the term "person." In contrast, the principle of specific identity does not require that the members of a nation be acquainted with one another at all as long as acquaintance implies that, at one point in time, one enters a personal relation of "I" and "you" in the present instance of discourse. Even when an individual does not know—"knowing" in the sense of being affiliated with—a single other member of the nation, she can claim she belongs to it because, in essence, the nation is a community of strangers.[3] The element in which it can exist is that of imagination. This is why the nation is above all else an imagined community.

Under the principle of specific identity, belonging no longer means that one is put in a face-to-face relation to a particular person; one need not engage in a personal relation to belong to the community. Now, belonging is a matter of an abstract relationship between an individual and the totality of the community when the person engaged in the community is thus determined.[4]

Once again, let me emphasize that the community at stake here is the national community, one that supposedly consists of individuals, even though, as I have explicated with regard to the transition in the mode of identification, the dictates of individuation and totalization are effectuated in modernity. So I suggested that, precisely because of this historical transformation in the mode of personal/individual identification, what one might call "fascism" is inherent in the formation of national community in general. With its constituent members being individuated, the nation form is projected as an organic unity of individuals; according to the principle of specific identity, the national community is imagined to be a gathering of individuated human beings, and it is believed that precisely the unity of these individuals requires a communion to form its cohesiveness.[5]

Under the dictates of specific identity, an individual human being is said to belong to a nation of similar individual humans according to the same classificatory scheme, just as a domestic cat is a carnivorous mammal subsumed under the species *Felis catus* or just as a potato is under the species *Solanum tuberosum*. Operating in this logical scheme is the hierarchical cataloguing formula of inclusion and exclusion, in classical or Aristotelian logic, a formula consisting of three distinct tiers of individual-species-genus, even though, strictly speaking, the Aristotelian classification does not necessarily correspond to the modern biological taxonomy of Carl Linnaeus, for instance. All human individuals belonging to the genus of humanity can be classified into distinctly different species because of the species differences among them. The nation is a class of this kind; it exists as a particular species distinguished from another particular species by a certain species difference even though, in strictly biological terms, humanity (*Homo sapiens*) cannot be further divided into multiple species. The speciation—classifying a genus into subsets or species—of humanity in terms of nationality is not relevant at all in biology but significant only in the politics of myth. In this respect, scientific racism is a confusionism or premeditated confusion that mixes up the biological speciation with the political. Yet it projects the logic of classification particular to the modern international world onto the level of the biological or physiological constitution of the individual human body.

The international world is organized by the following formula of speciation: at the level of genus, every human being belongs to humanity, but at the level of species, every human individual is supposedly subsumed under one of the many existing nations; all human beings belong to the general class of humanity, but an individual human is supposed to belong to a particular species or subset: French, Chinese, Russian, Thai, and so on. Normally and normatively, if a human individual belongs to a particular nation, he or she does not belong to another one. Thus, a nation is a taxonomic unity that corresponds to the level of species, while humanity as the general class of *Homo sapiens* corresponds to that of genus. Thus the nation exists only among many nations—as one species among many species—and the totality of a nation can be given only in contradistinction to other nations. Logically speaking, in other words, the nation would not exist outside the system of internationality, an assembly of nations juxtaposed to one another in a horizontal relationship of disjunction.

In the system of international law, the subsumption of an individual human being under the species of the nation used to indicate the expectation of abiding by the law of disjunction: in the regime of internationality, if one belongs to one state, one cannot belong to others. This used to imply that, if one belonged to one nation, one could not belong to others at the same time since it is assumed by the classical dictates of international law that one nation is defined as the totality of a population resident within one territory and governed by one territorial state sovereignty. Today, there are not many nation-states, such as Japan, where multiple citizenship is not accepted; however, the modern international world is ostensibly based upon the presumption that every human being must be classified exclusively into one of the nations. It may appear, accordingly, that we have yet to discard the predisposition that an individual with multiple nationalities is somewhat abnormal, and that an immigrant with multiple citizenships is a deviant who disturbs the assumed coherence of a nation. This outdated predisposition is reemerging as inward-looking tendencies predominate nowadays, as if in tandem with the return of outdated propaganda of the decline of the West.

Thus, the dictate of totalization advocates compellingly that by belonging to a national community, an individual is able to transcend such particular statuses, ranks, and castes as articulated in the kinship he is affiliated with, as defined in his professional networks, and as received from past familial, class, and religious heritages. Thanks to this dictate, it is now possible to prescribe that every member of the nation should be treated as an equal because an individual member is directly affiliated with the whole nation without any mediation by status, rank, or caste. Instead of relating to his kin, neighbors, ancestors, and so on, an individual is directly affiliated with the totality of the national community in imagination. An individual may be recognized in terms of kinship, professional specialty, caste, social rank, religious affiliation, and so on, but these properties attributed to him must be bracketed or reduced as far as his nationality—the fact of belonging to the totality of the nation—is concerned. In this imagined adherence to the totality of the nation, every member is directly involved with the national community and belongs to it, since he does not need to be related to his fellow citizens in any personal situation, that is, in the present instance of discourse where "I" addresses "you."

The Dictates of Individuation and Totalization

Until the collapse of the Tokugawa Shogunate in 1868, the federal system under which most of the Japanese archipelago was ruled was called the Baku-Han Taisei (the governing federation of the military shogunate and domains 幕藩体制), a feudal confederacy in which the ruling samurai class justified their governments in terms of pseudo-Confucian moral values and customs. The Baku-Han system was feudalistic in the sense that hundreds of *daimyo* (domainal lords with fiefs) maintained relative legal and financial independence while pledging loyalty to the most powerful daimyo, the Tokugawa Shogun. Japan was not politically centralized, and there was no authority that could have served to represent state sovereignty in the international world. What is remarkable about the moral universe of late Tokugawa Japan is that there was no value equivalent to equality. As touched upon in chapter 2, the idea of equality came into existence suddenly, as soon as the new emperor system of "one sovereign for all" (一君万民) was introduced in 1868 (Hirota 1990).

Why was it not possible, not only for peasants but also for the samurai, to conceive of a political society based upon the value of equality until the idea of the modern national community was introduced? Of course I do not claim that, as soon as the Meiji state introduced modernization policies, Japanese society became a modern nation-state overnight. Nevertheless, we cannot overlook the persistence of the Meiji government's policies of modernization in that the Japanese state never abandoned the dictates of individuation and totalization. This is why the Tokugawa caste systems based on hereditary rank were overturned within several years of the Meiji Restoration, and the Meiji state undertook concerted efforts to liberate the people of Japan from restrictions originating in kinship and social rank as well as to build an unprecedented type of community called "nation" around the newly established institution of the emperor system. To introduce the sense of communality regulated by the dictates of individuation and totalization, it persistently degraded institutions governed by the principle of relational identity so that the people were expected to internalize the new principle of specific identity.

According to the dictates of individuation, an individual must be freed from the network of familial, tribal, and neighborhood communities and instead must be expected to compete as an independent actor in the abstract field of the market. According to the dictate of totalization, on the other hand, such an atomized and alienated individual is expected to identify with the totality of the community without mediation. The structure of power outlined here is nothing other than what Michel Foucault called "pastoral power" (*le pouvoir pastoral*), and the modern emperor, as instituted by the Meiji state, is an apparatus essential for this arrangement of power. Indeed, Foucault conceived of pastoral power as a technique that originated in religious traditions of the ancient Orient, but he also implied that such a technology is not totally foreign to the sort of modern governmentality observed in Western Europe and North America in the last several centuries. The emperor system of "one sovereign for all" is a case in point. Even though the emperor system employs additional technologies—modern national service, modern universal education, social welfare, modern typography, photography, telegraph communication, cinematography, and so on—it is a pastoral power operative in the general fields of governmentality, which Foucault called biopower (*bio-pouvoir*).[6]

As I analyzed in chapter 2, in this arrangement of power, an individual becomes a member of the national community under the universal gaze of the emperor. In this individualized relationship to the emperor, in which an individual is subjected to the totality and fantasizes himself or herself as an infant seeking the protection and recognition of the universal parent ("a baby of the Emperor"「天皇之赤子」was an expression used extensively in Japanese legal and governmental publications until the collapse of the Japanese Empire in 1945), an individual is directly connected, in fantasy, to the totality of the national community as represented by the figure of the emperor, who plays the role of the shepherd and is willing to sacrifice his own life to save even one stray sheep. In this fantastic relationship between the totality of the community, represented by the figure of the emperor, and each member of this community, the member is severed from his or her kinship or clan ties and captured as an isolated and lonely stranger, that is, an individual in individualism. It is precisely because of this solitude or individuality vis-à-vis the universal gaze of the emperor that an individual subject is said to belong to the totality of the national community.[7] And the aesthetic form that mediates the individuality of a lonely subject with the totality of the national community is called fraternity. Essentially, this national community is a collectivity of strangers gathered together thanks to the gaze of the emperor, the benevolent shepherd. Under this universal gaze (一視同仁) that distributes equal charity and love to everyone in the community, the value "equality" is implemented as a principle that cements the rights of all individuals belonging to the nation.

In this pastoral power it is important to note that an individual's relation to other individuals is totally overlooked. The whole scene seems to be dictated by the statement, "You must behave as if, in this universe, there exists only the emperor and you." What is reproduced in this fantasized relation with the emperor is almost identical to the intimate and unmediated relationship between a shepherd and a stray sheep. Since the emperor symbolizes the unity of the nation, adhering to him is synonymous with belonging to the nation. Under the guidance and guardianship of the shepherd, a stray sheep can return to the herd and become integrated into its community. Thus, in the idiom "one gaze, equal mercy" (一視同仁), two distinct moments, the individual's devotion to the emperor through her or his solitude (the dictate of individuation) on the one hand and the totality embracing every member of the Japanese nation (the dictate of totalization) on the other are adeptly synthesized. This is an entirely new way of forming a community without involving the principle of relational identity, without the mediation of personal acquaintance between "I" and "you" (except for the very relationship between each isolated individual and the shepherd). Whereas the nation is essentially a community of strangers, an individual may well be disposed emotive-sentimentally in a positive way toward other members of the nation and negatively toward nonmembers, even though the members and nonmembers should be equally strangers.[8] From the first year of the Meiji state (1868) right up to the end of the Japanese Empire (1945), this idiom was repeatedly cited in governmental laws, ordinances, and regulations; they expressed the organizational doctrine upon which the nation-state of the Japanese Empire was legitimated.

This idiom came from Chinese publications that Christian missionaries prepared for the purpose of propagating Christian teachings in China. It is usually used in a combination such as "one gaze and equal mercy, four seas and all brotherhood" (「一視同仁、四海兄弟」), which expresses the spirit of universal fraternity. While concealing its original source, the Meiji government adopted the tactics of Christian missionaries in order to newly institute the relationship between Japan's modern state, symbolically represented by the figure of the emperor, and the subjects of the Japanese nation-state.

Within the regime of equality thus introduced, it is possible to anticipate two opposing political dynamics: the first is an exclusionist dynamic according to which the members of the nation, on whom the equal mercy of the emperor is endowed, must be able to enjoy such rights, whereas the nonmembers must not. Those individuals who do not belong to the nation should not be given the same privileges as its members, and these nonmembers must be unambiguously excluded. Otherwise, the nation, which after all is a community of strangers, cannot be sustained. On the other hand, it is equally possible to emphasize the universalistic tendency inherent in the emperor system. The range of equal mercy must be infinitely expandable, just as the community of individuals recognized under the gaze of the emperor must be. The totality of the nation is defined by the figure of the emperor so that, just as the idiom "one gaze, equal mercy" implied in the context of the proselytization activities of Christian missionaries, the nation could be redefined just as the range of the emperor's gaze is redefined. This dynamic was best represented by the propaganda dictum "eight corners of the world under one roof" (「八紘一宇」), which means that all the peoples in the eight corners of the world can live harmoniously under one roof.[9]

This second dynamic implies that the totality of the national community is not fixed; it can be extended as the nation-state expands its territory and conquers a larger population. It is not difficult to see that the logic of "one gaze, equal mercy" can be readily appropriated by imperial nationalism. Since this dynamic was intrinsic to Japan's imperial nationalism of the first half of the twentieth century, anticolonial ethnic nationalisms that viewed the nation as a fixed entity that could not be integrated into the larger nation were suppressed and sometimes violently censored by the Japanese state.

After the collapse of the Japanese Empire, the second dynamic was eliminated—that the Japanese public committed themselves to such a notion of universal brotherhood was deliberately forgotten—and only the first dynamic survived, to guarantee equality for all the members of the national community. From Japan's defeat in the Asia-Pacific War up to the present day, the view of the nation as fixed and substantial has been dominant in Japan, as I discuss in chapter 1. Indeed, the idiom "one gaze, equal mercy" was abandoned once and for all when popular sovereignty was implemented as the basic form of the state. However, the idea of the emperor as "the symbol of the unity of the nation," a new definition introduced in Article 1 of the Constitution of Japan, retained the structure of pastoral power as outlined in the prewar emperor system. Precisely because the emperor was stripped of all administrative, legislative, and judiciary powers, the essence of pastoral power inherent in the emperor system became all the more apparent. Clearly the first dynamic in the assumption of equality was intensified as time went by; it was generally accepted within the Japanese public sphere that, in contradistinction to the universalistic tendency manifested in the United Nations' Universal Declaration of Human Rights, the Japanese do not show much interest in the application of basic human rights as guaranteed in the constitution for nonmembers of the Japanese national community. Except for a relatively few activists, lawyers, journalists, and other intellectuals, the idea of equality seems strictly confined to national membership.

The Fantastic Representation of the Inside and the Outside of the Nation

Of course, it is a matter of political choice as to whether one belongs to a national community or not. Furthermore, this community itself changes in shape and constitution over time so that the nation's inside and outside are reinscribed and redefined many times in history. Japanese history offers one of the most illustrative examples in this respect. Until the Meiji Restoration, there was no well-articulated notion of national territory, and hardly any national border existed in the northern end of the Baku-Han federation of the Tokugawa Shogunate and Domains. But, as Japan emerged as a nation-state and joined the modern system of international law, the national territory had to be clearly defined for the first time. Yet a series of adjustments took place almost every decade from the 1870s until 1945, with each instance of territorial annexation of Hokkaido, Okinawa, Taiwan, the Korean Peninsula, Sakhalin, the Pacific islands (previously occupied by Germany), Tsingtao, and Manchuria as well as the areas the Japanese military had occupied during the Asia-Pacific War. Finally as a result of the defeat, Japan lost many of these territories, along with over 30 percent of its population. Thus the inside and outside of the Japanese nation were repeatedly redefined, and what constituted this nation could never be unambiguously determined. Furthermore, it is essential to remember that the inside and outside of the nation are not necessarily restricted to issues of territorial sovereignty; the outside of the nation is differentiated from its inside not only in terms of geography but also in terms of factors such as cultural traits, racial features, linguistic identities, and religious affiliations. In short, the inscription of a border is a matter of social encounter between one individual and another, or between one group and another, and this encounter—or what Sandro Mezzadra and Brett Neilson once called "bordering"—which inscribes the border separating the inside from the outside, is always mediated by the techniques of fantasy, including cartography.[10]

It may appear that the inside of the nation is distinct from the outside thanks to the geopolitical and geographic configuration of a space, where two different kinds of people are distinct from one another because of their geographic locations. A membership of the nation, however, is never one of geography. Even if a space is divided by a national border, it does not follow that an individual located on one side automatically belongs to the nation while an individual on the other side does not. Only when a border is articulated to the social relation of one individual to another does it acquire its social significance as a national border. Accordingly, it is in fact misleading to say that the inscription of a border is an event exclusively of a geographic nature. The national border is an apparatus of social discrimination such that each time a person encounters another, it must be inscribed and reinscribed as an institution that attributes certain social relations to the geographic relation. To stress this social aspect, I have relied upon the verb "bordering" rather than the noun "border."

From the outset, therefore, the distinction between the inside and the outside of the nation is a trope, a metaphoric linkage to multiple variables, such as geopolitical configuration, administrative classification, majoritarian-minoritarian gradients, social hierarchy, racial classification, and police surveillance.

In order to comprehend the inward-looking tendencies of nationalism and the surge of anti-immigrant racism in many postindustrial societies, therefore, we must investigate how the trope of the national border functions in our collective fantasy or how the inside of the national community has been narrated, modified with fantastic episodes, and articulated to anxieties concerning people's precarious conditions in their everyday life. Certainly this is one reason why I deliberately chose the topic of the nationalism of hikikomori in this book. We need to understand why a large number of people are persuaded by fantastic episodes in which they believe they can withdraw into the security of a secluded community, into the sanctuary of a utopian refuge so as to be exempt from any fierce competition in a neoliberal market, or into the communal comradery of a natal village. Provided that the most dominant image of a community in the modern international world is, besides that of the modern family, what Thongchai Winichakul (1994) called "the geo-body of a nation," it is no surprise that the space thus imagined is, almost without exception, equated to the national community. Nonetheless, let us keep in mind that this way of fantasizing the national community is not exceptional but idiosyncratic of the era in which anti-immigrant racism, reactionary populism, and anti-intellectual conservatism are prevalent.

In present-day Japan the dichotomy of the inside and the outside is articulated to the sanctuary of the national community in specific ways. The old fantasy of the nation under the universal gaze of the emperor is now projected onto the ethnicized nation where people are unified through the fantastic sense of communion, in contrast to the outside of the national community where the intimacy of national comradery is replaced by the logic of survival of the fittest. Thus the binary opposition of the inside and the outside is rearticulated, with the binary of the inside as the place of comfort and security, as opposed to the outside as the place of brutal rivalry and neoliberalism. It is under this fantasized configuration of the nation's inside and outside that the interior of the national community is modified in the collective fantasy with the connotation of the sanctuary for comfort, into which one would be tempted to withdraw from an outside fraught with merciless competition and neoliberal ruthlessness.

It goes without saying that, regardless of whether one is situated inside or outside the national community, one is in actuality never endowed with the sense of communion. One lives separated from others in an extremely atomized social environment, yet this fundamental distance between one person and another makes it possible to live and work together in modern social formations. Competition is the fundamental reality of modern life. Virtually every aspect of life is governed by the logic of rivalry. And this spirit of competition is hardly distinguishable from the ethical norm of fairness on which meritocracy is built.

As we have explored, the word "nationality" has many connotations, one of them being nationality in the sense of an individual's exclusive membership in the nation. Japanese nationality, for instance, may warrant a set of privileges that foreigners cannot enjoy, but Japanese nationality alone never serves as a total guarantee of security; it would never warrant one's well-being or insulate one from the reality of market competition and meritocracy. In many nation-states an individual is endowed with a formal equality of opportunity, but this does not signal an equality of outcome. A formal equality is necessary for the market to function most efficiently, and what the formal equality of opportunity guarantees is an orderly competition in which all participants strive to excel and outdo every other competitor. No member of the nation should be excluded from opportunities available to all its members regardless of his or her heritage, social rank, wealth, religious affiliation, or residential location. The principle of equality serves to legitimate the very process of competition as well as its outcome; it is expected from the outset that the participants are eventually ranked in a hierarchy according to their performance, and that their ranks are determined in terms of commensurate measures. Thus the principle of formal equality is categorically necessary in order for the consequences of market competition to be legitimated. Market competition may well give rise to a vastly different result for each participant, as a consequence of which new social ranks and different hierarchy can be established. In this respect, the principle of formal equality is a required premise upon which inequality ensues in outcome. At the same time, it is a necessary condition for legitimacy that inequality among competitors be actualized in fairness.

We are fully aware that, in our everyday life in a modern capitalist society, the vision of communality based on equality as portrayed by the dictum "one gaze, equal mercy" is no more than a figment of our imagination. For those of us who live in a modern society regulated by the principle of specific identity, to insist upon the security and intimacy in the personal relationship characterized by the principle of relational identity is tantamount to withdrawing from the public realm that is dictated by individualism and meritocracy based upon competition. As one lives more thoroughly engaged in a public realm dominated by meritocracy and individualism, one might be tempted all the more to fantasize the idealized vision of a national community—let us recall that John Stuart Mill (1972) called the nation "a society of sympathy"—where everybody is harmoniously integrated into the peoplehood in a state of personal comradery, while the outside is presumably a scene of bloody battle where the only dictate is the survival of the fittest. The very distinction of the inside from the outside can never be independent of the politics of sentimentality and fantasy. It is not because of some malice, hidden plot, or intrusion that one is deprived of the sense of communal belonging and empathy that should be enjoyed on the inside of the national community.

The premise that the nation is a community of equal members where unconditional comradery and sympathy prevail is one of the most distinctive characteristics of the social collectivity called "nation." Its essential feature consists in its imaginary and fantastic dynamics. While, as I have argued above, the nation is a community of strangers, each member is directly affiliated with its totality in imagination. The imaginary character of the nation does not at all mean that this collectivity is either illusionary or arbitrary. It is precisely due to this imaginary character that the national community is an objective and substantive existence for which people are willing to kill and die. And this historically specific form of collectivity—let me stress once again that the nation is particular to the modern international world—is in essence an aesthetic construct. Precisely because of this dynamic, this social formation assumes a tremendous capacity to induce its members to aspire and act—in other words, to fantasize collectively and politically—for the vision of this community. Accordingly, the dynamics of the national community lie in this potential capacity to inspire its members to fantasize their communality, a capacity that may well be called myth or mything.

It follows, however, that the interior of the national community thus fantasized is not something empirically determinable; its inside cannot be delimited solely in terms of geography, nor is its border identifiable exclusively in cartographic terms. Nevertheless, people aspire to consolidate the fantasized realm of the national interiority against its outside, particularly when many of them are in distress, the perception of social disparity and economic inequality is intensified, and an increasing number of members of the nation feel left out in capitalist competition games. They desperately seek to reestablish the fantasized interior of the national community by marking its border, reifying the separation between its inside and outside, and eventually building a physical obstacle to prevent movement between them.

It is generally agreed that fascism is a tendency inherent in nationalism that manifests itself in antiparliamentarian authoritarianism, violent oppression of oppositional forces, racist identity politics, the rhetoric of anti-immigration, an insistence on mythological national origins, and so forth. The word "fascism" is notorious for its overuse as a pejorative, especially since the defeat of the Axis Powers in 1945. The historical context of today's politics is vastly different from that of the early 1920s, when the term itself was put forth as a name for a political agenda by Benito Mussolini in opposition to liberalism, Marxism, and representative parliamentarianism. Nonetheless, the word somewhat captures the urgency and exclusionist violence with which contemporary radical authoritarian anti-immigration politics has been associated, but it is clear that this term should be used with deliberate caution.

No doubt the fantastic tropes of the national community are extensively appropriated by fascist politics. It is in this respect that this politics relies upon the basic vocabulary of nationalist tropes and is inextricably entwined with nationalism. What we sketchily and equivocally refer to as fascism today would be hardly comprehensible without this fantastic dynamics of the imagined community and the geo-body of a nation. Fascists' exclusion of immigrants, hostility toward ethnic and sexual minorities, and insistence on the rhetoric of racial purity are motivated by the fantastic seclusion of the inside from the outside of the national community, and are all actualized in terms of the basic vocabulary of the tropes of the imagined community.

What I want to suggest by the nationalism of hikikomori is marked by the resurgence of the collective fantasy of the imagined community, as well as the increasing demand for an economy in collective fantasy that reinforces the unambiguous and decisive distinction of the inside and the outside of the national community, for a fantastic dynamics somewhat reminiscent of "one gaze, equal mercy." It is against the backdrop of the fantasy of the national border, I believe, that the problematics of shame is acquiring significance once again.

Of course, the idea of equality is indispensable in our modern life. It is one of the vital instruments by which to fight against injustice in modern societies; it incites us to be attentive to existing discrimination; it urges us to engage in collective endeavors to transform social formations; it is one of the vital sources of social dynamism and communal solidarity in modernity. Yet when nationality is articulated to the geo-body of the nation, it could be mobilized to excuse violent exclusion and racist discrimination. What I call the nationalism of hikikomori accomplishes this particular synthesis of the geo-body of the nation with resentment toward foreigners.

The Feeling of Shame and the Comfort Women Problem

The problem of the Comfort Women or wartime sex slavery helps us comprehend how intimately the issue of the nationalism of hikikomori is associated with the phenomenology of shame. It also helps us in our search for mediation between collective aesthetics as a social formation and the individual's emotive and sentimental reaction to the legacies of history. Of course, I am not seeking to conceptualize the Comfort Women problem as a moment in the dialectic development of the spirit toward some sublation. Neither am I concerned with this problem as a challenge to be overcome or surmounted for Japan's or any other society's modernization.

I have repeatedly emphasized, mainly in my Japanese publications, that the Comfort Women problem was like a blessing, an exceptional gift, to people with Japanese nationality. A great number of Japanese regard this problem as a sort of natural disaster that should be dealt with among themselves without the involvement of foreigners, as if it were a case of family dishonor not to be broadcast outside the family. One can easily detect the nationalism of hikikomori in their reaction to this problem. But, regardless of whether one likes it or not, it has already been publicized internationally. Moreover, the system of Comfort Stations (従軍慰安所) was first introduced in the 1930s in China in response to a large number of rapes committed by Japanese soldiers against local civilian women. Originally, it was an institution designed to deal with struggles between members of the Japanese military and the foreign—in this case, Chinese—population. It was and still is an international problem. To the extent that this is a problem concerning the political responsibility of the Japanese nation, it necessarily involves people who do not identify with that nation, outsiders to the Japanese national community. As I argue in chapter 1, the question of nationality cannot be raised unless a different nationality is implicated. In this respect, the problem appears to be instigated by foreigners who came from outside the fantasized interior of the Japanese nation; this is also thanks to the fact that the gravity of this problem was publicly enunciated for the first time in 1991 when Korean Comfort Women sued the Japanese government for its responsibility for the system of Comfort Stations established all over the territories occupied by the Japanese military during the latter half of the Asia-Pacific War (1931–1945).

Let us not forget, however, that the Korean Comfort Women who actually sued the Japanese government were, as a matter of fact, Japanese nationals when recruited into the system of Comfort Stations. In this regard too, the problem is an exceptional gift from the outside world that prevents the Japanese from withdrawing into the fantasized interior of the imagined community. In other words, the problem of the Comfort Women is potentially a remedy given in the feeling of shame for the nationalism of hikikomori. For a Japanese individual must get out or be exposed to somebody outside the Japanese community in order to confront responsibility for the Comfort Women problem; he cannot do so while remaining withdrawn in the fantasized interior of the national community.

Moreover, this problem cannot be discussed without reference to sexuality and masculinity. The significance of the word "comfort" cannot be overlooked in the deliberate choices made in the "military Comfort Stations" (「従軍慰安所」) and the "military Comfort Women" (「従軍慰安婦」): these women were supposed to provide the soldiers of the Japanese imperial army and navy with a certain "comfort," and this sense of comfort must have been composed of a number of emotive and sentimental gratifications for the soldiers who needed them: the comfort of not being constantly scrutinized and scolded by their superiors; the comfort of being in an intimate and private relationship; the comfort of being safely away from battlegrounds; the comfort of being sexually recognized as a male by a female and thus being treated, however temporarily, not as a disposable commodity but rather as an indispensable human being; the comfort of being worshipped as a man representing an imperial force in a colonial relationship by a woman belonging to a nation or people apparently subordinate to such an imperial authority; and so forth.

It becomes immediately obvious that what was euphemistically portrayed as "comfort" for a soldier to enjoy as a male client at a Comfort Station was irresolvably associated with the exaggerated self-esteem and self-confidence one would boast of when identifying with a powerful imperial nation. Sexuality, masculinity, and (imperial) nationalism were thus articulated to one another in such a way that an individual's masculinity and self-esteem would not be dissociated from his membership in an imperial nation. Neither one's masculinity nor self-esteem is independent of the status of the nation to which he belongs in the international world.

This is why an inquisition into the status of Comfort Women, and the calling into question of the very normalcy of military prostitution, is perceived as an embarrassment for those who regard themselves as males and who identify with the Japanese nation. What is at stake is the fact that those held somewhat responsible—not necessarily responsible for the actual criminal conduct of sexual slavery but for being affiliated with the imperial nation that once committed such acts—are made to feel ashamed in confronting the problem of the Comfort Women.[11] The feeling of shame is, however, crucial in urging a response to those third-country members who would otherwise be totally ignored.

For the issue one must take into account in outlining the possible passage toward decolonization is how to invoke the courage with which to expose oneself to the gaze of foreigners (nonnational), of those who do not belong to the interior of the nation. This would be the first step toward the outside of the society of sympathy, of a community of those gathered together by sharing the sense of collective self-pity, a move away from the nationalism of hikikomori. Yet let me emphasize, once again, that the very image of a national community as an enclosure, a space marked by a definite border line, is viable only in the dimension of collective fantasy. There is no such organic entity as the Japanese nation; there is no outside of the Japanese national community, unless it is deciphered in terms of a fantastic geo-body that the trope of the nation evokes. The exterior of the nation is rendered tangible only when one encounters the otherness of others through the experience of shame; the exteriority that one thus faces is fundamentally different from the outside that is spatially representable. In other words, even among compatriots, you can come across a foreigner, a non-Japanese, who might well guide you to the outside of the nation.

Shame and Equality beyond Nationality

In the context of postcolonial subjective technology, therefore, the significance of shame cannot be overstated; shame is the first step toward an encounter with a foreigner, toward the experience of exposing oneself to the gaze of foreigners, those who do not immediately reside in the interior of the national community. Apparently shame signifies a modality of encounter with others, a modality of social action in which you are liberated from the confinement of hikikomori. And conversely, this is why hikikomori is, above all else, a defense against the feeling of shame; it always gives rise to actions intended to dodge a possibly shameful encounter. Through the humiliation and embarrassment of shame, you connect with another person, a foreigner, and the very otherness of the other; in the feeling of shame, you are destabilized and deterritorialized, opened up, and led out of the incarceration of hikikomori. Through the feeling of shame, you can realize that you can be a non-Japanese or an individual not completely determined by nationality. Thus shame is a concept that illustrates the fundamental sociality of our existence; shame is a modality of being exposed to others in the being-in-common. Being in touch with exteriority, you are helped by others, but you are simultaneously helping others and changing them. For shame is in neither the active nor the passive voice. To become able to be helped by others is to become able to help them; it is to enter a different dimension of communality in which the type of communality called "nationality" no longer matters.

What I want to undertake in this conclusion is to disengage the idea of equality from the feeling of nationality and to rearticulate it to the feeling of shame.

Decolonization and the End of Pax Americana

By now it is obvious that what is at stake in this volume is not a transition from Pax Americana to some other structure of global hegemony such as Pax Sinica. By the end of Pax Americana I do not anticipate a global transformation of the international world somewhat comparable to the one from Pax Britannica to Pax Americana.

A set of questions that have led me to an inquiry into the end of Pax Americana come from my concern with decolonization, the survival of the imperial-colonial order, the radical transformation of the international world, the resurgence of white supremacy, and, of course, the loss of empire. I understand that Pax Americana was a name given to the global order established after the Second World War in an attempt initiated by the United States and the United Kingdom to resurrect the system of international law. It was an attempt to preserve the basic structure of the modern world that was gradually established by introducing the system of international law starting in the seventeenth century.

It is in this historical context that the topic of decolonization gains prominence. What is at issue is not limited to the decolonization of a people who have been subjugated to colonial rule. Decolonization is not only a process in which the legacies of colonial governmentality are invoked, analyzed, and denounced; it is also a project to dismantle the very structure of the classical international world by which the distinction of Europe (more recently, the West) from the rest of the world was legitimated by international law until the outbreak of World War I. Even since then, the discourse of the West-and-the-Rest has continued to differentiate the world into the colonizers and the colonized. Even after the independence of colonized people under Pax Americana, the bipolarity of the world did not dissipate. This is why the topic of decolonization cannot evade the issues about the loss of empire. In discussing decolonization, we must address the postcoloniality of the colonizers, those who had regarded themselves as imperial subjects in the colonial relationship.

The loss of empire is not a problem only for the British. As I tried to illustrate, it is a problem from which the Japanese have suffered even though, unlike Britain or the United States, Japan was defeated in World War II and lost its colonizer status immediately. Under the subjugation to the global hegemony of the United States, however, the Japanese people could not discard their colonizer mindset. As I outlined in chapter 6, the loss of empire is closely connected to two problems we face today: anti-immigrant racism on the one hand and the inward-looking society on the other.

Thus, I hope, the idiom "loss of empire" captures the general tendencies observable in societies that used to be seen as advanced and developed. Today some portions of their populations suffer from a tremendous sense of loss, are overwhelmed by a collective anxiety. There is no doubt that the resurgence of white supremacy is a typical response to the loss of empire. It is true that the United States of America has remained imperial and is the only nation-state in the world to still enjoy the status of empire. Yet, the loss of empire can apply to, if not the whole of American society, to some portions of it. By the end of Pax Americana, I would like to intimate the coming of an age when decolonization is an urgent matter, not only for those who have been colonized but also for those who fashioned themselves as colonial masters.

Edwin O. Reischauer, "Memorandum on Policy towards Japan," September 14, 1942; with materials collected by War Department General Staff, Organization and Training Division, G-3. Concerning "Enlistment of loyal American citizens of Japanese descent into the Army and Navy," December 17, 1942; 291.2, Army-AG Classified Decimal File 1940–42; Records of the Adjunct General's Office, 1917–, record group 407, entry 360, box 147, National Archives, College Park, MD.

Memorandum on Policy towards Japan
I should like to present for consideration two small but extremely important points which are closely connected with our war effort in Asia and particularly with our post-war objectives in that area. Military victory is, of course, the essential prerequisite for any war objective, but certain of the more fundamental problems of winning the peace cannot be overlooked in the meantime.

The Japanese are an extremely self-conscious and intensely nationalistic people. Military defeat will unquestionably embitter even the few remaining liberals among them. It will be an extremely difficult task after the war to win over to a policy of sincere cooperation with us sufficient numbers of Japanese to bring Japan back into the family of friendly and cooperating nations. Many Americans believe that Japanese good-will and cooperation will be of little significance after this war, but it is all too clear to serious students of the Far East that a healthy political and economic situation can not be created in that area without the participation of the people of Japan.

One of the major difficulties in attempting to win the Japanese over to our system after this war will be the absence of suitable scapegoats to bear the onus of defeat. In Germany and Italy the Nazi and Fascist parties, and still more Hitler and Mussolini, the personifications of the whole totalitarian system, make most convenient scapegoats. The defeated Germans and Italians can destroy their dictatorial party government and discard their present leadership and by these very acts convince themselves that not they, the people, but their evil leaders were at fault and were defeated.

In Japan no such face-saving repudiation of leadership is possible. That the Emperor is not responsible, all the people know full well, and to repudiate him would be no more satisfactory than to blame the flag. Actual leadership in Japan tends to remain anonymous, there is no party to be blamed, and there are few, if any, prominent individuals who could serve as scapegoats. The army would be the only institution which could be singled out as the false leader and evil genius, but almost the whole nation now is identified with the army in one way or another, and with their long tradition of respect for the military man, the Japanese would derive no satisfaction from attacking their army. In fact, military defeat might well serve to strengthen rather than to overthrow military dictatorship in Japan.

In Germany and Italy we can expect to see a natural revulsion against Nazi and Fascist rule, a revulsion so strong that it will carry a large percentage of the population over to a policy of cooperation with the United Nations. In Japan, on the contrary, no such easy road to post-war victory is possible. There we shall have to win our ideological battles by carefully planned strategy. A first step would naturally be to win over to our side a group willing to cooperate. Such a group, if it represented the minority of the Japanese people, would be in a sense a puppet regime. Japan has used the strategem of puppet governments extensively but with no great success because of the inadequacy of the puppets. But Japan itself has created the best possible puppet for our purposes, a puppet who not only could be won over to our side but who would carry with him a tremendous weight of authority, which Japan's puppets in China have always lacked. I mean, of course, the Japanese Emperor.

No one in this country is in a position to know what the Japanese Emperor personally believes, but there is good reason to judge from his education and from the associates he has had for the greater part of his life that, as things are measured in Japan, he is a liberal and a man of peace at heart. It is not improbable that he could be won over to a policy of cooperation with the United Nations far more easily than the vast majority of his subjects. He, and possibly, he alone, could influence his people to repudiate their present military leadership. If he proves to have the potentialities of a real leader like his grandfather, so much the better. If he proves to be no more able than his half-demented father, his value as a symbol of cooperation and good will can still be extremely valuable.

The possible role of the Japanese Emperor in the post-war rehabilitation of the Japanese mentality has definite bearing upon the present situation. To keep the Emperor available as a valuable ally or puppet in the post-war ideological battle we must keep him unsullied by the present war. In other words, we cannot allow him to be portrayed to the American people as the counterpart of Hitler and Mussolini in Asia or as the personification of the Japanese brand of totalitarianism. General reviling of the Emperor by our press or radio can easily ruin his utility to us in the post-war world. It would make the American people unprepared to cooperate with him or even to accept him as a tool. And naturally it would make the Emperor himself and the men who surround him less ready to cooperate with our government. During the past several months there has been considerable use of the name Hirohito as a symbol of the evil Japanese system. With the post-war problem in mind, it would be highly advisable for the government to induce the news-disseminating organs of this country to avoid reference to the Emperor as far as possible and to use individuals, such as Tojo or Yamamoto or even a mythical toothsome Mr. Moto (in uniform!) as personifications of the Japan we are fighting.

The second and more important point I wish to make has to do with the inter-racial aspects of the conflict in Asia. Japan is attempting to make her war against the United Nations into a holy crusade of the yellow and brown peoples for freedom from the white race. China's courageous stand has prevented Japan from exploiting this type of propaganda too much, but it has apparently met with a certain degree of success in Siam and the colonial lands of southeastern Asia and even in a few circles in China. If China were to be forced out of the war, the Japanese might be able to transform the struggle in Asia in reality into a full-scale racial war.

The best proof of the falsity of Japanese claims is America's record both in the Philippines and in China. However, on the other side, we have also unwittingly contributed to Japan's dangerous propaganda campaign. The removal from the West Coast of the American citizen of Japanese ancestry along with the Japanese aliens was no doubt a move made necessary by immediate military considerations, but it provided the Japanese with a powerful argument in their attempt to win the Asiatic peoples to the view that the white race is not prepared to recognize them as equals and even now continues to discriminate against them.

Up to the present the Americans of Japanese ancestry have been a sheer liability to our cause, on the one hand presenting a major problem of population relocation and military surveillance in this country and on the other hand affording the Japanese in Asia with a trump propaganda card. We should reverse this situation and make of these American citizens a major asset in our ideological war in Asia. Their sincere and enthusiastic support of the United States at this time would be the best possible proof that this is not a racial war to preserve white supremacy in Asia, but a war to establish a better world order for all, regardless of race, and, when the military victory is achieved, these American citizens of Japanese ancestry could serve as an opening wedge into the minds and hearts of the Japanese people. That they had fought willingly and gladly for our side would prove to the Japanese people that this was not simply a war to defeat them as a people, but was a war to crush the wild schemes of their military clique and to win Japan back to a system of international cooperation.

There are probably many methods by which the Japanese Americans can be made an asset rather than a liability, but among the most effective methods would be to encourage them to join the armed forces, and to give them training in political thinking and for specialized services, military or civilian, they can render during and after the war. If they knew they were wanted and that opportunities for advancement were open to them, large numbers of young Japanese would certainly be glad to volunteer. A special volunteer unit of Japanese Americans and other Americans who desired to serve with them could easily be formed for combat service in the European or African zones, where it would probably be as effective as any other unit and where it would cause no special disciplinary or organizational difficulties.

The inclusion of large numbers of Japanese Americans in combat units would strengthen the morale of the whole Japanese American group and would help to keep it loyal to the United States. More important, when the war in the Pacific is ended, such a unit might prove an invaluable asset in lessening the inevitable animosity of the Japanese populace for us and our troops. If liberal numbers of Japanese Americans were to be among the troops of occupation we may station in Japan or were to be among the units which receive the surrender of the Japanese armies, the bitterness of the defeat would be alleviated slightly and cooperation with the victor nations would seem more possible to the Japanese. The enthusiastic and active participation of 100,000 Japanese Americans and of these Japanese American troops in the cause of the United Nations could be made into a tremendous strategical advantage in the great struggle to win the peace in Asia.

Edwin O. Reischauer
Faculty Instructor in Far Eastern Languages
September 14, 1942, @Harvard University

Appendix 2

Statement on Racism
Prepared by William Haver and Naoki Sakai,

March 20, 1987, in Chicago
We must acknowledge at the outset that a certain difficulty will undoubtedly continue to haunt any project which undertakes both to investigate that phenomenon or those phenomena which we designate as racism and to accomplish an investigation into the politics of racism. This certain difficulty concerns the status of "racism" as the object of our discourse and practice, that which we investigate, that of which we would speak, that which we would denounce. It will suffice neither merely to assume that we know with any surety or clarity what racism is, although we are continually witnesses to a wide range of racism's entirely unambiguous effects: nor can we merely propose a perhaps more self-conscious but finally no less ambiguous definition which would finally establish "racism" as an isolated conceptual object: nor yet again, however, will we be able to rest content with merely having established the fact of the unavoidable ambiguity of "racism," salutary propaedeutic gesture though it undoubtedly is. We must recognize that our entire project is bound to the equivocal status of racism as object, and in that sense bound to a certain impossibility; but it is only in acknowledging this certain impossibility that we might hope to contest rather than merely reproduce discourses which seem all too often to authorize racist oppressions.

On the one hand, if we confidently undertake to establish racism in an unambiguous objectivity; that is to say, if we define or determine the limits of an object denominated as "racism," and if, therefore, we distinguish that which is racist from that which is not racist, we have at least implicitly posited that we ourselves occupy a perspective which is necessarily distanced from its object, a perspective which, because it is one from which the difference between racism and its "outside" is clearly identifiable, is a perspective which, wittingly or not, is held to be exempt from "racism." Here the question is not, in the first instance, one of soul-searching, self-criticism or confession. It is perhaps more important to point out that to adopt a perspective taken to be preternaturally distanced from its object would make it impossible even to conceive the possibility that the presuppositions according to which such a perspective is constituted might in fact be entirely consonant with the presuppositions of explicitly racist discourse. Embedded in the claim to speak from a perspective "outside" of "racism" there is a claim that, at least in the matter of "racism," our discourse both says nothing other than what it intends to say and that it knows what it says, a claim to a secure purchase upon the truth about racism, a claim that there is a perspective from which a discourse might be enunciated which would presumptively guarantee a prophylaxis against racism. We cannot afford to lose sight of the possibility that it is by virtue of its very elusiveness as object that "racism" might saturate entire discursive fields and in fact constitute the conditions of possibility for more than one discursive practice.

On the other hand, we cannot thereby naively refuse to objectify racism altogether. Such a refusal would suggest not only that "racism" does not exist as object, but that racism "itself" does not exist. Worse, it would suggest (a "suggestion" with which we are all too familiar) that "racism," because it would be devoid of any exteriority, is thereby essential, inherent in being, natural. Thus it would be impossible to specify racism in its discrete articulations, obliging us to a political cynicism within which no practice of critique would be possible. Any serious and rigorous critique of racism must at least posit the hope that there is an "outside" of racism, that to retain a hope in the existence of an "outside" of racism, that hope cannot be essentially a matter of faith, that outside of racism cannot be merely a fiction or "speculative" Utopia.

If we are to undertake, then, to contest racisms both hidden and disclosed, we can neither merely refuse its status as object, resigning ourselves to its elusive ubiquity, nor merely have faith in its objectivity in its determined limits. No investigation can afford to find itself always already resigned to either cynicism or stoicism.

Thus, we cannot attempt to produce an "outside" of racism according to the various protocols which produce both racism as object and racism as impossible object, protocols which would thereby produce and enfranchise a discourse about racism as a knowledge, a knowledge which in turn would ratify those very protocols. Rather, it will be necessary to call into question the terms according to which objectivity is constituted, terms which enable all objectification and specifically the objectification of "racism." It may be necessary to challenge the oppositions of "inside" and "outside," "subject" to "object," and to ask whether these terms are indeed mutually exclusive. Concomitantly, such a reconsideration might require us to think the exteriority of the other otherwise than as the exteriority of an interiority. Such concerns have of course long been concerns of certain philosophical practices: we would seek in this rethinking not a resolution to such problems but their pertinence.

It is in this sense that the project finds itself as project (that is, as the search for the possibility of a hope, a future) bound to a certain theoretical obligation. Clearly, this theoretical obligation must not be construed to obligate us to detailing the scene of an agreement, or to the production of "a theory of racism" adequate to its object. Neither does this theoretical obligation demand a refusal of specificity, of specific discussions of particular instances of racist oppression. But it must, if as a theoretical intervention it is to be a political intervention, call into question the terms according to which specificity is constituted— both in its specificity and as specificity. That is, both with attention to the particular situation or circumstances of any particular instance of racism, and with attention to the constitution of such an instance as an "instance of racism."

We have stressed the invasive but elusive ubiquity of racism, the fact that racism is not only capable of saturating entire discursive fields, but possibly might also constitute the necessary conditions of possibility for certain discursive practices. This implies that racism is not merely a certain psychological attitude or prejudice which appropriates knowledge for its own untoward usages. (This is not to deny that it does so. What such a formulation cannot articulate, however, is why and how such a relation between racism and knowledge can be so evidently persuasive.) In other words, we cannot assume that racism is no more than a perversion forced upon a knowledge or discursive practice which, presumptively, had once been innocent. It may well be, for example, that certain specific conceptualizations of the constitution and practice of certain practices—for example, "anthropology," what in the United States is called "area studies," "Japanology"—are all finally implicated in and serve to perpetuate racism by virtue of their inaugural epistemological gestures, and that these gestures are repeated not merely in the positivities or "facts" which they represented. The issue is complicated, however, by the possibility (probably demonstrable) that a critique of such inaugural epistemological gestures, results and forms of representation is not itself necessarily free of racist possibilities.

This contradiction wherein critique too frequently betrays its own impulse is especially evident in instances where an insistence upon particularity is counterposed to the hegemonic domination exercised by discursive practices which take the conditions of possibility of their own practices to be universal. While a rigorous critique of the claim to universality is undoubtedly not only justified but urgently necessary, critiques based upon the primordial validity of the particular too often take the terms which constitute that particularity "in itself" to justify the suppression of differences within that particularity itself. Furthermore, such critiques too often forget that the very terms which enable the articulation of that particularity are assumed themselves to be universal. An insistence upon the particular or upon relativism does not of itself preclude racism.

Clearly, our concern here (to begin to speak in historically specific terms) is with humanism and its critique. Anthropocentric humanism assumes—or, in its interrogative form as "philosophical anthropology," has sought to identify—a specifically human essence, an essence which would in its recognition not only differentiate the human species from the nonhuman, but which would also designate a universal commonality transcending differences of time and place and uniting the "human race" in community. The consequence of such a view, such an aspiration, as many critiques of anthropocentric humanism have argued, is that humanism thereby renders itself incapable of recognizing the otherness of human beings, the exteriority of other human beings to the universal essentiality of "man." In short, anthropocentric humanism as universalist pretention annihilates the very possibility of encountering the other. Conversely, however, critiques which would reject the universalist aspirations of anthropocentric humanism have not infrequently insisted upon the particularity and ultimate validity of "cultural," "national" or "racial" experience. Such critiques, however, have perhaps too often forgotten that notions of culture, nation, nation-state and race (in some cases, terms which are thought to be identical) are entirely commensurate with the nomenclature of anthropocentrism, terms which are often said to articulate universal values. As such, they occlude differences, alterities and exteriorities within any particular "culture," "nation," "nation-state" or "race."

Once again, it is a question of exteriority. We cannot, it seems, merely assume ourselves to be "outside" or "beyond" either humanism, particularism or the aporia of their apparent opposition. But if these terms within which we have attempted, however clumsily, to broach the question of racism are in any sense valid, we might be able to see our question as one put to a history (or histories). Which is to say, among much else, that just as the "man" of anthropocentric humanism is a historical phenomenon—one which, whether it be admitted or not, has appeared within and as an effect of history—and therefore possessed of exteriority (therefore possessed of that which can never be "possessed"), possessed by the exteriority of history, so too is "race" and "racism." Which suggests that there is a historically articulated relation between humanism, its critique and racism. Which is not to say that we assume a causal relation among these terms, but that we provisionally admit at least the possibility of a certain complicity among them. We admit the possibility that different constructions of identity and community, as "man," "nation," "nation-state," "race," are inextricably historical, subject to a certain historicity and to the certainty of historicity, a historicity which as the necessary condition for critique is the necessary condition of possibility for the political practice of a critique of racism. For we would attempt to think beyond the platitudes of denunciation—which is not to say that denunciation is not, in fact, in order.

William Haver
The State University of New York–Binghamton
Department of History
Binghamton, New York 13901

or

Naoki Sakai
Cornell University
Department of Asian Studies
370 Rockefeller Hall
Ithaca, New York 14853

Notes

INTRODUCTION

1 For instance, Truman's inaugural address of January 20, 1949, stated some of the objectives of his foreign policies.

2 What is usually referred to as "modernization theory" in area studies was produced during the 1950s and 1960s and applied to a number of areas in East Asia. Among the well-known projects of modernization is Walter W. Rostow's *The Stages of Economic Growth: A Non-Communist Manifesto.*

3 *Traces: A Multilingual Series of Cultural Theory and Translation* was published in English, Korean, Chinese, and Japanese for the first, second, and third issues; in English, Korean, and Chinese for the fourth; and English, Chinese, Korean, and Spanish for the fifth issue.

4 In contrast to the delimitation of the state's objectives by raison d'état, a new form of government, the police or police state, with unlimited objectives, was introduced. "When it is a question of an independent power facing other powers, the government according to raison d'état has limited objectives. But there is no limit to the objectives of government when it is a question of managing a public power that has to regulate the behavior of subjects. Competition between states is precisely the hinge connecting these limited and unlimited objectives, because it is precisely so as to be able to enter into competition with other states, that is to say, maintain an always uneven, competitive equilibrium with other states, that government [has to regulate the life of] its subjects, to regulate their economic activity, their production, the price [at which] they sell goods and the price at which they buy them, and so on" (Foucault, 2004a; 2008, 7).

5 Of course, this observation was related to the analysis of subject in the sense of grammatical subject, or *shugo* (主語). The idea of the grammatical subject, which was discovered in the process of translation between modern European and Northeast Asian languages, was a modern invention. For more details, see Sakai (1991).

6 I can make this generalized statement only on the condition that Confucian discourses can be conflated with other kinds of discourses on ethical conduct.

I relied upon Yasumaru Yasuo's (安丸 良夫) historical study of subjectivation in the peasant rebellions during the Tokugawa period. He argued that, toward the end of the Tokugawa period, rich peasantry had appropriated Confucian ethics into the contexts of their everyday life to invent what Yasumaru called 通俗道徳 (popular ethics), in which he identified the preliminary form of modern subjectivity (Yasumaru 1974).

7 There are many different modes by which an individual human can identify a collectivity. An interpersonal dynamics is one mode. In relation to my son, I can be identified as a mother. Or in contrast to a buyer, I can be a seller. But, convinced that I belong to the totality of a nation such as Britain or Vietnam, I can be identified as British or Vietnamese. I can identify myself with the nation. The question of identification is open to the vast field of inquiry concerning collectivity and the speciation of humanity (the classification of humanity into species). Chapter 2 of this volume explores historical transformations in the mode of identification.

8 Of course, it is absolutely necessary to discuss anthropological difference in order to comprehend the structure of the modern international world. It is also important to note that both the West and the Rest must be capitalized since, as a directional adverb, "west" cannot have a fixed referent. Only when a west is delimited by the rest can it be "the West" that can be located. Only when it is accompanied by the Rest can the West claim itself to be unique and fixated. When not capitalized, a west is dislocated; it cannot have a fixed location; neither can the rest be postulated as the Rest. This is why Stuart Hall (1996) hyphenated the West-and-the-Rest in his discussion of the discourse of the West and the Rest.

9 Martin Heidegger analyzed the mode of projecting ourselves into the world in terms of "Dasein's being-in-the-world" in chapters 1–3 of "Division One: The Preparatory Fundamental Analysis of Dasein" in *Being and Time* (Heidegger 1996, 39–106). In the early 1930s, Tanabe Hajime critically appropriated the problems of schema from Heidegger and published a series of articles on the topic of the world as a schema (cf. Tanabe 1963a, 1963b). I learned much from Tanabe's reading of Kant and Heidegger.

With regard to the topic of lifeworld, Edmund Husserl introduced the concept of passive doxa in his posthumous work *Experience and Judgment*, arguing, "before every movement of cognition the object of cognition is already present as a dynamis which is to turn into an entelecheia. . . . an actual world always precedes cognitive activity as its universal ground, and this means first of all a ground of universal passive belief in being which is presupposed by every particular cognitive operation." A passive doxa is "this universal ground of belief in a world which all praxis presupposes, not only the praxis of life but also theoretical praxis of cognition" (1973, 30).

10 Historically, two geopolitical or civilizational indexes, the West and Europe, must be differentiated, even though the terms are used almost interchangeably in some contexts. An extensive inquiry is necessary, so in the future I will thematically discuss the overdetermined nature of the West and Europe. In the meantime, I refer to "the West" as if it were almost synonymous with "Europe."

11 For a more detailed discussion of the modern regime of translation, see Sakai (1997b; 2013b, 15–31).

12 I used to use a variety of expressions, "colonial difference," "civilizational differ- ence," and so on, in addition to "anthropological difference." It is mainly thanks to Jon Solomon's intervention that I decided to unify the terminology (cf. Solo- mon 2014).

13 Husserl argued that theory is exclusively European. See, for instance, "The Vienna Lecture" (Husserl 1970c, 269–299).

14 I follow the economy of genus and species in classical logic and rely upon the defi- nition of species difference (diaphora) given by Aristotle in book 10 of *Metaphysics* (1054–1058).

15 The exceptions are Malaysia, Hong Kong, and a few other colonies. Malaysia became independent twelve years after Japan's unconditional surrender to the Allied Powers. The United Kingdom did not return Hong Kong to the People's Republic of China until 1997, fifty-two years after the evacuation of Japanese troops.

16 The representative work on the loss of British empire is Gilroy (1991).

17 Per capita G D P purchasing power parity value is G D P converted to international dollars using purchasing power parity rates and divided by total population.

18 *Statista Infographic Bulletin*, July 3, 2020, "Number of International Students Study- ing in the United States in 2019/2020, by Country of Origin."

19 This figure may appear extraordinarily low, but it used to be within the range of 8–9 percent in the 1990s. I relied on information provided by the Tourism Strategy Division (2017).

20 An article based upon the 2015 survey conducted by Sangyô Nôritsu University in Tokyo, reported by *Nihon Keizai Shinbun* on October 25, 2015.

21 Japan is an archipelago, so there is no social movement for the building of a wall at the national border. Due to immigration policies adopted since the collapse of the Japanese Empire in 1945, the officially registered number of immigrants to Japan has been very small. Yet the last few decades have seen the rise of an anti-immigrant racist movement called Association of Citizens against the Special Privileges of the Zainichi (在日特権を許さない市民の会), which openly targets resident Koreans and Chinese.

CHAPTER 1. HISTORY AND RESPONSIBILITY

This chapter was originally prepared for a public lecture at Hanyang University in Seoul and included as "History and Responsibility: On the Debates on the *Shōwa History*" in *Mass Dictatorship and Memory as Ever Present Past*, edited by Lim Jie- Hyun, Barbara Walker, and Peter Lambert (Basingstoke, UK: Palgrave Macmillan, 2014), 120–138.

1 This is exactly what Takata Yasuma (高田 保馬), perhaps the most important sociol- ogist of modern Japan, advocated in his publications in the 1930s and early 1940s. He talked about "the integration in the future" (将来における統合) and an "integral nation" (広民族) and sought to find social scientific knowledge to design a multi- ethnic nationality and construct the ideological justification for the oppression of anticolonial ethnic nationalisms. Precisely because his sociology harbored antiracist

rhetoric and anticipated the agenda of postwar American social sciences, he was purged as a collaborator in the wartime regime of Japan (see Takata 1939, 1942).

2 A small number of intellectuals, including Watsuji Tetsurô (和辻 哲郎), who was very much inspired by German National Socialism, advocated for the purity of Japanese blood and objected to the political formation in which different bloods were mixed. Accordingly, Watsuji denounced Japanese integrationist propaganda in Korea, where Japanese and Korean ethnicities were to be synthesized by the Japanese state policy of "Japan and Korea as one" (内鮮一体; see Sakai, 1997b, 72–116).

3 Let me acknowledge the problematic nature of the concept of culture here. I am not sure what is meant by "being culturally homogeneous" since what is signified by the word "culture" is not clear.

4 At the Tokyo War Crimes Tribunal, the category "crimes against humanity" was not applied. This does not mean that no war criminal was prosecuted under this category in war criminal courts held in Asia. One must not overlook that a number of war crime courts were held outside Japan. There are a great number of publications on the Tokyo War Crimes Tribunal. One of the most reliable and concise books on this topic is Hayashi (2005).

5 It is in this context that the verdict reached at the Women's International War Crimes Tribunal on Japan's Military Sexual Slavery (December 8–12, 2000) is particularly significant. Emperor Hirohito was found guilty of the Japanese government's crimes against humanity. It was an absolutely necessary correction to the Tokyo War Crimes Tribunal.

6 Such an attempt can be found in *Total War and "Modernization"* (Yamanouchi, Koschmann, and Narita 1998).

7 A notable exception that discusses the grassroots of Japanese ultranationalism is Nakano (2012).

8 The representative figure of this anti-Marxist group was Kamei Katsuichirô (亀井 勝一郎). He was once involved in Marxist literary movements before his conversion in the 1930s (Kamei 1956).

9 More detailed discussion of the modality of belonging in the nation is included in chapter 2.

10 I would like to thank Katsumata Mitsumasa (勝股 光政), CEO of Ibunsha publishers, for his generosity in letting me read secondary literature in his personal collection about *The Showa History* during the 1950s and 1960s.

CHAPTER 2. FROM RELATIONAL IDENTITY TO SPECIFIC IDENTITY
This chapter was presented at the University of British Columbia in August 2013 and published as "From Relational Identity to Specific Identity: On Equality and Nationality" in *Values, Identity and Equality in 18th and 19th-Century Japan*, edited by Peter Nosco et al. (Boston: Brill, 2015), 290–320. It was translated into Japanese and published as「関係的同一性から種的同一性へ ― 平等と国体(ナショナリティ) について」(From relational identity to specific identity: On equality and nationality, translated by Noberto Ono, in『江戸の中の日本、日本の中の江戸』, edited by Peter Nosco et al. (Tokyo: Kashiwa-shobo, 2016), 246–291.

1 This chapter developed from a manuscript prepared for a public debate with Paul Standish on the topic of social justice at Kyoto University in December 2011. A modified manuscript was also presented at the international symposium on early modern Japanese values and individuality at the University of British Columbia in August 2013.

2 The etymology of the word "legitimacy" is important. Legitimacy is the social acceptance of an authority or an institution. In moral spheres, the term "legitimacy" often is positively interpreted as the normative status conferred by subordinate people upon their family lineage, inheritance, and decisions based upon the belief that the family head's actions are appropriate uses of authority by the rules of kinship tradition. Hence, the terms "legitimate" and "illegitimate" refer to the proper or improper handlings of the matters of lineage and inheritance. In the sphere of politics, legitimacy is the popular acceptance of an authority or government. Whereas "authority" denotes a specific position in an established government, the term "legitimacy" denotes a system of government—wherein "government" denotes "sphere of influence." Political legitimacy is considered a basic condition for governing, without which a government will suffer legislative stalemate and collapse. As a matter of fact, the etymological transition of "legitimacy" outlines a historical transformation of ethical legitimacy from the regime of relational identification to that of specific identification.

3 For instance, Yasumaru Yoshio (安丸 良夫) conducted an impressive analysis of revolutionary subjectivity by studying peasant ideology and peasant rebellions during the Tokugawa period (Yasumaru 1974).

4 In the nineteenth century, the English word "nation" was translated into several combinations of Chinese characters and began to be widely used in Japan, Korea, China, and so on in regions in Northeast Asia where the notational systems of Chinese ideography were widely used. Two points must be underlined: the first is that this translation took place largely before the formation of national languages in Northeast Asia. The second is that, as the institutions of national languages were established, the same combinations began to be used in different national contexts. Consequently a complex system of polysemy exists among words or combinations connoting "nation." The most important combinations are 「国民」, 「民族」, 「種族」, and 「人種」.

5 It is well known by now that the concept of religion was newly introduced into Japan during the Meiji period. On the historicity of the concept of religion and its association with colonialism, see Asad (1993). On the critique of religion and religion studies, see Isomae (2003, 2012).

6 In his study of pronouns in Indo-European languages, Émile Benveniste introduced an important distinction between the shifters of "I" and "you" and those of the so-called third-person pronouns. He observed that every utterance of the third person assumes the conditions of a possible polarity between I and you. From this Benveniste concluded that the third-person pronoun should not be regarded as *personal*. The so-called third-person pronoun is not a *personal* pronoun. Confucian ethics relies upon the instance of discourse in which the I and you polarity is virtual, even though, in the Confucian classics, the first- and second-person pronouns are not very often explicitly referred to because the shifter function was carried out in terms of various

linguistic measures, including the honorific in Classical Chinese. See Benveniste (1971, 195–204).

7 The third person acts under the conditions of the possibility of this polarity between the first and second persons. "The first-person singular 'I' signifies 'the person who is uttering the present instance of the discourse containing *I*.' This instance is unique by definition and has validity only in its uniqueness. . . . *I* can only be identified by the instance of discourse that contains it and by that alone." *You*, on the other hand, is defined in this way: "by introducing the situation of 'address,' we obtain a symmetrical definition for *you* as the individual spoken to in the present instance of discourse containing the linguistic instance of *you*." These definitions refer to *I* and *you* as a category of language and are related to their position in language (Benveniste 1971, 223–230). The third person pronoun does not participate in this polarity.

8 By the ie family, Nishikawa means the unity of the social network that was regarded as the authentic form of a family by the feudal authority. For her "ie" means an extended family, which could include many nuclear families and servants, and its legitimacy is sustained by ancestral genealogy. The Meiji states adopted this notion of ie and established the system of the family registry (戸籍) following the ie model. However, it also adapted the modern institutions of the bourgeois family and tried to create something like "home" ("katei" [家庭] is a neologism for the English word "home"), as a result of which the family instituted by the Meiji state manifested itself as a hybrid between the worlds of relational and specific identities until the 1970s, when the modern family based upon the ideals of the nuclear family and romantic love between a husband and a wife began to decline (see Nishikawa 1998; 2000, 7–93).

9 The triad individual–species–genus was known to be originally conceptualized by Aristotle. This logical format was applied in the modern taxonomy of creatures in *Systema Naturae* (1735) by Carl Linnaeus. All creatures were divided into three kingdoms—mineral, vegetable, and animal—and each kingdom was further classified through the repetitive use of the classical formula of genus and species. Linnaean taxonomy still remains popular, but scientists no longer take this taxonomy as universally valid, but scientific racism, for instance, still believes that humanity can be classified according to this logical formula.

10 See, for instance, the preface to『学問のすゝめ』(*An Encouragement of Learning*) (Fukuzawa [1880] 1969) and chapter 6 of『文明論の概略』(*An Outline of a Theory of Civilization*) (Fukuzawa [1875] 1973, 183–212).

11 For an excellent historical analysis of the similar point, see Calhoun (1993, 229).

12 Elsewhere I have written about relational identity and specific identity. For more extensive discussions of the concepts, see Sakai (1996, 166–210; 2008, 85–148; 2011, 91–110).

13 As is well known, Maruyama Masao (1952, 1974) adopted Borkenau's analysis as one of his main themes in『日本政治思想史研究』(*Intellectual History of the Tokugawa Japan*).

14 The translation has been modified in order to show the connections between Fukuzawa Yukichi's and John Stuart Mill's arguments.

15 Concerning such central notions of nineteenth-century liberal representative government as "national feeling," "national character," and "the society of sympathy," see "Considerations of Representative Government" in Mill (1972, 187–428). Compare

Fukuzawa's explanation of nationality with Mill's: "A portion of mankind may be said to constitute a Nationality if they are united among themselves by common sympathies which do not exist between them and any others—which make them co-operate with each other more willingly than with other people, desire to be under the same government, and desire that it should be government by themselves or a portion of themselves exclusively. This feeling of nationality may have been generated by various causes. Sometimes it is the effect of identity of race and descent. Community of language, and community of religion, greatly contribute to it. Geographical limits are one of its causes. But the strongest of all is identity of political antecedents; the possession of a national history, and consequent community of recollections; collective pride and humiliation, pleasure and regret, connected with the same incidents in the past" (Mill 1972, 391).

16 Oguma Eiji shows that there have been many views about the ethnic constitution of Japanese society since the Meiji period, but he fails to recognize the problematic nature of the ethnic unity itself. It is rather astonishing that no definition of ethnicity is given in his entire book. He clearly wants to criticize the myth of the single ethnos prevalent in postwar Japan. But, not being aware of the theoretical complexities in the concept of ethnicity itself, he would eventually reproduce the very myth he wants to criticize in his subsequent publications (Oguma 1995).

17 Let me note that, although Fukuzawa rejected this characterization of the emperor, the idea of isshi dôjin (literally translated, it is "one gaze, equal love" and connotes that every subject is absolutely equal before the emperor, or, that the emperor's love does not discriminate) was adopted to determine the relation of the emperor to his subjects from the outset of the modern emperor system. The expression "isshi dôjin" has appeared repeatedly in governmental ordinances and publications since the first year of Meiji. For more detailed discussion on the use of this expression and social discrimination in modern Japan, see Hirota (1990, 436–516) and Kuno and Tsurumi (1956, 126–129) in particular.

18 We must not lose sight of the duality in the sentiment of nationality. Equality among all the members of the nation is, above all else, a demand or claim that we all be equal qua members of the nation. The unity of the nation cannot be legitimated unless this demand is sincerely acknowledged. On the other hand, it is precisely because people are not equal qua members of the nation that the demand for equality is meaningful. Those who are most ardently aspiring to equality are those who are most severely discriminated against.

19 The anecdote that the emperor volunteered to sacrifice himself for the sins committed by his Japanese subjects was skillfully manipulated by General Douglas MacArthur's staff. In 1988, the time of Hirohito's death, the publicity campaign undertaken at the end of the Asia-Pacific War for the reinstallment of the emperor system under the Allied Powers occupation was played out again. Jiro Yamaguchi and I wrote a letter to the editor of the *New York Times* (October 10, 1988) to criticize an essay by Faubion Bowers (1988), who served as a translator and publicity representative for General MacArthur in 1945–1946. The Supreme Commander for the Allied Powers (SCAP) justified the emperor system on the basis of the episode of a self-sacrificial pastor; it involved the familiar fable of a shepherd and a flock of sheep.

20 Hirota Masaki, for instance, attributes the emergence of the idea of equality to the institutionalization of the emperor in what he calls the system of one emperor over myriad subjects (「一君万民制」; Hirota 1990, 456–470).

21 The term "emperor system" was introduced by Marxist historical scholarship in the 1920s but was deliberately censored by the Japanese state then. The term meant an anachronistic monarchical state power just like czarism in the Russian Empire. According to Marxist historians, the emperor system was a remnant in an industrial capitalist society of a premodern absolutist state, indicating the backwardness of Japanese capitalism. Only after Japan's defeat in 1945 was state censorship lifted and the term used widely. It continues to be used in academia as well as mass media. My use of "emperor system" unambiguously differs from that of Marxist scholarship. By this term I do not at all mean to imply that the emperor system had its origins in Japan's premodern history. It is a modern institution created in response to the need for a national community. In this respect, it is entirely cut off from the lineage of the imperial family that has supposedly existed since the sixth century C.E. It goes without saying that the emperor system created in the Meiji Restoration adopted the person of the Meiji emperor himself (who came from the imperial family) but also many rituals, institutions, and terms associated with the imperial family such as "the linear succession of emperors for ages" (「萬世一系」) and so on, and pretended to be a continuation of the traditional imperial lineage. The emperor system is an illuminating case of what Eric Hobsbawm called "the invention of tradition."

22 The public use of the photographic picture started in 1874, six years after the Meiji Restoration. In 1891, the preservation of the emperor's photograph at each school was legislated by the Japanese state. In the 1920s, the Hôanden, a small building on school campuses in which photographs of the emperor and the empress were enshrined, became universal in education in many parts of the Japanese Empire. Among many outstanding historical works on this topic, I cite several from which I learned much (Taki 1988; Fujitani 1998; Yasumaru 1992).

23 It is important to ascertain that the emperor system is essentially a modern institution and distinct from the lineage of the imperial family. The governmentality represented by the emperor system was entirely different from the previous institution of the imperial familial lineage. The emperor system was preliminarily established as the symbol of national sovereignty at the time of the Meiji Restoration when the authority of the Tokugawa Shogun was officially transferred to the new government. However, as an institution, it evolved and underwent many transformations since there was no governing legal system at the beginning of the Meiji period. Judicially, the emperor was instituted as the head of the territorial sovereign state in 1890 when the Meiji Constitution was promulgated. In 1890 the Imperial Rescript on Education was also issued, according to which the symbolic relationship of the emperor and the nation was outlined. Only after the 1910s was the idea of the school shrine, Hôanden, implemented. In the 1930s, particularly, many such shrines were built at schools nationwide in the national territories, including the annexed territories of Taiwan and Korea.

Takashi Fujitani captures this modern feature of the emperor system succinctly in his *Splendid Monarchy* (1998).

24 Once again let me note that Fukuzawa Yukichi emphasized the difference between the two types of legitimacy: 血統, legitimacy based upon kinship lineage, and 政統, legitimacy of national state sovereignty. The emperor system of the Japanese Empire was undoubtedly a modern institution, yet it was still legitimated on the basis of kinship lineage. Eventually and after World War II, all the other countries in Northeast Asia gave up the old legitimacy of familial succession and adopted the new legitimacy of popular sovereignty and constituted themselves as republican states (perhaps the only exception is the People's Democratic Republic of Korea—North Korea—which seems to follow the convention of monarchical succession). Even under the new constitution enforced during the Allied occupation (1945–1952), the Japanese emperor system continues to appeal to the familial lineage for its sole legitimacy.

25 John Stuart Mill (1972, 139–145) discusses the functions of sympathy and antipathy in the formation of the nation in chapter 4, "Representative Government."

26 The nation-state did not immediately become the predominant form of sovereignty when the Treaty of Westphalia was signed in 1648. First, the modern state emerged as territorial state sovereignty. Only after a series of events, including the independence of the United States of America and the French Revolution, was state sovereignty gradually redefined as territorial national state sovereignty. By the time Fukuzawa Yukichi began to write in the 1860s and 1870s, a shift from the old type of legitimacy (based on kinship lineage) to the new type of legitimacy (based on popular sovereignty) was occurring.

27 In Japan, the compound "Zainichi" (「在日」) generally means "resident aliens" or "alien residents." However, because of the postimperial history of Japan, it refers to the Zainichi Koreans, often known simply as Zainichi: the permanent ethnic Korean residents of Japan. The term "Zainichi Korean" refers only to long-term Korean residents of Japan who trace their roots to Korea under Japanese rule, distinguishing themselves from the later wave of Korean migrants who came mostly in the 1980s and also from premodern immigrants dating back to antiquity. Yet the term "Zainichi Korean" is extended to describe settled permanent residents of Japan—those who have retained either their North or South Korean nationalities and even, sometimes, Japanese citizens of Korean descent who acquired Japanese nationality by naturalization or by birth, from one or both parents with Japanese citizenship. "Buraku" is an abbreviation of "Burakumin" (hamlet people or village people). Traditionally, the Burakumin are an outcast group at the bottom of the Japanese social ladder that has historically been the victim of severe discrimination and ostracism. They were originally members of outcast communities in the Japanese feudal era, composed of those with occupations considered impure or tainted by death (such as executioners, undertakers, workers in slaughterhouses, butchers, or tanners), which had severe social stigmas of pollution attached to them.

28 Because of complicated histories that I cannot summarize here, these resident Koreans have been treated differently from other foreigners in Japan under a number of laws. One must take into account some conditions: the population in the Korean peninsula used to hold Japanese citizenship; in the late 1940s and early 1950s, the labor market in both North and South Korea was extremely unstable due to the Korean

War; the division of the Korean Peninsula created an extremely difficult situation for resident Koreans, whose families were often divided between the North and the South, and so on.

29 According to Yasuda Kôichi (2012), one of the functions of the Zaitokukai's street demonstrations is to create confrontations with their opponents, which are then filmed on the spot; the footage is uploaded onto YouTube, thereby securing wide dissemination of the news of the Association of Citizens Who Denounce the Privileges Accorded to Resident Koreans and Chinese well beyond the small circle of eyewitnesses to the street demonstrations.

CHAPTER 3. ASIAN THEORY AND EUROPEAN HUMANITY

This chapter was published as "Theory and Asian Humanity: On the Question of *Humanitas* and *Anthropos*" (*Postcolonial Studies* 13, no. 4 [2010]: 441–464).

1 Husserl repeatedly argued that theory is exclusively European. See, for instance, "The Vienna Lecture" (Husserl 1970c).

2 A crisis of European humanity was always of the European man, rarely of the European woman. As Edward Said (1979) illustrated this point convincingly in his *Orientalism*, the gender dimension cannot be overlooked in our assessment of anthropological difference. Also important to note is that the word "theory" is not free of gender bias.

3 Husserl (1970c) uses the phrase "the spiritual shape of Europe" in "The Vienna Lecture."

4 Husserl's denunciation of the European political and cultural climate of the late 1930s does not cohere at a number of points. We must take into account, first of all, the fact that he belonged to the minority explicitly marked by the political fiction of the German nation as well as European civilization. Above all, "Europe" is multivalent and polysemic: this means many different modes of identification are possible. Particularly important is an analysis of the fiction/myth of the political pursued by Philippe Lacoue-Labarthe and Jean-Luc Nancy (1991).

5 For the question of the victim speaking for the victimizer, see my article that explored the case of Japanese Americans who were kept in U.S. internment camps during World War II (Sakai 2004, 229–257).

6 Certainly it is beyond the scope of this chapter to explore the exceptionally ambiguous relationships among those mythemes as implicated in the anti-Semitic exclusion of Jewry. With anti-Semitism deriving from Europe's or the West's identity politics, it is absolutely imperative to comprehend how the figure of the Jew plays in the putative unity of Europe or the West. Furthermore, it is important to keep in mind that the term "Europe" was increasingly replaced by the idiom "the West" from the end of the nineteenth century to the 1930s in Western Europe. Husserl, for example, always referred to Europe, whereas his disciple Martin Heidegger frequently used "the West" in such terms as "Western metaphysics." Even today Europe is not clearly delineated from the West in so many contexts. On some other occasion I would like to undertake a more thorough and extensive analysis of the dynamics of Eurocentrism

in relation to anti-Semitic racism, but tentatively let me list those topoi/themes that must be investigated in order to apprehend Husserl's involvement, in antiminority rhetoric, for example:

On what grounds is Europe or the West said to constitute a community? What variables—language, rationality, tradition, religious heritages, race, political sovereignty, and so on—serve to produce the figure of Europe as a community?

How is Europe or the West determined as a geographic unity in contradistinction to Asia, Africa, and the Americas? How are Europeans distinguished from peoples belonging to non-European territories, particularly when Europeans were supposed to be the most mobile immigrants/conquerors who occupied and settled in so many different places all over the earth?

How are ambiguous boundaries drawn between Europe or the West and its others? Where can such boundaries be drawn, on the geographic surface, or in terms of religious affiliation, of scientific rationality, of level social capital, or of racial constitutions?

What is the relationship between a national community such as Germany and Europe as a community? Are East European nations less European than West European nations such as France? Is Turkey excluded from Europe while Ukraine is included? What kind of criteria does one utilize in order to include or exclude some individuals in or from Europe or the West?

7 In *The* Nomos *of the Earth in the International Law of the* Jus Publicum Europaeum (2003), Schmitt discussed the spatial order of the international world as the basic design of international law, thanks to which world peace had been maintained since the mid-seventeenth century, until the first collapse of the system of international law, namely, World War I in the early twentieth century. By the spatial order, Schmitt meant the division of the world into Europe and non-Europe, the structuring distinction of Europe from the rest of the world. Four decades later, Hall approached the issue of the spatial order of the modern world from the viewpoint of the discourse of the West and the Rest. Hall's diagnosis is diametrically opposed to Schmitt's; Hall denounced the colonial formation of the modern world, while Schmitt enthusiastically supported its Eurocentric structure and sought to conserve it. In many respects, however, Schmitt's analysis endorses Hall's apprehension of the modern world. Undoubtedly Schmitt was a Nazi who believed in the exceptional status of European humanity; even after the collapse of the Third Reich, he spoke as an authentic Nazi and did not hesitate to express his conviction on European exceptionalism in 1950 when the original version of *The* Nomos *of the Earth* was published in Germany (see Schmitt 2006; also see Hall 1996, 185–227).

8 Donatella Di Cesare (2018) discusses Heidegger's implication in anti-Semitism from the 1930s until the 1970s in her *Heidegger and the Jews*. Heidegger studied with Husserl and adopted the phenomenological approach in his first major work, *Being and Time*, whose first edition was devoted to Husserl. It is well known that he did not attend Husserl's funeral even though he succeeded to his position as professor of philosophy at Freiburg University. Today, after the posthumous publication of

Ponderings (II–XV), many intellectual historians claim that Heidegger never got rid of his anti-Semitic convictions. It is important to remember that, in the 1930s, Husserl had to work alongside a number of German intellectuals committed to Eurocentric visions (see Heidegger 2016–2017).

9 Toward the end of his life, Husserl (1970b) wrote "The Origin of Geometry," in which the teleology of reason he advocated in *The Crisis of European Sciences and Transcendental Phenomenology* was put into practice. Also important is Jacques Derrida's introduction to the French translation of *Husserl's Origin of Geometry* (1989).

10 In the *Crisis* book, Husserl defines the objective of his philosophical project as follows: "For the primal establishment of the new philosophy is, according to what was said earlier, the primal establishment of modern European humanity itself— humanity which seeks to renew itself radically as against the foregoing medieval and ancient ages, precisely and only through its new philosophy" (Husserl 1970a, 12).

11 What is at issue is the nature of phenomenological investigation. Phenomenological reduction invalidates the sociological particularities of the human agent who engages in the production of scientific and philosophical knowledge. It postulates some idealized subject who carries out philosophical inquiries about objects in the world. Does phenomenological reduction postulate two distinct states of the human being, an agent of thinking who does not reflect upon its own thinking, and an agent of reflective thinking who relates to itself as a sort of metalanguage? In this sense, as Husserl claimed, his phenomenology is a continuation of modernity in philosophy, a version of what Foucault called the "empirico-transcendental doublet" (see Husserl 1999; also see Foucault 1966b, 1973).

12 The spatial demarcation that gives rise to the distinction of Europe and non-Europe must be articulated to what Marx referred to in his analysis of "so-called primitive accumulation of capital." The implicit affiliation of Foucault's investigation of biopolitics with Marx's analysis of the capitalist mode of accumulation is explored extensively by Gavin Walker (2011, 2019).

13 According to Sandro Mezzadra and Brett Neilson, "The term *fabrica mundi* came to denote the 'proportion,' the 'order,' or 'texture' of the world the map is supposed to represent. . . . The use of the expression *fabrica mundi* signals, in the form of a slippage, the cartographer's awareness of the fact that representing the world on a map also means producing it." (Mezzadra and Neilson 2013, 31–32) Mezzadra and Neilson also remind us that the production of the world proposed in the modern theological notion of fabrica mundi resonates with the general problematics of modernity as addressed by Heidegger ("The Age of the World Picture" [2002, 57–85]) and Foucault (*The Order of Things* [1966b, 1973]). "While modern cartography was emerging in Europe, new lines were being traced, on both European land (in the forms of the enclosures of the commons that marked what Karl Marx called the so-called primitive accumulation of capital and the new maps of the Americas), to legally organize the colonial conquest and expansion of European power" (Mezzadra and Neilson 2013, 32).

14 Generally speaking, Husserl maintained that the theoretical attitude has been monopolized by Europeans since Greek antiquity. But this monopoly may well fall into

an uncritical use of "theory" in the technical fetishization of specialized knowledge. This is indeed one of the implications of the crisis of European sciences.

15 Obviously, the West and Europe are two clearly distinct designations, and it is important to differentiate them historically. However, I cannot take up an extensive historical analysis of Europe and the West in this chapter, mainly for lack of space, so I only offered a brief remark about the task of historically differentiating these two geopolitical, cartographic, racial, and/or civilizational terms. For both Europe and the West are overdetermined in themselves; furthermore, the combination/dichotomy of the two would give rise to even more complicated questions. As is commonly accepted in the use of Eurocentrism—one does not bother to fabricate such terms as Westocentrism or West-centeredness to differentiate the West's global domination from Europe's—I would like to allow myself to proceed provisionally in my demonstration in this chapter as if the West and Europe were interchangeable.

16 For Takeuchi's discussion of Asian modernity, see Sakai (1988) and Takeuchi ([1947] 1993, [1948] 2005).

17 Against American scholars of modernization theory, a number of Japanese social scientists and intellectual historians tried to offer a different model of modernization in the 1950s and '60s. Takeuchi (1993, 2005, 149–165) referred to Tsurumi Kazuko (鶴見 和子), who advocated for two distinct types of modernization: the *naihatsu* type, "motivated from within" or "development from within," and the *gaihatsu* type, or "imposition from outside," that imitates the outside model. As a critical endeavor against American imperialism, Tsurumi's attempt and Takeuchi's endorsement must be appreciated, but what should be called into question is the trope of the inside and the outside that underlines this typology.

18 This point is further elucidated in chapter 4, "'You Asians': On the Historical Role of the Binary of the West and Asia," in this volume.

19 Let me issue a disclaimer here. I do not believe that there is anything abnormal or exceptional in the derivative nature of the designation "Asia" in relation to Europe. Self-referentiality is impossible without the presence of alterity. Although the use of pronominals may well impose a prejudice on our analysis in this case, it is appropriate to say that "I" is a derivative of "you." Unless "you" can be postulated, "I" cannot be "here" (see Nishida 1965).

20 In the modality of spontaneity or receptivity, the relationship between subject and object is construed in terms of either activity or passivity. Therefore, the proposition "A sees B" in the active voice is rendered "B is seen by A" in the passive voice. A social relation of "you and "I" should not be construed in terms of activity and passivity. Foucault's attempt to comprehend power is important in this regard, for his notion of power is liberated from the constraints of the activity and passivity. It is an attempt to conceptualize power in the middle voice.

21 Cited in GoGwilt (1995). (GoGwilt relied on an earlier English translation of *The Decline of the West* than mine.)

22 I want to draw attention to a prevalent confusion over the terms "universality" and "generality." As in the classic logic, the definitions of generality and particularity derive from the logical economy of genus and species in which one species is

identified in terms of species difference from another species as long as both belong to the same genus. Red and blue are different from one another and identifiable as such because both are subsumed under the same genre of color. Generality (color in general) and particularity (red or blue in particular) are thus dictated by the classificatory economy of genus and species. The concept of universality is not governed by this logical rule; it is not opposed to particularity, but to singularity. However, it is also important to note that, in nonphilosophical parlance, universality and generality are hardly distinguished from one another.

23 According to Foucault (1966b, 395; 1973, 371), "man" is fundamentally historical precisely because he can never be exhaustively determined in his positivity because the limitlessness of history, inherent in the modern determination of the human being, "perpetually refers certain positivities determining man's being to the finitude that causes those same positivities to appear."

24 See Chakrabarty (1993), Nishitani (1998, 287–288), and Lacoue-Labarthe (1990). "The awakening of the power of myth—the auto-poietic act—becomes a necessity once the inconsistency of the abstract universals of reason has been revealed and the beliefs of modern humanity (Christianity and belief in humanity itself), which were at bottom only bloodless myths, have collapsed. But here again we should be careful: Nazism is a humanism in so far as it rests upon a determination of *humanitas* which is, in its view, more powerful—i.e. more effective—than any other. The subject of absolute self-creation, even if, occupying an immediately natural position (the particularity of the race), it transcends all the determinations of the modern subject, brings together and concretizes these same determinations (as also does Stalinism with the subject of absolute self-production) and constitutes itself as the subject, in absolute terms. The fact that this subject lacks the universality which apparently defines the *humanitas* of humanism in the received sense, still does not make Nazism an anti-humanism" (Lacoue-Labarthe 1990, 95).

25 Undoubtedly due to his Jewish background, Husserl was a victim of racial and anti-immigrant discrimination in Germany and later in Europe at large, and he could have spoken as one of the terrorized minorities in Europe in the 1930s before his death in 1938. His commitment to the historical mission of European humanity, which is the basis of his diagnosis of the crisis of European sciences, reminds me of a few other questions—in addition to the ones I have hinted at above—that I would like to explore in my future project. They must include the following: How can a minority intellectual evade repeating the very logic of racial and national exclusion of which he is a victim, if and when the nation presents itself as an ethnic or racial community? How can a target of racial execution manage to find a way to survive such an execution without succumbing to the majority's pronounced patriotism?

26 See Hall (1996). In this explicitly Foucauldian article, Hall indirectly showed Foucault's blindness to the problematic of Occidentalism on the one hand and illustrates how productive the archaeological approach to modernity in knowledge could be on the other. By hyphenating the West-and-the-Rest, he reminds us that the

West and the Rest are not postulated separately prior to the discursive enactment but rather in the bipolar projection in the discourse of the West and the Rest.

27 For "comparusion," see Nancy (1991). I followed Peter Connor for his translation of "comparusion" into "compearance."

28 Of course, Derrida (1991, 1992) adopted Valéry's rhetoric in his discussion of the fate of Europe.

CHAPTER 4. "YOU ASIANS"

This chapter was delivered at the Millennium Regional Conference "'WeAsians' between Past and Future" held in Singapore in February 2000 and included in the conference publication of the same title, edited by Kowk Kian-Woon, Indira Aru-mugam, Karen Chia, and Lee Chee Kenge (Singapore: Singapore Heritage Society/National Archive of Singapore, 2000), 212–247. It was reprinted as "Millennial Japan: Rethinking the Nation in the Age of Recession," edited by Harry Harootu-nian and Tomiko Yoda (*South Atlantic Quarterly* 99, no. 4 [2000]), 789–817.

1 The West is an identity that is postulated figuratively by mythical identification. For more rigorous discussions of mythical identification, see Lacoue-Labarthe and Nancy (1991).

2 In this respect, *Siam Mapped: A History of the Geo-body of a Nation*, in which Thongchai Winichakul (1994) explores the imaginary constitution of the national community in reference to modern cartography, is of a decisive importance. I learned much from this work. I also acknowledge that Sandro Mezzadra and Brett Neilson taught me much, particularly with regard to *fabrica mundi* and how modern cartography contributed to the fabrication of the modern world (cf. Mezzadra and Neilson 2013, 27–93).

3 It goes without saying that the identity of Europe cannot be discussed without reference to mythical elements of the past, including such lineages, threads, and traditions as legacies from ancient Greece, Hebrew and Christian scriptures, Indo-Aryan heritages, the clerical uses of Latin, Germanic folklore, Roman laws, and so on. These elements were assembled and reassembled to constitute the continuing image of Europe in response to historical conditions (Bernal 1987, 189–223). Particularly important is the mythical identification with the originary Greece. At any rate, the identity of Europe is essentially mythical, and the most significant factor in its identification is the work of contradistinction or bordering between Europe and that which is not European.

4 *Intellectual History of Tokugawa Japan* (『日本政治思想史研究』) consists of three essays, which were originally published in the journal 国家学会雑誌 (State Study Association journal) from 1940 to 1944. The first two were written earlier, during the Asia-Pacific War. The last essay, which differs much from the previous two in its orientation, was published in 1944 when it was almost certain that Japan was going to be defeated. Also important as a contemporary work of historiography based on the concept of negativity is by Ienaga Saburo ([1938] 1997). The concept of negativity played a central role in both Maruyama's studies of Tokugawa

intellectual history and Ienaga's studies of Japanese Buddhism. Initially the concept was elaborated on in Tanabe Hajime's social ontology in the early 1930s. However, unlike Takeuchi's, neither Maruyama's nor Ienaga's negativity implied "the defeat" or "being colonized."

5 Dipesh Chakrabarty (2000) explores such a possibility, but my attempt does not agree with his on a few points.

6 At the moment when this manuscript was prepared, before COVID-19 was detected, the most recent and infamous pandemic was the Ebola virus desease that spread in West Africa from December 2013 to January 2016.

7 An extensive analysis of the collapse of the emanation model of the modern world from the perspective of anthropology is offered by Michel-Rolph Trouillot (2003).

8 Many other instances that exemplify the internal heterogeneity of the West can easily be mentioned. Yet the identity politics of the West does not dissipate. On the contrary, insistence on the putative unity of the West would be intensified. This is why the study of National Socialism is so important, even today (cf. Lacoue-Labarthe and Nancy 1991; Lacoue-Labarthe 1990; and Nancy, "Myth Interrupted," in Nancy 1991).

9 For extensive analyses concerning "the end of area," see "Guest Editors' Introduction," and "The Regime of Separation and the Performativity of Area" in Walker and Sakai (2019, 1–31, 241–279).

10 A number of works by authors such as John Dower, Harry D. Harootunian, Rey Chow, Masao Miyoshi, Edward Said, and many others have already critically examined area studies.

11 The adjective "objectal" is distinguished from another adjective, "objective," derived from "object": Whereas "objective" connotes the impartial or unbiased validity of a judgment or statement—that is, the property of knowledge that is intersubjectively ascertainable—"objectal" emphasizes the directionality of knowing, away from the subject of knowing toward the target of knowing. Therefore, "objectal" suggests the purpose or target of knowledge at which the transitive verb "to know" aims, in contrast to its subjective register pertaining to what Kant suggested by the concept "transcendental apperception." See the introduction in Haver (2012).

12 First of all, it must be underlined that translation is not a means of communication; it is an exposure in the sense that Jean-Luc Nancy articulates to speech: an addresser is exposed to an addressee (see Nancy 1986, 9–105; 1991, 1–42).

13 Empress Masako received her postgraduate education at Harvard prior to her engagement to then-Crown Prince Naruhito. In total, the area studies program on Japan at Harvard had probably received the largest donation from Japan among all universities in the United States prior to Masako's marriage into the Japanese imperial family. Since her marriage, Harvard University has continued to receive large donations from the Japanese government and its subsidiary organizations. Such a mutually dependent relationship between the postwar Japanese emperor system and Japanese studies clearly marks those particular political and economic conditions under which the studies of Japan have been developed in both Japan and the United States. This insight should imply that a different kind of Japanese studies should

be developed in countries such as China, Australia, Malaysia, Canada, Indonesia, India, France, England, Singapore, Hong Kong, Korea, Taiwan, Germany, Russia, Poland, Turkey, New Zealand, Mexico, Italy, and so forth. In adopting the accomplishments of U.S. Japanology and Japanese Nihonshi and Nihon-bungaku, one must be acutely aware of the ideological and political limitations within which Japanese studies have been developed in the United States and Japan.

14 See the roundtable discussion "'America's Japan/America's Voice'" by Takashi Fujitani, Ryûichi Narita, and Naoki Sakai (1995). Also see my interview of Harry D. Harootunian (Harootunian and Sakai 1997/1999).

15 Reischauer's *Wanted: An Asian Policy* (1955) is an early example. You can also find a number of typically jingoistic declarations in Bellah's "Values and Social Changes in Modern Japan" (1962). Of course, the war in which they were so patriotically involved was no longer the Pacific War, but the Cold War.

16 As to Japan's ideological goal in Pacific Asia, Reischauer continued, "China's courageous stand has prevented Japan from exploiting this type of propaganda too much, but it has apparently met with a certain degree of success in Siam and the colonial lands of southeastern Asia and even in a few circles in China. If China were to be forced out of the war, the Japanese might be able to transform the struggle in Asia in reality into a full-scale racial war" (Reischauer 1942; see appendix 1).

17 Reischauer continues, "The best proof of the falsity of Japanese claims is America's record both in the Philippines and in China. However, on the other side, we have also unwittingly contributed to Japan's dangerous propaganda campaign. The removal from the West Coast of the American citizen of Japanese ancestry along with the Japanese aliens was no doubt a move made necessary by immediate military considerations, but it provided the Japanese with a powerful argument in their attempt to win the Asiatic peoples to the view that the white race is not prepared to recognize them as equals and even now continues to discriminate against them" (see appendix 1).

18 During the war, Watsuji continued to adhere to the ideal of pure blood and opposed the multiethnic principle of the Greater East Asian Co-prosperity Sphere by taking a stance similar to that of Nazism. See "Return to the West/Return to the East: Watsuji Tetsurô's Anthropology and Discussions of Authenticity," chapter 3 in *Translation and Subjectivity* (Sakai 1997b, 72–116). Also of interest is the fact that Watsuji was often celebrated as the representative thinker of Japanese thought in Japanese studies in the United States and Western Europe. It is of note that those in the missionary positionality deliberately overlooked the Japanese thinkers who were engaged in the construction of universalistic ideology during the war, such as Tanabe Hajime, Ienaga Saburo, Miki Kiyoshi, and Kôsaka Masaaki, and they celebrated particularistic thinkers like Watsuji as being typical of Japanese culture. The most emblematic argument of this kind can be found in Bellah (1965); also noteworthy is Berque (1982).

19 Starting with the Independence Movement of 1919 and the genocide of Korean residents in the Tokyo area in the aftermath of the 1923 earthquake, the Japanese leadership was preoccupied with a possible mutiny among the colonized. As indicated by

the announcement by Ishihara Shintarô (石原 慎太郎), the governor of Tokyo, on the occasion of the seventy-seventh anniversary of the 1923 earthquake, the majority of the Japanese are still anxious about a possible mutiny by foreign and former colonial residents in Japan. As war in China intensified in the late 1930s, an increasing number of policy makers and political leaders called for the recruitment of Korean youth into the Japanese military. However, there was always some opposition in the Japanese parliament to the new national service legislation designed to expand the military draft pool. Hitherto, individuals from the annexed territories had not qualified to apply for universal national service, despite an apparent shortage of soldiers in the Japanese military. It should not be forgotten that to integrate Koreans into the Japanese military meant arming them. The Japanese state could not overcome its anxiety about potential Korean mutiny until the last stage of World War II. Recall what was rumored about black soldiers in the U.S. military in Vietnam during the Vietnam War and one will understand how anxious the Japanese leadership must have been. In due course, the Japanese army had to carefully allocate soldiers from Korea at every level in such a way that they would never constitute a majority (see Higuchi 1991, 89–93).

20 In his monumental work *Race for Empire: Koreans as Japanese and Japanese as Americans during World War II*, Takashi Fujitani (2011) introduced the idioms "vulgar racism" and "polite racism" as analytical categories. The term "polite racism" captures Reischauer's stance very well. Fujitani's is a significant attempt to analyze the formation of the welfare state in both the United States and Japan, in which the system of racial discrimination was elaborated upon into the fabric of national community.

21 In contrast, integrationist rhetoric disappeared in Japan on its unconditional surrender to the Allied Powers. I offer more detailed analysis in chapter 6 on how polite racism disappeared in postwar Japan.

22 Edwin Reischauer was also involved in the postwar treatment of Korean residents in Japan. Here, too, his racist attitude not only toward Asians in general but toward Koreans in particular was manifest. See Reischauer's foreword to Edward Wagner's *The Korean Minority in Japan, 1904–1950* (1951).

23 In recent years, some attempts have been made to study how wartime human rights violations have been treated and what measures were taken in response to these incidents. Since I cannot devote much space to this topic, I will mention a work of exceptional importance: *Cold War Ruins: Transpacific Critique of American Justice and Japanese War Crime* (Yoneyama 2016).

24 For the problem of shamelessness and of guilt, see Ukai (2000, 3–36).

25 It is interesting that the Keizo Obuchi cabinet's effort from 1998 to 2000 to produce a new vision of twenty-first-century Japan is still very much based on the old premises of Watsuji-style cultural nationalism. See *The Prime Minister's Commission on Japan's Goals in the Twenty-first Century* (Kawai et al. 2000). The commission is headed by well-known Nihonjin-ron (Japanese uniqueness nationalist) author Hayao Kawai, who was also director-general of the International Research Center for Japanese Studies, a governmental research institute with strong connections with

war criminal conservatives. Also see Harry D. Harootunian's (1989) analysis of the Policy Research Bureaus of the Masayoshi Ohira cabinet.

26　See Balibar (1991).

This chapter was published as the introduction to the special issue "Translation, Biopolitics, Colonial Difference" of *Traces: A Multilingual Series of Cultural Theory and Translation* (Hong Kong: Hong Kong University Press, 2006, 1–35).

1　The Japanese translation was not available to us at the time this text was composed. Parts of this argument have been published in Chinese (Solomon 2005).

2　The monks included Omori Sôgen; significantly, the others are not named.

3　"What is equally curious is that Foucault plays to the hilt here—and indeed throughout his interview—upon the grand oppositions and the grand habitual baggage: world-thought, East-West, etc." (Jullien 2000, 18).

4　"Homosociality" here refers to the mode of communal solidarity that is obtained by the boundary of distinction. This use of homosociality should not be confused with the well-known one coined by Eve K. Sedgwick. The assumed homogeneity of the inside is no other than an effect of the erection or marking of distinction by which the outside is posited and excluded. Let us take the example of a xenophobic joke: this sort of joke isolates certain foreigners as an object of laughter, and against this object "we," who are distinguished from "them" by virtue of the fact that "we" can laugh at "them," are consolidated as a community. Laughter serves as the act of the marking of distinction, which gathers "us" together.

5　Jean-Luc Nancy writes: "The philosophical requirement of hermeneutics is, thus, one that concerns preliminary faith, that is to say, a precomprehensive anticipation of that very thing which is the question to be comprehended, or the question which comprehension must finally command" (1982, 17; 1990, 213, English translation slightly modified).

6　Address "precedes" communication only if we allow that its "coming first" (pre-) occurs only by having already given "itself" up (*cedere*). Communication is thus "exposed" by address: it is simultaneously revealed and displaced.

7　Cheng-Zhu Neo-Confucianism refers to the school of interpretation of Confucian texts initiated by the Cheng brothers (Cheng Hao 程顥, 1032–1085, and Cheng Yi 程頤, 1033–1107) and Zhu Xi 朱熹 (1130–1200).

8　See Nancy (1993, 15; 1997, 5): "Consequently, when I say that the end of the world is the end of the *mundus*, this cannot mean that we are confronted merely with the end of a certain 'conception' of the world, and that we would have to go off in search of another one or to restore another one (or the same). It means, rather, that there is no longer any assignable signification of 'world,' or that the 'world' is subtracting itself, bit by bit, from the entire regime of signification available to us."

9　Deconstruction largely set the stage for a growing body of work exploring this matrix, what we call the national institution of translation, particularly in relation to German philosophy. Compare the pivotal role—unthematized—of translation in Philippe Lacoue-Labarthe's *La fiction du politique* (1987, 1990); and the works of Antoine Berman (1984, 1992, 1999) and Sathya Rao (2003).

10 Brian Holmes's brilliant critique of the "flexible personality" behind cultural studies suggests ways in which the figure of the sociologist (previously critiqued by the Frankfurt School notion of the authoritarian personality) is undergoing historical metamorphosis (Holmes 2003, 106–137).

11 The classic example, in philosophical terms, of an "amphiboly" is, of course, found in the common theoretical premise that secretly joins materialism to idealism. Foucault recognized that this amphibological problem would find its apex in the figure of "modern man," who oscillates between transcendental and empirical positions. While deconstructive philosophy excels at demonstrating the undecidability of the terms, it still cannot explain why the typical formula "the real = x" always includes some sort of recursivity between the terms, nor, for that matter, why Science has no need for the Concept. In Laruelle's "nonphilosophy" (which holds for us the prospect of being the sort of philosophy-of-the-future for which Foucault calls), amphibological figures such as "the concept of man" or "the theory of x" are structured by an economy of decision that invariably relies upon a combination of two and a half or three terms (i.e., the terms of a dyad, such as theory and matter, plus a synthetic term, such as "man the sociologist," which is the reflection of one or both of the terms of the dyad). The problem of philosophical decision in Laruelle's account covers the entirety of the recursive relation between philosophy and the real in which either empirical forms surreptitiously become the basis for transcendental postulates or transcendental forms are installed as the basis for empirical judgments. Laruelle's nonphilosophy is not a form of deconstruction that plays upon undecidability to destabilize metaphysical presuppositions, but is rather a rigorous critique of idealist materialism from the point of view of the nonrelational identity of the real, which has the specific structure of determination in the last instance. See Laruelle (1981), part of which has been translated into English as "The Decline of Materialism in the Name of Matter" (Laruelle 2001, 33–40).

12 Edward Soja's erudite argument for a postmodern geography astutely dilates Foucault's apprehension of the amphibological nature of spatiality, yet Soja's fecund materialist understanding of spatiality still cannot avoid repeating the hermeneutic circle ("As a social product, spatiality is simultaneously the medium and outcome, presupposition and embodiment, of social action and relationship" (Soja 1989, 129). No wonder Soja characterizes Foucault's vision of spatiality as "ambivalent." Evidently, the amphibolies discovered by Foucault appear ambivalent only when seen from the indecision of philosophy, including its materialist variant. Here, we cannot elaborate an alternative concept of the region that is not based on the traditional amphibological determination, both transcendental and immanent, of "being" + "at" + "there." We are merely concerned with Foucault's inability to open up the problem of amphibological spatiality in relation to the location of the West, evinced in a 1976 interview between Foucault and specialists in the discipline of geography (Foucault 1980, 2001b). In this interview, Foucault is confronted by geographers concerned

over his general deployment of spatial tropes and metaphors along with a studious avoidance of the terms of geography per se. His interlocutors offer a challenge: "Your domains of reference are alternately Christendom, the Western world, Northern Europe and France, without these spaces of reference ever really being justified or specified" (Foucault 1980, 67; 2001b, 31). Foucault cursorily defends his approach, as Soja points out, by "reassert[ing] the spatiality of power/knowledge" (Soja 1989, 20). Here we simply want to show that Foucault's notion of power/knowledge as spatiality must be turned, not, as the geographers imply, toward a new, more precise definition of the location of the West, nor even toward the marvelous, infinite dispersion of locality championed by Soja, but by moving in the direction of a new conception of totality, such as Foucault seems to have intended for the concept of discourse. Needless to say, this totality would need to be defined in a rigorously democratic, nonhierarchical way with the sort of extreme care displayed by Laruelle's (2000) concept of determination in the last instance.

13   We would like to advance a formula that would highlight the radical transition implicitly suggested by Foucault's future philosophy: Whereas philosophy in its most general form as a pretense of knowing the real (either in terms of a materialist identification of the real with matter or a phenomenological identification of the real with the phenomenon) produces bodies of knowledge that capitalize upon the amphibological regions of the world (understood, in philosophical fashion of course, as given), a nonphilosophy of the future begins, without donation or essence, from the identity of the multitude as foreigner. According to this nonphilosophy, "Me and the Foreigner are identical," but this identity is only to be determined "in-the-last-instance"—before which point the two are radically (i.e., unilaterally) distinguished (see Laruelle 1996, 159–169).

14   The term "foreigner without the foreign" is used to designate an identity that is a donation without being given, "a radically transcendental and therefore rigorously unenvisageable form of exteriority" (Brassier 2001, 144). Naturally, it has nothing to do with the mediation of a nation-state or the fantasy of a specular unity; other alternative names might include "the stranger without estrangement," "the outsider without outside," and/or "the alien without alienation" (cf. Holmes and Solomon 2003; Solomon 2001).

15   On the non-European origins of Western modernity, see Viswanathan (1989) and Cohn (1996).

16   For an informed and critical reading of the psychoanalytic critique of Foucault's notion of normalcy, see Sakai (2001).

17   Carl Schmitt (2003) advances this argument in *The Nomos of the Earth*. See part III, "The Jus Publicum Europæum." The implications of Schmitt's argument for biopolitics have been succinctly argued by Hideaki Tazaki 田崎秀明 (2000).

18   Two related works in the Chinese language come to mind (Gang 2005; Chao 2001).

19   "The social sciences try to grasp the new situation by defining the society of control as a society of risk. A negative and ambiguous way of saying that the evental creation of the new is no longer an exception, that the power of the creation of multiplicities is the source of the constitution of the real" (Lazzarato 2004, 256).

20   The work cited is included as chapter 4 in this volume.

This chapter has origins in two separate manuscripts: "Trans-Pacific Studies and U.S.-Japan Complicity," published in *The Trans-Pacific Imagination: Rethinking Boundary, Culture and Society*, edited by Naoki Sakai and Hyon Joo Yoo (Singapore: World Scientific, 2012), and "The End of *Pax Americana* and the Nationalism of *Hikikomori*," delivered as a public lecture at the University of Hong Kong in October 2014 and at Kobe University in November 2014. The latter was also published as "On Nishikawa Nagao's *Neo-Colonialism*: The End of *Pax Americana* and the Nationalism of *Hikikomori*" (*Shisô*, no. 1095, July 2015) and included in the Japanese anthology 『ひきこもりの国民主義』(The nationalism of hikikomori [reclusive withdrawal]) (Tokyo: Iwanami Shoten, 2017).

1 When I presented my assessment of the future of the global hegemony of the United States of America in the original version of this chapter in 2014, it was beyond my imagination to anticipate such a swift collapse of Pax Americana. Since Donald Trump's astonishing presidential election victory, I now have to entertain the possibility of the American empire's suicide or a self-destructive recklessness that would give rise to an entirely different configuration of global power politics.

2 After the Allied occupation, Japan resumed its diplomatic relations with the USSR through the Joint Declaration in 1956, with the Republic of Korea through the Treaty on Basic Relations between the Republic of Korea and Japan in 1965, and with the People's Republic of China through the Joint Communiqué of the Government of the People's Republic of China and the Government of Japan in 1972.

3 Since a large section of this chapter was first delivered at the University of Hong Kong in October 2014 during the Umbrella Revolution, a number of explicit signs of an inward-looking society have emerged in many parts of the world: Brexit in the United Kingdom, the Donald Trump presidency in the United States, the popularity of the National Front in France, and anti-immigrant racist movements in countries such as Hungary, Poland, the United States, and even Germany.

4 Émile Benveniste argues: "Language is possible only because each speaker sets himself up as a *subject* by referring to himself as *I* in his discourse. Because of this, *I* posits another person, the one who, being, as he is, completely exterior to "me," become my echo to whom I saw *you* and who says *you* to me" (emphasis in original) (Benveniste 1971, 225).

5 In reference to Gilles Deleuze and Félix Guattari's (1994) discussion of "the shame of being a man" in *What Is Philosophy?*, Satoshi Ukai (鵜飼 哲) explores the problematic of shame in his article "The Future of an Affect: The Historicity of Shame" (Ukai 2000), from which I learned much.

6 "Poietics" comes from the Greek word *poiesis*, meaning manufacture or production, and poietics thus connotes the technology or knowledge of poiesis. For a description of Ito Jinsai's critique of Cheng-Zhu rationalism, see Ito (1966, 1971; Sakai 1991, 21–112).

7 The 2008 Status of Forces Agreement (SOFA) that Iraq made with the United States of America meant an entirely different legal status for American military personnel after the withdrawal of U.S. military forces from Iraqi territory as compared to the

U.S.-Japan SOFA signed and ratified under the system of the San Francisco Peace Treaty. The U.S.-Iraq SOFA cannot be viewed as a similar bilateral treaty. It was signed on November 16, 2008, and included the total withdrawal of U.S. troops from Iraqi territory by the end of 2011. In due course, the agreement expired on December 31, 2011. So there was no possibility for the United States to maintain military bases in Iraq after its withdrawal. In contrast, the U.S.-Japan SOFA protects the extraterritorial privileges of American military personnel in Japanese territories as well as offering legal justifications for the maintenance of U.S. military bases and facilities in Japan.

8　The most typical mystification can be found in an article titled "The Day the General Blinked" on the occasion of Hirohito's serious illness—preceding his eventual death on January 7, 1989—by Faubion Bowers (1988), personal secretary to General Douglas MacArthur.

9　Perhaps Etô Jun (江藤 淳) was the most typical conservative ideologue to yield willingly to the sentimental logic of self-pity inherent in Japanese populism and argued that Japan did not surrender unconditionally. He, perhaps unwittingly, served to endorse American propaganda for Japan under Pax Americana. In this respect, I cannot think of a better manifestation of civilizational transference between the United States and Japan than Etô Jun (Etô [1979] 1996; [1989] 1994).

10　The system of state bureaucracy based upon the sovereignty of the emperor has been called the "emperor system." This term was coined through an analysis provided by a school of Marxists known as the Lecture School during the interwar period. While censored by the state until the end of the Asia-Pacific War, this analysis became widely accepted after the war. There are, however, two shortcomings in the Lecture School's analysis. The first is a developmental teleology implicit in the term "emperor system." It is understood as a form of absolutism, comparable to Russian czarism, characteristic of an already surpassed stage in the development of capitalism. The second is ahistoricality—a lack of historical awareness concerning the constitution of the national community. Marxists did not adequately historicize the existence of the Japanese nation but instead assumed that it was always there before the constitution of the modern national state. In respect to viewing the nation as a natural given, these Marxists were no different from nationalists; after all, they were no more than Marxist nationalists.

11　The political scheme according to which the Chinese were encouraged to unify their country and establish their sovereign state was first introduced by leftist intellectuals in the early 1930s. The idea of the East Asian Community (東亜共同体) was advocated by Japanese intellectuals, some of whom were affiliated with the Showa Research Association (昭和研究会), but this scheme was appropriated in the late 1930s by conservative forces into the strategy of the Greater East Asia Co-prosperity Sphere.

12　As I discussed in chapter 2, the term "kokutai" was initially a neologism for the English word "nationality" in the early Meiji period (Fukuzawa [1875] 1973).

Here, let me reiterate. I rely upon the classical notion of nationality as in British liberalism. According to John Stuart Mill, nationality means that "a portion of mankind are united among themselves by common sympathies which do not exist between them and any others—which make them co-operate with each other more willingly than with other people, desire to be under the same government, and desire that it should be government by themselves or a portion of themselves exclusively. This feeling of nationality may have been generated by various causes. Sometimes it is the effect of identity of race and descent. Community of language, and community of religion greatly contribute to it. Geographical limits are one of its causes. But the strongest of all is identity of political antecedents; the possession of a national history, and consequent community of recollections; collective pride and humiliation, pleasure and regret, connected with the same incidents in the past" (1972, 391).

As I mentioned in the previous footnote, Fukuzawa Yukichi translated the English term "nationality" as kokutai (national body) in the 1870s in the early Meiji period. Later kokutai was used to express the sovereignty of the Japanese emperor system. The preservation of nationality (*kokutai goji*) was the idiom around which it was frequently argued that the negotiation between the U.S. Occupation Administration and the Japanese government was conducted toward the end of World War II. The term "nationality" or "national body" had acquired almost a sacrosanctity and proscriptiveness by the end of the Meiji period. In his *Outline of the Theory of Civilization* (Fukuzawa [1875] 1973), however, Fukuzawa includes Mill's explications of nationality and the feeling of nationality almost verbatim in his exposition of kokutai.

13   The Planning Agency included some who had been involved in Marxist activities and had strong ties with the Shôwa Kenkyû-kai (昭和研究会, Shôwa Research Association), a think tank created in 1933 by intellectuals close to Konoe Fumimaro (近衛文麿). When Konoe became prime minister in 1936, the Shôwa Research Association was integrated into the Cabinet Secretariat, where many of the top intellectuals of Japan at that time participated in the discussions and planning of policy proposals. It was abolished in 1940.

14   Of exceptional importance in this respect is Takashi Fujitani's monumental work *Race to Empire: Koreans as Japanese and Japanese as Americans during World War II*, in which the policies of racial integration were designed and implemented as supplements to the racist structure of the Japanese and American empires (Fujitani 2011).

15   Let me assert, once again, that the West is a putative unity, and that it is overdetermined so that it is impossible to determine its meaning—cartographic location, civilizational identity, political alliance and otherwise—in multiple contexts simultaneously. Yet, during the period of the Cold War, such statements were blatantly propagated and readily accepted in mass media: "As an anticommunist bastion, Taiwan proudly belongs to the West"; "However hard they may try, the local populace cannot acquire the spirit of Western democracy in Iraq"; and "One of the indispensable goals of education in the United States is to nurture the love of Western civilization."

16   I would like to thank Sandro Mezzadra and Brett Neilson (2013, 46) for drawing my attention to this article, "Development," by Gustavo Estava (2010).

17   Of course, the expression "something inherited transhistorically" is an oxymoron in itself. Inheritance always implies that the succession is mediated by historical action.

Therefore, one cannot inherit anything without the potential for historical disruption. Inheritance is of necessity historical. It is important to note that it is always possible to find conceptual contradictions of this kind in the discourse of ethnicity and race.

18 Here I issue a warning disclaimer. Scientific racism believed that the concept of race concerns itself with the physiological constitution of an individual human. This is a belief according to which race derives from a system of classifications based upon physiological and biological properties of an individual human being, but I have no intention of confirming this definition of racism in general. Racism also exists outside scientific racism, and this is one of the reasons why, as I argue here and elsewhere, an analysis of nationality with regard to racism is indispensable.

19 It is said that the idiom "sangokujin" (third-country person) meant an individual or people who belonged neither to victor nations such as the United States of America, the United Kingdom, China (prior to the establishment of the People's Republic of China), or Australia, nor to defeated nations such as Japan and Germany. The third-country person meant a member of the excess population within Japanese territory who used to be a Japanese subject of the Japanese Empire but ceased to be Japanese because the colony he or she was from became independent as a result of the loss of the empire. This idiom was almost dormant until Ishihara Shintaro (石原 慎太郎), governor of the Tokyo prefecture, revived it in his notoriously racist statement in 2000.

20 Excluding the territories recently obtained during the latter half of the Asia-Pacific War—French Indochina, the Philippines, Dutch East Indies, British Malaya, Burma, and so on—the Japanese Empire retained its territories in many regions in Asia and the Pacific such as Okinawa, Taiwan, Korea, Sakhalin, the Pacific Islands, protectorates in China, and Manchuria. One of the ways in which the secondary status of the colonized was legally marked as distinct from the Japanese was the institution of the *koseki* (戸籍, family registry). The family registry requires the registration of the permanent domicile (*honseki* 本籍), and those from the annexed territories had to register their permanent domiciles in the territories outside Japan proper. Thus the subject population under Japanese sovereignty was classified into two major categories, those whose permanent domicile was in Japan proper (*naichi* 内地), and those with permanent domicile outside Japan proper. Generally, sangokujin (third-country person or people) designated those who were resident in Japan without family registers within Japan proper. At the end of the Asia-Pacific War, several million Japanese subjects from outside Japan proper were resident in Japan proper. The largest groups among them were from Taiwan and Korea; Korean and Taiwanese (Chinese) sovereignties were returned after Japan's defeat in 1945. During the Allied occupation of Japan (1945–1952), most of these third-country people were eventually deprived of their Japanese citizenship, but because of the different historical conditions for Taiwan, which became virtually the sole territory governed by the Chinese Nationalist Party as a result of their defeat in the civil war in China in 1949, and Korea, which was divided into North and South Korea in 1948, Taiwanese and Korean residents in Japan would be treated differently by the U.S. Occupation Administration and the Japanese government in subsequent

years. Racial discrimination against Korean residents has been particularly intense throughout the postwar period. Since the North Korean government's disclosure of its scheme of kidnapping Japanese individuals in 2001, racism against the Korean minority has been even stronger.

21 "Antinominal" is an adjectival form of the noun "antinomy" (*anti-nomos* in Greek) that refers to a real or apparent mutual incompatibility of two laws.

22 The Imperial Shrine of Yasukuni, informally called the Yasukuni Shrine, was founded by Emperor Meiji adjacent to the Imperial Palace in Tokyo in 1869. It commemorates those who died in service of the Japanese state from 1868 through 1964. At the Yasukuni Shrine, the glory of the Japanese Empire is still celebrated, and Class A war criminals are enshrined with soldiers who died as Japanese, some of whom would have been called "sangokujin," if alive in postwar Japan. Some conservative politicians pay visits there contrary to the constitutional separation of the state and religious organizations.

23 In 1951, when Japan was still occupied by the Allied Powers, Japan and the United States of America signed the "Agreement under Article VI of the Treaty of Mutual Cooperation and Security between Japan and the United States of America, Regarding Facilities and Areas and the Status of United States Armed Forces in Japan" in preparation for Japan's so-called independence. This agreement defined the status and privileges U.S. military personnel were granted in Japan and other administrative regulations under which U.S. armed forces were allowed to operate in Japan. In 1960, as the U.S.–Japan Security Treaty was revised, it was renamed the "U.S.–Japan Status of Forces Agreement." This agreement serves as the legal base upon which the semicolonial relationship between Japan and the United States is largely built. As part of Pax Americana, the United States signed a number of SOFAs with its satellite states including Italy, the United Kingdom, South Korea, and Germany.

24 See Gustavo Estava's argument on development (Estava 2010).

25 Of course, we now know that the Obama administration's transpacific initiative ("Pivot to Asia" in 2013), announced by Secretary of State Hillary Clinton, was reversed by the Donald Trump administration as soon as Trump entered the White House. The recession of Pax Americana was thereby further promoted. But long before the Trump administration, American global hegemony had been receding. The inward-looking tendency so obvious in the Trump presidency is no more than a reaction to, as well as an admission of, the loss of American empire on the global stage. "Make America Great Again!"

26 As I mentioned above, the *New York Times* reported that Kishi Nobusuke and his brother, Satô Eisaku, were agents on the CIA payroll operating against socialist and progressive forces in Japan (cf. Weiner 1994). What is remarkable about this information is that, in Japan, no national news outlet, be it newspaper or TV network, reported this full-page article in the *New York Times*. This information was totally disavowed by Japanese media at the time. For the general historical background of the CIA's connections with war criminal conservatives, see Weiner (2007).

27 It is noteworthy that, first of all, the term "war criminal conservative" is an oxymoron. Those war criminals who were imprisoned as class A war criminals at Sugamo

Prison did not necessarily adhere to the political ideas of conservatism. Sasakawa Ryô'ichi and Kodama Yoshio were fascists who rejected the conservatism of the 1930s and early 1940s. Kishi Nobusuke was known as a reform bureaucrat who promoted policies of a planned economy for the Greater East Asia Co-prosperity Sphere. Sasakawa, Matsukata, and Kodama manifested their fascistic and therefore nationalistic orientation until Japan's surrender, but after the war, they became promoters of American colonial interests in East Asia; they worshipped American authority in Japan and served American interests in East Asia. In this sense, they cannot be portrayed as nationalists who advocated for the autonomy of their own nation against colonial or imperial maneuvers by external forces. In fact, they were colonial agents who would not hesitate to worship their colonial masters. Yet they extensively relied upon the rhetoric of nationalism and fashioned themselves as nationalists. The fascist ideology they retained after the war could only be found in their persistent anticommunism. Therefore, I am hesitant to introduce the term "war criminal conservatives"; they may well be called "war criminal reactionaries" or "war criminal anticommunists." Although it is evident that they were not nationalists, they consistently presented themselves as either official members of, or associated with, the conservative party, that is, the LDP, and appealed to the rhetoric of nationalism.

28 "The Image Expected of the Japanese" (「期待される人間像」) was the title of the governmental leaflet prepared by the Central Council for Education (中央教育審議会) and published by the Japanese Ministry of Education (Central Council for Education 1966). Literally translated, the title should be rendered "the image expected of the human being," but it should be translated as "the image expected of the Japanese," since the deliberate confusion of "human being" and "Japanese" occurred in this document in exactly the same way as I depicted national humanism in chapter 1. Here what is referred to as "human being" (人間) is a person of Japanese nationality. The leaflet divides the world into two blocks, the block of liberal democratic states and that of totalitarian states, and it characterizes Japan as a country belonging to the group of liberal democracies. It describes the guidelines for advanced secondary education—senior high school education normally for children between the ages of fifteen and eighteen. These guidelines include the following moral principles: (1) liberal individualism emphasizing the spirit of independence; (2) the spirit of free enterprise; (3) the monogamous nuclear family as the basis of society as a whole; (4) respect for creativity and innovation; (5) scientific and technological knowledge as guidance for the future; (6) respect for law and social harmony; (7) love of the emperor as the basis for Japanese society as a whole; and (8) respect for national tradition and the ethnic culture of Japan. The leaflet discusses what and how the Japanese high school children are expected to learn, but it also illustrates the moral norms expected of the Japanese under Pax Americana. The image of the authentic Japanese person expected of Japanese high school pupils is the same as the image expected of the Japanese in general under the gaze of the United States of America.

29 In psychoanalysis, transference refers to projection of a patient's feelings or desires for a significant person onto the therapist. Transference is often manifested as an

erotic attraction to a therapist but can be seen in many other emotive-sensational modes such as hostility, mistrust, extreme dependence, or even giving the therapist godlike or guru status. By "civilizational transference," I see a comparable dynamic of projection or redirection of feelings and desire in the colonial relationship—between the colonizer and the colonized. Here, two processes must be discerned. The first is the identification of an individual with either the colonizer or the colonized. The second is for the colonized to accept the colonizer's desire. The analysis of transference was actually a work consisting of two directions: how the social positions of the colonizer and the colonized are mutually constituted as a shared constitutive binary configuration in which colonial power is conducted, on the one hand, and how the colonized mimics the desire of the colonizer, on the other. Yet it is also essential to remember that the very relationship in reference to which transference occurs is always directional or inclined. It takes place within a gradient from a majoritarian positionality toward a minoritarian one, and therefore it is always in the context of a power relation. The transference, which, whether affectionate or hostile, operates in the identity politics of colonial governmentality, must be objectified in order to comprehend the working of colonial power, particularly in knowledge production. Both the colonizer and the colonized must recognize the transference relationship and explore its significance in order for both parties to decolonize themselves. Decolonization is not a matter only for the colonized. On the contrary, it is a matter of utmost importance for the colonizer.

30 The International Federation for Victory over Communism (国際勝共連合) was established by anticommunist politicians and activists such as Moon Sun Myung, Sasakawa Ryô'ichi, and Kishi Nobusuke in 1968 under the direction of the Central Intelligence Agency (CIA). It included many right-wing politicians, relatively young and old, including Abe Shinzô, Abe Shintarô (Abe Shinzô's father), Inada Tomomi (稲田 朋美), Nakasone Yasuhiro (中曽根 康弘), Kase Hideaki (加瀬 英明), and so on.

31 Sasakawa Ryôichi (1899–1995) was one of the leaders of the prewar fascist party (国粋大衆党, Patriotic People's Party), who joined the Japanese parliament in 1942. He was arrested as a Class A war criminal after the war, but he managed to establish connections with other Class A criminals during his detention at Sugamo Prison, from which he was released during the American Reverse Course toward Japan. He successfully established the Japan Shipbuilding Foundation (日本船舶振興会) in 1951 and managed a motorboat gambling business from which he amassed a huge fortune; this was then invested in many different activities through the same foundation. Together with Kishi Nobusuke he was most active in the anticommunist campaigns that were surreptitiously initiated and sponsored by the CIA. For instance, he was one of the major supporters of the aforementioned Holy Spirit Association for the Unification of World Christianity and founded the International Federation for Victory over Communism in 1968. The Japan Shipbuilding Foundation was gradually transformed into the Sasakawa Foundation and later, in 1995, into the Nippon Foundation. In addition to activities in support of the anticommunist campaign, Sasakawa served as a representative of American interests and remained influential in many political agendas under the guise of philanthropy.

Shôriki Matsutarô (1885–1969) worked for the Tokyo metropolitan police in the Ministry of the Interior before Japan's defeat. As an expert in censorship, he dealt with a number of governmental activities suppressing social movements and anarchist and socialist activism. He was also a specialist in propaganda techniques; he openly admitted that he deliberately propagated the unfounded rumor of a Korean uprising immediately after the Great Kanto Earthquake of 1923. After resigning from the metropolitan police in 1924, he bought the *Yomiuri Shimbun* (Yomiuri newspaper) and moved into journalism and fields of propaganda management. In 1934, Shôriki established Japan's first professional baseball team, later named the Tokyo Giants. During the war, he worked for the Information Bureau of the Cabinet and served as the general director of the Imperial Rule Assistance Association (大政翼賛会). He was arrested for his war crimes but later released from Sugamo Prison; he actively represented American political and strategic interests in Japan as an agent for the CIA, in particular through the medium of *Yomiuri Shimbun*. It is no exaggeration to say that, in the 1950s and '60s, *Yomiuri* was a propaganda organ for the CIA in Japan.

Shôriki was also farsighted with respect to qualitative changes in society at large in Japan by promoting professional sports such as baseball. After the war, he shifted the baseball team he owned to the control of *Yomiuri Shimbun*. With the growing popularity of professional baseball in Japan, *Yomiuri Shimbun* expanded its business into the fields of mass entertainment and mass communication, far beyond the classical fields of journalism. In 1953, as the recipient of the first television technology transfer from the United States, he started the Nippon Television Company, the first television broadcasting corporation in Japan, which still operates as one of the major national television networks today. It was during a period of high economic growth after the war that *Yomiuri Shimbun* outpaced the *Asahi* and *Mainichi* newspapers and grew to be the national paper with the largest readership; it was estimated to have more than nine million daily readers in Japan toward the end of the twentieth century.

Kodama Yoshio (1911–1984) was a member of the fascist party, the Patriotic People's Party (国粋大衆党), and for a brief period worked with Sasakawa Ryôichi. He was arrested for his attempts to assassinate some politicians in the 1930s, and when released from prison, he moved to China, where he got involved in the supply chain for goods, including opiates from the territories occupied by Japanese military forces. Through these underground operations Kodama accumulated huge wealth, which he used in his various political and criminal maneuvers after the war. With Japan's defeat, he was arrested for war crimes and ultranationalist activities as a Class A war criminal, and was imprisoned at Sugamo, where he resumed his old connection with Sasakawa Ryôichi and got acquainted with a number of prominent detainees. U.S. government intelligence officials requested his release in exchange for his collaboration with the CIA. After being freed from Sugamo, he was active in national politics and the criminal *yakuza* (crime syndicate) world; the LDP was connected to them through a number of channels after 1955, when it was formed as a coalition of the Liberal Party and the Democratic Party. The CIA found Kodama most reliable in its anticommunist activities, and, just like Kishi and Shôriki, he was on the CIA payroll as a willing collaborator. By utilizing his connections with yakuza figures in the criminal underworld as well as with conservative politicians, he was active in suppressing labor disputes, obstructing labor unions, eradicating socialist sympathizers, and promoting anticommunist campaigns.

32 See note 28 above.

33 The double structure of U.S.-Japan complicity is reconfirmed even in Abe's own publications, such as *Toward a Beautiful Country*『美しい国へ』(Abe 2006). Abe cites Kevin Doak, an American Japan expert known for his antiquated anticommunism and antimodernity, to endorse Koizumi and Abe's visit to the Yasukuni Shrine. Perhaps he wanted such Japan experts as Doak to be the representative voice of American public opinion (Abe 2006, 74). The endorsement is mutual and illustrates the typical structure of U.S.-Japan complicity that was evidently anachronistic by 2006 (cf. Doak 2006, 82–89). Grotesque and anachronistic though it may appear, there is no better example than this of the old complicity between American area studies on Japan and Japan's ultranationalism.

34 U.S. House Resolution 121: "A resolution expressing the consensus of the House of Representatives that the Government of Japan should formally acknowledge, apologize, and accept historical responsibility in a clear and unequivocal manner for its Imperial Armed Forces' coercion of young women into sexual slavery, known to the world as 'comfort women,' during its colonial and wartime occupation of Asia and the Pacific Islands from the 1930s through the duration of World War II" (introduced January 31, 2007, and amended July 30, 2007).

35 Abe Shinzô is well known for his historical revisionism. He openly interfered with the broadcast of the NHK television series on wartime violence, one episode of which touched upon the problem of the Comfort Women (see Yoshimi and Yoneyama 2006; Media-Crisis Citizens' Network 2005.)

36 In the 1960s, some outstanding studies were done on the American occupation of Japan. One, to which I have already referred, is by an author who participated in the business of the Allied occupation of Japan (Dunn 1963). In the 1980s, another important work was published (Schaller 1997).

37 Carl Schmitt wanted to see the United States rescue the very imperial-colonial order of international law: he argued, "the term 'Western Hemisphere' was opposed precisely to Europe, the old West, the old Occident. . . . The new West claimed to be the true West, the true Occident, the true Europe. The new West, America, would supersede the old West, would reorient the old world historical order, would become the center of the earth. The West, and all that belonged to it in the moral, civilizing, and political sense of the word 'Occident,' would neither be eliminated nor destroyed, nor even dethroned, but only displaced. International law ceased to have its center of gravity in old Europe. The center of civilization shifted further west, to America" (2006, 290).

38 In every instance of social conduct, every singular being is separated from other social beings. Precisely because of this spacing, a singular being is in common with other singular beings. Jean-Luc Nancy also calls this spacing *aléarité*. See "La Comparution" in *La Comparution* (Nancy 1986; Nancy and Bailly 1991). "Being in common means that singular beings are, present themselves, and appear only to the

extent they compear [*comparassent*], to the extent that they are exposed, presented, or offered to one another. Their compearance [*comparution*] is not something added on to their being; rather their being comes into being in it" (Nancy, "Myth Interrupted," in Nancy 1991, 58).

39 As I alluded to in chapter 2, the formation of the modern family offers an important context in which the paradigm of gender positions is institutionalized. Of course, masculinity cannot be apprehended without reference to the modern paradigm of gender positions in the institution of the modern family. For the formation of the modern family in Japan, see Nishikawa (2000, 7–93).

40 Any reader of popular literature of the Tokugawa period (1600–1868) knows that same-sex love among males was openly discussed with little inhibition; what was then called *nanshoku* (男色)—"male color" or men's erotic attraction to other males—was one of the most popular topics in the literary genre of popular novellas. In this respect, sexual orientation in men toward other men was not regarded as immoral or abnormal. Perhaps it could be viewed as rather unconventional or inconvenient, but this sexual orientation observable among certain male figures was not marked as irregular, abnormal, or pathological. This situation drastically changed during the Meiji period (1868–1911), by the end of which such an orientation was publicly condemned and began to be seen as a manifestation of pathological abnormality or mental deficiency in such an individual.

41 Of course, as I have explored above, the national community is in the element of imagination. The fantastic constitution of national community must be further construed in the case of the nationalism of hikikomori.

42 It is in this reference to the imagined enclosure of the national community that the idea of the national body (kokutai) is articulated to the geographic representation of the nation. On the one hand, the national body invokes a fantastic relationship between the emperor (representing the totality of the nation) and an individual member of the national community. On the other hand, the national body is often equated with what Thongchai Winichakul (1994) called "the geo-body of a nation."

43 The terms "polysemy" and "sememe" were coined in structural semiotics. Polysemy is a function of a sign having multiple meanings or multiple sememes, and "sememe" is a semantic language unit of meaning. Here, the meaning referred to is a sense of such a unit of sign as word, phrase, or symbol, and not a signification for sentence. A sememe is a proposed unit of intended meaning, which is indivisible or atomic. For example, "top" means the summit of a mountain or tower. It also means the dominant position in an organization, as in the expression "top executive of a company." It also means somebody who is listed first in a list of players, such as a "top runner." Each of these senses is a sememe, and the word "top" is potentially open to these different sememes, and thus polysemic.

CONCLUSION

1 Let me stress again that the principle of relational identity is not totally rejected in modern societies. It is confined to the sphere of privacy while the public sphere is regulated by the principle of specific identity. One of the characteristic features

of modern social formations is the strict separation of the public and the private spheres.

2 See note 15 in chapter 2, this volume.

3 One might as well claim that a nation consists of individuals of the third person singular. It is interesting to note that, prior to the social transformations of the Meiji period, the grammatical category of the third person singular did not exist in academic, political, and literary discourses in Japan (cf. Noguchi 1994).

4 What connects individuals and the totality of the community that those individuals are supposed to form is of myth or mything. For a more detailed analysis, see Jean-Luc Nancy, "Myth Interrupted," in *The Inoperative Community* (Nancy 1991, 43–70).

5 As I have repeatedly emphasized, the community in the sense of being-in-common must not be confused with the typical social imaginary of the national community. For an extensive analysis of the relationship between community and myth, see "The Inoperative Community" and "Myth Interrupted" in *The Inoperative Community* (Nancy 1991, 1–42, 43–70; Lacoue-Labarthe and Nancy 1991).

6 Foucault (2004b, 2007) investigated the history of power particular to the West. First he identified a particular arrangement of power, "pastoral power," in the Oriental religious traditions of Judaism, Christianity, and so on, and attributed it to the ancient Orient. He also characterized the modern arrangement of power in governance in Europe and called it biopolitics. Here I want to modify Foucault's diagnosis, first because I want to distance myself from his Occidentalism and, second, because it seems more productive to comprehend pastoral power and biopolitics in continuity.

7 An individual and a singular being must be rigorously distinguished from one another. Let me state once again, following Jean-Luc Nancy (1991), that one who is exposed to another and engages in being-in-common is not an individual but a singular being. Whereas an individual is in the conceptual paradigm of individual-species-genus, that is, in the logical economy of particularity and generality, a singular being inheres in the opposition of singularity and universality.

8 The nation is an aesthetic constitution in this respect. The totality of the nation is dependent upon the distinction of the members of the nation from its nonmembers while one is not required or expected to be acquainted with either kind of people. Only when one can differentiate the nation's members from its nonmembers can the totality of the nation be made representable. For this reason, aesthetics is of great importance in nationalism. It is in this respect that nationalism is impossible to segregate from racism.

9 "Eight corners of the world under one roof" is said to be quoted from the *Chronicle of Japan* (日本書紀). This dictum was adopted by the Japanese administration of Prime Minister Konoe Fumimaro in 1940. It expressed the spirit of Japanese imperial nationalism and the vision of the Greater East Asia Co-prosperity Sphere. It was banned by the supreme commander of the Allied Powers as soon as the Japanese Empire was defeated in 1945.

10 I learned the term "bordering" from Sandro Mezzadra and Brett Neilson's paper presented at the international conference "Italian as Second Language: Citizenship,

Language, and Translation" held in Rimini, Italy, in February 2008. Their research was further developed and published as a monograph (Mezzadra and Neilson 2013).

11 Let us not forget that the vast majority of those who were involved in the creation, expansion, management, and maintenance of the system of the Comfort Stations, as well as those who recruited Comfort Women, benefited from work at those stations, or received the services of the Comfort Women, are now dead, so the question of responsibility cannot be simply equated with that of criminal guilt. As I argue in chapter 1, I do not believe that those born after the Asia-Pacific War but who share Japanese nationality can be immediately accountable for the problem of the Comfort Women. Today it is not because they are of Japanese nationality that they are guilty of the Comfort Stations. It is important not to yield to the rhetoric of guilt by association. The Japanese people born after the war are not criminally accountable for the various criminal acts connected to the system of the Comfort Stations. Yet I claim that these Japanese are responsible politically to those who insist upon Japanese responsibility for the Comfort Station system and for Japanese colonialism. In other words, I believe the Japanese must respond to those who call attention to the responsibility of the Japanese nation. And they must be responsible either by clearly and rigorously explaining why and how they are not guilty of the crimes or by admitting why and how they are implicated in the legacies of colonial responsibility. Here I mean that the problem of responsibility must not be confused with that of guilt.

References

Abe, Shinzô. 2006. *Toward a Beautiful Country*『美しい 国 へ』. Tokyo: Bungei Shunjû.

Anderson, Benedict. 1983. *Imagined Communities: Reflections on the Origin and Spread of Nationalism*. London: Verso.

Asad, Talal. 1993. *Genealogies of Religion: Discipline and Reasons of Power in Christianity and Islam*. Baltimore, MD: Johns Hopkins University Press.

Balibar, Étienne. 1991. "Racism and Nationalism." In *Race, Nation, Class: Ambiguous Identities*, translated by Chris Turner, 37–67. London: Verso.

Balibar, Étienne. 1994. "Racism as Universalism." In *Masses, Classes, Ideas*, translated by James Swenson, 191–204. London: Routledge.

Balibar, Étienne, and Immanuel Wallerstein. 1991. *Race, Nation, Class: Ambiguous Identities*. Translated by Chris Turner. London: Verso.

Bauman, Zygmunt. 1989. *Modernity and the Holocaust*. Ithaca, NY: Cornell University Press.

Bellah, Robert N. 1962. "Values and Social Changes in Modern Japan." *Asian Cultrual Studies*, no. 3: 13–56.

Bellah, Robert N. 1965. "Japan's Cultural Identity: Some Reflections on the Work of Watsuji Tetsuro." *Journal of Asian Studies* 24, no. 4: 573–594.

Benveniste, Émile. 1971. *Problems in General Linguistics*. Translated by Mary Elizabeth Meek. Coral Gables, FL: University of Miami Press.

Berman, Antoine. 1984. *L'épreuve de l'étranger*. Paris: Gallimard.

Berman, Antoine. 1992. *The Experience of the Foreign: Culture and Translation in Romantic Germany*. Translated by S. Heyvaert. Albany: State University of New York Press.

Berman, Antoine. 1999. *La traduction et la lettre ou l'auberge du lointain*. Paris: L'ordre philosophique.

Bernal, Martin. 1987. *Black Athena: The Afroasiatic Roots of Classical Civilization*. New Brunswick, NJ: Rutgers University Press.

Berque, Augustin. 1982. *Vivre l'espace au Japon*. Paris: Presses Universitaires de France.

Borkenau, Franz. 1934. *Der Übergang vom Feudalen zum Bürgerlichen Weltbild*. Paris: Felix Alcan.

Borkenau, Franz. 1965. 『封建的世界像から市民的世界像へ』. Translated by Mizuta Hiroshi et al. Tokyo: Misuzu Shobô.

Bowers, Faubion. 1988. "The Day the General Blinked." *New York Times*, September 30.

Brassier, Ray. 2001. "Alien Theory: The Decline of Materialism in the Name of Matter." PhD diss., Department of Philosophy, University of Warwick.

Buck, Pearl S. 1942. *American Unity and Asia*. New York: John Day.

Calhoun, Craig. 1993. "Nationalism and Ethnicity." *Annual Review of Sociology* 19: 211–232.

Central Council for Education 中央教育審議会. 1966. "The Image Expected of the Japanese" 『期待される人間像』. Leaflet prepared by Central Council for Education.

Chakrabarty, Dipesh. 1993. "Marx after Marxism: Subaltern Histories and the Question of Difference." *Polygraph* 6, no. 7.

Chakrabarty, Dipesh. 2000. *Provincializing Europe*. Princeton, NJ: Princeton University Press.

Chang, Iris. 1997. *The Rape of Nanking: The Forgotten Holocaust of World War II*. New York: Basic Books.

Chao, Yen-ning (Antonia) 趙彥寧. 2001. *On the Road with a Straw Hat* 『《戴著草帽到處旅行》台北: 巨流出版社』. Taipei: Daizhe caomao daochulüxing.

Chow, Rey. 1995. *Primitive Passions: Visuality, Sexuality, Ethnography, and Contemporary Chinese Cinema*. New York: Columbia University Press.

Cohn, Bernard S. 1996. *Colonialism and Its Forms of Knowledge*. Princeton, NJ: Princeton University Press.

Deleuze, Gilles, and Félix Guattari. 1980. *Milles Plateaux*. Paris: Éditions de Minuit.

Deleuze, Gilles, and Félix Guattari. 1987. *A Thousand Plateaus*. Translated by Brian Massumi. Minneapolis: University of Minnesota Press.

Deleuze, Gilles, and Félix Guattari. 1994. *What Is Philosophy?* Translated by Hugh Tomlinson and Graham Burchell. New York: Columbia University Press.

Derrida, Jacques. 1989. "Introduction." In *Husserl's Origin of Geometry, with an Introduction by Jacques Derrida*. Translated by John P. Leavy Jr., 23–153. Lincoln: University of Nebraska Press.

Derrida, Jacques. 1990. *Du droit à la philosophie*. Paris: Galilée.

Derrida, Jacques. 1991. *L'autre cap*. Paris: Éditions de Minuit.

Derrida, Jacques. 1992. *The Other Heading*. Translated by Pascale-Anne Brault and Michael B. Haas. Bloomington: Indiana University Press.

Derrida, Jacques. 2004. *Eyes of the University*. Translated by Jan Plug et al. Stanford, CA: Stanford University Press.

Di Cesare, Donatella. 2018. *Heidegger and the Jews: The Black Notebooks*. Translated by Murtha Baca. Cambridge: Polity.

Doak, Kevin. 2006. "The Vatican City Endorses the Prime Minister's Visit to the Yasukuni Shurine" 「ヴァチカンは靖国を認めている」. Translated by Tomiyama Yasushi. *Seiron* (Tokyo), September, 82–89.

Dower, John. 1979. *Empire and Aftermath: Yoshida Shigeru and the Japanese Experience, 1978–1954*. Cambridge, MA: Council on East Asian Studies.

Dower, John. 1987. *War without Mercy: Race and Power in the Pacific War*. New York: Pantheon.

Dower, John. 2000. *Embracing Defeat: Japan in the Wake of World War II*. New York: W. W. Norton.

Dunn, Frederick S. 1963. *Peace-Making and the Settlement with Japan*. Princeton, NJ: Princeton University Press.

Erber, Pedro R. 2015. *Breaching the Frame: The Rise of Contemporary Art in Brazil and Japan*. Berkeley: University of California Press.

Estava, Gustavo. 2010. *The Development Dictionary: A Guide to Knowledge as Power*. Edited by Wolfgang Sachs. London: Zed Books.

Etô, Jun 江藤 淳. (1979) 1996. *What We Have Forgotten and What We Were Forced to Forget*『忘れたことと忘れさせられたこと』. Reprint, Tokyo: Bungei Shunjū.

Etô, Jun 江藤 淳. (1989) 1994. *Enclosed Language Space: Censorship by Allied Powers and Postwar Japan*『閉ざされた言語空間: 占領軍検閲と戦後日本』. Serially published in *Shokun*. Reprint, Tokyo: Bungei Shunjū.

Fabian, Johannes. 1983. *Time and the Other*. New York: Columbia University Press.

Foucault, Michel. 1966a. "La pensée du dehors." *Critique* 229 (June): 523–546.

Foucault, Michel. 1966b. *Les mots et les choses: Une archéologie des sciences humaines*. Paris: Gallimard.

Foucault, Michel. 1973. *The Order of Things: An Archaeology of the Human Sciences*. New York: Vintage.

Foucault, Michel. 1980. "Questions on Geography." Translated by Colin Gordon. In *Power/Knowledge: Selected Interviews and Other Writings 1972–1977*, edited by C. Gordon, 63–77. New York: Pantheon.

Foucault, Michel. 1999. "Michel Foucault and Zen: A Stay in a Zen Temple (1978)." Translated by Richard Townsend. In *Religion and Culture / by Michel Foucault*, edited by Jeremy R. Carrette, 110–114. New York: Routledge.

Foucault, Michel. 2001a. "Michel Foucault et le zen: Un séjour dans un temple zen." In *Dits et Écrits II, 1976–1988*, 618–624. Paris: Gallimard.

Foucault, Michel. 2001b. "Questions à Michel Foucault sur la géographie." In *Dits et Écrits II*, 28–40. Paris: Gallimard.

Foucault, Michel. 2003. "The Thought of the Outside." Translated by Brian Massumi. In *The Essential Foucault*, edited by Paul Rabinow and Nikolas Rose, 423–441. New York: New Press.

Foucault, Michel. 2004a. *Naissance de la biopolitique: Cours au Collège de France, 1978–1979*. Paris: Gallimard et Seuil.

Foucault, Michel. 2004b. *Sécurité, Territoire, Population: Cours au Collège de France, 1977–1978*. Paris: Gallimard et Seuil.

Foucault, Michel. 2007. *Michel Foucault, Security, Territory, Population: Lectures at the Collège de France, 1977–1978*. Edited by Michel Senellart. Translated by Graham Burchell. New York: Palgrave Macmillan.

Foucault, Michel. 2008. *The Birth of Biopolitics: Lectures at the Collège de France 1978–1979*. Translated by Graham Burchell. New York: Palgrave Macmillan.

Freud, Sigmund. 1991. *On Narcissism: An Introduction*. New Haven, CT: Yale University Press.

Fujitani, Takashi. 1998. *Splendid Monarchy: Power and Pageantry in Modern Japan*. Berkeley: University of California Press.

Fujitani, Takashi. 2000. "Reischauer's Plan for a Puppet Regime Emperor System." *Sekai*, no. 672, 137–146.

Fujitani, Takashi. 2001. "The Reischauer Memo: Mr. Moto, Hirohito, and Japanese American Soldiers." *Critical Asian Studies* 33, no. 3: 379–402.

Fujitani, Takashi. 2011. *Race to Empire: Koreans as Japanese and Japanese as Americans during World War II*. Berkeley: University of California Press.

Fujitani, Takashi, Ryûichi Narita, and Naoki Sakai. 1995. "Round-Table Discussion: 'America's Japan/America's Voice'"「アメリカの日本／アメリカの 声」. *Gendai Shisô*『現代思想』23, no. 23: 8–37.

Fujiwara, Akira 藤原 彰 et al. 1955. *The Showa History*『昭和史』. Tokyo: Iwanami Shoten.

Fukuzawa, Yukichi 福沢 諭吉. (1875) 1973. *An Outline of the Theory of Civilization*『文明論之概略』. Translated by David A. Dilworth and G. Cameron Hurst. Tokyo: Sophia University.

Fukuzawa, Yukichi 福沢 諭吉. (1880) 1969. *An Encouragement of Learning*『学問のすゝめ』. Translated by David A. Dilworth and Umeyo Hirando. Tokyo: Sophia University.

Fukuzawa, Yukichi 福沢 諭吉. (1882) 1959. *On Moral Education*『徳育如何』. Originally published in *Jiji Shinpô*『時事新報』. Reprint,『福沢諭吉全集』(*Fukuzawa Yukichi Zenshû*) [Complete works of Fukuzawa Yukichi], vol. 5: 349–364. Tokyo: Iwanami Shoten.

Fushimizu, Osamu 伏水 修, dir. 1940. *China Night*『支那の夜』. Tôhô Company.

Gallicchio, Marc. 2000. *The African American Encounter with Japan and China*. Chapel Hill: University of North Carolina Press.

Gang, Luo 羅岡. 2005. "Empire, City, and Modernity"「帝國、都市與現代性」(Diguo, dushi yu xiandaixing). In『知識分子論叢第四卷』(*Zhishifenzi luncong* [Intellectual papers]), vol. 4, edited by Luo Gang. Jiangsu: Jiangsu Renmin Publishers.

Gilroy, Paul. 1991. *There Ain't No Black in the Union Jack*. Chicago: University of Chicago Press.

Gluck, Carol. 2002. "Operation of Memory: 'Comfort Women' and the World"「記憶の作用—世界の中の「慰安婦」」, translated by Umezaki Toru. In *Cultural History of Modern Japan*, vol. 8, 191–234. Tokyo: Iwanami Shoten.

GoGwilt, Christopher. 1995. *The Invention of the West: Joseph Conrad and the Double-Mapping of Europe and Empire*. Stanford, CA: Stanford University Press.

Gramsci, Antonio. 1992. *Prison Notebooks I*. Edited and translated by Joseph A. Buttigieg, New York: Columbia University Press.

Gramsci, Antonio. 1996. *Prison Notebooks II*. Edited and translated by Joseph A. Buttigieg, New York: Columbia University Press.

Gramsci, Antonio. 2007. *Prison Notebooks III*. Edited and translated by Joseph A. Buttigieg, New York: Columbia University Press.

Hall, Stuart. 1996. "The West and the Rest: Discourse and Power." In *Modernity: An Introduction to Modern Societies*, edited by Stuart Hall, David Held, Don Hubert, and Kenneth Thompson, 184–227. London: Wiley-Blackwell.

Harootunian, Harry D. 1989. "Visible Discourse/Invisible Ideologies." In *Postmodernism and Japan*, edited by Masao Miyoshi and H. D. Harootunian, 63–92. Durham, NC: Duke University Press.

Harootunian, Harry D., and Naoki Sakai. 1997. "Japanese Studies and Cultural Studies" 「日本研究と文化研究」. Translated by Okazaki Haruteru. *Shisô*『思想』, no. 877: 4–53.

Harootunian, Harry D, and Naoki Sakai. 1999. "Japan Studies and Cultural Studies." *Positions: East Asia Cultures Critique* 7, no. 2: 593–647.

Haver, William. 2012. *Ontology of Production*. Durham, NC: Duke University Press.

Hayashi, Hiroshi 林 博史. 2005. *War Crime Trials for the Class B and Class C War Criminals*『BC 級戦犯裁判』. Tokyo: Iwanami Shoten.

Heidegger, Martin. 1996. *Being and Time*. Translated by Joan Stambaugh. Albany: State University of New York Press.

Heidegger, Martin. 2002. "The Age of the World Picture." In *Off the Beaten Track*, translated by Julian Young and Kenneth Haynes, 57–85. Cambridge: Cambridge University Press.

Heidegger, Martin. 2016a. *Ponderings II–VI: Black Notebooks 1931–38*. Translated by Richard Rojcewicz. Bloomington: Indiana University Press.

Heidegger, Martin. 2016b. *Ponderings II–VI: Black Notebooks 1938–39*. Translated by Richard Rojcewicz. Bloomington: Indiana University Press.

Heidegger, Martin. 2017. *Ponderings II–VI: Black Notebooks 1939–41*. Translated by Richard Rojcewicz. Bloomington: Indiana University Press.

Higuchi, Yûichi 樋口 雄一. 1991. *Koreans Who Were Made Emperor's Soldiers*『皇軍兵士にされた朝鮮人』. Tokyo: Shakai Hyoronsha.

Hirota, Masaki ひろた, まさき. 1990. Afterword to *Aspects of Discrimination*『岩波近代日本思想体系『差別の諸相』の解説』, 436–516. Tokyo: Iwanami Shoten.

Hitler, Adolf. 1999. *Mein Kampf*. Translated by Ralph Manheim. New York: Houghton Mifflin.

Holmes, Brian. 2003. "The Flexible Personality—for a New Cultural Critique." In *Hieroglyphs of the Future: Art and Politics in a Networked Era*, 106–137. Paris: What, How and for Whom.

Holmes, Brian, and Jon Solomon. 2003. "Towards a Science of Foreigners? (Interview with Michael Hardt Prepared by Jon Solomon and Brian Holmes)." *Multitudes* (Paris: Exils), no. 14: 73–80.

Husserl, Edmund. 1970a. *The Crisis of European Sciences and Transcendental Phenomenology*. Translated by David Carr. Evanston, IL: Northwestern University Press.

Husserl, Edmund. 1970b. "The Origin of Geometry." Appendix VI to *The Crisis of European Sciences and Transcendental Phenomenology*, translated by David Carr, 353–378. Evanston, IL: Northwestern University Press.

Husserl, Edmund. 1970c. "The Vienna Lecture." Appendix I to *The Crisis of European Sciences and Transcendental Phenomenology*, translated by David Carr, 269–299. Evanston, IL: Northwestern University Press.

Husserl, Edmund. 1973. *Experience and Judgment*. Edited by Ludwig Landgrebe. Translated by James S. Churchill and Karl Ameriks. London: Routledge and Kegan Paul.

Husserl, Edmund. 1999. *Cartesian Meditations: An Introduction to Phenomenology*. Translated by Dorion Cairns. Dordrecht: Kluwer Academic.

Ienaga, Saburo 家永 三郎. (1938) 1997. *The Development of the Concept of Negativity in Japanese Intellectual History*『日本思想史における否定の論理の 発達』. *Historical Studies*『歴史学研究』8, nos. 10–12. Reprint, *Ienaga Saburô Shû*, vol. 1, 3–78, Tokyo: Iwanami Shoten.

Imai, Seiichi 今井 清一 et al. 1955. *The Showa History*『昭和史』. Tokyo: Iwanami Shoten.

Ishiguro, Kazuo. 1989. *The Remains of the Day*. London: Faber and Faber.

Isomae, Jun'ichi 磯前 順一. 2003. *Discourse on Religion in Modern Japan and Its Genealogy*『近代日本の宗教言説とその系譜』. Tokyo: Iwanami Shoten.

Isomae, Jun'ichi 磯前 順一. 2012. *The Concept of Religion and the Death of Religious Studies*『宗教概念あるいは宗教学の死』. Tokyo: Tokyo University Press.

Ito, Jinsai 伊藤 仁斎. 1932. *The Manchukuo Declaration of Independence* (『満州国建国宣言』). Tokyo: National Archive of Japan.

Ito, Jinsai 伊藤 仁斎. 1966. *An Infant Asks*『童士問』. Edited by Shigeru Shimizu. 『日本古典文学大系 近世思想家文集』[Japanese classical literature series], vol. 97, 25–291. Tokyo: Iwanami Shoten.

Ito, Jinsai 伊藤 仁斎. 1971. *Characters and Meanings in the Analects and Mencius*『語孟字義』. Edited by Kôjirô Yoshikawa. 『日本思想大系 伊藤仁斎・伊藤東涯』[Japanese thought series], vol. 23, 11–167. Tokyo: Iwanami Shoten.

Johnson, Chalmers. 2000. *Blowbacks: The Costs and Consequences of American Empire*. New York: Metropolitan.

Johnson, Chalmers. 2004. *The Sorrows of Empire: Militarism, Secrecy, and the End of the Republic*. New York: Metropolitan.

Jullien, François. 2000. *Penser d'un dehors (la Chine)* [Thinking from outside (China)]. Paris: Seuil.

Kamei, Katsuichirô 亀井 勝一郎. 1956. "A Question to Present-Day Historians"「現代歴史家への疑問」. *Bungei Shunjû*, March.

Kawai, Hayao 河合隼雄 et al. 2000. *The Prime Minister's Commission on Japan's Goals in the Twenty-first Century*. Tokyo: Cabinet Secretariat.

Kôsaka, Masaaki 高坂 正顕. 1942. *Philosophy of Nationality*『民族の哲学』. Tokyo: Iwanami Shoten.

Kuno, Osamu 久野 収, and Tsurumi Shunsuke 鶴見 俊輔. 1956. *Contemporary Japanese Thought*『現代日本の思想』. Tokyo: Iwanami Shoten.

Lacoue-Labarthe, Philippe. 1987. *La fiction du politique*. Paris: Christian Bourgois.

Lacoue-Labarthe, Philippe. 1990. *Heidegger, Art and Politics: The Fiction of the Political*. Translated by Chris Turner. Oxford: Basil Blackwell.

Lacoue-Labarthe, Philippe, and Jean-Luc Nancy. 1991. *Le mythe nazi*. La Tour d'Aigues: Éditions de L'aube.

Laruelle, François. 1981. *Principe de Minorité*. Paris: Aubier Montaigne.

Laruelle, François. 1996. *Théorie des Étrangers*. Paris: Kimé.

Laruelle, François. 2000. *Introduction au non-marxisme*. Paris: Actuel Marx.

Laruelle, François. 2001. "The Decline of Materialism in the Name of Matter." Translated by Ray Brassier. *Pli* 12: 33–40.

Lazzarato, Maurizio. 2004. *Les Révolutions du Capitalisme*. Paris: Les empêcheurs de penser rond.

Lipsitz, George. 1998. *The Possessive Investment in Whiteness*. Philadelphia: Temple University Press.

Maruyama, Masao 丸山 眞男. 1952. *Intellectual History of Tokugawa Japan*『日本政治思想史研究』. Tokyo: Tokyo University Press.

Maruyama, Masao 丸山 眞男. 1964. *Thought and Behavior in Modern Japanese Politics*『現代政治の思想と行動』. Tokyo: Mirai-sha.

Maruyama, Masao. 1966. *Thought and Behavior in Modern Japanese Politics*. Translated by Ivan Morris. London: Oxford University Press.

Maruyama, Masao. 1974. *Studies in Intellectual History of Tokugawa Japan*. Translated by Mikiso Hane. Princeton, NJ: Princeton University Press.

Matsuzawa, Hiroaki 松澤 弘陽. 1959. "Book Review: The New Edition of *The Showa History*"「書評：昭和史新版」. *Shisô*, October.

Mazower, Mark. 2000. *Dark Continent: Europe's Twentieth Century*. New York: Vintage.

Media-Crisis Citizens' Network. 2005. *An Erased Verdict: The Distortion of the NHK Program and Political Intervention*『消された裁き—NHK番組改変と政治的介入事件』. Tokyo: Gaifu-sha.

Mezzadra, Sandro, and Brett Neilson. 2013. *Border as Method, or, The Multiplication of Labor*. Durham, NC: Duke University Press.

Miki, Kiyoshi 三木 清. (1939) 1968. *The Principle of Thought for a New Japan*, vols. 1 and 2『新日本の思想原理』and『新日本の思想原理（続篇）』.Translated by Lewis Harrington. Tokyo: Iwanami Shoten. Originally published by Showa Research Association 昭和研究会 in *Miki Kiyoshi Zenshü* [Complete works of Miki Kiyoshi], vol. 17: 507–533, 534–588.

Mill, John Stuart. 1972. *John Stuart Mill*. Edited by H. B. Action. London: J. M. Dent and Son.

Miyoshi, Masao, and Harry D. Harootunian, eds. 2002. *Learning Places: The Afterlives of Area Studies*. Durham, NC: Duke University Press.

Moulier Boutang, Yann. 1998. *De l'esclavage au salariat: Économie historique du salariat bridé*. Paris: PUF.

Murayama, Michio 村山 道雄. 1943. *The Construction of Greater East Asia*『大東亜建設論』. Tokyo: Shôkô Gyôsei Shuppan-sha [Administrative publishers for the Ministry of Commerce and Industry].

Mutô, Ichiyô 武藤 一羊. 1999. *The Problem Called <Postwar Japanese State>*『＜戦後日本国家＞という問題』. Tokyo: Renga Shobo Shinsha.

Nakano, Toshio 中野 敏男. 2012. *Poetry and War*『詩歌と戦争』. Tokyo: NHK Shuppan.

Nancy, Jean-Luc. 1982. *Le partage des voix*. Paris: Galilée.

Nancy, Jean-Luc. 1986. *La communauté désoeuvrée*. Paris: Chirsitan Bourgois Editeur.

Nancy, Jean-Luc. 1990. *Transforming the Hermeneutic Context*. Edited by Gayle Ormiston and Alan Schrift. Translated by Gayle Ormiston. Albany: State University of New York Press.

Nancy, Jean-Luc. 1991. *The Inoperative Community*. Edited by Peter Connor. Translated by Peter Conner, Lisa Garbus, Michael Holland, and Simon Sawhney. Minneapolis: University of Minnesota Press.

Nancy, Jean-Luc. 1993. *Le sens du monde*. Paris: Galilée.

Nancy, Jean-Luc. 1997. *The Sense of the World*. Translated by Jeffrey Librett. Minneapolis: University of Minnesota Press.

Nancy, Jean-Luc (Shang-Luke, Nongxi). 2003. 『解構共同體』 [*La communauté désoeu-vrée*]. Translated by Jon Solomon 蘇哲安. Taipei: Laureate.

Nancy, Jean-Luc, and Jean-Christophe Bailly. 1991. *La comparution*. Paris: Christian Bourgois Editeur.

Nancy, Jean-Luc, and Philippe Lacoue-Labarthe. 1991. *Le mythe nazi*. La Tour d'Aigues: Editions de l'Aube.

Narita, Ryûichi 成田 龍一, Takashi Fujitani, and Naoki Sakai. 1995. Round-Table Discussion: "America's Japan/America's Voice" 「アメリカの日本／アメリカの 声」. *Gendai Shisô*『現代思想』23, no. 23: 8–37.

Nishida, Kitarô 西田 幾多郎. 1965. "I and Thou" 「我と汝」. In *Apperceptive Determination of Mu*『無の自覚的限定』, in *Nishida Kitarô Zenshû* [Complete works of Nishida Kitarô], vol. 6, 341–427. Tokyo: Iwanami Shoten.

Nishikawa, Yûko 西川 祐子. 1998. *Literary History of the Rented Houses and the Owned Houses*『借家と持ち家の文学史』. Tokyo: Sanseidô.

Nishikawa, Yûko 西川 祐子. 2000. "The Era of the Family" 「家族の時代」. In *Modern State and the Model of Family*『近代国家と家族モデル』. Tokyo: Yoshikawa Kôbundô.

Nishitani, Osamu 西谷 修. 1998. "Translator's Postface II." In *Le Crime du caporal Lortie*, by Pierre Legendre, 287–288. Kyoto: Jinmon Shoin.

Nishitani, Osamu 西谷 修, and Naoki Sakai. 1999. *Destruction of World History*『世界史の解体』. Tokyo: Ibunsha.

Noguchi, Takehiko 野口 武彦. 1994. *Toward the Discovery of the Third Person*『三人称の発見まで』. Tokyo: Chikuma Shobô.

Oguma, Eiji 小熊 英二. 1995. *The Origins of the Myth of the Mono-Ethnic Society*『単一民族神話の起源』. Tokyo: Shinyôsha.

Park, Keun Ho 朴 根好. 2003. "Vietnam War and 'East Asian Miracle'" 「ヴェトナム 戦争と「東アジアの奇跡」」. In *From Total War to Globalization: Globalization Studies*, vol. 1 『総力戦体制からグローバリゼーションへ』, edited by Yasushi Yamanouchi and Naoki Sakai, 80–120. Tokyo: Heibonsha.

Rao, Sathya. 2003. "Philosophies et non-philosophie de la traduction." PhD diss., Department of Philosophy, University of Paris X, Nanterre, March.

Read, Jason. 2003. *The Micro-politics of Capital: Marx and the Prehistory of the Present*. Albany: State University of New York Press.

Reischauer, Edwin O. 1942. "Memorandum on Policy towards Japan," September 14, with materials collected by War Department General Staff, Organization and Training Division, G-3. Concerning "Enlistment of loyal American citizens of Japanese descent into the Army and Navy," December 17, 291.2, Army-AG Classified Decimal File 1940–42, Records of the Adjunct General's Office, 1917–, record group 407, entry 360, box 147, National Archives, College Park, MD.

Reischauer, Edwin O. 1947. *Japan Past and Present*. New York: A. A. Knopf.

Reischauer, Edwin O. 1955. *Wanted: An Asian Policy*. New York: Knopf.

Rostow, Walter W. 1960. *The Stages of Economic Growth: A Non-Communist Manifesto*. Cambridge: Cambridge University Press.

Said, Edward. 1979. *Orientalism*. New York: Vintage.

Sakabe, Megumi 坂部 恵. 1989. *Poetics of Persona*『ペルソナの詩学』. Tokyo: Iwanami Shoten.

Sakabe, Megumi 坂部 恵. 2009. *Hermeneutics of the Mask*『仮面の解釈学』. Tokyo: Tokyo University Press.

Sakai, Naoki 酒井 直樹. 1988. "Critique of Modernity: The Problem of Universalism and Particularism." *South Atlantic Quarterly* 87, no. 3 (summer): 93–122. Originally published in Japanese, *Gendai Shisô* 15, no. 15 (1987): 184–207.

Sakai, Naoki 酒井 直樹. 1991. *Voices of the Past: The Status of Language in Eighteenth-Century Japanese Discourse*. Ithaca, NY: Cornell University Press.

Sakai, Naoki 酒井 直樹. 1996. *Stillbirth of the Japanese as an Ethnos and as a Language* 『死産される日本語・日本人』. Tokyo: Shinyô-sha.

Sakai, Naoki 酒井 直樹. 1997a. "On Being Japanese"「日本人であること」. *Shisô*, no. 882 (December): 5–48.

Sakai, Naoki 酒井 直樹. 1997b. *Translation and Subjectivity: On "Japan" and Cultural Nationalism*. Minneapolis: University of Minnesota Press.

Sakai, Naoki 酒井 直樹. (1997c) 2015. *Still-birth of the Japanese as Ethnos and as a Language*『死産される日本語・日本人』. Tokyo: Shinyô-sha. Reprint, Tokyo: Kodansha.

Sakai, Naoki. 1999. "Japan Studies and Cultural Studies." *Positions: East Asia Cultures Critique* 7, no. 2: 593–647.

Sakai, Naoki. 2000a. "Subject and Substratum." *Cultural Studies* 14, nos. 3–4: 462–530.

Sakai, Naoki. 2000b. "'You Asians': On the Historical Role of the West and Asia Binary." *South Atlantic Quarterly* 99, no. 4 (fall): 789–817.

Sakai, Naoki 酒井 直樹. 2003. "Editor's Postscript"「編者あとがき」. In *From Total War to Globalization: Globalization Studies*, vol. 1『総力戦からグローバリゼイションへ: グローバリゼイション研究』, edited by Yasushi Yamanouchi and Naoki Sakai, 319–324. Tokyo: Heibonsha.

Sakai, Naoki. 2004. "Two Negations: Fear of Being Excluded and the Logic of Self-Esteem." *Novel* 37, no. 3 (summer): 229–257.

Sakai, Naoki 酒井 直樹. 2007. *Japan/Image/the United States: The Community of Sympathy and Imperial Nationalisms*『日本/ 映像/ 米国: 共感の共同体と帝国的国民主義』. Tokyo: Seidosha.

Sakai, Naoki 酒井 直樹. 2008. *Hope and the Constitution*『希望と憲法』. Tokyo: Ibunsha.

Sakai, Naoki. 2009a. "How Do We Count a Language? Translation and Discontinuity." *Translation Studies* 2, no. 1: 71–88.

Sakai, Naoki. 2009b. "Transpacific Complicity and Comparatist Strategy." *Positions: East Asia Cultures Critique* 17, no. 1: 159–207.

Sakai, Naoki. 2011. "The Body of the Nation: The Pastorate, the Emperor System, and the Society of Sympathy of Japan's Intellectual Modernization." In *Biopolitics, Ethics and Subjectivation*, edited by Alain Brossat, Yuan-Horng Chu, Rada Ivekovic, and Joyce C. H. Liu, 91–120. Paris: L'Harmattan.

Sakai, Naoki. 2013a. "Postscript." In *Imagining Mass Dictatorships: The Individual and the Masses in Literature and Cinema*, edited by Michael Schoenlas and Karin Sarsenov, 285–312. Basingstoke: Palgrave Macmillan.

Sakai, Naoki. 2013b. "Transnationality in Translation." *Translation* 2 (spring): 15–31.

Sakai, Naoki. 2018. "The Modern Regime of Translation and Its Politics." In *A History of Modern Translation Knowledge: Sources, Concepts, Effects*, edited by Yves Gambier and Lieven D'hulst. Amsterdam: John Benjamins.

Sakai, Naoki 酒井 直樹, and Harry D. Harootunian. 1997. "Japanese Studies and Cultural Studies" 「日本研究と文化研究」. Translated by Okazaki Haruteru. *Shisô* 『思想』 no. 877: 4–53.

Sakai, Naoki 酒井 直樹, and Osamu Nishitani. 1999. *Destruction of World History* 『世界史の解体』. Tokyo: Ibunsha.

Sakai, Naoki, and Hyon Joo Yoo, eds. 2012. *The Trans-Pacific Imagination: Rethinking Boundary, Culture and Society.* Singapore: World Scientific.

Sakai, Takashi 酒井 隆史. 2001. *On Freedom: "The Genealogy of the Present"* 『自由論—'現在性の系譜学'』. Tokyo: Seitosha.

Sangyô Nôritsu University 産業能率大学. 2015. "Report on the New Employees." *Nihon Keizai Shinbun,* October 25.

Schaller, Michael. 1997. *Altered States.* Oxford: Oxford University Press.

Schmitt, Carl. 1950. *Der Nomos der Erde in Völkerrecht des Jus Publicum Europaeum.* Berlin: Duncker and Humbolt.

Schmitt, Carl. 1976. 『大地のノモス— ヨーロッパ公法という国際法における』（上・下、新田邦夫訳. Tokyo: Fukumura Shuppan.

Schmitt, Carl. 2006. *The Nomos of the Earth in the International Law of the Jus Publicum Europaeum.* Translated by G. L. Ulman. New York: Telos Press.

Shinmei, Masamichi 新明 正道. 1940. *Race and Society* 『人種と社会』. Tokyo: Kadokawa Shobô.

Soja, Edward. 1989. *Postmodern Geographies: The Reassertion of Space in Critical Theory.* London: Verso.

Solomon, Jon. 2001. "No-soberanía para las multitudes: Recursos para una Democracia de Extranjeros, a partir de François Laruelle" [Nonsovereignty for the multitudes: Resources for a democracy of foreigners from François Laruelle's non-philosophy]. Translated by Erik del Bufalo. In *Revista Latinoamericana de Estudios Avanzados* [Latin American journal of advanced studies] RELEA, no. 17 (Caracas: Central University of Venezuela).

Solomon, Jon. 2003a. "Impero e il regime della traduzione unilaterale: Un dibattito a Taiwan." Translated by Federica Matteoni. *DeriveApprodi,* no. 23: 155–159.

Solomon, Jon. 2003b. "L'empire et le régime de la traduction unilatérale" [Empire and the regime of unilateral translation]. Translated by Brian Holmes, Bérénice Angremy, François Matheron, and Charles Wolfe. *Multitudes,* no. 13: 79–88.

Solomon, Jon 蘇哲安. 2003c. 〈翻譯的共同體, 共同體的翻譯〉, 序尚呂克 · 儂曦著《解構共同體》, 蘇哲安譯, 台北, 櫃冠出版社, 2003 年, I–XV 頁。, "Translation of Community, Community of Translation" [Fanyi de gongtongti, gongtongti de fanyi]. Preface to *Jiegou Gongtongti* [*La communauté désoeuvrée*], by Nongxi Shang-Luke (Jean-Luc Nancy). Translated by Zhean Su (Jon Solomon), i–xv. Taipei: Laureate Books.

Solomon, Jon. 2004a. "La traduction métaphysicoloniale et les Sciences Humaines: La région amphibologique comme lieu biopolitique" [Metaphysicolonial translation and the Human Sciences: The amphibological region as biopolitical site]. Translated by Frédéric Neyrat and Jerôme Maucourant. *Rue Descartes,* no. 48.

Solomon, Jon. 2004b. "Taiwan Incorporated: A Survey of Biopolitics in the Sovereign Police's East Asian Theater of Operations." In *Traces: A Multilingual Series of Cultural Theory and Translation,* vol. 3, edited by Kang Nae-hui and Thomas Lamarre, 229–254. Hong Kong: University of Hong Kong.

Solomon, Jon 蘇哲安 著. 2005. 〈未來的哲學：論傅柯的西方主義與翻譯問題〉, 收錄於黃瑞祺編,《瞄準傅柯》, 台北：松慧, 2005 年 [Philosophy of the future: Foucault's occidentalism and the problem of translation]. In *Miaozhun Fuke* [Aiming at Foucault], edited by Jui-chyi Huang. Taipei: Sunghui.

Solomon, Jon. 2014. "Invoking the West: Giorgio Agamben's 'Romantic Ideology' and the Civilizational Transference." *Concentric: Literary and Cultural Studies* 40, no. 2 (September): 125–147.

Solomon, Jon, and Brian Holmes. 2003. "Towards a Science of Foreigners?" (Interview with Michael Hardt Prepared by Jon Solomon and Brian Holmes). *Multitudes*, no. 14: 73–80.

Spengler, Oswald. 1991. *The Decline of the West*. Translated by Charles Francis Atkins. Oxford: Oxford University Press.

Stadler, Friedrich. 1995. "The Emigration and Exile of Austrian Intellectuals." In *Vertreibung der Vernunft: The Cultural Exodus from Austria*, edited by Friedrich Stadler and Peter Weibel. Vienna: Springer-Verlag.

Takata, Yasuma 高田 保馬. 1939. *On East Asian Nations*『東亜民族論』. Tokyo: Iwanami Shoten.

Takata, Yasuma 高田 保馬. 1942. *On the Nation*『民族論』. Tokyo: Iwanami Shoten.

Takeuchi, Yoshimi 竹内 好. (1947) 1993. "Chinese Modernity and Japanese Modernity"「中国の近代と日本の近代」. In *Japan and Asia*『日本とアジア』, 11–57. Tokyo: Chikuma Shobo.

Takeuchi, Yoshimi. (1948) 2005. "What Is Modernity?" In *What Is Modernity? Writings of Takeuchi Yoshimi*, edited and translated by Richard F. Calichman, 53–81. New York: Columbia University Press.

Takeuchi, Yoshimi 竹内 好. 1993. "Asia as Method"「方法としてのアジア」. In *Japan and Asia*『日本とアジア』. Tokyo: Chikuma Shobo.

Takeuchi, Yoshimi. 2005. "Asia as Method." In *What Is Modernity? Writings of Takeuchi Yoshimi*, edited and translated by Richard L. Calichmann, 149–165. New York: Columbia University Press.

Taki, Kôji 立木 浩二. 1988. *The Portrait of the Emperor*『天皇の肖像』. Tokyo: Iwanami Shoten.

Tanabe, Hajime 田邊 元. 1963a. "From the Schema of Time to the Schema of the World"「図式「時間」から図式「世界へ」. In *Tanabe Hajime Zenshû* [Complete works of Hajime Tanabe], vol. 6, 1–49. Tokyo: Chikuma Shobo.

Tanabe, Hajime 田邊 元. 1963b. "The Logic of Social Being"「社会存在の論理」. In *Tanabe Hajime Zenshû* [Complete works of Hajime Tanabe], vol. 6, 51–167. Tokyo: Chikuma Shobo.

Tazaki, Hideaki 田崎 秀明. 2000. "Nietzsche in Contemporary Biopolitics"「今日の生政治の中のニーチェ」. *Shisô*, no. 919. Tokyo: Iwanami Shoten.

Tourism Strategy Division. 2017.「観光庁による若者旅行振興の取組」[Japan Tourism Agency's promotion of tourism for young people]. Tokyo: Japan Tourism Agency, Japanese Ministry of Land, Infrastructure, Transport and Tourism. http://www.mlit.go.jp/common/001083168.pdf.

Tôyama Shigeki 遠山 茂樹, Imai Sei'ichi, and Fujiwara Akira. 1955. *The Showa History*『昭和史』. Tokyo: Iwanami Shoten.

Trouillot, Michel-Rolph. 2003. *Global Transformations: Anthropology and the Modern World*. New York: Palgrave Macmillan.

Tsurumi, Shunsuke 鶴見 俊輔, and Osamu Kuno. 1956. *Contemporary Japanese Thought* 『現代日本の思想』. Tokyo: Iwanami Shoten.

Ukai, Satoshi 鵜飼 哲. 2000. "The Future of an Affect: The Historicity of Shame." *Traces: A Multilingual Journal of Cultural Theory and Translation* 1: 3–36.

Viswanathan, Gauri. 1989. *Masks of Conquest*. New York: Columbia University Press.

Wagner, Edward W. 1951. *The Korean Minority in Japan, 1904–1950*. New York: Institute of Pacific Relations.

Walker, Gavin. 2011. "Primitive Accumulation and the Formation of Difference: On Marx and Schmitt." *Rethinking Marxism* 23, no. 3: 384–404.

Walker, Gavin. 2019. "The Accumulation of Difference and the Logic of Area." *Positions: Asia Critique* 27, no. 1: 67–98.

Walker, Gavin, and Naoki Sakai, eds. 2019. "The End of Area: Biopolitics, Geopolitics, History." Special issue, *Positions: Asia Critique* 27, no. 1.

Watsuji, Tetsurô 和辻 哲郎. 1962. "The Symbol of the National Unity" 「国民統合の象徴」. In *Watsuji Tetsurô Zenshû* [Complete works of Tetsurô Zenshû], vol. 14: 313–396. Tokyo: Iwanami Shoten.

Weiner, Tim. 1994. "C.I.A. Spent Millions to Support Japanese Right in 50s and 60s." *New York Times*, October 9.

Weiner, Tim. 2007. *Legacy of Ashes: The History of the CIA*. New York: Anchor.

Winichakul, Thongchai. 1994. *Siam Mapped: A History of the Geo-body of a Nation*. Honolulu: University of Hawai'i Press.

Yamanouchi, Yasushi, J. Victor Koschmann, and Ryûichi Narita, eds. 1998. *Total War and "Modernization."* Ithaca, NY: Cornell East Asia Program.

Yasuda, Kôichi 安田 浩一. 2012. *Internet and Patriotism* 『ネットと愛国 — 在特会の「闇」を追って』. Tokyo: Kôdansha.

Yasumaru, Yoshio 安丸 良夫. 1974. *Japanese Modernization and Popular Ethics* 『日本の近代化と民衆思想』. Tokyo: Aoki Shoten.

Yasumaru, Yoshio 安丸 良夫. 1992. 『近代天皇像の形成』 [The formation of the image of modern emperor]. Tokyo: Iwanami Shoten.

Yoneyama, Lisa 米山 リサ. 2016. *Cold War Ruins: Transpacific Critique of American Justice and Japanese War Crime*. Durham, NC: Duke University Press.

Yoshimi Shunya 吉見 俊哉, and Lisa Yoneyama, eds. 2006. *Why Was the Program Distorted? The Hidden Truth of the NHK ETV Incident* 『番組はなぜ改竄されたか NHK ETV 事件の真相』. Tokyo: Impaction.

Yoshimoto, Takaaki 吉本 隆明. 1962. *The End of a Fiction* 『擬制の終焉』. Tokyo: Gendai Shichôsha.

Yoshimoto, Takaaki 吉本 隆明. 1976. *The Logic of Lyricism* 『抒情の論理』. Tokyo: Miraisha.